Business Process Execution Language for Web Services

Second Edition

An architect and developer's guide to orchestrating web services using BPEL4WS

Matjaz B. Juric
With Benny Mathew and Poornachandra Sarang

BIRMINGHAM - MUMBAI

Business Process Execution Language for Web Services

Second Edition

First published: October 2004

Second edition: January 2006

Published by Packt Publishing Ltd.
32 Lincoln Road
Olton
Birmingham, B27 6PA, UK.

ISBN 1-904811-81-7

www.packtpub.com

Cover Design by www.visionwt.com

Credits

Author
Matjaz B. Juric

Co-Authors
Benny Mathew
Poornachandra Sarang

Reviewers
Mark Little
Dave Shaffer
Prasad Yendluri

Technical Editor
Ashutosh Pande

Editorial Manager
Dipali Chittar

Development Editor
Louay Fatoohi

Indexer
Ashutosh Pande

Proofreader
Chris Smith

Production Coordinator
Manjiri Nadkarni

Cover Designer
Helen Wood

About the Authors

Matjaz B. Juric holds a Ph.D. in computer and information science. He is Associate Professor at the University of Maribor. In addition to this book, he has coauthored *Professional J2EE EAI*, *Professional EJB*, *J2EE Design Patterns Applied*, and *.NET Serialization Handbook*, published by Wrox Press. He has published chapters in *More Java Gems* (Cambridge University Press) and in *Technology Supporting Business Solutions* (Nova Science Publishers). He has also published in journals and magazines, such as *Java Developer's Journal*, *Java Report*, *Java World*, *Web Services Journal*, *eai Journal*, *theserverside.com*, *OTN*, and ACM journals, and presented at conferences such as OOPSLA, Java Development, XML Europe, OOW, SCI, and others. He is a reviewer, program committee member, and conference organizer. Matjaz has been involved in several large-scale object technology projects. In cooperation with IBM Java Technology Centre, he worked on performance analysis and optimization of RMI-IIOP, an integral part of the Java platform.

Matjaz is an author of courses and consultant for the BPEL and SOA consulting company **BPELmentor.com**. For more information, please visit `http://www.bpelmentor.com/`

My efforts in this book are dedicated to my family. Special thanks to Jerneja, my friends at the University of Maribor, and to Louay and Damian at Packt Publishing.

Benny K. Mathew is a Sr. Software Engineer at IBM Global Services (India), Bangalore. He holds a Masters degree in Computer Applications. His fascination for computers started at the age of 14, when he first experienced the delight of programming on a Sinclair ZX Spectrum+.

He has co-authored books and articles on technologies like .NET, BizTalk, BPEL, etc.

During his free time, Benny likes to read blogs and help people on the newsgroups related to .NET and BizTalk. He has been awarded Microsoft Most Valuable Professional (MVP) for two consecutive years.

Before joining IBM, he was with companies like Hewlett Packard, Thomson Financials, and Delphi Software.

I'd like to thank Louay for giving me the opportunity to contribute to this book and to Matjaz for giving me valuable suggestions. I'd also like to take this opportunity to thank my parents and family for their support in writing this book.

Poornachandra Sarang, Ph.D., is CEO of ABCOM Information Systems. Dr. Sarang is one of the leading software architects in the industry, has more than 20 years of IT experience and provides consulting services to worldwide clients in architecting and designing IT solutions based on Java, CORBA, Oracle, and .NET platforms. He has been a Visiting Professor of Computer Engineering at the University of Notre Dame, USA and is currently a visiting professor for Post-Graduate Computer Science studies at the University of Mumbai. He conducts lectures/seminars on emerging technologies across the world and has made several presentations at international conferences. He has authored/coauthored several books and journal articles on Java, C++, J2EE, e-Commerce, Open-Source Technologies, and .NET.

In this book, Matjaz B. Juric wrote Chapters 1, 3, 4, 5, 6 and Appendix A; Benny Matthew wrote Chapter 7; and Poornachandra Sarang wrote Chapter 2.

About the Reviewers

Mark Little is one of the primary authors of the OMG Activity Service specification and is on the expert group for the same work in J2EE (JSR 95). Mark is also the specification lead for JSR 156: Java API for XML Transactions. He is on the OTS Revision Task Force and the OASIS Business Transactions Protocol specification. Before joining HP he was, for over 10 years, a member of the Arjuna team within the University of Newcastle upon Tyne (where he continues to have a Visiting Fellowship). His research within the Arjuna team included replication and transaction support, including the construction of an OTS/JTS-compliant transaction processing system. Before Arjuna Technologies, Mark was a distinguished Engineer/Architect within HP Arjuna Labs, Newcastle upon Tyne, England, where he led the HP-TS and HP-WST teams, developing J2EE and web services transactions products respectively. Mark has published extensively in the *Web Services Journal*, *Java Developers Journal*, and other journals and magazines.

Dave Shaffer has held senior consulting, management, and software development roles over the last 15 years in a wide-range of technology companies including Oracle, Collaxa, Apple Computer, NeXT Software, and Integrated Computer Solutions. He has helped organizations ranging from early-stage startups to Fortune 10 companies to design, implement, and manage mission-critical software systems for e-commerce and business process automation in the financial services, telecommunications, and manufacturing sectors. At Oracle, Dave is responsible for BPEL customer success, for both pre-sales POCs and post-sales project implementations. Dave is a former faculty member of the Computer Science department at the University of Vermont and holds an MS in Computer Science from the University of Massachusetts.

Table of Contents

Preface 1

Chapter 1: Introduction to BPEL and SOA 5

Why Business Processes Matter 5

Automation of Business Processes 6

Exposing and Accessing the Functionality of Applications as Services 7

Enterprise Bus Infrastructure for Communication and Management of Services 7

Integration between Services and Applications 7

Composition of Exposed Services into Business Processes 7

Web Services 8

How Web Services Differ from their Predecessors 9

Web Services Technology Stack 9

Enterprise Service Bus 10

ESB Features 11

Service Oriented Architecture 12

SOA Concepts 12

Services 13

Interfaces 13

Messages 13

Synchronicity 13

Loose Coupling 14

Registries 14

Quality of Service 14

Composition of Services into Business Processes 14

Service Composition 16

BPEL for Service Composition 17

BPEL Features 18

Orchestration and Choreography 19

Executable and Abstract Processes 21

Relation of BPEL to Other Languages 22

ebXML BPSS 22

BPML 23

WSCI 24

WS-CDL 24

BPEL Servers Overview 25
Oracle BPEL Process Manager 27
Microsoft BizTalk 27
IBM WebSphere Business Integration Server Foundation 27
IBM BPWS4J 28
ActiveBPEL Engine and ActiveWebflow 28
OpenStorm Service Orchestrator 29
The Future of BPEL 29
Conclusion 30

Chapter 2: Web Services Technology Stack 31

E-Business Collaborations 31
WS-Security 34
Example 34
Binary Security Token 35
Referencing an External Security Token 35
Faults 36
Typical Business Transaction Scenario 36
WS-Coordination 37
The Framework 38
Scenario 38
CoordinationContext 40
CreateCoordinationContext 40
CreateCoordinationContextResponse 41
Register 41
RegisterResponse 41
Faults 41
Web Services Transaction Specifications 42
Atomic Transaction 42
Sharing Context Information 42
Coordination Protocols 43
Business Activity 44
Sharing the Context Information 45
Coordination Protocols 45
OASIS BTP 46
The BTP Stack 48
The BTP Model 48
Atomic Transactions 49
Cohesive Transactions 49

Reliable Messaging **49**
Messaging Model 50
Example 51
Requesting Acknowledgement 51
Delivery Assurances 51
Other Assertions 52
Faults 52
WS-Addressing **53**
Endpoint Reference 53
Faults 55
WS-Inspection **55**
Inspection Document Hierarchy 56
WS-Policy **56**
Policy Outline 57
The <wsp:All> Operator 57
The <wsp:ExactlyOne> Operator 57
The <wsp:OneOrMore> Operator 57
The <wsp:Policy> Operator 57
Policy Assertions 57
Example 58
Policy Inclusion 58
WS-Eventing **59**
Event Subscription 59
Response to Event Subscription 60
Subscription Renewal 61
Unsubscribing 61
Subscription End Message 62
Conclusion **63**
Chapter 3: Service Composition with BPEL **65**
Developing Business Processes with BPEL **65**
Core Concepts **67**
Invoking Web Services 70
Invoking Asynchronous Web Services 71
Synchronous/Asynchronous Business Processes 72
Understanding Links to Partners 73
Partner Link Types 75
Defining Partner Links 77
BPEL Process Tag 78

Variables 78
Providing the Interface to BPEL Processes: <invoke>, <receive>, and <reply> 79
Assignments 81
Conditions 84
BPEL Business Process Example **85**
Involved Web Services 88
Employee Travel Status Web Service 88
Airline Web Service 90
WSDL for the BPEL Process 92
Partner Link Types 93
Business Process Definition 95
BPEL Process Outline 97
Partner Links 97
Variables 98
BPEL Process Main Body 99
Asynchronous BPEL Example **102**
Modify the BPEL Process WSDL 103
Modify Partner Link Types 104
Modify the BPEL Process Definition 104
Conclusion **106**
Chapter 4: Advanced BPEL **107**
Advanced Activities **108**
Activity Names 108
Loops 108
Delays 110
Deadline and Duration Expressions 110
Empty Activities 111
Process Termination 112
Fault Handling and Signaling **112**
WSDL Faults 112
Signaling Faults 113
Signaling Faults to Clients in Synchronous Replies 114
Signaling Faults to Clients in Asynchronous Scenarios 115
Handling Faults 117
Selection of a Fault Handler 118
Synchronous Example 119
Asynchronous Example 121
Inline Fault Handling 122

Scopes **123**
Example 125
First Scope 127
Second Scope 129
Third Scope 131
Serializable Scopes 132
Compensation **132**
Compensation Handlers 133
Example 135
Invoking Compensation Handlers 136
Managing Events **137**
Pick Activity 138
Message Events 138
Alarm Events 139
Example 139
Event Handlers 140
Example 142
Business Process Lifecycle **143**
Correlation and Message Properties **145**
Message Properties 145
Mapping Properties to Messages 146
Extracting Properties 147
Properties and Assignments 147
Correlation Sets 148
Using Correlation Sets 149
Concurrent Activities and Links **150**
Sources and Targets 151
Example 151
Transition Conditions 157
Join Conditions and Link Status 158
Join Failures 159
Suppressing Join Failures 160
Dynamic Partner Links **161**
Abstract Business Processes **162**
Model Driven Approach: Generating BPEL from UML Activity Diagrams **164**
Conclusion **165**

Chapter 5: Oracle BPEL Process Manager and BPEL Designer: Overview 167

Overview and Architecture 167
BPEL Server 169
Core BPEL Engine 169
WSDL Bindings 169
Integration Services 170
BPEL Console 170
BPEL Designer 171
Database 171
Process Deployment Example 171
Process Descriptor 172
Configuration Properties 174
Setting the Environment 175
BPEL Compiler and Revision Numbers 176
Deployment and Domains 177
Ant Utility 177
Process Management with the BPEL Console 178
Visual Flow 181
Instance Auditing 182
Debugging 182
Overview of Other BPEL Console Functions 184
Deploying Processes 186
Management 187
Performance Tuning 188
Domains and Administration 190
Administration of Server-Related Parameters 191
Managing BPEL Domains 192
Graphical Development with BPEL Designer 193
JDeveloper BPEL Designer 194
Importing Existing BPEL Processes 195
Partner Links and Web Services 195
Variables 196
Process Activities 198
Copy Rule Editor 199
XPath Expression Builder 200
XSLT Mapper 201
BPEL Validation Browser 203
Building and Deploying 204
Eclipse BPEL Designer 206
Partner Links and Web Services 207

Variables 208
XML Type Browser 209
Process Map 210
Copy Rule Editor 211
Function Wizard 211
Building and Deploying 212
Summary **213**

Chapter 6: Oracle BPEL Process Manager: Advanced Features **215**

Extension Functions and Activities **215**
Transformation and Query Support 217
Data and Array Manipulation 218
XML Manipulation 220
Date and Time Expressions 220
Process Identification 221
LDAP Access and User Management 221
Dynamic Parallel Flow **222**
Dynamic Flow Example 223
Providing a List of Partner Links 224
Dynamic Parallel Invocation of Airline Services 224
Dynamic Partner Links 225
Offer Selection Loop 226
Deploying and Testing the Example 227
Web Services Invocation Framework **228**
Advantages of WSIF 229
Java to XML Bindings 230
XML Façades 231
Invoking a Java Class through WSIF 233
Defining WSIF Bindings in WSDL 233
WSIF Bindings for Java Classes 234
Testing the Example 235
Exception Handling 237
User Exceptions in Java 238
Defining Faults in WSDL 238
Defining WSIF Binding for an Exception 239
Custom Exception Serializers 241
Invoking EJB through WSIF 243
WSDL for Session Bean 244
WSIF Binding for EJB 245
Generating WSIF Bindings from JDeveloper 247

Java Code Embedding 249
Invoking a Java Class from Embedded Code 250
Notification Service 253
Email Example 254
Notification Wizard 255
Review of Code 258
Testing the Example 258
Mail and JMS Services 259
Workflow Service 259
Workflow Patterns 260
Example 261
Checking User Outcome 267
Worklist Application to Approve Ticket 268
Identity Service 271
BPEL Server APIs 273
Summary 274

Chapter 7: MS BizTalk Server 275

Overview 275
Support for BPEL and XLANG/s 276
Architecture 276
Ports 277
Receive Locations 278
Adapters 278
Receive Pipelines 279
Message Contexts 280
Promoted Properties 280
Distinguished Fields 280
The MessageBox 281
How Publish-Subscribe works 281
Orchestrations 281
Maps 282
Business Rules Engine 283
Send Pipeline 283
Building a Sample Orchestration in BizTalk 284
Scenario 284
Implementation 285
Exporting Orchestration to BPEL 291
Importing BPEL Processes into BizTalk 294

Do's and Don'ts for BPEL Compliance in BizTalk 305
Comparing BizTalk Orchestration Constructs with BPEL 306
Receive and Send Shapes (<receive>, <invoke>, <reply>) 307
Port and Role Link Shapes (<partnerLink>, <partnerLinkType>, <role>) 307
Expression and Message Assignment Shapes (<assign>, <copy>, <from>, <to>) 308
Decide Shape (<switch>, <case>, <otherwise>) 309
Delay Shape (<wait>) 310
Parallel Actions Shape (<flow>) 310
Loop Shape (<while>) 311
Suspend Shape 311
Terminate Shape (<terminate>) 311
Advanced BPEL Functions using BizTalk 312
Listen Shape (<pick>, <onMessage>, <onAlarm>) 312
Scope Shape (<scope>) 313
Throw Exception Shape and Exception Handling (<throw>, <faultHandler>, <catch>, <catchAll>) 314
Compensate Shape and Compensation Block (<compensate>, <compensationHandler>) 315
Correlation (<correlations>, <correlationSets>) 316
Other BizTalk-Specific Features 316
Integration with other BizTalk Servers 316
Integration with Web Services 317
Integration with the .NET Framework 317
Human Workflow Services (HWS) 317
Business Activity Monitoring (BAM) 318
Health and Activity Tracking (HAT) 318
BizTalk Server 2006 and Beyond 318
Summary 319
Appendix A: BPEL Syntax Reference 321
Important BPEL Activities and Elements 321
<assign>, <copy>, <from>, <to> 321
<catch>, <catchAll> 322
<compensate> 323
<compensationHandler> 324
<correlations>, <correlation> 325
<correlationSets>, <correlationSet> 325
<empty> 325
<eventHandlers> 326

<faultHandlers>, <faultHandler> 326
<flow> 327
<invoke> 328
<links>, <link> 329
<onAlarm> 329
<onMessage> 330
<partnerLinks>, <partnerLink> 330
<partnerLinkType>, <role> 330
<partners> 331
<pick> 331
<process> 332
<property> 333
<propertyAlias> 333
<receive> 334
<reply> 334
<scope> 334
<sequence> 335
<source> 335
<switch>, <case> 336
<target> 337
<terminate> 337
<throw> 337
<variables>, <variable> 338
<wait> 338
<while> 338
BPEL Functions **339**
getLinkStatus() 339
getVariableData() 340
getVariableProperty() 340
Deadline and Duration Expressions **340**
Standard Elements **341**
Standard Attributes **341**
Default Values of Attributes **342**
Standard Faults **342**
Namespaces **343**
Index **345**

Preface

Business Process Execution Language for Web Services (BPEL, WS-BPEL, or BPEL4WS) is the new standard for defining business processes with composition of services. It is the cornerstone of Service Oriented Architecture (SOA). With its ability to define executable and abstract business processes it opens new doors in business process management and represents the top-down approach to the realization of SOA.

BPEL is supported by the majority of software vendors including Oracle, Microsoft, IBM, BEA, SAP, Hewlett-Packard, Siebel, and others. Most of them already have products that support BPEL; others will follow soon.

This book explains the BPEL standard, provides a step-by-step guide to designing and developing business processes in BPEL, defines the role of BPEL in SOA, and discusses how BPEL relates to the web services stack and to other standards. It also covers two important BPEL servers—the Oracle BPEL Process Manager and Microsoft BizTalk Server. The book presents the service-oriented approach to business process definition using web services, which enables us to develop loosely coupled solutions.

What This Book Covers

Chapter 1 provides a detailed introduction to BPEL and Service Oriented Architecture (SOA). It discusses business processes and their automation, explains the role of BPEL, web services, and Enterprise Service Buses (ESB) in SOA, provides insight into business process composition with BPEL, explains the most important features, compares BPEL to other specifications, provides an overview of BPEL servers, and discusses the future of BPEL.

Chapter 2 provides a detailed introduction to the Web Services Technology Stack. It discusses the important standards and specifications for using BPEL and implementing SOA with web services, such as WS-Security, WS-Addressing, WS-Coordination, WS-AtomicTransaction, WS-BusinessActivity, WS-Reliable Messaging, etc.

Chapter 3 discusses the composition of web services with BPEL. The chapter introduces the core concepts of BPEL and explains how to define synchronous and asynchronous business processes with BPEL. The reader gets familiar with BPEL process structure, partner links, sequential and parallel service invocation, variables, conditions, etc.

Chapter 4 goes deeper into the BPEL specification and covers advanced features for modeling complex business processes. Advanced activities, scopes, serialization, fault handing, compensations, event handling, correlation sets, concurrent activities and links, process lifecycle, and dynamic partner links are covered in detail.

Chapter 5 explains how to use the Oracle BPEL Process Manager for deploying and executing business processes defined in BPEL. It describes the server architecture, tools, features, and common approaches for managing and debugging BPEL processes. The chapter also looks at graphical development of BPEL processes using Oracle BPEL Designer for JDeveloper and for Eclipse.

Chapter 6 takes a detailed look at the advanced features of the Oracle BPEL Process Manager including extension functions, dynamic parallel flows, Web Services Invocation Framework, Java embedding, Notification service, Workflow service, Identity service, and Oracle BPEL Server APIs.

Chapter 7 discusses MS BizTalk Server 2004 and its support for BPEL. It explains how to develop business processes in BizTalk and export them to BPEL. It also explains how to import BPEL processes into BizTalk and how to use the Orchestration Designer tool to define processes graphically, and compares BizTalk and BPEL constructs.

Appendix A provides a syntax reference for BPEL version 1.1. The appendix covers standard BPEL activities and elements, functions, attributes, and faults.

What You Need for Using This Book

To test the examples in Chapters 3, 4, 5, and 6, you need to have Oracle BPEL Process Manager 10g installed on your system (`http://www.oracle.com/technology/products/ias/bpel/`), and for Chapter 7 you need Microsoft BizTalk Server 2004 (`http://www.microsoft.com/biztalk/`).

Conventions

In this book, you will find a number of styles of text that distinguish between different kinds of information. Here are some examples of these styles, and an explanation of their meaning.

There are three styles for code. Code words in text are shown as follows: "We can include other contexts through the use of the `include` directive."

A block of code will be set as follows:

```
<operation name="TravelApproval">
    <input message="tns:TravelRequestMessage" />
    <output message="aln:TravelResponseMessage" />
    <fault name="fault" message="tns:TravelFaultMessage" />
</operation>
```

When we wish to draw your attention to a particular part of a code block, the relevant lines or items will be made bold:

```
<operation name="TravelApproval">
    <input message="tns:TravelRequestMessage" />
    <output message="aln:TravelResponseMessage" />
    <fault name="fault" message="tns:TravelFaultMessage" />
</operation>
```

Any command-line input and output is written as follows:

```
schemac Employee.wsdl
```

New terms and **important words** are introduced in a bold-type font. Words that you see on the screen, in menus or dialog boxes for example, appear in our text like this: "clicking the Next button moves you to the next screen".

> Warnings or important notes appear in a box like this.

Reader Feedback

Feedback from our readers is always welcome. Let us know what you think about this book, what you liked or may have disliked. Reader feedback is important for us to develop titles that you really get the most out of.

To send us general feedback, simply drop an email to `feedback@packtpub.com`, making sure to mention the book title in the subject of your message.

If there is a book that you need and would like to see us publish, please send us a note in the SUGGEST A TITLE form on `www.packtpub.com` or email `suggest@packtpub.com`.

If there is a topic that you have expertise in and you are interested in either writing or contributing to a book, see our author guide on `www.packtpub.com/authors`.

Customer Support

Now that you are the proud owner of a Packt book, we have a number of things to help you to get the most from your purchase.

Downloading the Example Code for the Book

Visit `http://www.packtpub.com/support`, and select this book from the list of titles to download any example code or extra resources for this book. The files available for download will then be displayed.

> The downloadable files contain instructions on how to use them.

Errata

Although we have taken every care to ensure the accuracy of our contents, mistakes do happen. If you find a mistake in one of our books—maybe a mistake in text or code—we would be grateful if you would report this to us. By doing this you can save other readers from frustration, and help to improve subsequent versions of this book. If you find any errata, report them by visiting `http://www.packtpub.com/support`, selecting your book, clicking on the Submit Errata link, and entering the details of your errata. Once your errata have been verified, your submission will be accepted and the errata added to the list of existing errata. The existing errata can be viewed by selecting your title from `http://www.packtpub.com/support`.

Questions

You can contact us at `questions@packtpub.com` if you are having a problem with some aspect of the book, and we will do our best to address it.

1
Introduction to BPEL and SOA

BPEL (Business Process Execution Language for Web Services, also WS-BPEL, BPEL4WS) is a language used for composition, orchestration, and coordination of web services. It provides a rich vocabulary for expressing the behavior of business processes. In this chapter, we introduce BPEL, define its role in the **SOA** (Service Oriented Architecture), and explain the process-oriented approach to SOA and the role of BPEL. We also provide short descriptions of the most important BPEL servers—the run-time environments for execution of business processes specified in BPEL—and compare BPEL to other business process languages. In this chapter, we:

- Discuss the role of business processes and their automation
- Overview web services, ESB (Enterprise Service Bus), and SOA
- Discuss the composition of services
- Explain the role of BPEL in web service composition
- Explain the most important BPEL features
- Overview BPEL orchestration servers
- Compare BPEL with other standards
- Discuss the future of BPEL

Why Business Processes Matter

Enterprise applications and information systems have became fundamental assets of companies. Companies rely on them to be able to perform business operations. Enterprise information systems can improve the efficiency of businesses through automation of business processes. The objective of almost every company is that the applications it uses should provide comprehensive support for business processes. This means that applications should align with business processes closely.

Although this requirement does not sound very difficult to fulfill, the real-world situation shows us a different picture. Business processes are usually of dynamic nature. Companies have to improve and modify, act in an agile manner, optimize and adapt business processes to their customers, and thus improve the responsiveness of the whole company. Every change and improvement in a business process has to be reflected in the applications that provide support for them. Only companies where applications can be quickly and efficiently adapted to the changing business needs can stay competitive on the global market.

We all know that changing and modifying applications is a difficult job, which requires time. This means that information systems cannot react instantly to changes in business processes—rather they require some time to implement, test, and deploy the modifications. This time is sometimes referred to as the *information systems gap time*. It is obvious that the information systems gap time should be as short as possible. However, in the real world this is again not always the case. Let us discuss the reasons.

The time required for modifying applications is related to several factors. The most important factor, in addition to the complexity and size of the modification, is the state of the application being modified. If an application has a well-defined architecture and has been constructed keeping in mind future modifications, then it will be easier to modify. However, each modification to the application makes its architecture less robust with respect to future changes. Applications that have been maintained for several years and have gone through many modifications usually do not provide robust architecture anymore (unless they have been refactored constantly). Modifying them is difficult, time consuming, and often results in unexpected errors.

The situation gets even more complicated. Several applications still in use in companies (particularly legacy applications) have not been developed with the objective of providing support for entire business processes. Such applications, often called stovepipe applications, provide support for certain functions or tasks only. For an information system to provide complete support for business processes, it has to be able to use the functionalities of several existing applications in a coordinated and integrated way. This makes the primary objective of information systems—to provide timely, complete, and easy modifiable support for business processes—even more difficult to achieve.

Automation of Business Processes

Based on what we have said so far, we can conclude that for efficient automation of business processes through IT we need to:

- Provide a standardized way to expose and access the functionality of applications as services.
- Provide an enterprise bus infrastructure for communication and management of services, including message interception, routing, transformation, etc.
- Provide integration architecture between the various services and existing and newly developed applications used in business processes.
- Provide a specialized language for composition of exposed functionalities of applications into business processes.

For many years the software industry has been searching for efficient architectures, technologies, and methods that would make the realization of the above mentioned aspects as simple and as quick as possible. Let us briefly describe each of the four aspects.

Exposing and Accessing the Functionality of Applications as Services

The requirement to expose functionalities of applications and access them remotely has resulted in several distributed architectures and middleware products, which emerged over time. The latest distributed architecture, which combines both synchronous and asynchronous communications, is **Web Services**. Web services are the most suitable distributed architecture for exposing the functionality of applications as services.

Enterprise Bus Infrastructure for Communication and Management of Services

The enterprise bus infrastructure for communication and management of services provides answers related to the usage of services in complex enterprise information systems. In such environments support for centralized, declarative, and well-coordinated management of services and their communications is required. Because of existing middleware, the integration of different middleware products and interoperability with web services is required. These features are provided by the **Enterprise Service Bus (ESB)**.

Integration between Services and Applications

Integration between applications is a well-known topic. This integration is needed because enterprise information systems usually consist of several different applications, which address certain (sometimes isolated) functions and tasks and not whole business processes. Achieving efficient integration is related to the definition and realization of sound integration architectures, which are often very complex, particularly in large companies. Best methods and practices for building integration architectures are today known as **Service Oriented Architectures (SOA)**.

Composition of Exposed Services into Business Processes

The final aspect is the composition of exposed services of integrated applications into business processes. The most popular, commonly accepted, and specialized language for business process definition is **BPEL**, the main topic of this book. BPEL promises to acheive the holy grail of enterprise information systems—to provide an environment where business processes can be developed in an easy and efficient manner and quickly adapted to the changing needs of enterprises without too much effort.

The following figure shows the relation between SOA, web services, ESB, and BPEL:

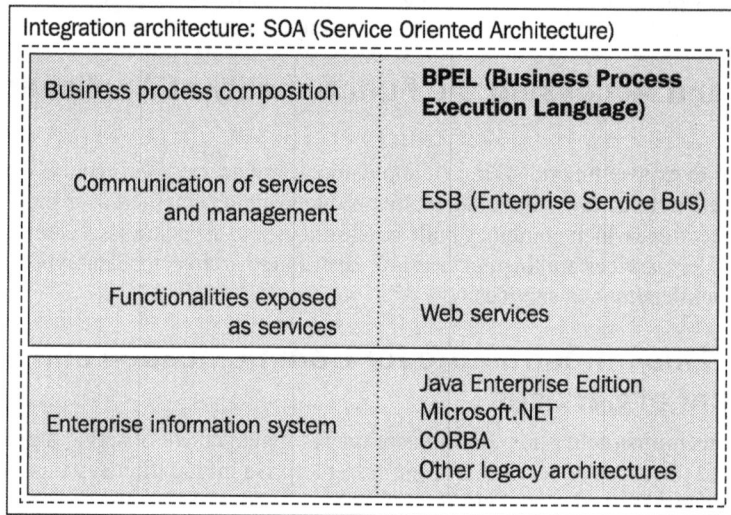

Integration architecture: SOA (Service Oriented Architecture)

Business process composition	**BPEL (Business Process Execution Language)**
Communication of services and management	ESB (Enterprise Service Bus)
Functionalities exposed as services	Web services
Enterprise information system	Java Enterprise Edition Microsoft.NET CORBA Other legacy architectures

Before starting the discussion on BPEL let us first have a quick look at web services, the enterprise service bus, and SOA.

Web Services

Web services are the latest distributed technology and, as we will see, the most suitable technology for realization of SOA. They have become the commonly used technology for interoperability and integration of applications and information systems. Web services provide the technological foundation for achieving interoperability between applications using different software platforms, operating systems, and programming languages. They are built on XML. While XML is the de facto standard for data-level integration, web services are becoming the de facto standard for service-level integration between and within enterprises.

From the technological perspective, web services are a distributed architecture. The distributed computing paradigm started with DCE (Distributed Computing Environment), RPC (Remote Procedure Call), and messaging systems, also called message-oriented middleware (products such as MQ Series, MSMQ, etc.). Then distributed objects and ORBs (Object Request Brokers), such as CORBA (Common Object Request Broker Architecture), DCOM (Distributed Component Object Model), and RMI (Remote Method Invocation), emerged. Based on them component models, such as EJB (Enterprise Java Beans), COM+ (Component Object Model), .NET Enterprise Services, and CCM (CORBA Component Model) have been developed. RPC, ORBs, and component models share similar communication model, which is based on synchronous operation invocation. Messaging systems are based on the asynchronous communication model.

How Web Services Differ from their Predecessors

Web services are similar to their predecessors, but also differ from them in several aspects. Web services are the first distributed technology to be supported by all major software vendors. Therefore they are the first technology that fulfills the promise of universal interoperability between applications running on disparate platforms. The fundamental specifications that web services are based on are SOAP (Simple Object Access Protocol), WSDL (Web Services Description Language), and UDDI (Universal Description, Discovery, and Integration). SOAP, WSDL, and UDDI are XML based, making web services protocol messages and descriptions human readable.

From the architectural perspective, web services introduce several important changes compared to earlier distributed architectures:

- Web services support loose coupling through operations that exchange data only. This differs from component and distributed object models, where behavior can also be exchanged.
- Operations in web services are based on the exchange of XML-formatted payloads. They are a collection of input, output, and fault messages. The combination of messages defines the type of operation (one-way, request/response, solicit response, or notification). This differs from previous distributed technologies. For more information, please refer to WSDL and XML Schema specifications.
- Web services provide support for asynchronous as well as synchronous interactions.
- Web services introduce the notion of endpoints and intermediaries. This allows new approaches to message processing.
- Web services are stateless. They do not follow the object paradigm.
- Web services utilize standard Internet protocols such as HTTP (Hyper Text Transfer Protocol), SMTP (Simple Mail Transfer Protocol), FTP (File Transfer Protocol), and MIME (Multipurpose Internet Mail Extensions). So, connectivity through standard Internet connections, even those secured with firewalls, is less problematic.

Web Services Technology Stack

In addition to several advantages, web services also have a couple of disadvantages. One of them is performance, which is not as good as that of distributed architectures that use binary protocols for communication. The other is that plain web services do not offer infrastructure and quality-of-service (QoS) features, such as security, transactions, and others, which have been provided by component models for several years. Web services fill this important gap by introducing additional specifications:

- **WS-Security**: Addresses authentication and message-level security, and enables secure communication with web services.
- **WS-Coordination**: Defines a coordination framework for web services and is the foundation for WS-AtomicTransaction and WS-BusinessActivity.

- **Transactions specifications** (**WS-AtomicTransaction** and **WS-BusinessActivity**): Specify support for distributed transactions with web services. AtomicTransaction specifies short duration, ACID transactions, and BusinessActivity specifies longer running business transactions, also called compensating transactions.
- **WS-Reliable Messaging**: Provides support for reliable communication and message delivery between web services over various transport protocols.
- **WS-Addressing**: Specifies message coordination and routing.
- **WS-Inspection**: Provides support for dynamic introspection of web service descriptions.
- **WS-Policy**: Specifies how policies are declared and exchanged between collaborating web services.
- **WS-Eventing**: Defines an event model for asynchronous notification of interested parties for web services.

These specifications constitute the web services technology stack, which is described in detail in Chapter 2, and is required (at least partially) for serious use of web services in enterprise applications.

Because of their flexibility, interoperability, and other features, web services are regarded as the most appropriate technology for exposing the functionalities of applications as services and are therefore the most appropriate technology for realization of SOA. Because of their wide support by all major software vendors, web services provide the possibility to use the same technology to expose services implemented in a variety of different applications ranging from mainframe-based legacy applications to the modern multi-tier applications.

Enterprise Service Bus

While web services are an appropriate technology for SOA, some other aspects need to be considered:

- In most enterprises, web services are not the only middleware solution used. Usually enterprises already have one or more middleware products, such as messaging systems and ORBs. They cannot afford to replace them overnight with web services. Therefore, there is a need to integrate different middleware products, and provide interoperability with web services.
- In order to provide connectivity between services, the use of SOAP in complex environments is not adequate. In such environments, we need ways to connect, mediate, manage, and control the services and particularly the communication between them.
- SOAP over HTTP might not be robust enough for heavy enterprise use. Enterprise information systems require dependable, robust, and secure service infrastructure.

The Enterprise Service Bus (ESB) is the software infrastructure, acting as an intermediary layer of middleware that addresses the above-mentioned requirements. An ESB adds flexibility to communication between services and simplifies the integration and reuse of services. An ESB makes it possible to connect services implemented in different technologies (such as EJBs, messaging systems, CORBA components, and legacy applications) in an easy way. An ESB can act as a mediator between different, often incompatible protocols and middleware products.

The ESB provides a robust, dependable, secure and scalable communication infrastructure between services. It also provides control over the communication and control over the use of services, including:

- **Message interception capabilities**: This allows us to intercept requests to services and responses from services and apply additional processing to them. In this manner, the ESB acts as an intermediary.
- **Routing capabilities**: This allows us to route the messages to different services based on their content, origin, or other attributes.
- **Transformation capabilities**: These allow us to transform messages before they are delivered to services. For XML formatted messages, such transformations are usually done using XSLT (Extensible Stylesheet Language for Transformations) or XQuery engines.
- **Control over the deployment, usage, and maintenance of services**: This allows logging, profiling, load balancing, performance tuning, charging for use of services, distributed deployment, on-the-fly reconfiguration, etc.
- Other important management features include the definition of correlation between messages, definition of reliable communication paths, definition of security constraints related to messages and services, etc.

ESB Features

Currently there are several products on the market that claim to provide ESB functionality. A good ESB should provide at least quality-of-service support of enterprise level, including reliability, fault-tolerance, and security. If provided by an ESB, services can depend on these features and do not need to implement them themselves. The ESB should also allow configuring any combination of these quality-of-service features and provide flexibility.

An ESB should provide support for a variety of technologies on which services are implemented. In addition to web services, an ESB should provide connectors for a broad range of technologies, such as J2EE and .NET components, messaging middleware, legacy applications, and TP monitors. The ESB needs to provide flexibility to bind any combination of services without technological constraints. It should also support a combination of different interaction models, such as queuing, routing, etc., without changing the services or requiring writing code.

An ESB should make services broadly available. This means that it should be easy to find, connect, and use a service irrespective of the technology it is implemented in. With broad availability of services, an ESB can increase reuse and can make the composition of services easier. Finally, an ESB should provide management capabilities, such as message routing, interaction, and transformation, which we have already described.

An ESB that provides these features becomes an essential part of the SOA. It provides several benefits, including increased flexibility, reduced deployment, development, and maintenance costs, and increased reliability and manageability. Therefore the ESB is an essential part of SOA, which we will discuss in the next section.

Service Oriented Architecture

Information systems need to support business changes quickly and efficiently. However, they also need to adapt to the fast development of new technologies. The majority of enterprise information systems are heterogeneous, containing a range of different systems, applications, technologies, and architectures. Integration of these technologies is crucial as only integrated information systems can deliver business values, such as efficient decision-making support, instant access to information, data integrity, along with decreased cost of software development and maintenance.

To manage problems related to changing requirements, technology development, and integration, different methods have been proposed and used over time. Service-oriented architecture is the latest architectural approach related to the integration, development, and maintenance of complex enterprise information systems.

SOA is not a radically new architecture, but rather the evolution of well-known distributed architectures and integration methods. Integration between applications has evolved from early days to well-defined integration methods and principles, often referred to as EAI (Enterprise Application Integration). EAI initially focused on integration of applications within enterprises (intra-EAI). With the increasing need for integration between companies (B2B, business-to-business), the focus of EAI has been extended to inter-EAI.

SOA improves and extends the flexibility of earlier integration methods (EAI) and distributed architectures, and focuses on reusability of existing applications and systems, efficient interoperability and integration of applications, and composition of business processes out of services (functionalities) provided by applications. An important objective of SOA is also the ability to apply changes in the future in a relatively easy and straightforward way.

SOA defines the concepts, architecture, and process framework, to enable cost-efficient development, integration, and maintenance of information systems through reduction of complexity, and stimulation of integration and reuse. Let us look at the definition of SOA, as provided in a paper by Bernhard Borges, Kerrie Holley, and Ali Arsanjani:

SOA is the architectural style that supports loosely coupled services to enable business flexibility in an interoperable, technology-agnostic manner. SOA consists of a composite set of business-aligned services that support a flexible and dynamically re-configurable end-to-end business processes realization using interface-based service descriptions.

SOA Concepts

SOA is more than just a set of technologies. SOA is not directly related to any technology, although it is most often implemented with web services. Web services are the most appropriate technology for SOA realization. However, using web services is not adequate to build SOA. We have to use web services according to the concepts that SOA defines.

The most important SOA concepts are:

- Services
- Self-describing interfaces with coarse granulation
- Exchange of messages
- Support for synchronous and asynchronous communication
- Loose coupling
- Service registries
- Quality of service
- Composition of services into business processes

Services

Services provide business functionalities, such as an application for a business travel, an application for a loan, etc. This differs considerably from technology-oriented functionalities, such as retrieving or updating a table in a database. Services in SOA must provide business value, hide implementation details, and be autonomous. Service consumers are software entities, which call the service and use its functionality.

Interfaces

Service consumers access the service through its interface. The interface of a service defines a set of public operation signatures. The interface is a contract between the service provider and a service consumer. The interface is separated from the implementation, is self-describing, and platform independent. Interface description provides a basis for the implementation of the service by the service provider and a basis for the implementation of the service consumers. Each interface defines a set of operations. In order to define business services, we need to focus on correct granulation of operations. SOA services are best modeled with coarse granulation.

Messages

Operations are defined as a set of messages. Messages specify the data to be exchanged and describe it in a platform- and language-independent way using schemas. Services exchange only data, which differs considerably from object-oriented and component approaches, where behavior (implementation code) can also be exchanged. Operations should be idempotent (an operation is idempotent if repeated invocations have the same effect as one invocation). WSDL is a service description language that meets SOA criteria.

Synchronicity

Service consumers access the services through the service bus. This can be either a transport protocol, such as SOAP, or an ESB. Service consumers can use synchronous or asynchronous communication modes to invoke operations of services. In synchronous mode, a service operation returns a response to the service consumer after the processing is complete. The service consumer has to wait for the completion. Usually we use synchronous mode with operations complete processing in a short time. In asynchronous mode a service operation does not return a response to the consumer, although it may return an acknowledgement so that the consumer knows that the operation has been invoked successfully. If a response is needed, usually a callback from the service to the consumer is used. In such a scenario, correlation between messages is needed.

Loose Coupling

Through the self-describing interfaces, coarse granulation, exchange of data structures, and support for synchronous and asynchronous communication modes, loose coupling of services is achieved. Loosely coupled services are services that expose only the necessary dependencies and reduce all kinds of artificial dependencies. This is particularly important when services are subject to frequent changes. Minimal dependencies assure that there will be a minimal amount of changes required to other services when one service is modified. Such an approach improves robustness, makes systems more resilient to changes, and promotes reuse of services.

Registries

To simplify and automate searching for the appropriate service, services are maintained in service registries, which act as directory listings. Service providers publish services in registries; service consumers look up the services in the registries. Lookup can be done by name, service functionality, or business process properties. UDDI is an example of a service registry.

Quality of Service

Services usually have associated quality-of-service attributes. Such attributes include security, reliable messaging, transaction, correlation, management, policy, and other requirements. The infrastructure must provide support for these attributes. Quality-of-service attributes are often important in large information systems. In web services, quality-of-service attributes are covered by WS-* specifications, such as WS-Security, WS-Addressing, WS-Coordination, etc. Quality of service is also provided by the ESB.

Composition of Services into Business Processes

The final, and probably the most important, SOA concept is composition of services into business processes. Services are composed in a particular order and follow a set of rules to provide support for business processes. Composition of services allows us to provide support for business processes in a flexible and relatively easy way. It also enables us to modify business processes quickly and therefore provide support to changed requirements faster and with less effort. For composition, we will use a dedicated language, BPEL, and an engine on which business process definitions will be executed. Only when we reach the level of service composition can we realize all the benefits of SOA.

The figure bellow shows the architectural view of SOA and positions the above-mentioned concepts:

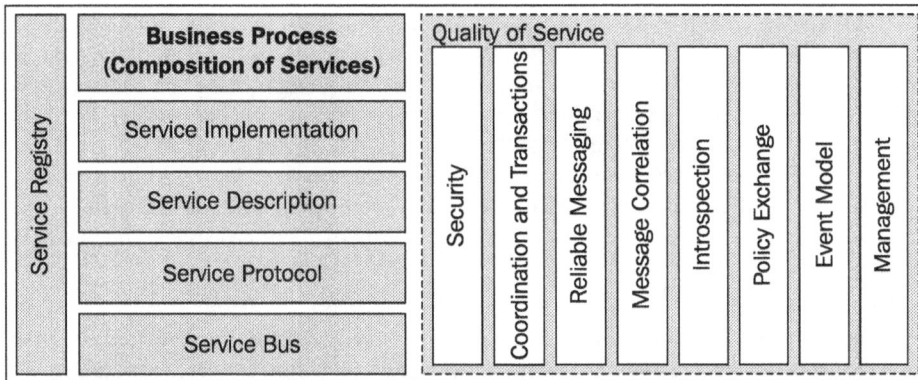

Service Registry
Business Process (Composition of Services)
Service Implementation
Service Description
Service Protocol
Service Bus
Quality of Service
Security
Coordination and Transactions
Reliable Messaging
Message Correlation
Introspection
Policy Exchange
Event Model
Management

Let us now fill the technologies into the above picture to understand the connection between SOA concepts and technologies that provide means for their realization. Notice that the mere use of a specific technology does not guarantee that we build SOA-compliant architecture. For example, with web services we can develop business services (for example, a loan application), but we can also develop technology-focused services (updating the database, for example). So, it is essential that technologies are used according to the guidelines provided by SOA concepts:

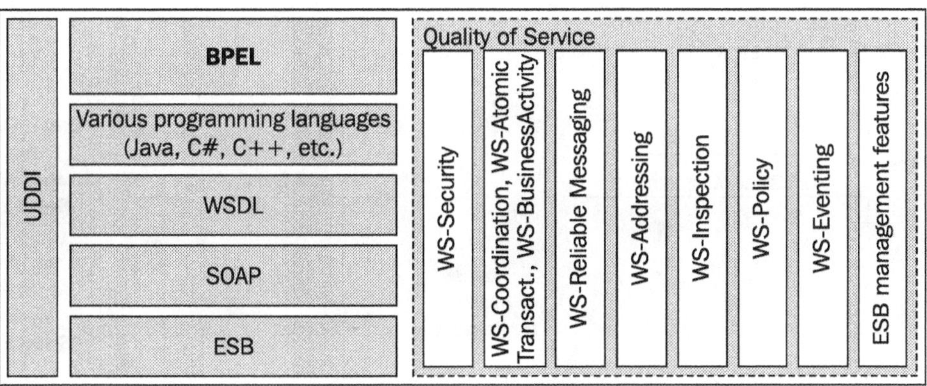

For this picture, we can have two views. The bottom-up view of SOA sees different applications exposing their functionalities through business services. This enables access to functionalities (services) of different existing and newly developed applications in a standard way. Access to services is important because a typical enterprise has a large number of applications, which have to be integrated.

Developing business services, either through reuse of existing applications or by new development, is not sufficient. We also need to compose services into business processes—this is the second, the top-down or process-oriented approach to SOA. We would obviously prefer a relatively simple and straightforward way to compose and modify business processes. This is where the BPEL becomes important. In the next section we will discuss service composition and BPEL.

Service Composition

We have seen that services provide business-aligned operations. To fulfill the SOA promise services need to be composed into new larger services. We compose services until the aggregate services provide support for the whole business processes. Business processes are thus defined as a collection of activities through which services are invoked. For the outside world—that is for the clients—a business process looks like any other service. In real-world scenarios we will usually create two kinds of business processes: those that will contain services from within enterprise only, and those that will consume services provided by several companies. With service composition we can use services provided by business partners in our processes, and business partners can use our services in their processes.

> A business process is a collection of coordinated service invocations and related activities that produce a business result, either within a single organization or across several.

For example, a business process for planning of business travel will invoke several services. In an oversimplified scenario, the business process will require us to specify the employee name, destination, dates, and other travel details. Then the process will invoke a web service to check the employee status. Based on the employee status it will select the appropriate travel class. Then it will invoke web services of several airline companies (such as American Airlines, Delta Airlines, etc.) to check the airfare price and buy the one with the lowest price. The structure of services composed into the business process is shown in the following figure. In Chapter 3 we will discuss this example in detail and show how to define this process using BPEL:

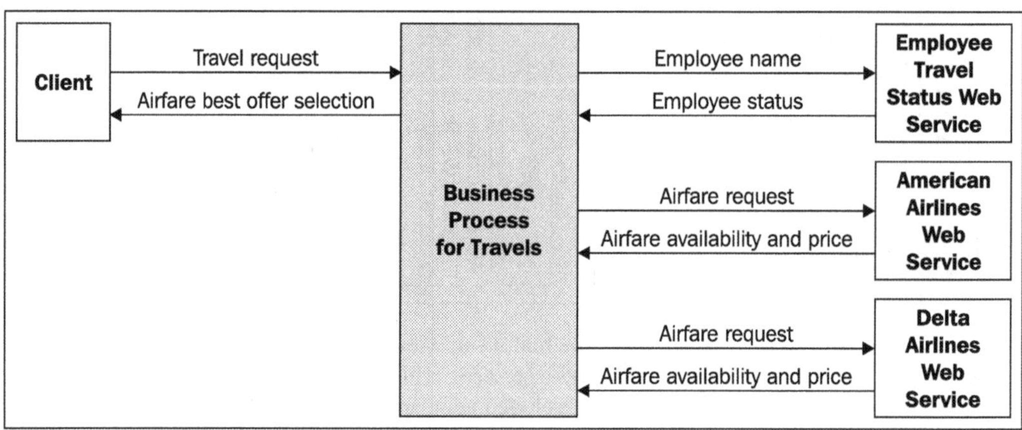

From the perspective of our business process, we do not care whether the web service for checking the employee status accesses a legacy system, a database directly, or retrieves the status in any other way. We also do not care whether the web services of airline companies are composed of other, lower-level services. From the perspective of the client for our business process the client sees the process as any other service and does not care whether the process is implemented through composition of other services, or some other way. This stimulates reuse and further composition. Real-world business processes will usually be much more complicated than our example. Usually they will contain several services and invoke their operations either in sequence or in parallel. They will also contain flow logic, handle faults, take care of transactions and message correlation, etc.

Composition of services into business processes requires the definition of collaboration activities and data-exchange messages between involved web services. WSDL provides the basic technical description and specifications for messages that are exchanged. However, the description provided by WSDL does not go beyond simple interactions between the client (sender) and the web service (receiver). These interactions may be stateless, synchronous, or asynchronous. These relations are inadequate to express, model, and describe complex compositions of multiple web services in business activities, which usually consist of several messages exchanged in a well-defined order. In such complex compositions, synchronous and asynchronous messages can be combined, and interactions are usually long running, often involving state information that has to be preserved. An important aspect is also the ability to describe how to handle faults and other exceptional situations. Given the limitations of WSDL, we need a mechanism to describe the composition of web services into more complex processes.

The composition of services into business processes could be realized using one of the well-known programming languages (Java, C#, ...). But it turns out that the composition of services differs somehow from traditional programming. With composition, we merge functionalities (services) into larger services and processes. In other words, we do programming in the large, which differs from traditional programming in the small. Programming in the large refers to representation of the high-level state transition logic of a system. Using programming languages, such as Java, C#, etc., for composition often results in inflexible solutions, particularly because there is no clear separation between the process flow and the business logic, which should not be tightly coupled.

In addition to these facts, the composition of business processes has other specific requirements, such as support for many process instances, long-running processes, compensation, etc. All this makes the use of dedicated solutions reasonable. This is why over the years several proprietary BPM (Business Process Management) products have been developed, such as Dralasoft Workflow and Tibco Business Process Management. The disadvantage of using proprietary BPMs is that these are traditionally niche products, sold from a top-down perspective to large business users. Such products usually are expensive and bound to a certain provider.

BPEL for Service Composition

General adoption of business process automation solutions requires a standard foundation and a specialized language for composing services into business processes that provides the ability to express business processes in a standardized way, using a commonly accepted language. BPEL is such a language and is quickly becoming the dominant standard. The main goal of BPEL is to standardize the process of automation between web services.

> With BPEL we can define business processes that make use of services and business processes that externalize their functionality as services.

Within enterprises, BPEL is used to standardize enterprise application integration and extend the integration to previously isolated systems. Between enterprises, BPEL enables easier and more effective integration with business partners. BPEL stimulates enterprises to further define their business processes, which in turn leads to business process optimization, reengineering, and the selection of the most appropriate processes, thus further optimizing the organization. Definitions of business processes described in BPEL do not influence existing systems. BPEL is the key technology in environments where functionalities already are or will be exposed via web services. With increases in the use of web service technology, the importance of BPEL will rise further.

IBM, BEA, and Microsoft developed the first version of BPEL in August 2002. Since then SAP and Siebel have joined, which has resulted in several modifications and improvements and adoption of version 1.1 in March 2003. In April 2003, BPEL was submitted to OASIS (Organization for the Advancement of Structured Information Standards) for standardization purposes, where the WSBPEL TC (Web Services Business Process Execution Language Technical Committee) has been formed. Many vendors have joined the WSBPEL TC (`http://www.oasis-open.org/committees/tc_home.php?wg_abbrev=wsbpel`) since. This has led to even broader acceptance in industry.

BPEL represents a convergence of two early workflow languages, **WSFL** (Web Services Flow Language) and **XLANG**. WSFL was designed by IBM and is based on the concept of directed graphs. XLANG was designed by Microsoft and is a block-structured language. BPEL combines both approaches and provides a rich vocabulary for the description of business processes.

> In this book, we use BPEL version 1.1.

BPEL uses an XML-based vocabulary to specify and describe business processes. BPEL version 1.1 is based on the WSDL 1.1, XML Schema 1.0, and XPath 1.0 specifications. Familiarity with them is helpful for learning BPEL.

BPEL Features

With BPEL we can define simple and complex business processes. To a certain extent, BPEL is similar to traditional programming languages. It offers constructs, such as loops, branches, variables, assignments, etc. that allow us to define business processes in an algorithmic way. BPEL is a specialized language focused on the definition of business processes. Therefore, on one hand it offers constructs, which make the definition of processes relatively simple. On the other hand, it is less complex than traditional programming languages, which simplifies learning.

The most important BPEL constructs are related to the invocation of web services. BPEL makes it easy to invoke operations of web services either synchronously or asynchronously. We can invoke operations either in sequence or in parallel. We can also wait for callbacks. BPEL provides a rich vocabulary for fault handling, which is very important as robust business processes need to react to failures in a smart way. BPEL also provides support for long-running process and compensation, which allows undoing partial work done by a process that has not finished successfully. Listed below are the most important features that BPEL provides. With BPEL we can:

- Describe the logic of business processes through composition of services
- Compose larger business processes out of smaller processes and services
- Handle synchronous and asynchronous (often long-running) operation invocations on services, and manage callbacks that occur at later times
- Invoke service operations in sequence or parallel
- Selectively compensate completed activities in case of failures
- Maintain multiple long-running transactional activities, which are also interruptible
- Resume interrupted or failed activities to minimize work to be redone
- Route incoming messages to the appropriate processes and activities
- Correlate requests within and across business processes
- Schedule activities based on the execution time and define their order of execution
- Execute activities in parallel and define how parallel flows merge based on synchronization conditions
- Structure business processes into several scopes
- Handle message-related and time-related events

Orchestration and Choreography

Depending on the requirements, composition of services can address private or public processes, for which two terms are used:

- Orchestration
- Choreography

In **orchestration**, a central process (which can be another web service) takes control over the involved web services and coordinates the execution of different operations on the web services involved in the operation. This is done as per the requirements of the orchestration. The involved web services do not know (and do not need to know) that they are involved into a composition and that they are a part of a higher business process. Only the central coordinator of the orchestration knows this, so the orchestration is centralized with explicit definitions of operations and the order of invocation of web services. Orchestration is usually used in private business processes and is schematically shown overleaf:

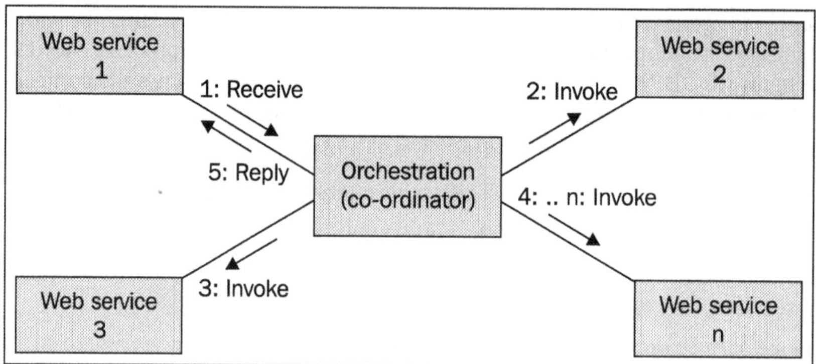

Choreography on the other hand does not rely on a central coordinator. Rather, each web service involved in the choreography knows exactly when to execute its operations and whom to interact with. Choreography is a collaborative effort focused on exchange of messages in public business processes. All participants of the choreography need to be aware of the business process, operations to execute, messages to exchange, and the timing of message exchanges. Choreography in web services composition is as shown in the following figure:

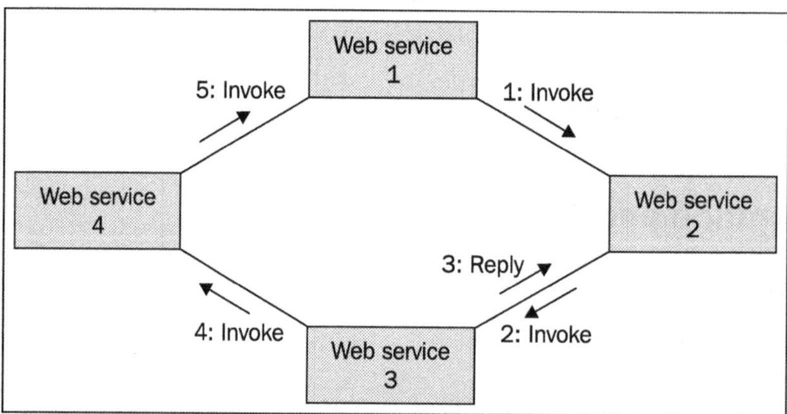

From the perspective of composing web services to execute business processes, orchestration has an advantage over choreography. Orchestration is a more flexible paradigm, although the line between orchestration and choreography is vanishing. Orchestration has the following advantages:

- We know exactly who is responsible for the execution of the whole business process.
- We can incorporate web services, even those that are not aware that they are a part of a business process.
- We can also provide alternative scenarios when faults occur.

BPEL provides support for orchestration and choreography through executable and abstract business processes.

Executable and Abstract Processes

With BPEL, we can describe business processes in two distinct ways:

- We can specify the exact details of business processes. Such processes are called **executable business processes** and follow the orchestration paradigm. They can be executed by an orchestration engine.
- We can specify the public message exchange between parties only. Such processes are called **abstract business processes**. They do not include the internal details of process flows and are not executable. They follow the choreography paradigm.

Executable business processes are processes that compose a set of existing services and specify the exact algorithm of activities and input and output messages. Such processes are executable by BPEL engines. Executable processes are important because they are the direct answer to the problem of business process automation through IT that we have discussed earlier in this chapter. With BPEL executable processes, we are able to specify the exact algorithm of service composition in a relatively simple and straightforward way, and execute it on a BPEL-compliant engine. Executable processes fill the gap between the business process specifications and the code responsible for their execution.

When we define an executable business process in BPEL, we actually define a new web service that is a composition of existing services. The interface of the new BPEL composite web service uses a set of port types, through which it provides operations like any other web service. To invoke an executable business process, we have to invoke the resulting composite web service. You can see that executable business processes are the most important way of using BPEL. In the majority of cases, BPEL is used to specify executable processes.

Abstract business processes, on the other hand, are not executable. They specify public message exchange between parties only—the externally observable aspects of process behavior. The description of the externally observable behavior of a business process may be related to a single service or a set of services. It might also describe the behavior of a participant in a business process. Abstract processes will usually be defined mainly for two scenarios:

- To describe the behavior of a service without knowing exactly in which business process it will take part.
- To define collaboration protocols among multiple parties and precisely describe the external behavior of each party.

Abstract processes are rarely used. The most common scenario is to use them as a template to define executable processes. Abstract processes can be used to replace sets of rules usually expressed in natural language, which is often ambiguous. In this book, we will first focus on executable processes and come back to abstract processes in Chapter 4.

Relation of BPEL to Other Languages

BPEL is not the only language for business process management and modeling. Before we start discussing the technical aspects of BPEL let us overview the relation of BPEL to other languages. Recently, several languages have been proposed, including:

- XLANG and the new version XLANG/s from Microsoft
- BPML (Business Process Modeling Language) from BPMI.org, the Business Process Management Initiative
- WSFL (Web Services Flow Language) from IBM
- WSCL (Web Services Conversation Language) from HP, submitted to W3C
- BPSS (Business Process Specification Schema), part of the ebXML framework
- WSCI (Web Services Choreography Interface), co-developed by Sun, SAP, BEA, and Intalio and submitted to W3C
- WS-CDL (Web Services Choreography Description Language), at the time of writing a W3C Working Draft

The following figure shows a timeline of the mentioned languages, as they have been developed:

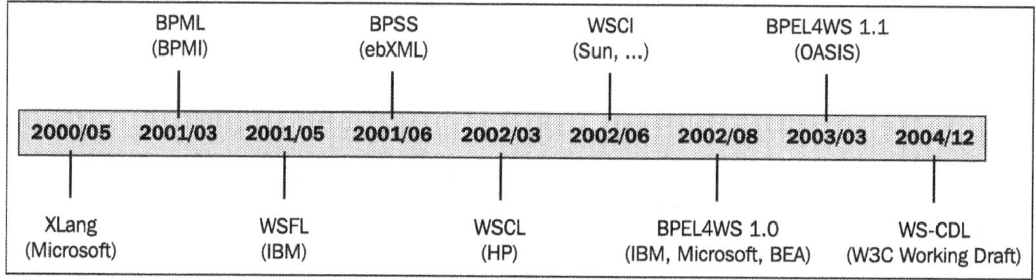

We have already mentioned that BPEL represents a convergence of XLANG and WSFL. HP's WSCL has been submitted to W3C in 2002 as a W3C Note. Since then it has not been very active and has not gained much support from the industry. In the following sections we will briefly describe ebXML BPSS, BPML, WSCI, and WS-CDL.

ebXML BPSS

ebXML (Electronic Business XML) is a framework that provides a set of technologies, BPSS (Business Process Specification Schema) being one of them. ebXML has been developed under the initiative of OASIS and UN/CEFACT and consists of the following technologies:

- **Messaging**: Uses SOAP with attachments for communication between partners
- **Registry and repository**: Similar to UDDI registry, but offers additional functionality through the repository
- **Core Components**: Used for construction of business documents

- **CPP (Collaboration Protocol Profile)**: Used to express a partner profile
- **CPA (Collaboration Protocol Agreement)**: Used to express an agreement between partners
- **BPSS (Business Process Specification Schema)**: Used for the specification of business processes

BPSS covers the same domain as BPEL. The BPSS approach to the process specification follows the choreography pattern and is therefore comparable to abstract BPEL processes. In addition to specifying the process logic, BPSS also specifies the communication protocol details.

BPSS is designed around the concept of business transactions, which is, however, not fully conformant with the Web Services Transactions specifications. A BPSS business transaction is used to describe message exchange between two abstract roles: the sender and the responder. Each message consists of an XML document and optional attachments, which can be XML or binary. For each responding message, we specify whether it is a positive or negative message. Each message is associated with a business transaction protocol. Collaboration in BPSS can be bilateral or multi-party and is described by the business transaction protocol.

We can see that BPSS is not a direct alternative to BPEL and is used in environments where ebXML is applied. For more information on ebXML, read the following books:

- *ebXML: Concepts and Application* by Brian Gibb and Suresh Damodaran, John Wiley & Sons, October 21, 2002, ISBN: 0-7645-4960-X
- *ebXML: The New Global Standard for Doing Business over the Internet* by Alan Kotok and David RR Webber, SAMS, August 23, 2001, ISBN: 0-7357-1117-8
- *ebXML Simplified: A Guide to the New Standard for Global E-Commerce* by Eric Chiu, John Wiley & Sons, June 15, 2002; ISBN: 0-471-20475-7

BPML

BPML (Business Process Markup Language) has been developed by BPMI.org (Business Process Management Initiative). Intalio has played an important role, and has been the initiator of BPML. BPML is a meta-language for modeling business processes and provides an abstract execution model for describing collaborations and transactions. It defines a formal model for expressing abstract and executable processes, and supports:

- Data management
- Conformity
- Exception handling
- Operation semantics

BPML can describe a process in a specific language, defined on top of the extensible BPML scheme. Business processes are defined as groups of flows (control flows, data flows, and event flows). Formatting features, security rules, and transactional contexts can also be defined. BPML offers support for synchronous and asynchronous distributed transactions and can be used for process components of existing applications.

Comparing BPML to BPEL shows that both share similar roots in web services and leverage other web services specifications, particularly WS-Security, WS-Coordination, and WS-Transactions. BPML, however, supports modeling more complex business processes through its support for advanced semantics such as nested processes and complex compensated transactions. BPML can therefore be regarded as a superset of BPEL. The extensions of BPEL with business rules, task management, human interactions, etc. are defined in BPXL (Business Process Extension Layers). The fact that both BPEL and BPML share the same idioms and have similar syntax can be a basis for possible future convergence. This is interesting because BPMI.org provides solutions for analysis and design of business processes (Business Process Modeling Notation—BPMN), a semantic model (Business Process Semantic Model—BPSM), and a query language (Business Process Query Language—BPQL). Find out more at `http://www.bpmi.org/`.

WSCI

WSCI (Web Services Choreography Interface) version 1.0 has been developed by Sun, BEA, SAP, and Intalio. WSCI is a language for describing flows of messages exchanged by web services in the context of a process. It allows us to describe the observable behavior of a web service in a message exchange. WSCI also describes the collective message exchange among interacting web services, providing a global and message-oriented view of a process involving multiple web services.

In WSCI, message exchange is described from the viewpoint of each web service. Each exchange can be qualified by message correlations, transactions descriptions, and location capabilities. WSCI therefore describes the observable behavior of web services. However, WSCI does not address the definition of the processes driving the message exchange. It also does not address the definition of the internal behavior of each web service.

Since WSCI follows the choreography pattern and does not address defining executable business processes, it compares directly only to BPEL abstract processes. WSCI has a cleaner interface, which makes it a little easier to learn than BPEL. The WSCI specification has also been submitted to W3C, which has published it as a W3C Note. Further, W3C has formed a WS-Choreography working group, which will address the choreography of web services, but has only released the requirements specification so far.

WSCI has not gained industry support comparable to BPEL and the only company that has provided support in tools is Sun with the SunONE WSCI Editor. The industry consensus seems to support BPEL. The WSCI specification is accessible at `http://www.w3.org/TR/wsci/`.

WS-CDL

WS-CDL is a language for specifying the choreography of collaborating services. It targets the composition of interoperable collaborations between services. With WS-CDL we can specify peer-to-peer collaboration of web services through the definition of their observable behavior. We can define sets of rules that define how and in what order different services should act together. Such specification provides a flexible systemic view of the process.

Its authors position WS-CDL as a complementary language to BPEL (and other business process languages). While BPEL focuses on behavior specification of a specific business partner, WS-

CDL focuses on the description of message interchanges between business partners. WS-CDL provides the global model needed by BPEL processes to ensure that the behavior of endpoints is consistent across all cooperating services.

A business partner can use the WS-CDL choreography specification to verify if their internal processes have their outside behavior defined in a way that will allow them to participate in choreography. WS-CDL choreography specifications can be used to generate public interfaces, for example, specified using BPEL abstract processes. WS-CDL specifications are also useful at run time to verify the execution of message exchange between business partners.

As WS-CDL is a complementary language to BPEL we cannot make a direct comparison. However, WS-CDL differs considerably from BPEL. With WS-CDL we define the message flows exchanged by all partners, while with BPEL we focus on message flow and the behavior of a specific partner—that is on the internal behavior of a business process. The WS-CDL description of message flows is done from a general perspective, while BPEL specifies message exchange from the point of view of a specific partner. A BPEL process specifies activities that are executed. WS-CDL specifies reactive rules, which are used by all participants of a collaboration.

At the time of writing WS-CDL has been under development and has been published as a W3C Working Draft. This is why WS-CDL has not yet gained wide industry support. It is also difficult to predict how important the role of WS-CDL will be in the future. The WS-CDL specification is accessible at `http://www.w3.org/TR/ws-cdl-10/`.

BPEL Servers Overview

BPEL servers provide a run-time environment for executing BPEL business processes. BPEL is strongly related to web services and to the modern software platforms that support web service development, particularly to Java Enterprise Edition and Microsoft .NET. BPEL servers leverage Java Enterprise Edition or .NET application server environments, where they can make use of the services provided by application servers, such as security, transactions, scalability, integration with databases, components such as EJBs (Enterprise Java Beans) and COM+ (Component Object Model), messaging systems such as JMS (Java Message Service) or MSMQ (Microsoft Message Queue), etc.

BPEL servers exist for Java Enterprise Edition, .NET, and other platforms. The most important commercial servers are listed below:

- Oracle BPEL Process Manager (`http://www.oracle.com/technology/products/ias/bpel/index.html`)
- Microsoft BizTalk (`http://www.microsoft.com/biztalk/`)
- IBM WebSphere Business Integration Server Foundation (`http://www.ibm.com/software/integration/wbisf`)
- IBM alphaWorks BPWS4J (`http://www.alphaworks.ibm.com/tech/bpws4j`)
- BEA WebLogic Integration and the related AquaLogic (`http://www.bea.com/framework.jsp?CNT=index.htm&FP=/content/products/weblogic/integrate/`)

- OpenStorm Service Orchestrator (`http://www.openstorm.com/`)
- Active Endpoints ActiveWebflow (`http://www.active-endpoints.com/products/index.html`)
- Sun Java Integration Suite for Java Enterprise Suite (`http://www.sun.com/software/javaenterprisesystem/`), formerly known as SeeBeyond eInsight Business Process Manager (`http://www.seebeyond.com/software/einsight.asp`)
- Cape Clear Orchestration Studio (`http://www.capeclear.com/products/`)
- OpenLink Virtuoso Universal Server (`http://virtuoso.openlinksw.com/`)
- Parasoft BPEL Maestro (`http://www.parasoft.com/jsp/products/home.jsp?product=BPEL`)
- Fiorano Business Integration Suite (`http://www.fiorano.com/products/fesb/fioranobis.htm`)
- PolarLake Integration Suite (`http://www.polarlake.com/en/html/products/integration/index.shtml`)
- Fuego BPM (`http://www.fuegotech.com/fuego_software.html`)
- Digité Enterprise Business Process Management (`http://www.digite.com/4.0/products/digite_ent_business-process.htm`)

There are also a few open-source implementations:

- ActiveBPEL Engine (`http://www.activebpel.org/`)
- FiveSight Process eXecution Engine PXE (`http://www.fivesight.com/pxe.shtml`)
- bexee BPEL Execution Engine (`http://sourceforge.net/projects/bexee`)
- Apache Agila (`http://wiki.apache.org/agila/`), formerly known as Twister (`http://www.smartcomps.org/twister/`)

Several BPEL design and development tools are also available. These tools enable graphical development of BPEL processes. Some design tools are bundled with servers. Provided below is a list of important stand-alone design and development tools that support BPEL:

- Oracle JDeveloper 10g (`http://www.oracle.com/technology/products/jdev/index.html`)
- Oracle BPEL Designer for Eclipse (`http://www.oracle.com/technology/products/ias/bpel/index.html`)
- IBM WebSphere Studio Application Developer Integration Edition (`http://www.ibm.com/software/integration/wsadie/`)
- iGrafx BPEL (`http://www.igrafx.com/products/bpel/index.html`)
- itp Process Modeler for Microsoft Visio (`http://www.itp-commerce.com/`)

The following sections provide an overview of some BPEL servers.

Oracle BPEL Process Manager

The Oracle BPEL Process Manager 10g supports BPEL version 1.1. It provides a complete run-time environment for orchestration of web services with support for long-running transactions. The server is developed in Java and comes in three versions:

- The regular version uses the Oracle 10g Application Server (Oracle Containers for Java—OC4J).
- Versions for BEA WebLogic application server (with native integration with BEA Workshop) and JBOSS are available.
- Manual installation and configuration is possible on top of IBM WebSphere and SunONE application servers.

In addition to the usual features Oracle BPEL Process Manager provides support for automatic passivization of processes that wait for asynchronous callbacks. This is called dehydration. Through the BPEL console, it is possible to visually monitor the execution of BPEL process definitions. It is also possible to review audit trails and track transactions. The server also provides a BPEL Debugger, which simplifies the debugging of BPEL processes considerably. An important feature is native integration with Java Enterprise Edition, which simplifies inclusion of Java Enterprise Edition resources, such as EJB (Enterprise Java Beans), JMS (Java Message Service), JCA (Java Connector Architecture), or JDBC databases, through Web Services Invocation Framework (WSIF).

Oracle also provides two graphical development tools. Oracle JDeveloper 10g provides integrated support for graphical development of BPEL processes and related WSDL and XML documents. It also provides support for direct deployment, testing, and debugging. Oracle BPEL Designer for Eclipse is an Eclipse plug-in that provides a graphical environment for the development of BPEL processes and related WSDL documents. Preview versions of all Oracle BPEL products can be downloaded from the company's website. Chapter 5 and Chapter 6 are dedicated to Oracle BPEL Process Manager and BPEL features of JDeveloper.

Microsoft BizTalk

Microsoft BizTalk Server 2004 and the upcoming 2006 use the Microsoft .NET framework. BizTalk is more than just a BPEL execution environment. It is an integration server product with support for integrated business processes and web services. It provides integration between messaging and orchestration as well as security. The changes in the BizTalk Server 2004 and 2006 architecture, compared to previous versions, reflect the focus on more comprehensive support for web services. One of the functions is support for BPEL version 1.1, which enables existing BizTalk processes to be exported to BPEL, or BPEL processes from other partners to be imported. Chapter 7 is dedicated to Microsoft BizTalk Server.

IBM WebSphere Business Integration Server Foundation

IBM WebSphere Business Integration Server Foundation (WBISF) is a BPEL server built on top of the IBM WebSphere Application Server. It is a Java Enterprise Edition based product, which supports BPEL version 1.1. It can be used in conjunction with WebSphere Studio Application

Developer, Integration Edition, which is a graphical integrated development environment and enables visual drag-and-drop development of BPEL processes. It also provides a visual debugger.

The WBISF server provides full support for BPEL. It also provides dehydration, compensation, clustering, and versioning capabilities. It provides a built-in XSLT engine as well as integration capabilities with the Java platform, particularly through JCA (Java Connector Architecture). Through JCA we can integrate BPEL processes with CICS, IMS, and other IBM products. Other interesting features of WBISF include Business Rules Beans, which enable us to define and manage business rules in an easy way, and human workflow support, which enables us to include human interactions in BPEL processes.

IBM BPWS4J

IBM BPWS4J version 2.1 has been developed by alphaWorks and provides support for BPEL version 1.1. The acronym stands for the IBM Business Process Execution Language for Web Services Java Run Time and includes the run-time support for execution of BPEL processes, a BPEL validating tool, and an Eclipse plug-in with a simple editor for creating and modifying BPEL documents.

BPES4J is developed in Java and has to be deployed on top of an existing Java Enterprise Edition application server. It has been tested with IBM WebSphere Application Server and with Apache Tomcat. It provides process integration with web services and EJBs. The product can be downloaded from the IBM alphaWorks website.

ActiveBPEL Engine and ActiveWebflow

ActiveBPEL engine is an open-source BPEL implementation written in Java. It supports BPEL version 1.1. In addition to BPEL process execution the engine provides support for persistence, queues, and alarms. It runs within a Java Enterprise Edition compliant web or application server, such as Tomcat or any other commercial or open-source Java Enterprise Edition server. ActiveBPEL is currently the only open-source BPEL engine, which gives it a unique position, comparable to JBoss among application servers. JBoss and ActiveBPEL have even announced that they will combine their technologies to deliver a comprehensive open-source BPEL development and deployment platform.

The ActiveBPEL engine is developed and maintained by Active Endpoints. Therefore ActiveBPEL is also the foundation for BPEL solutions developed by Active Endpoints, particularly for the ActiveWebflow BPEL Server and Designer. ActiveWebflow is a commercial business process management solution based on BPEL standard. It includes a visual designer, which is based on the Eclipse platform, and a Java Enterprise Edition server. In addition to visual design of BPEL processes, the designer offers the ability to perform visual simulations of execution scenarios. The server offers native integration with Java Enterprise Edition, particularly with EJBs and JMS.

OpenStorm Service Orchestrator

OpenStorm provides versions of its Service Orchestrator suite for Java Enterprise Edition as well as .NET. Full lifecycle development of BPEL processes is supported. For design and development there is an integrated studio, which provides the ability to visually define XML mappings using XPath, in addition to designing the BPEL processes and corresponding WSDLs. The Java Enterprise Edition version of the server provides integration with Java Enterprise Edition technologies and the .NET version provides integration with .NET technologies. At the time of writing OpenStorm does not provide demo or preview versions of its products.

The Future of BPEL

OASIS is responsible for further development of BPEL since April 2003. An OASIS Technical Committee, called WSBPEL TC, has been formed for the development of a new BPEL version, called WS-BPEL 2.0. The technical committee, which supervises and influences further development of BPEL, has many new members. This ensures that BPEL will be extended with new features and also ensures continuity of development. The number of participants involved in BPEL shows that industry support is large and still increasing. More information on WSBPEL TC can be found at `http://www.oasis-open.org/committees/tc_home.php?wg_abbrev=wsbpel`.

WS-BPEL version 2.0 is at the time of writing in the working draft stage, without any dates announced for final release. Based on the working drafts, WS-BPEL 2.0 does not show major differences from BPEL 1.1. The concepts on which BPEL is based on will stay unchanged. Version 2.0 will, however, introduce improvements and enhancements to the language, which will make it even more powerful. There will be a few new activities for loops (such as `<repeatUntil>` and `<forEach>`), variable assignments will be simplified, and improvements will be made to fault handling, compensation, and event handling. Partner links will be improved and will enable automatic initialization. There will probably also be some minor changes in function names and a few new standard faults will be defined. At the time of writing it is not clear whether WS-BPEL 2.0 will also provide support for user interactions, a field not covered by the current BPEL specification.

We can see that WS-BPEL 2.0 will be an evolution of the current BPEL version 1.1. To upgrade business processes specified in BPEL 1.1 to version 2.0 will take only minor effort.

Conclusion

In this chapter, we have become familiar with the BPEL, its role in the SOA, and basic concepts related with service composition and the definition of business processes. BPEL provides a rich vocabulary for defining processes and has several features not found in programming languages. This makes BPEL the preferred choice for composition of services. Major software vendors on Java and Microsoft platforms support BPEL, and even open-source implementations exist. Based on the comparison to other technologies and languages, we have seen that BPEL plays important role in service composition.

BPEL fits very well into the SOA, and with BPEL, we can define executable business processes and abstract business processes. Executable processes are the most important and allow us to define the exact order in which services are composed.

> To continue reading, you have two choices:
>
> If you are interested in the web services technology stack, which covers WS-Addressing, WS-Security, WS-Coordination, WS-AtomicTransaction, WS-BusinessActivity, and other specifications, you should continue with Chapter 2.
>
> If you are interested in BPEL only then you should proceed directly to Chapter 3.

2
Web Services Technology Stack

Chapter 1 introduced you to SOA and BPEL—a language for composing web services. The composition of web services requires several new considerations in the protocol stack. Such collaborations require exchange of security tokens, transaction contexts, reliable delivery of messages, etc. Thus, the existing web services protocol stack must be modified to account for the additional information that must be carried as a part of the message.

In this chapter, we will study the modified protocol stack and the various new components added to the stack. Several new standards have been created for accommodating these components in the new stack. These are WS-Security, WS-Coordination, WS-AtomicTransaction, WS-BusinessActivity, WS-Reliable Messaging, WS-Addressing, WS-Eventing, etc.

E-Business Collaborations

The development of web services technology and its use for integrating widely spread legacy applications for a multi-location company was not sufficient. Something more was needed: the integration (composition) of web services deployed by different companies. A typical business transaction requires the use of diverse web services. Let us take an example of a travel booking. When you use a website for booking your flights, you are using the service provided by the website and also the service provided by the airline. You may even request the lowest quote from different airlines during this transaction. So, you will be using the services offered by several companies in a single business transaction. This kind of composition of web services introduces many more considerations. The participating web services (partners) must collaborate with other participants and a coordinator to perform the desired business operation. The operation may be to achieve a simple buyer-seller transaction or a complex supply chain transaction. All such transactions require a workflow to be defined between different collaborating parties. Defining and executing such workflows is called **orchestration**. In this book, you will learn the emerging standards for defining the workflows for e-business collaborations.

When two companies collaborate and allow the composition of their services into an aggregate service to be invoked by yet another partner (a client), we need to implement proper coordination for all involved activities. A client determines the workflow for the execution of different services. A typical business activity for travel booking is depicted in the following figure:

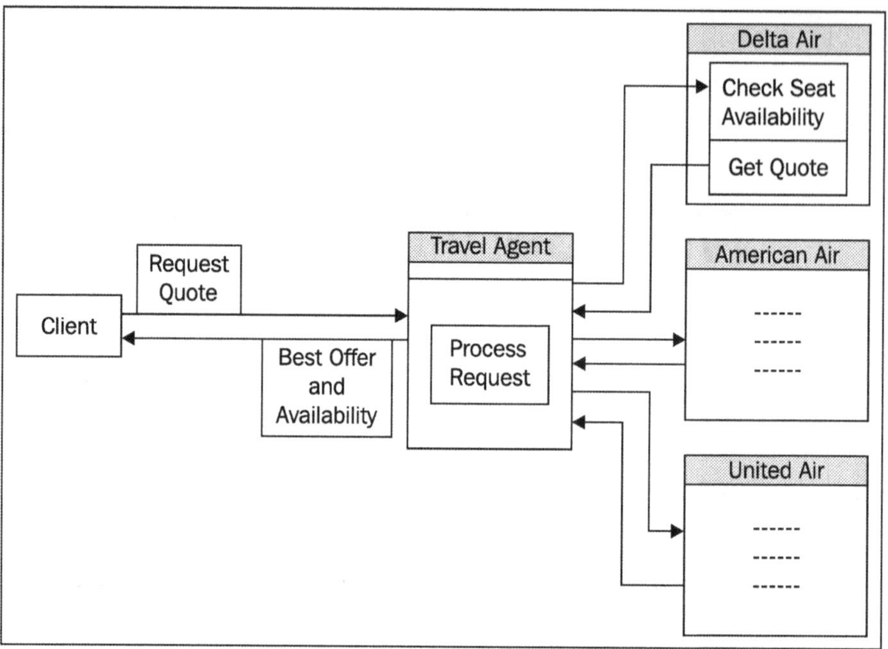

Clients interested in making an airline reservation at the cheapest rate log on to a travel agent's site. They fill in the request for travel, specifying the origin, destination, and proposed travel dates. The travel agent's service now passes on this information to various airlines to obtain the availability of seats and their best quotes. The availability, along with the lowest fare offer is then communicated to the clients. Clearly, such business activity requires collaboration between diverse parties.

We need a proper standardized language for describing such a workflow. As the workflow requires transport of several messages between coordinating partners, we need to establish an infrastructure for the reliable transmission of messages. The messages must be secured and their delivery should be guaranteed. The client may initiate a business process as a part of a transaction that may involve diverse partners. Such transactions must meet the usual requirements of a DTC (Distributed Transaction Control); this is discussed later in depth. As the messaging is XML-based, we need to create standards for transporting transaction contexts through an XML document, which is purely text based. The same thing applies even to security context—such context must be transported through a text-based document. Note that typically these contexts are binary and not text based.

Having seen the need for orchestrating web services to achieve e-business collaborations, let us first look at the various standards defined for such collaborations. The following diagram positions the various standards in the stack:

<table>
<tr><td colspan="8">BPEL</td></tr>
<tr><td>WS-Atomic Transaction</td><td>WS-Business Activity</td><td rowspan="2">WS Security</td><td rowspan="2">WS Addressing</td><td rowspan="2">WS Reliable Messaging</td><td rowspan="2">WS Inspection</td><td rowspan="2">WS Policy</td><td rowspan="2">WS Eventing</td></tr>
<tr><td colspan="2">WS Coordination</td></tr>
<tr><td colspan="8">UDDI</td></tr>
<tr><td colspan="8">Web Services
SOAP, WSDL</td></tr>
<tr><td colspan="8">Component Architecture
COM+, CORBA, Java EE</td></tr>
</table>

At the bottom of the stack, we have various specifications for component architecture. These may be Microsoft's .NET/COM+ architecture, Sun's Java EE architecture, or OMG's CORBA architecture. On top of the component architecture, we have specifications for creating web services. This consists of mainly SOAP and WSDL. Above this, we have several new specifications to support the integration and composition of web services. This chapter discusses all such new specifications, why they are needed, and the purpose they satisfy. At the top we have BPEL, which is the subject of this book. In this section, we will describe the various specifications that will be discussed in the rest of this chapter:

- **WS-Security**: Addresses the transport of security context.
- **WS-Coordination**: Defines a framework for achieving coordination between partners.
- **Web Services Transaction Specifications**: Specifies the standard for creating a distributed transaction involving multiple web services. This consists of.
    - WS-AtomicTransaction: Specification for creating Atomic transactions that typically last for a short duration.
    - WS-BusinessActivity: Specifies the standard for creating long duration distributed transactions.
- **WS-Reliable Messaging**: Specifies standards for reliable delivery of messages between partners.
- **WS-Addressing**: Defines the endpoint of communication.
- **WS-Inspection**: Defines specifications used for dynamic discovery of service description documents.
- **WS-Policy**: Specifies the policy of a web service provider for the benefit of service consumers.
- **WS-Eventing**: Defines event sources and consumers in the event model.

WS-Security

In the distributed web-services model, messages are exchanged between collaborating parties. During this message exchange, end-to-end message security must be addressed. As we have seen in earlier examples of typical business processes, a message may hop between many participating service providers. XML provides a platform-independent and network-neutral format for data transport. However, such messages must be secured. There may be a need to encrypt sensitive data. Also, once a service requester sends a message for a service to a service provider, the service provider may ask for the sender's identity. The request message should be able to transport the user credentials securely to the provider. Overall, message transport in a business process has many more requirements than are typically required for point-to-point messaging, where a single transport and a single protocol is used for communication.

Message security primarily involves the following:

- Message integrity
- Message confidentiality
- Message authentication

To implement security, a new standard has been defined—**WS-Security**. This defines enhancements to SOAP by providing a mechanism for associating security tokens with messages. The security token may be a binary token, X.509 certificate, Kerberos ticket, and so on. The standard is fully extensible and can support many types of tokens. It provides support for multiple security tokens, trust domains, signature formats, and encryption technologies.

WS-Security defines several tags to include security-related information in the XML document. Such information is embedded in the SOAP header.

Security-related information is enclosed in the `Security` element:

```
<S:Header>
  <wsse:Security
    xmlns:wsse="http://schemas.xmlsoap.org/ws/2002/04/secext">
      ...
  </wsse:Security>
</S:Header>
```

This security information may consist of a username and password required for server-side authentication, or may contain a digital certificate or information on the algorithms used for encrypting the message body.

Example

The following code illustrates how a security token is embedded in the message header:

```
<?xml version="1.0" encoding="utf-8"?>
<S:Envelope xmlns:S="http://www.w3.org/2001/12/soap-envelope"
            xmlns:ds="http://www.w3.org/2000/09/xmldsig#">
  <S:Header>
    <wsse:Security
          xmlns:wsse="http://schemas.xmlsoap.org/ws/2002/04/secext">
      <wsse:UsernameToken>
        <wsse:Username>ABCOM</wsse:Username>
```

```
        <wsse:Password>Mumbai123</wsse:Password>
      </wsse:UsernameToken>
    </wsse:Security>
  </S:Header>
  ...
</S:Envelope>
```

This code first defines the required namespaces and then opens the `Header` element. This element may contain some message routing information (not shown in the above example). The security-related information is enclosed in the `Security` element. The current example encodes the user credentials in the message header. The `UsernameToken` encloses the `UserName` and `Password` elements. As the XML document is a text document that is readable by human beings, you will not send the password this way unless you are using secured transport (HTTPS) for sending the message. You need to send the username and password to the server for authentication. Once the server authenticates the user, the user is assigned permissions (authorized) to access the services provided by the server.

Instead of sending credentials in the form of a username and password, you can send them in the form of certificates. Such certificates are in binary format. For this purpose, WS-Security standard allows you to include binary tokens in XML documents, as explained in the next section.

Binary Security Token

You can include a binary security token by using the `BinarySecurityToken` element. The following code illustrates how to include a binary security token:

```
<?xml version="1.0" encoding="utf-8"?>
<S:Envelope xmlns:S="http://www.w3.org/2001/12/soap-envelope"
            xmlns:ds="http://www.w3.org/2000/09/xmldsig#">
  <S:Header>
    <wsse:Security
         xmlns:wsse="http://schemas.xmlsoap.org/ws/2002/04/secext">
       <wsse:BinarySecurityToken
             Id="myToken"
             ValueType="wsse:X509v3"
             EncodingType="wsse:Base64Binary">
         ...
       </wsse:BinarySecurityToken>
    </wsse:Security>
  </S:Header>
```

The `ValueType` indicates the type of token (in this case it is X.509), and the `EncodingType` specifies the encoding method (in this case it is base-64 encoding).

You can also *reference* an external token rather than encoding a token in the message header.

Referencing an External Security Token

Sometimes, a security token may be located elsewhere, identified by a URI. Such external tokens are referenced using the `SecurityTokenReference` element. The syntax for `SecurityTokenReference` is given below:

```
<SecurityTokenReference Id="...">
  <Reference URI="..."/>
</SecurityTokenReference>
```

The following code illustrates how an external token is referenced:

```
<wsse:SecurityTokenReference
    xmlns:wsse="http://schemas.xmlsoap.org/ws/2002/04/secext">
  <wsse:Reference URI="http://mysite.com/tokens/ABCOM#X509token"/>
</wsse:SecurityTokenReference>
```

In this case, the security token is taken from `mysite.com` at the specified location.

Faults

Several kinds of errors may occur during the processing of security information. For example, an invalid security token or signature could give rise to an error. The WS-Security specification defines several **fault types**. The different fault types and their meanings are listed below:

- `wsse:UnsupportedSecurityToken`: Indicates that an unsupported token was encountered
- `wsse:UnsupportedAlgorithm`: Indicates the use of an unsupported signature or encryption algorithm
- `wsse:InvalidSecurity`: Indicates an error during the processing of a security header
- `wsse:InvalidSecurityToken`: Indicates that an invalid token was encountered
- `wsse:FailedAuthentication`: Indicates that a token could not be authenticated
- `wsse:FailedCheck`: Indicates an invalid signature or decryption.
- `wsse:SecurityTokenUnavailable`: Indicates failure to retrieve the referenced token

If there is a fault, the message header will contain one of the appropriate elements from the above list to indicate the type of fault.

In addition to the above elements, the specification defines several more elements that allow you to include encrypted data, specify a signature, sign an algorithm, and so on. The reader is encouraged to look up the WS-Security specification (`http://www-106.ibm.com/developerworks/webservices/library/ws-secure/`) for further details.

Before we discuss more specifications, we will describe a typical business process that requires a distributed transaction involving many parties.

Typical Business Transaction Scenario

When you make a business trip, you typically require an airline booking, a hotel booking, and a car rental booking. Generally, all three bookings must be done before you confirm your trip. If any of these bookings is not available, you may have to re-schedule your business trip. This kind of business transaction involves confirmations from more than one participant.

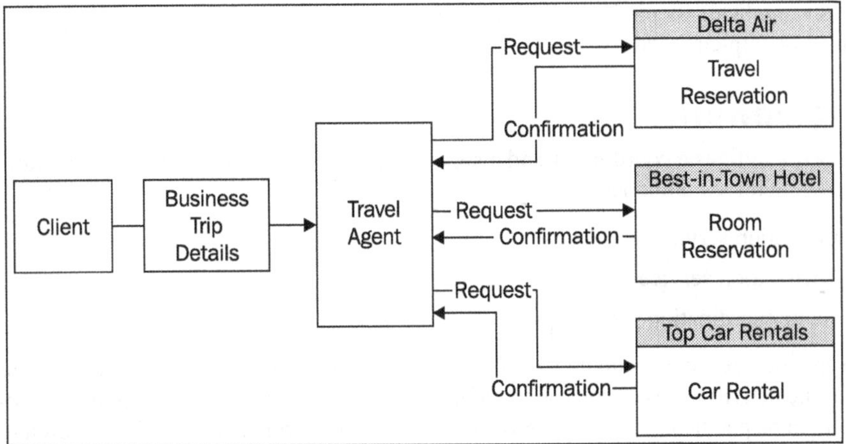

Each participant is an independent business entity and will not like an outer business process, such as the one initiated by your travel agent, to get hold of the company's resources. An initiating process (your travel agent) makes a request to each of the involved parties and obtains a commitment from them.

For example, you may request a direct flight to the destination on the specified day, the hotel booking for a couple of nights starting on the arrival day, as well as a car rental for the number of days of your trip. The travel agent makes a request to each of the concerned parties and asks each one to hold the reservation for a certain period of time, perhaps a couple of hours. When all the involved parties respond with a positive acknowledgement indicating that the specified bookings are available, the travel agent sends a confirmation to each of the involved parties. Each party now commits the change and informs the travel agent of the confirmation. When the travel agent receives confirmation from each, the transaction is treated as complete.

What if one of the bookings is not available? In such a case, the travel agent will send a cancellation to the other parties, requesting them to undo the earlier booking. This may require compensating transactions to be run on the individual systems that may even involve cancellation charges to the requester.

Clearly such a business scenario requires proper coordination between participating parties. For this purpose, a new specification called WS-Coordination was developed, which is discussed in the following section.

WS-Coordination

In a typical business scenario, web services may be required to share information, such as security context, transaction context, and so on while participating in a composite business process. The **WS-Coordination** specification defines a framework for this purpose. This is an extensible framework and allows existing applications to hide their proprietary protocols while coordinating with other applications in a heterogeneous environment. It is used in conjunction with other specifications and does not provide a complete solution on its own. WS-Coordination is used whenever coordination between applications developed using different vendor specifications is desired. Such applications obviously run under different trust domains and so appropriate access control must be implemented.

The Framework

The framework defines a coordinator and a set of coordination protocols. The coordinator consists of the following three components:

- Activation service
- Registration service
- Set of coordination protocols

A service that decides to coordinate its activity with another service first creates a coordination context for the activity. This is done with the help of the activation service component. This context is then dispatched to the service with which coordination is desired. The receiving service uses the coordination context to register into the activity. This is done with the help of the registration service component. The receiving application may use the registration service component provided by the sender to register the activity. Alternatively, it may use the registration service component of any interposing, trusted coordinator. The context itself contains sufficient information that describes the behavior that the sender application will follow.

Scenario

To understand the model used by the WS-Coordination framework, we will now discuss a scenario in which two applications having their own coordinators collaborate with each other. Each application has its own coordinator, as depicted in the following figure:

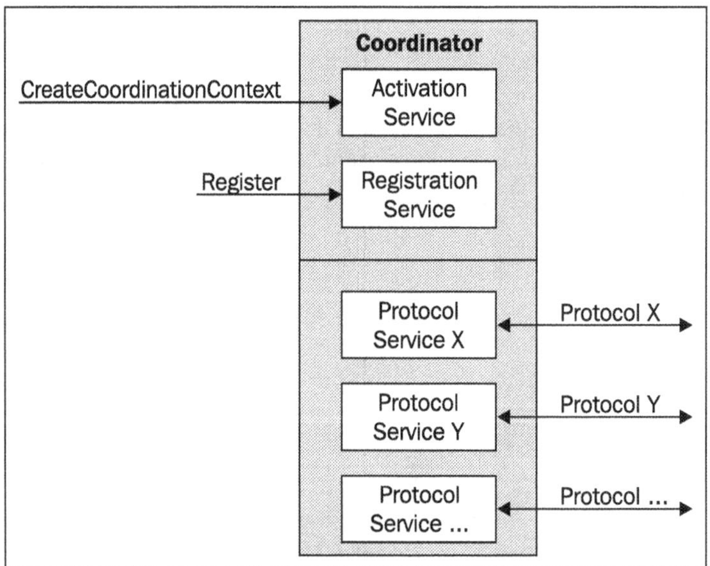

The steps involved in the coordination are as follows:

1. Application A creates a coordination context by calling the `CreateCoordinationContext` operation on the `ActivationService` provided by coordinator A.
2. The coordinator returns a coordination context to application A.
3. The coordination context contains:
   - Activity identifier
   - Coordination type
   - Endpoint reference to the registration service of coordinator A
4. Application A sends a message to Application B containing the above coordination context.
5. Application B calls the `CreateCoordinationContext` operation on coordinator B by passing the received coordination context as input.
6. Coordinator B returns a new coordination context to application B.
7. The coordination context contains following:
   - The same activity identifier as above
   - The same coordination type as above
   - Endpoint reference to the registration service of coordinator B
8. Application B determines the coordination protocol from the coordination context.
9. Application B registers the protocol with coordinator B, thereby exchanging the endpoint references between application B and the protocol service B.
10. Coordinator B now forwards the registration to Coordinator A's registration service, exchanging the endpoint references between the protocol services A and B.
11. The two applications now use the protocol defined in the coordination type to collaborate with each other.

The entire process is depicted in the following figure:

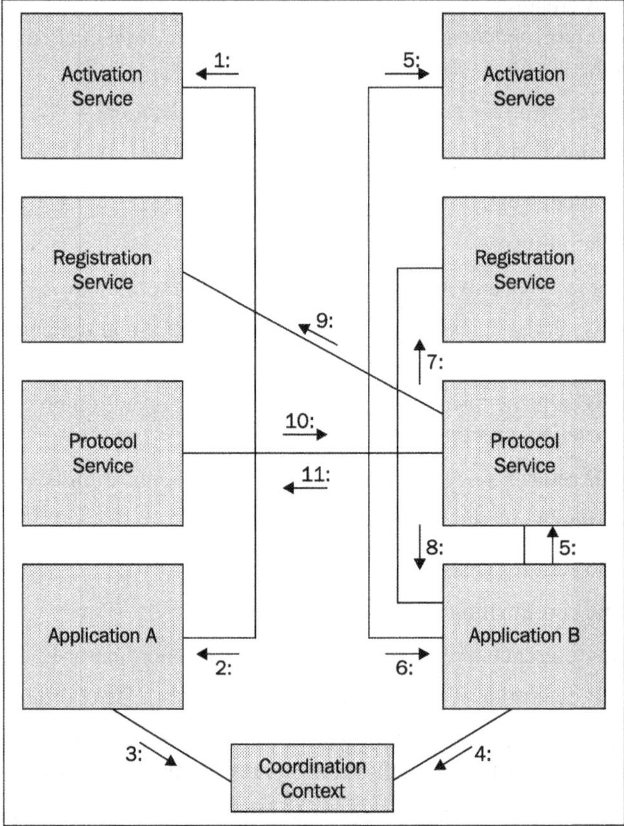

Note: The numbered arrows indicate the respective steps outlined above.

Having seen the coordination operation between two applications, let's now look at the various elements provided in the schema definition.

CoordinationContext

`CoordinationContext` is a `Context` type as defined in the `wscoor.xsd` schema definition. The `Context` type defines two elements, `Identifier` and `Expires`. The `Expires` element specifies the expiration time for the context.

The application sends the `CreateCoordinationContext` message to the activation service by passing the above `CoordinataionContext`.

CreateCoordinationContext

The `CreateCoordinationContext` message defines the coordination type, the expiry time, and the current context.

CreateCoordinationContextResponse

The application receives a message from the coordinator containing the coordination response. The response structure is shown below:

```
<CreateCoordinationContextResponse>
  <CoordinationContext>
    <wsu:Identifier> ... </wsu:Identifier>
    <CoordinationType> ... </CoordinationType>
    <RegistrationService>
      <wsa:Address> ... </wsa:Address>
    </RegistrationService>
  </CoordinationContext>
</CreateCoordinationContextResponse>
```

Note that the response contains the coordination context containing the identifier, the type, and the endpoint for the registration service.

The application registers the coordination context with the registration service by sending a `Register` message to it.

Register

The message contains the identifier obtained from the coordinator and the address of the protocol service. The application receives a `RegisterResponse` in response to the `Register` message.

RegisterResponse

The response contains the endpoint for the protocol service provided by the coordinator.

Faults

During message communication, errors could be generated. The specification defines the following error codes:

- `wscoor:InvalidState`: Generated by coordinator or a participant to indicate that the endpoint has entered an invalid state
- `wscoor:InvalidProtocol`: Indicates that a message from an invalid protocol has been received
- `wscoor:InvalidParameters`: Indicates that invalid parameters have been received within a message
- `wscoor:NoActivity`: Sent by the coordinator to indicate that the participant has presumably ended communication
- `wscoor:ContextRefused`: Indicates that the received context is unacceptable
- `wscoor:AlreadyRegistered`: Indicates that the same protocol with the same activity is already registered

The coordinating applications receive one or more of these faults in the case of any failures. These applications are responsible for processing them and taking an appropriate action.

The WS-Coordination specifications are used along with other specifications to achieve an end-to-end solution. One of the most significant applications of this specification is to share a transaction context between multiple applications running on different platforms and developed using different vendor technologies. In the next section, we will discuss the Web Services Transaction specifications that are used along with WS-Coordination for achieving a consistent agreement on the outcome of distributed processing.

Web Services Transaction Specifications

The Web Services Transaction specifications define the coordination types discussed in the previous section. These specifications are used along with WS-Coordination and WS-Security to implement distributed transactions across a set of diverse web services.

The Web Services Transaction Specifications define two specifications:

- Atomic transaction (AT)
- Business activity (BA)

An **atomic transaction** is a typical single-domain transaction that requires the ACID properties to be satisfied. This is typically used for activities of short duration and is applicable within a limited trust domain.

A **business activity** is used for activities having long duration. In this case, due to the long duration, the changes made by each participant are not hidden from others for an unduly long time and so are immediate and permanent. Exceptions are handled by the business logic and compensating transactions are used to guarantee consistency.

Both AT and BA allow coordination between applications that use different proprietary protocols and are running across different hardware and software infrastructures. Additionally, BA allows coordination across trust boundaries.

Atomic Transaction

In the case of atomic transactions, actions taken by all the involved participants before committal are tentative. If the coordinator commits the transactions, the actions are made persistent and are visible to others. If the coordinator aborts the transaction, all the actions by participating processes are rolled back and the application returns to its former state as if nothing occurred.

Atomic transactions leverage the WS-Coordination specification to coordinate the activities of all the involved parties. As seen in the previous section, WS-Coordination uses `CoordinationContext` to share the context information between participants.

Sharing Context Information

We use the `CoordinationContext` as follows:

```
<?xml version="1.0" encoding="utf-8"?>
<S:Envelope xmlns:S="http://www.w3.org/2001/12/soap-envelope"
```

```
    <S:Header>
        ...
        <wscoor:CoordinationContext

          xmlns:wscoor="http://schemas.xmlsoap.org/ws/2002/08/wscoor"
          xmlns:wsu="http://schemas.xmlsoap.org/ws/2002/07/utility"
          ...
          <wsu:Identifier> ... </wsu:Identifier>
          <wsu:Expires> ... </wsu:Expires>
          <wscoor:CoordinationType>
            http://schemas.xmlsoap.org/ws/2002/08/wstx
          </wscoor:CoordinationType>
          <wscoor:RegistrationService>
            <wsu:Address> ... </wsu:Address>
          </wscoor:RegistrationService>
          ...
        </wscoor:CoordinationContext>
        ...
    </S:Header>
    ...
</S:Envelope>
```

The `CoordinationContext` is defined in the message header. The `CoordinationType` is set to the specified URI. As discussed in the previous section, the `CoordinationContext` element defines the identifier, expiry date, and the address of the registration service. Additionally, it can contain any application-specific information.

As seen in the previous section, the application sends a `CreateCoordinationContext` message to the coordinator. The message may contain a `CurrentContext`. If the current context is provided, the coordinator will act as a subordinate to the current coordinator. If the current context is not provided, this will be treated as a new transaction and a new transaction context, along with its associated protocols, is created and returned to the application.

Coordination Protocols

After obtaining the context, the application sends a `Register` message to the coordinator to register a desired protocol with the coordinator. An application may register with the coordinator for multiple protocols by sending multiple messages to it.

We will now look at the coordination protocols that are defined in this specification. The specification defines the following five protocols:

- Completion
- CompletionWithAck
- Two-Phase Commit (2PC)
- PhaseZero
- OutcomeNotification

Completion

Applications use this protocol to tell the coordinator to either commit or roll back the current transaction. The coordinator returns the status of the final outcome.

CompletionWithAck

This is similar to the completion protocol, except that an acknowledgement of the status is returned to the coordinator. Until such time, the coordinator remembers the outcome of the transaction.

Two-Phase Commit

When there are multiple participants in a transaction, each participant registers with the coordinator using a **2PC** protocol. The coordinator manages the commit or abort decision across all the involved resource managers. During phase one, all the resource managers are informed of the updates they are required to perform. Once all resource managers agree to perform the updates, during the second phase of the commit, the coordinator requests them to write the updates. This protocol is required for distributed transaction processing.

PhaseZero

A participant may cache the data and want to write the data to the database before a two-phase commit begins. In such cases, the application registers with the coordinator using a PhaseZero protocol. The coordinator now notifies the registered application before it begins a 2PC protocol.

OutcomeNotification

A participant interested in the outcome of a transaction registers with the coordinator with this message. The coordinator informs the registered participant whether the current transaction is committed or rolled back. The participant may use this information to release resources held by it or to perform any other desired operation, depending on the transaction outcome.

Business Activity

The **business activity** transaction type is used whenever coordination for achieving a distributed transaction between several participants having different vendor implementations, such as IBM, Sun, Microsoft, and so on is desired. A business activity consists of a series of tasks, each executed independently of the others. For example, a purchase business activity may consist of sending requests for quote (RFQ), selecting the lowest quote, negotiations, and eventually generating and sending a purchase order to the winner. The entire business process may require human interventions and is usually a long-running activity. The process requires several cooperating partners. The partner processes are not under direct control of the initiating process. Thus, the entire activity consists of several tasks executed in a specified sequence. Such a sequence may be specified in BPEL. Each task may be an atomic transaction. However, the entire business activity cannot be implemented as an atomic transaction. The reasons for not doing this are:

- The process is long running and it is not advisable to lock the resources for unknown time durations.
- The partners may not allow the initiating process to put locks on their resources.

The business activity coordination type used in WS-Coordination allows you to coordinate the activities of several participants in such situations. The coordination process and the flow of events remain the same as in the previous sections.

Each task runs as an atomic transaction. If the initiating process decides to abort the business activity, a compensating transaction is sent to the involved participants requesting them to reverse the activities they have performed so far as part of the current business activity.

Sharing the Context Information

The application sends a message to the coordinator for defining the coordination context. The message header uses the `CoordinationContext` element as shown below:

```
<?xml version="1.0" encoding="utf-8"?>
<S:Envelope xmlns:S="http://www.w3.org/2001/12/soap-envelope"
  <S:Header>
    ...
    <wscoor:CoordinationContext
        xmlns:wscoor="http://schemas.xmlsoap.org/ws/2002/08/wscoor"
        xmlns:wsu="http://schemas.xmlsoap.org/ws/2002/07/utility"
         ...
        <wsu:Identifier> ... </wsu:Identifier>
        <wsu:Expires> ... </wsu:Expires>
        <wscoor:CoordinationType>
            http://schemas.xmlsoap.org/ws/2002/08/wsba
        </wscoor:CoordinationType>
        <wscoor:RegistrationService>
            <wsu:Address> ... </wsu:Address>
        </wscoor:RegistrationService>
    ...
    </wscoor:CoordinationContext>
    ...
  </S:Header>
  ...
</S:Envelope>
```

This header is similar to the one used for an atomic transaction, except that the URI used in the `CoordinationType` is different. As in the earlier case, the header may contain additional application-specific information. Similar to the previous case, if the message contains the `CurrentContext`, the target coordinator is interposed as a subordinate to the current coordinator, else a new business activity context is created.

Coordination Protocols

The specification defines two protocols for the business activity coordination type:

- BusinessAgreement
- BusinessAgreementWithComplete

A business activity is initiated by some business task; we call it a parent task. The parent task delegates several business activities to child tasks. The child task registers with its parent and keeps the parent updated on its state. The two agreements defined here address the proper coordination between the parent and the child scopes.

BusinessAgreement

The child scope participant registers with the parent scope coordinator. The child knows the scope of business activities or tasks it is supposed to perform as part of the outer business activity. During the business activity, a child may send the following messages to the coordinator:

- `Exited`: The child scope sends this message after completing all required activities.
- `Completed`: After completing the required tasks, a child may decide to continue its participation in the business activity and notify the coordinator of such intent. After completing such activities, the child sends a `Completed` message to the coordinator.
- `Closed`: The parent may request the child to close. The child then sends a `Closed` message to the coordinator after closing.
- `Compensated`: The parent may request the child to compensate an earlier activity. The child sends a `compensated` message to the coordinator after performing the desired compensation.
- `Canceled`: At the request of the parent, the child will cancel the current activity and send a `canceled` message to the coordinator after doing so.
- `Faulted`: If an error occurs while performing the task, the child sends this message to the coordinator.

BusinessAgreementWithComplete

This protocol is similar to BusinessAgreement, except that now the parent informs the child whenever it has completed all the desired tasks. Thus, the child keeps on performing the tasks on behalf of the parent until the parent sends a `Completed` message to the child marking the end of all the requests to the child as a part of the current business activity.

Having seen the Web Services Transaction specifications, we will now study another protocol for implementing business transactions.

OASIS BTP

As mentioned earlier, a typical business activity spans several independent organizations. Implementing a transaction that requires ACID properties to be satisfied may not be possible in such cases, as a single transaction could last for hours or even days together. It may not be possible to hold locks on the participants' resources for such a long duration. OASIS has defined a protocol called **BTP** (Business Transaction Protocol) that allows the coordination of business transactions spanning multiple participants. The transaction ensures consistency irrespective of the disparate applications running on different technologies deployed at different organizations. As it is not possible for a single controller to hold the resources belonging to different organizations, each participating organization is responsible for making a commitment required by a business transaction. The requester assumes that the party who has committed a portion of a business process will honor its commitment whenever asked to do so and accordingly proceeds with the outer business transaction. The requester or consumer may commit or cancel the request at a later time. The provider honors the earlier commitment, or it cancels all the operations by undoing whatever was done earlier as a part of the commitment, if it receives a request for canceling the transaction. This is depicted in the following figure:

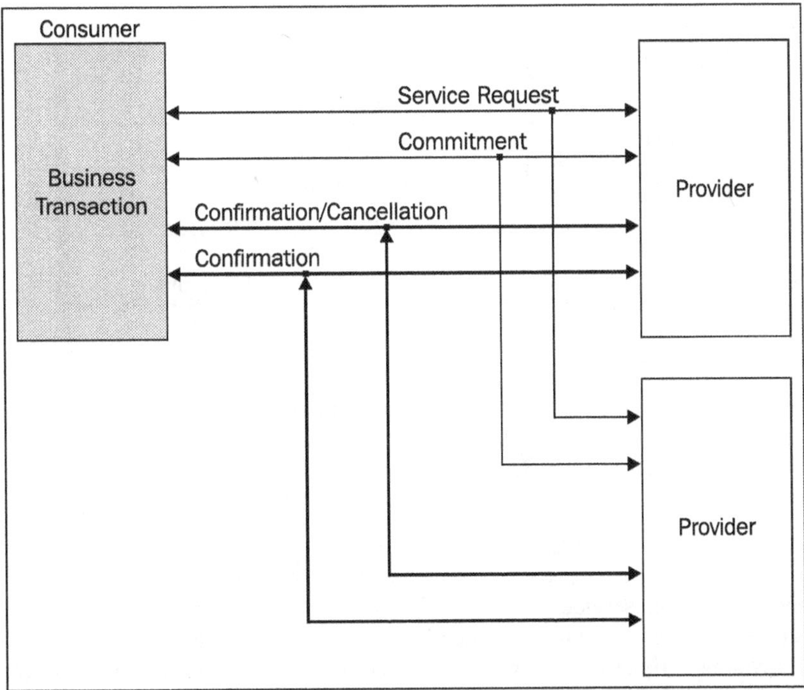

In the above diagram, the consumer requests a service from a provider(s) by sending a service request message. The consumer may request the provider(s) to participate in a transaction. The provider(s) send a response to the consumer agreeing to participate in the specified transaction. Each participating provider agrees to participate in a transaction in the manner specified by the consumer.

At a later time in the business process, the consumer sends either a confirmation or the cancellation to the participating providers. In the case of a confirmation, the providers would commit their respective commitments to complete the transaction and acknowledge to the consumer. In the case of cancellations, the provider may run a compensating transaction to reverse the internal changes made.

BTP defines a protocol for achieving a business transaction that involves disparate applications.

The BTP Stack

The BTP stack is shown in the following figure:

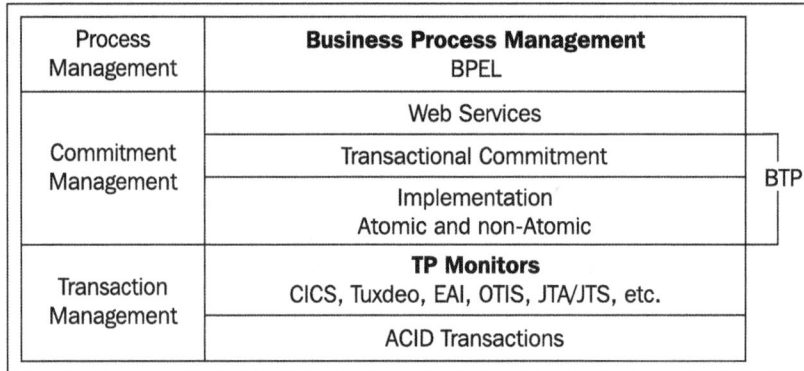

Process Management	**Business Process Management** BPEL	
Commitment Management	Web Services	
	Transactional Commitment	BTP
	Implementation Atomic and non-Atomic	
Transaction Management	**TP Monitors** CICS, Tuxdeo, EAI, OTIS, JTA/JTS, etc.	
	ACID Transactions	

At the bottom of the stack we have **transaction management**. This consists of typical TP (transaction processing) monitors consisting of one of several popular technologies. This may be an IBM Mainframe running CICS, CORBA transaction services, or Java EE transaction services, and so on. These services essentially provide ACID transactions and typically run at a single location.

Above this layer, we have **commitment management**. This consists of web services that use XML-based protocols. We have already studied the different transactional commitment specifications used by web services. The commitment management layer is responsible for providing support for atomic and non-atomic transactions. Non-atomic transactions are those that may require a compensating transaction to be run in case of a rollback. Web Services transactions and business activity protocols are implemented at this layer.

At the top, we have a layer for business **process management**. At this layer, the business processes defined using BPEL are executed.

The BTP Model

BTP defines a model for transactions that typically involve multiple participants over the Internet. The protocol:

- Addresses how to handle errors and communication failures over a channel
- Coordinates between multiple applications and provides a way to define the business activity workflow
- Supports loosely-coupled systems and both synchronous and asynchronous calls
- Provides for long-running transactions with support for running compensating transactions in case of failures

The model defines two types of transactions:

- Atomic
- Cohesive

Atomic Transactions

An atomic transaction requires one coordinator with zero or more sub-coordinators. Each coordinator is responsible for managing one or more participants within the transaction. The outcome of the transaction is atomic, that is either all participants confirm or all cancel. You must already have a fair idea about atomic transactions from the Web Services Transactions section in this chapter.

Cohesive Transactions

In a cohesive transaction there can be multiple sub-transactions. Some of the participants may confirm while others may cancel. The cohesive coordinator ensures output consistency by sending appropriate requests to the participants based on its agreement and interaction with the originator. Thus it has more complex functionality than an atomic coordinator.

Having seen the coordination and transaction specifications, we will now look at the specifications that allow reliable messaging. Reliable messaging is required for guaranteeing coordination between multiple parties in a distributed transaction.

Reliable Messaging

A typical business process is composed of several diverse web services. These services are provided by several coordinating partners. During the execution of the business process, several documents are exchanged between the partners. The means of exchange used for these documents must be reliable. This section discusses the standards for achieving reliable messaging between the partners.

In any communication, delivering a message reliably is of utmost importance to ensure the proper integrity of the system. Delivery of messages is subject to several error conditions arising due to:

- Network failures
- Component failures
- System failures

Under such unforeseen conditions, messages should still be reliably delivered. XML-based messages are usually exchanged between partners over HTTP. HTTP is a stateless protocol and is not reliable. While using HTTP, a message in split into several small packets during delivery. Such packets are numbered. The order in which these packets are received may not agree with the dispatch order. Packets may be lost during transit. HTTP does not provide for positive acknowledgement of a message delivery. Thus, it becomes important for us to define a standard for reliable messaging while exchanging messages in a business process.

Reliable messaging specifications were designed to address these issues associated with HTTP. These specifications define a new protocol that is responsible for:

- Identifying each message
- Tracking its delivery
- Guaranteeing delivery of the message from the source to the ultimate destination, in the correct order of dispatch

Messaging Model

The messaging model used for reliable message delivery is illustrated in the following diagram:

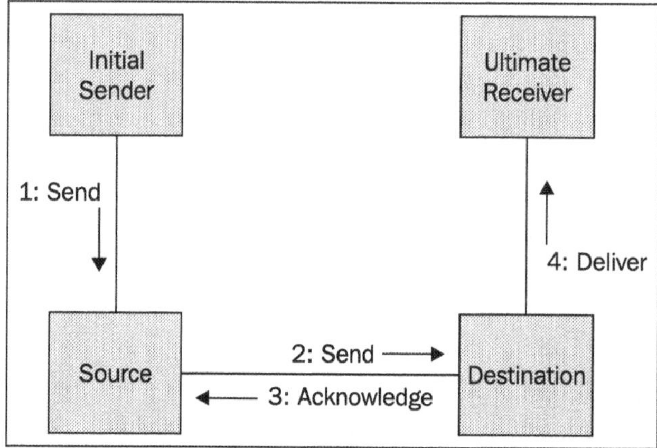

This model defines four components:

- Initial sender
- Source
- Destination
- Ultimate receiver

The initial sender sends a message to the source for delivery to the ultimate receiver. The source dispatches the message to the destination. After receiving the message, the destination acknowledges the message. If the source does not receive the acknowledgment, the source resends the message. The source will send the message multiple times until an acknowledgement is received. Finally, the destination delivers the message to the ultimate receiver.

For this model to work properly, the source must have an endpoint reference to the destination. The source must know the policies associated with the destination and must be capable of formulating messages that comply with these policies. Also, if a secured message exchange is desired, both source and destination must support associated security protocols.

The source assigns a sequence number to each message. The number starts with 1 and increments by exactly 1 for each subsequent reliable message. The destination acknowledges the message along with the sequence number of the received message.

Example

The RM protocol uses the `sequence` element for tracking messages and managing their delivery. The following example shows how the messages are sequenced:

```
<wsrm:Sequence>
  <wsu:Identifier>
    http://mysite.com/test
  </wsu:Identifier>
  <wsrm:MessageNumber>
    12
  </wsrm:MessageNumber>
  <wsrm:LastMessage/>
</wsrm:Sequence>
```

Each message contains a `MessageNumber`. If the current message is the last message in a sequence, the `LastMessage` element is included in the sequence.

The receiving endpoint acknowledges the message receipt using the following XML code:

```
<wsrm:SequenceAcknowledgment>
  <wsu:Identifier>
    http://mysite.com/test
  </wsu:Identifier>
  <wsrm:AcknowledgmentRange Upper="12" Lower="1"/>
</wsrm:SequenceAcknowledgment>
```

The range of received messages is specified in the acknowledgement. For example, the above acknowledgment indicates that the messages in the range 1 through 12 are received. If the messages are not received in order, the acknowledgement specifies the sub-ranges of received messages, as shown in the following code:

```
<wsrm:SequenceAcknowledgment>
  <wsu:Identifier>
    http://mysite.com/test
  </wsu:Identifier>
  <wsrm:AcknowledgmentRange Upper="2" Lower="1"/>
  <wsrm:AcknowledgmentRange Upper="8" Lower="5"/>
  <wsrm:AcknowledgmentRange Upper="12" Lower="10"/>
</wsrm:SequenceAcknowledgment>
```

The above acknowledgement indicates that the messages in the ranges 1-2, 5-8, and 10-12 are received, and that the messages 3, 4, and 9 are not yet received.

Requesting Acknowledgement

A message sender may request an acknowledgement from the destination at any time. It does so by sending a message containing the `AckRequested` element. The use of this element is as follows:

```
<wsrm:AckRequested ...>
  <wsu:Identifier> uri </wsu:Identifier>
  ...
</wsrm:AckRequested>
```

The destination must respond to the above message with the `SequenceAcknowledgment` message.

Delivery Assurances

The two endpoints that implement the Reliable Messaging protocol assure message delivery from the initial sender to the ultimate receiver. The following four delivery assurances are supported:

- `AtMostOnce`: No duplicate messages are permitted. Some may not be delivered.
- `AtLeastOnce`: May result in duplicate messages at the receiver end.
- `ExactlyOnce`: Every message is delivered without duplication.
- `InOrder`: Messages are delivered in the order received.

Delivery assurance is specified using the following syntax:

```
<wsrm:DeliveryAssurance Value="wsrm:AtMostOnce"/>
```

Other Assertions

The RM specification defines a few XML elements to specify other types of assertions. These assertions include:

- Inactivity timeout:
  ```
  <wsrm:InactivityTimeout Milliseconds="100" />
  ```
- Base re-transmission interval:
  ```
  <wsrm:BaseRetransmissionInterval Milliseconds="100"/>
  ```
- Acknowledgment interval:
  ```
  <wsrm:AcknowledgementInterval Milliseconds="100"/>
  ```
- Sequence lifetime specified using the `Expires` element of WS-Security:
  ```
  <wsu:Expires> time </wsu:Expires>
  ```

Faults

Faults, if any, during the transmission are indicated using the `SequenceFault` element.

The following example illustrates the `SequenceTerminated` fault.

```
<wsrm:SequenceFault>
  <wsu:Identifier> uri </wsu:Identifier>
  <wsrm:FaultCode>
    wsrm:SequenceTerminated
  </wsrm:FaultCode>
</wsrm:SequenceFault>
```

The `SequenceTerminated` fault indicates that the current sequence was terminated either by the source or the destination due to unrecoverable conditions.

The other pre-defined fault codes are:

- `wsrm:UnknownSequence`
- `wsrm:InvalidAcknowledgement`
- `wsrm:MessageNumberRollover`
- `wsrm:LastMessageNumberExceeded`
- `wsrm:SequenceRefused`

WS-Addressing

Every web service has an endpoint to which service messages are targeted. WSDL allows you to define endpoints for the messages using port types, bindings, service elements, and so on. However, the WSDL 1.1 model lacks flexibility. (For detailed information on WSDL refer http://www.cos.ufrj.br/~baiao/papers/cavalcantim_workflow.pdf.)

To achieve flexibility, a new specification for defining endpoints has been proposed. This is known as WS-Addressing. This specification facilitates the following:

- Endpoint descriptions may be dynamically generated and customized.
- During stateful interactions, new service instances may be created. The new specifications help in identifying these.
- Endpoint information may be shared between communicating parties in tightly coupled environments.

The specification defines new XML elements to address service endpoints. The following XML document illustrates the use of these new elements.

```
<S:Envelope xmlns:S="http://www.w3.org/2002/12/soap-envelope"
  xmlns:wsa="http://schemas.xmlsoap.org/ws/2003/03/addressing">
<S:Header>
  <wsa:ReplyTo>
    <wsa:Address>
      http://...
    </wsa:Address>
  </wsa:ReplyTo>
  <wsa:To>
    http://...
  </wsa:To>
  <wsa:Action>
    http://...
  </wsa:Action>
</S:Header>
<S:Body>
...
</S:Body>
</S:Envelope>
```

The Header contains ReplyTo, To, and Action elements. The To element specifies the URI to which the message is sent and the ReplyTo element specifies the URI to which a reply should be sent. The Address element specifies the desired URI. The Action element specifies the desired action on the target.

Endpoint Reference

The definition for the endpoint reference is shown below:

```
<wsa:EndpointReference>
  <wsa:Address>
    xs:anyURI
  </wsa:Address>
  <wsa:ReferenceProperties>
    ...
  </wsa:ReferenceProperties> ?
  <wsa:PortType>
```

```
        xs:Qname
    </wsa:PortType> ?
    <wsa:ServiceName PortName="xs:NCName"?>
        xs:Qname
    </wsa:ServiceName> ?
  <wsp:Policy/> *
  </wsa:EndpointReference>
```

The following elements are used in the definition:

- Address: Mandatory element; specifies the address property of an endpoint reference. This may be a logical address or identifier for the endpoint.
- ReferenceProperties: Optional element; may contain child elements that specify the reference properties of the reference.
- PortType: Specifies the port type property of the endpoint reference.
- ServiceName: Specifies the WSDL description of the endpoint. This is basically the <wsdl:service> element in the WSDL document.
- PortName: Specifies the <wsdl:port> definition for the endpoint.
- Policy: Specifies the policy for the current interaction.

With the addition of these new elements, the WS-Addressing endpoint specification overcomes the limitations of the WSDL 1.1 specification to provide the facilities discussed above.

The WS-Addressing specification takes the **next-hop** approach for routing. In the next-hop approach, only the single endpoint of an ultimate destination is stored. This is sufficient for the message sender and the message sender need not know the full message path to the destination. Each node in the path examines the destination endpoint address and forwards the message to the next node closer to the destination. As the message does not need to be modified on its way to the ultimate destination, message security is not compromised.

In WS-Addressing, the EndpointReference element defines the endpoint for the destination and the message source. Note that the wsa:from element also uses the same EndpointReference to specify the source location. The schema definition of the EndpointReferenceType is shown below:

```
<xs:complexType name="EndpointReferenceType">
<xs:sequence>
    <xs:element name="Address" type="wsa:AttributedURI" />
    <xs:element name="ReferenceProperties" type="wsa:ReferencePropertiesType"
            minOccurs="0" />
    <xs:element name="PortType" type="wsa:AttributedQName" minOccurs="0" />
    <xs:element name="ServiceName" type="wsa:ServiceNameType" minOccurs="0" />
    <xs:any namespace="##other" processContents="lax" minOccurs="0"
            maxOccurs="unbounded"/>
</xs:sequence>
<xs:anyAttribute namespace="##other" processContents="lax" />
</xs:complexType>
<xs:element name="EndpointReference" type="wsa:EndpointReferenceType"/> ...
```

The ReferenceProperties element allows you to specify additional information such as port name, service name, and policies, and is easily extensible. You can specify any number of additional custom properties.

Faults

During message transport, faults can occur along the message path. The fault element describes the reason for the fault. A typical fault element used in the path is shown below:

```
<m:fault>
  <m:code>812</m:code>
  <m:reason>Service Too Busy</m:reason>
  <m:retryAfter>300</m:retryAfter>
</m:fault>
```

The `code` element specifies the fault code. Codes starting with `8xx` indicate receiver faults and those starting with `7xx` indicate sender faults. The `reason` element describes the cause of the fault in string format and the `retryAfter` element states the retry time interval.

WS-Inspection

A web service provider publishes a service description for consumers. This is typically published as a WSDL document. The service provider registers a reference to the service description in a centralized registry, typically UDDI. The consumer locates a reference to the service description by looking up the registry and requests the service description from the service provider. The description document is usually emailed to the consumer, limiting the dynamic discovery and use of the service.

The **WS-Inspection** specification allows for dynamic discovery of service documents. WS-Inspection is XML-based and provides an aggregation of references to service descriptions. A WS-Inspection document does not describe a service—it just helps in locating a desired description document. Generally, a WS-Inspection document is made available at the point of contact of the service. The consumer parses this document to retrieve the references to the service descriptions and selects a desired description. This is depicted in the following diagram:

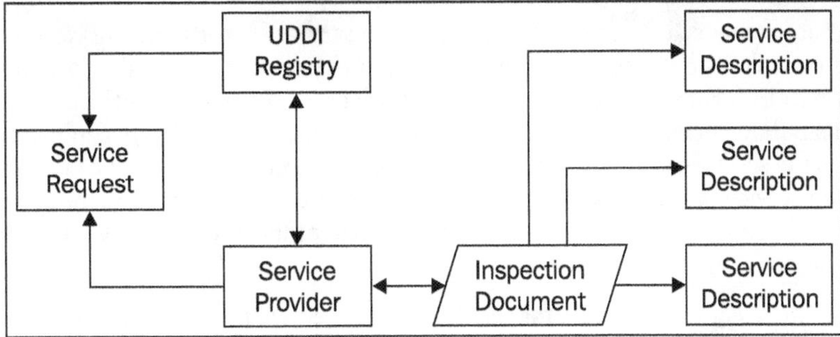

WS-Inspection defines service and description elements to describe references to service descriptions. A typical example would be:

```
<inspection xmlns="http://schemas.xmlsoap.org/ws/2001/10/inspection/">
  <service>
    <description referencedNamespace="http://schemas.xmlsoap.org/wsdl/"
          location="http://mysite.com/myservice.wsdl" />
  </service>
```

```
    <service>
      ...
    </service>
  </inspection>
```

The `inspection` element encloses one or more service elements. Each service element contains a reference to the web service description. In this example, the first service element describes a reference to a WSDL document. The `referencedNamespace` attribute describes the type of service description. The description itself may be defined in WSDL, UDDI, or plain HTML. Depending on the type of document, the attribute value for `referencedNamespace` would be different.

The following example shows how a UDDI reference is described in the inspection document:

```
<service>
  <description referencedNamespace="urn:uddi-org:api">
    <wsiluddi:serviceDescription
      location="http://mysite.com/uddi/myservice">
    <wsiluddi:serviceKey>
      ...
    </wsiluddi:serviceKey>
  </wsiluddi:serviceDescription>
  </description>
</service>
```

Inspection Document Hierarchy

A hierarchy of inspection documents can be created using the `link` element:

```
<wsil:link
referencedNamespace="http://schemas.xmlsoap.org/ws/2001/10/inspection/"
           location="uri">
```

The location specifies the URI of the other inspection document.

WS-Policy

Web services are composed to create an aggregate web service. A participating web service may need to communicate its policies to other participants. For example, one of the participants (a partner) may require a Kerberos security token for its access. This will be defined as a policy assertion in its policy document. Such policy documents must be shared between partners who wish to access the services provided by this partner site. A policy may consist of multiple assertions. The service provider may require all such assertions be satisfied by the requesting partner, or it may request the partner to satisfy at least one of the assertions. **WS-Policy** was designed for creating policy documents.

WS-Policy defines a set of constructs for specifying web service policies that can be communicated to others. The specification does *not* define how to transport or discover a policy. Policies may be associated with various entities and resources. The policy may be associated with arbitrary XML elements, WSDL documents, and UDDI elements. The WS-PolicyAttachment specifications define such mechanisms. The policy, specified in an XML document, is transmitted to the requester using messaging specifications discussed earlier.

Policy Outline

A general outline for defining a policy is as follows:

```
<wsp:Policy xmlns:wsp="http://schemas.xmlsoap.org/ws/2002/12/policy">
  ...
  Policy Assertions
  ...
</wsp:Policy>
```

The policy may include multiple policy assertions. The specification defines policy operators that decide the assertions to be used. The various operators are:

- `<wsp:All>`
- `<wsp:ExactlyOne>`
- `<wsp:OneOrMore>`
- `<wsp:Policy>`

The <wsp:All> Operator

The use of the `<wsp:All>` operator is illustrated in the following example:

```
<wsp:Policy xmlns:wsse="http://schemas.xmlsoap.org/ws/2002/12/secext"
    xmlns:wsp="http://schemas.xmlsoap.org/ws/2002/12/policy">
  <wsp:All>
    Assertion 1
    Assertion 2
    ...
    ...
  </wsp:All>
</wsp:Policy>
```

A typical policy defines multiple assertions. This example specifies the security assertions, so we have defined the security namespace. `<wsp:All>` specifies that all listed assertions must be satisfied.

The <wsp:ExactlyOne> Operator

If we use `ExactlyOne` in place of `All` in the above code, it indicates that exactly one of the assertions must be satisfied. Typically, this is useful when specifying the alternatives to an assertion. Thus, more than one alternative assertion may be listed in the policy and exactly one of the assertions must be satisfied.

The <wsp:OneOrMore> Operator

`OneOrMore` specifies that at least one of its child elements must be satisfied. With multiple assertions, it ensures that one or more assertions are satisfied.

The <wsp:Policy> Operator

This is equivalent to `<wsp:All>`.

Policy Assertions

The assertions within a policy are defined using following syntax:

```
<wsp:Policy TargetNamespace="..."? >
  <Assertion wsp:Usage="..."? wsp:Preference="..."? /> *
```

```
    ...
</wsp:Policy>
```

`wsp:Usage` specifies how the assertion is processed. It supports the following values:

- `wsp:Required`: Indicates that this is a required assertion. If this is not satisfied, a fault occurs.
- `wsp:Rejected`: Indicates that this assertion is explicitly not supported. If present, it causes a fault to occur.
- `wsp:Optional`: Indicates that this is an optional assertion.
- `wsp:Observed`: Indicates that the service requesters are informed that the policy is applied. The assertion is applied to all the subjects.
- `wsp:Ignored`: Indicates that the assertion is ignored.

The `wsp:Preference` operator specifies the preference given to the current assertion. This is specified as a numeric value; the higher the value, the higher is the preference.

Example

The following example illustrates how the policy is defined.

```
<wsp:Policy xmlns:wsse="http://schemas.xmlsoap.org/ws/2002/12/secext"
    xmlns:wsp="http://schemas.xmlsoap.org/ws/2002/12/policy">
  <wsse:SecurityToken wsp:Usage="wsp:Required">
    <wsse:TokenType>
      wsse:Kerberosv5TGT
    </wsse:TokenType>
  </wsse:SecurityToken>
</wsp:Policy>
```

We have defined two namespaces, one for the policy and the other for security. Policy assertions are usually related to security, so we need to define the security namespace. The policy assertion is the `SecurityToken`. It is specified as `Required`. The type of token is `Kerberos`.

Note that we have not specified the policy operator here. If we had specified more than one assertion, say one more security token of type X.509, we could have specified the operator as `ExactlyOne`, indicating that only one of the token types is to be used.

Policy Inclusion

The specification allows you to include an already-defined policy expression in another policy expression. The `<wsp:PolicyReference>` element is used for this purpose. The `PolicyReference` is specified as follows:

```
<wsp:Policy>
  ...
  <wsp:PolicyReference URI="..." ?/>
  ...
</wsp:Policy>
```

The URI specifies the location for the existing policy. The following example illustrates the use of this element:

```
<wsp:Policy wsu:Id="MyPolicy" xmlns:wsu="..." >
  ...
</wsp:Policy>

<wsp:Policy xmlns:wsse="...">
  <wsp:PolicyReference URI="#MyPolicy" />
  ...
</wsp:Policy>
```

In this code, the existing policy specified by `MyPolicy` is included in the new policy definition.

WS-Eventing

In a business process, a participating web service may be interested in receiving notifications whenever a certain type of event occurs in relation with other participating web services. A web service that is interested in such a notification should register its interest (subscribe) with other web services (event sources) where such events may be generated. The subscriber is called an event sink. The **WS-Eventing** specification allows you to create and delete event subscriptions. An expiration time may be set for each subscription. A subscriber may renew or unsubscribe its subscription with the event source.

All these requests are performed by sending an appropriate message to the event source. The WS-Eventing specification defines the message format for achieving this. Like the other specifications we discussed, this specification also relies on other service specifications for secure, reliable, and transacted message delivery.

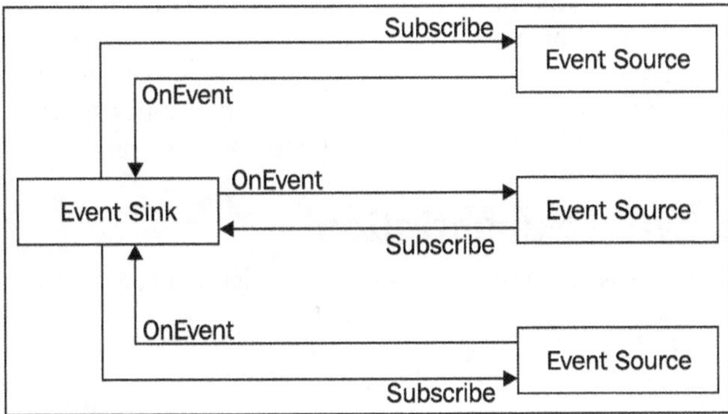

Event Subscription

An event sink subscribes to an event source by using the following message format:

```
<s:Envelope ...>
  <s:Header ...>
      <wsa:Action>
        http://schemas.xmlsoap.org/ws/2004/01/eventing/Subscribe
      </wsa:Action>
    <wsa:MessageID>
      xs:anyURI
    </wsa:MessageID>
    <wsa:FaultTo>
      endpoint-reference
    </wsa:FaultTo> ?
```

```
        <wsa:ReplyTo>
          endpoint-reference
        </wsa:ReplyTo>
        <wsa:To>
          xs:anyURI
        </wsa:To>
        ...
    </s:Header>
    <s:Body ...>
          <wse:Subscribe ...>
            <wse:NotifyTo>
              endpoint-reference
            </wse:NotifyTo>
            <wse:EndTo>
              endpoint-reference
            </wse:EndTo> ?
            <wse:Expires>
              [xs:dateTime | xs:duration]
            </wse:Expires> ?
            <wse:Filter Dialect="xs:anyURI"? >
              xs:string
            </wse:Filter> ?
            ...
          </wse:Subscribe>
    </s:Body>
</s:Envelope>
```

In the message header, the `Action` element indicates an interest in subscribing to an event. The `ReplyTo` defines the endpoint reference for a reply message and the `To` element defines the URI for the event source. The `<wse:subscribe>` element defines the subscription information. The `NotifyTo` element defines the endpoint reference where the notification messages are to be sent. The `EndTo` defines a URI where the message is sent whenever the subscription ends. The `Expires` element defines the requested expiration time for the subscription. The event source may provide the filtering of notification messages. The event source uses the values specified in the `Filter` element while generating a response or a fault message to the event sink.

Response to Event Subscription

The event source sends a message to the event sink on receipt of a request for subscription using the following format:

```
<s:Envelope ...>
  <s:Header ...>
    <wsa:Action>
      http://schemas.xmlsoap.org/ws/2004/01/eventing/SubscribeResponse
    </wsa:Action>
    <wsa:RelatesTo>
      xs:anyURI
    </wsa:RelatesTo>
    <wsa:To>
      xs:anyURI
    </wsa:To>
      ...
  </s:Header>
  <s:Body ...>
    <wse:SubscribeResponse ...>
      <wse:Id>
        xs:anyURI
```

```
      </wse:Id>
      <wse:Expires>
        [xs:dateTime | xs:duration]
      </wse:Expires>
        ...
      </wse:SubscribeResponse>
    </s:Body>
  </s:Envelope>
```

The RelatesTo element specifies the value of the message ID of the corresponding request. <wse:Id> specifies the unique identifier created by the event source. The Expires element defines the expiry time for the subscription.

Subscription Renewal

An event sink sends a renewal request to the event sink using something like the following message format:

```
<s:Envelope ...>
  <s:Header ...>
    <wsa:Action>
      http://schemas.xmlsoap.org/ws/2004/01/eventing/Renew
    </wsa:Action>
    ...
  </s:Header>
  <s:Body ...>
    <wse:Renew ...>
      <wse:Id>xs:anyURI</wse:Id>
      <wse:Expires>[xs:dateTime | xs:duration]</wse:Expires> ?
      ...
    </wse:Renew>
  </s:Body>
</s:Envelope>
```

The Action element specifies that this is a renewal request. The <wse:Renew> element defines the renewal request.

Unsubscribing

An event sink may unsubscribe for an event by sending a message to the event source using the following message format:

```
<s:Envelope ...>
  <s:Header ...>
    <wsa:Action>
      http://schemas.xmlsoap.org/ws/2004/01/eventing/Unsubscribe
    </wsa:Action>
    ...
  </s:Header>
  <s:Body>
    <wse:Unsubscribe ...>
      <wse:Id>
        xs:anyURI
      </wse:Id>
    ...
      </wse:Unsubscribe>
  </s:Body>
</s:Envelope>
```

In the Action element, the interest to unsubscribe for an event is specified. The <wse:Unsubscribe> element specifies the subscription ID.

Subscription End Message

Whenever the subscription ends, the source sends a notification to the endpoint reference using following message format:

```
<s:Envelope ...>
  <s:Header ...>
    <wsa:Action>
      http://schemas.xmlsoap.org/ws/2004/01/eventing/SubscriptionEnd
    </wsa:Action> ?
    <wse:SubscriptionEnd s11:mustUnderstand="xs:boolean" ?
                         s12:mustUnderstand="xs:boolean" ?
                         ...>
      <wse:Id>
        xs:anyURI
      </wse:Id>
      <wse:Code>
        [wse:Unsubscribed | wse:Expired | wse:NotifyToFailure |
         wse:SourceCanceling]
      </wse:Code>
      <wse:Reason xml:lang="language identifier" >
        xs:string
      </wse:Reason> ?
    ...
    </wsa:SubscriptionEnd>
    ...
  </s:Header>
  <s:Body ...>
    ...
  </s:Body>
</s:Envelope>
```

The `Action` element indicates that the subscription has ended. The event source specifies the reason for ending the subscription in the `Code` element. The `Unsubscribed` value indicates the acceptance of an unsubscribe request from the event sink. The `Expired` value indicates that the subscription has not been renewed and is now expired. The `NotifyToFailure` value indicates that the source terminated the subscription because it is not able to deliver the notifications to the URI specified in the `NotifyTo` element of the request. The `SourceCanceling` value indicates that the source terminated the subscription before it expired.

With the help of the above message formats, an infrastructure for notifying events between web services is made available to developers.

Conclusion

Web services expose interfaces of existing components using a standard web-based protocol. A client uses these interfaces to use the services provided by the components. A typical business process requires multiple web services. The involvement of web services from different developers required the creation of new standards to achieve proper coordination between them. Several new standards were developed to achieve this coordination. This chapter has discussed several such open standards that are required for the coordination of web services.

The WS-Security specification addresses how to transport security context between the participating processes and thus how to provide a secured distributed computing based on the collaboration of diverse web services. The WS-Coordination specification defines a framework that is used by participating processes to coordinate the desired activities between multiple processes.

Web Services Transactions require the coordination between multiple parties to implement a distributed transaction. They use the WS-Coordination specification for this purpose. As several messages are transported between diverse parties during a business process, reliable message delivery is required. The WS-Reliable Messaging specification addresses this issue. The messages are sent to endpoints. The WS-Addressing specification describes how to define such endpoints. Web services expose their interface with the help of service-description documents. The WS-Inspection specification helps in dynamic discovery of such documents. The WS-Policy specification describes the policies used by a process to its partners. Finally, the WS-Eventing specification helps in creating an event-based infrastructure for business collaborations.

When different web services are connected together to create a larger business process, there is a need to define the workflow to ensure the proper sequencing of these services. A new language, BPEL, is designed for this purpose. This chapter described briefly the need for this new language. Further chapters in the book will go into the depths of this language to understand how a business process is created in BPEL and describe the several tools that are available to develop BPEL documents.

3
Service Composition with BPEL

In this chapter, we will get familiar with the BPEL concepts and discuss composing services with BPEL. We will show how to develop executable business processes. In a nutshell, we:

- Discuss service composition with BPEL
- Explain how business processes are defined in BPEL
- Get familiar with core concepts including:
    - The structure of BPEL process definitions
    - Invoking web services
    - Synchronous and asynchronous processes
    - Partner links
    - The role of WSDL
    - Important activities and other constructs
- Define an example BPEL process

Developing Business Processes with BPEL

BPEL uses an XML-based vocabulary that allows us to specify and describe business processes. As mentioned in Chapter 1, with BPEL, you can describe business processes in two distinct ways:

- **Executable business processes** specify the exact details of business processes and can be executed by a BPEL engine. In the majority of cases we will use BPEL to specify executable processes.
- **Abstract business processes** specify only the public message exchange between parties, without including the specific details of process flows. They are not executable and are rarely used.

This chapter focuses on executable business processes. Abstract business processes are covered in the next chapter.

Executable business processes are processes that compose a set of existing services. When we describe a business process in BPEL, we actually define a new web service that is a composition of existing services. The interface of the new BPEL composite web service uses a set of port types, through which it provides operations like any other web service. To invoke a business process described in BPEL, we must invoke the resulting composite web service.

In a typical scenario, the BPEL business process receives a request. To fulfill it, the process then invokes the involved web services and finally responds to the original caller. Because the BPEL process communicates with other web services, it relies heavily on the WSDL description of the web services invoked by the composite web service.

Anyone developing BPEL processes requires a good understanding of WSDL and other related technologies. BPEL introduces WSDL extensions, which enable us to accurately specify relations between several web services in the business process. These relations are called **partner links**. The following figure shows a BPEL process and its relation to web services (partner links):

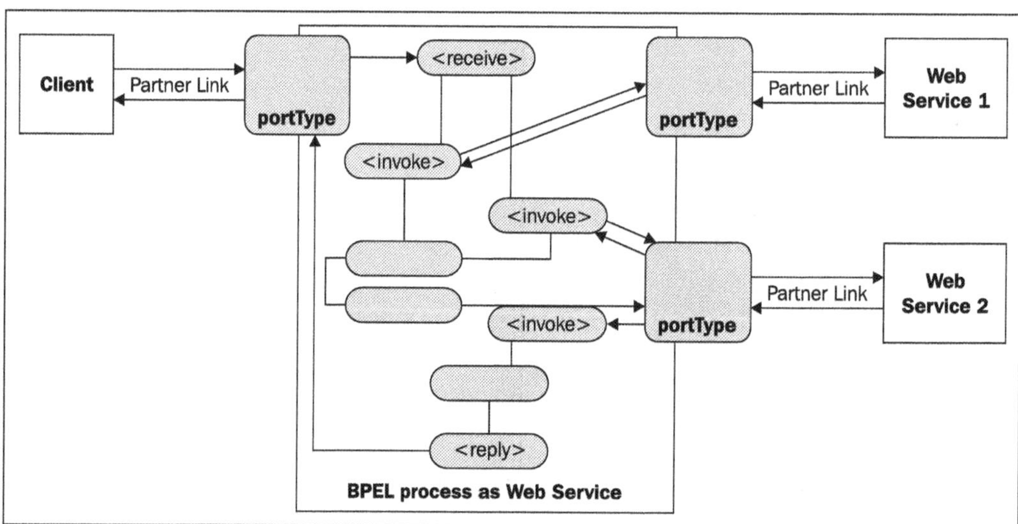

Any BPEL process specifies the exact order in which participating web services should be invoked. This can be done sequentially or in parallel. With BPEL, we can express conditional behavior, for example, a web service invocation can depend on the value of a previous invocation. We can also construct loops, declare variables, copy and assign values, define fault handlers, and so on. By combining all these constructs, we can define complex business processes in an algorithmic manner. We can describe deterministic as well as non-deterministic flows. Because business processes are essentially graphs of activities, it is sometimes useful to express them using **UML** (Unified Modeling Language) activity diagrams. To understand how business processes are defined in BPEL, we look at the core concepts in the next section.

Core Concepts

A BPEL process consists of steps. Each step is called an **activity**. BPEL supports basic and structured activities. Basic activities represent basic constructs and are used for common tasks, such as those listed below:

- Invoking other web services, using `<invoke>`
- Waiting for the client to invoke the business process through sending a message, using `<receive>` (receiving a request)
- Generating a response for synchronous operations, using `<reply>`
- Manipulating data variables, using `<assign>`
- Indicating faults and exceptions, using `<throw>`
- Waiting for some time, using `<wait>`
- Terminating the entire process, using `<terminate>`

We can then combine these and other basic activities and define complex algorithms that exactly specify the steps of a business process. To combine basic activities BPEL supports several structured activities. The most important are:

- Sequence (`<sequence>`) for defining a set of activities that will be invoked in an ordered sequence
- Flow (`<flow>`) for defining a set of activities that will be invoked in parallel
- Case-switch construct (`<switch>`) for implementing branches
- While (`<while>`) for defining loops
- The ability to select one of a number of alternative paths, using `<pick>`

Each BPEL process will also define partner links, using `<partnerLink>`, and declare variables, using `<variable>`.

To provide an idea of how a BPEL process looks, we show below a very simple BPEL process, which selects the best insurance offer from several.

We first declare the partner links to the BPEL process client (called `client`) and two insurance web services (called `insuranceA` and `insuranceB`):

```
<?xml version="1.0" encoding="utf-8"?>

<process name="InsuranceSelectionProcess"
         targetNamespace="http://packtpub.com/bpel/example/"
         xmlns="http://schemas.xmlsoap.org/ws/2003/03/business-process/"
         xmlns:bpws="http://schemas.xmlsoap.org/ws/2003/03/business-process/"
         xmlns:ins="http://packtpub.com/bpel/insurance/"
         xmlns:com="http://packtpub.com/bpel/company/" >

   <partnerLinks>
      <partnerLink name="client"
                   partnerLinkType="com:selectionLT"
                   myRole="insuranceSelectionService"/>

      <partnerLink name="insuranceA"
                   partnerLinkType="ins:insuranceLT"
```

```
                    myRole="insuranceRequester"
                    partnerRole="insuranceService"/>

      <partnerLink name="insuranceB"
                    partnerLinkType="ins:insuranceLT"
                    myRole="insuranceRequester"
                    partnerRole="insuranceService"/>

   </partnerLinks>
...
```

Next, we declare variables for the insurance request (`InsuranceRequest`), insurance A and B responses (`InsuranceAResponse`, `InsuranceBResponse`), and for the final selection (`InsuranceSelectionResponse`):

```
...
   <variables>
      <!-- input for BPEL process -->
      <variable name="InsuranceRequest"
                messageType="ins:InsuranceRequestMessage"/>
      <!-- output from insurance A -->
      <variable name="InsuranceAResponse"
                messageType="ins:InsuranceResponseMessage"/>
      <!-- output from insurance B -->
      <variable name="InsuranceBResponse"
                messageType="ins:InsuranceResponseMessage"/>
      <!-- output from BPEL process -->
      <variable name="InsuranceSelectionResponse"
                messageType="ins:InsuranceResponseMessage"/>
   </variables>
...
```

Finally, we specify the process steps. First we wait for the initial request message from the client (`<receive>`). Then we invoke both insurance web services (`<invoke>`) in parallel using the `<flow>` activity. The insurance web services return the insurance premium. Then we select the lower amount (`<switch>`/`<case>`) and return the result to the client (the caller of the BPEL process) using the `<reply>` activity:

```
...
   <sequence>

      <!-- Receive the initial request from client -->
      <receive partnerLink="client"
               portType="com:InsuranceSelectionPT"
               operation="SelectInsurance"
               variable="InsuranceRequest"
               createInstance="yes" />

      <!-- Make concurrent invocations to Insurance A and B -->
      <flow>

         <!-- Invoke Insurance A web service -->
         <invoke partnerLink="insuranceA"
                 portType="ins:ComputeInsurancePremiumPT"
                 operation="ComputeInsurancePremium"
                 inputVariable="InsuranceRequest"
                 outputVariable="InsuranceAResponse" />

         <!-- Invoke Insurance B web service -->
```

```
        <invoke partnerLink="insuranceB"
                portType="ins:ComputeInsurancePremiumPT"
                operation="ComputeInsurancePremium"
                inputVariable="InsuranceRequest"
                outputVariable="InsuranceBResponse" />

      </flow>

      <!-- Select the best offer and construct the response -->
      <switch>

        <case condition="bpws:getVariableData('InsuranceAResponse',
                          'confirmationData','/confirmationData/ins:Amount')
                       &lt;= bpws:getVariableData('InsuranceBResponse',
                          'confirmationData','/confirmationData/ins:Amount')">

          <!-- Select Insurance A -->
          <assign>
            <copy>
              <from variable="InsuranceAResponse" />
              <to variable="InsuranceSelectionResponse" />
            </copy>
          </assign>
        </case>

        <otherwise>
          <!-- Select Insurance B -->
          <assign>
            <copy>
              <from variable="InsuranceBResponse" />
              <to variable="InsuranceSelectionResponse" />
            </copy>
          </assign>
        </otherwise>
      </switch>

      <!-- Send a response to the client -->
      <reply partnerLink="client"
             portType="com:InsuranceSelectionPT"
             operation="SelectInsurance"
             variable="InsuranceSelectionResponse"/>

    </sequence>

  </process>
```

In the coming sections, we will explain the different parts of the BPEL process and the syntax of various BPEL activities.

> As BPEL processes are exposed as web services, we need a WSDL for the BPEL process.

Because each BPEL process is a web service, each BPEL process needs a WSDL document too. This is more or less obvious. As mentioned, a client will usually invoke an operation on the BPEL process to start it. With the BPEL process WSDL, we specify the interface for this operation. We also specify all message types, operations, and port types a BPEL process offers to other partners. We will show WSDL for the BPEL process later in this chapter.

Invoking Web Services

A BPEL process definition is written as an XML document using the <process> root element. Within the <process> element a BPEL process will usually have the top-level <sequence> element. Within the sequence, the process will first wait for the incoming message to start the process. This wait is modeled with the <receive> construct. Then the process will invoke the related web services, using the <invoke> construct. Such invocations can be done sequentially or in parallel. If we want to make them sequentially we simply write an <invoke> for each invocation and the web services will be invoked in that order. This is shown in the following code excerpt:

```
<process ...>
   ...
   <sequence>

      <!-- Wait for the incoming request to start the process -->
      <receive ... />

      <!-- Invoke a set of related web services, one by one -->
      <invoke ... />
      <invoke ... />
      <invoke ... />
      ...
   </sequence>
</process>
```

Here we have not shown the full syntax of <receive>, <invoke>, and other activities, which require that we specify certain attributes. This is explained later in this chapter, after we have become familiar with the basic structure of BPEL documents.

To invoke web services concurrently, we can use the <flow> construct. In the example below, the three <invoke> operations would perform concurrently:

```
<process ...>
   ...
   <sequence>
      <!-- Wait for the incoming request to start the process -->
      <receive ... />

      <!-- Invoke a set of related web services, concurrently -->
      <flow>
         <invoke ... />
         <invoke ... />
         <invoke ... />
      </flow>
      ...
   </sequence>
</process>
```

We can also combine and nest the <sequence> and <flow> constructs, which allows us to define several sequences executing concurrently. In the following example we have defined two sequences, one consisting of three invocations, and one with two invocations. Both sequences would execute concurrently:

```
<process ...>
   ...
   <sequence>

      <!-- Wait for the incoming request to start the process -->
      <receive ... />
```

```
        <!-- Invoke two sequences concurrently -->
        <flow>
           <!-- The three invokes below execute sequentially -->
           <sequence>
              <invoke ... />
              <invoke ... />
              <invoke ... />
           </sequence>
           <!-- The two invokes below execute sequentially -->
           <sequence>
              <invoke ... />
              <invoke ... />
           </sequence>
        </flow>

        ...
     </sequence>
  </process>
```

Invoking Asynchronous Web Services

We just explained how to invoke synchronous web service operations. There are actually two major types of web service operations:

- **Synchronous request/reply web service operations**: Here we send a request and wait for the reply. Such operations usually do not require much time to process, therefore it is reasonable for the sender (client) to wait for the reply. They are shown in the following figure:

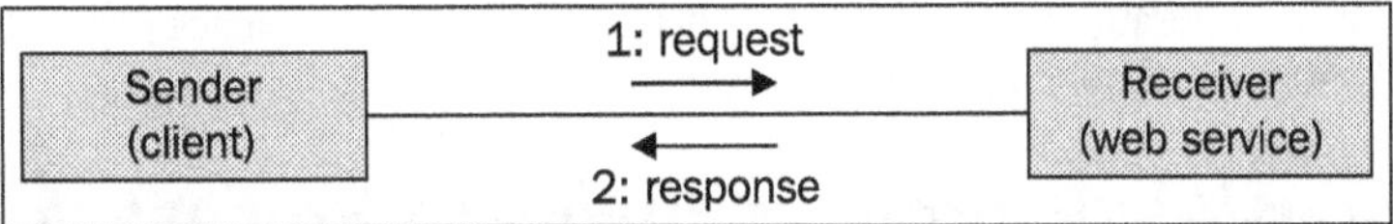

- **Asynchronous web service operations**: Usually, such operations perform processing that requires a longer time to finish. Therefore, they do not block the sender for the duration of the operation. If such operations require that results are sent back to the client, they usually perform callbacks. This is shown in the following figure:

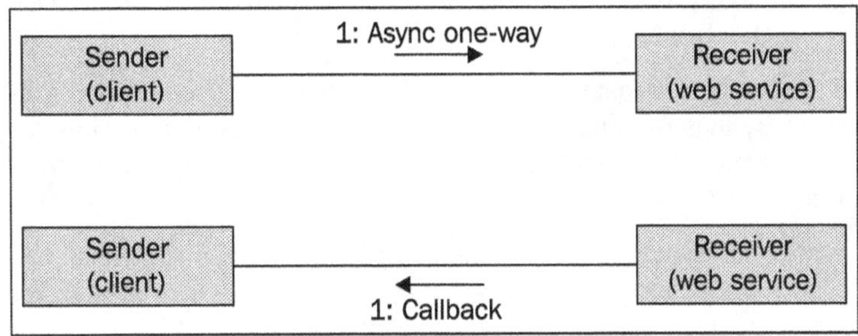

Callbacks usually need to be related to original requests. We call this message correlation. Message correlation can be achieved with WS-Addressing, explained in Chapter 2, or with BPEL correlation sets, which we explain in Chapter 4.

Using the <invoke> construct, we can invoke both types of operations, synchronous and asynchronous. If we invoke a synchronous operation, the business process waits for the reply. We do not need to use an explicit construct to retrieve the reply.

With asynchronous operations, <invoke> only takes care for the first part—for the operation invocation. To receive a result (if one is returned to the client), we need to use a separate construct, <receive>. With <receive>, the business process waits for the incoming message. Between the <invoke> and <receive> we could do some other processing instead of waiting for the reply, as is the case with synchronous operations. The code excerpt below shows how to invoke asynchronous operations:

```
<process ...>
   <sequence>

      <!-- Wait for the incoming request to start the process -->
      <receive ... />

      <!-- Invoke an asynchronous operation -->
      <invoke ... />

      <!-- Do something else... -->

      <!-- Wait for the callback -->
      <receive ... />

      ...
   </sequence>
</process>
```

Just like synchronous operations, we can use asynchronous <invoke>/<receive> pairs within <flows> to perform several concurrent invocations.

Synchronous/Asynchronous Business Processes

We have already mentioned that the BPEL modeled business process is exposed as a web service. The BPEL process itself can be synchronous or asynchronous. A synchronous BPEL process returns a response to the client immediately after processing and the client is blocked for the whole duration of the BPEL process execution.

An asynchronous BPEL process on the other hand does not block the client. To return a result to the client, an asynchronous process uses a callback, similar to any other web service. However, it is not required that such a BPEL process returns a response.

This brings us to the conclusion that the type of BPEL process we choose is very important. Most real-world processes are long running, so we model them as asynchronous. However, there may also be processes that execute in a relatively short time, or processes where we want the client to wait for completion. We model such processes as synchronous.

How do synchronous and asynchronous processes differ in the BPEL specification? We know that both first wait for the initial message, using a <receive>. Both also invoke other web services, either synchronously or asynchronously. However, a synchronous BPEL process will return a result after the process has completed. Therefore, we use a <reply> construct at the end of the process, as shown in the following excerpt:

```
<process ...>
   <sequence>

      <!-- Wait for the incoming request to start the process -->
      <receive ... />

      <!-- Invoke a set of related web services -->
      ...

      <!-- Return a synchronous reply to the caller (client) -->
      <reply ... />

   </sequence>
</process>
```

An asynchronous BPEL process does not use the `<reply>` clause. If such a process has to send a reply to the client, it uses the `<invoke>` clause to invoke the callback operation on the client's port type. Remember that an asynchronous BPEL process does not need to return anything.

```
<process ...>
   <sequence>

      <!-- Wait for the incoming request to start the process -->
      <receive ... />

      <!-- Invoke a set of related web services -->
      ...

      <!-- Invoke a callback on the client (if needed) -->
      <invoke ... />

   </sequence>
</process>
```

We will come back to the `<invoke>`, `<receive>`, and `<reply>` activities a little later to describe the whole syntax, including the necessary attributes. First, however, we have to introduce the concept of partner links and partner link types.

Understanding Links to Partners

From what have we said until now, we can see that BPEL processes interact with external web services in two ways:

- The BPEL process invokes operations on other web services.
- The BPEL process receives invocations from clients. One of the clients is the user of the BPEL process, who makes the initial invocation. Other clients are web services, for example, those that have been invoked by the BPEL process, but make callbacks to return replies.

Links to all parties BPEL interacts with are called **partner links**. Partner links can be links to web services that are invoked by the BPEL process. These are sometimes called **invoked partner links**. Partner links can also be links to clients, and can invoke the BPEL process. Such partner links are sometimes called **client partner links**. Note that each BPEL process has at least one client partner link, because there has to be a client that first invokes the BPEL process.

Usually a BPEL process will also have at least one invoked partner link, because it will most likely invoke at least one web service. The process invokes other web services using the `<invoke>` activity, where it has to specify the operation name and the port type used for invocation, as we will see later. Invoked partner links may, however, become client partner links—this is usually the case with asynchronous services, where the process invokes an operation. Later the service (partner) invokes the callback operation on the process to return the requested data.

BPEL treats clients as partner links for two reasons. The most obvious reason is support for asynchronous interactions. In asynchronous interactions, the process needs to invoke operations on its clients. This is used for modeling asynchronous BPEL processes. Such processes also invoke the callback on the initial caller, as mentioned in the previous section.

The second reason is based on the fact that the BPEL process can offer services. These services, offered through port types, can be used by more than one client. The process may wish to distinguish between different clients and offer them only the functionality they are authorized to use. For example, an insurance process might offer a different set of operations to car-insurance clients than to real-estate insurance clients.

To sum up, partner links describe links to partners, where partners might be:

- Services invoked by the process
- Services that invoke the process
- Services that have both roles—they are invoked by the process and they invoke the process

We have already described the first two scenarios. Let us now have a closer look at the third scenario: a typical asynchronous callback. Here a web service offers a `portType A`, through which the BPEL process invokes the operations on that web service. The BPEL process also has to provide a `portType` through which the web service invokes the callback operation—let us call that `portType B`. This is shown in the following figure:

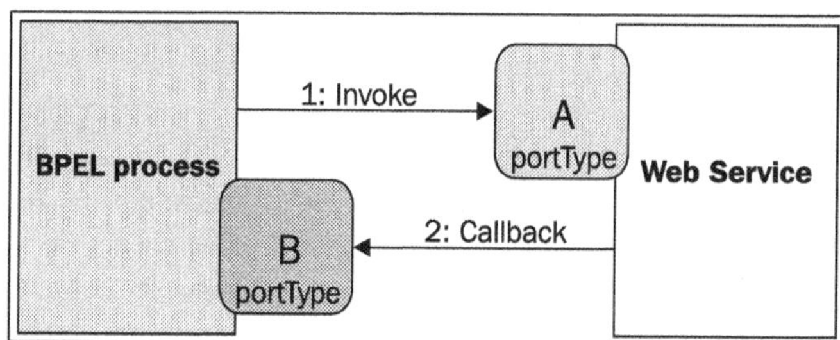

From the viewpoint of the BPEL process, the process requires `portType A` on the web service and provides `portType B` to the web service. From the perspective of the web service, the web service offers `portType A` to the BPEL process and requires `portType B` from the process.

Partner Link Types

Describing situations where the service is invoked by the process and vice versa requires selecting a certain perspective. We can select the process perspective and describe the process as requiring the `portType` A on the web service and providing the `portType` B to the web service. Alternatively, we select the web service perspective and describe the web service as offering `portType` A to the BPEL process and requiring `portType` B from the process.

To overcome this limitation BPEL introduces partner link types. They allow us to model such relationships as a third party. We are not required to take a certain perspective; rather we just define roles. A partner link type must have at least one role and can have at most two roles. The latter is the usual case. For each role we must specify a `portType` that is used for interaction.

> A partner link type declares how two parties interact and what each party offers.

In the following example, we define a `partnerLinkType` called `insuranceLT`. It defines two roles, the `insuranceService` and the `insuranceRequester`. The `insuranceService` offers the `ComputeInsurancePremiumPT` port type from the namespace `ins`, qualified by the corresponding URI (the namespace declarations are not shown here). The `insuranceRequester` offers the `ComputeInsurancePremiumCallbackPT` port type from the `com` namespace. As the name implies, the later port type is used for the callback operation. This declaration specifies the service and the callback roles:

```
<partnerLinkType name="insuranceLT"
                 xmlns="http://schemas.xmlsoap.org/ws/2003/05/partner-link/">

   <role name="insuranceService">
      <portType name="ins:ComputeInsurancePremiumPT"/>
   </role>

   <role name="insuranceRequester">
      <portType name="com:ComputeInsurancePremiumCallbackPT"/>
   </role>
</partnerLinkType>
```

Sometimes we may not need to specify two roles. A typical example is when we use synchronous request/response operations. If the operations in the `ComputeInsurancePremiumPT` port type returned results immediately, there would be no need for a callback. We would only need a single role:

```
<partnerLinkType name="insuranceLT"
                 xmlns="http://schemas.xmlsoap.org/ws/2003/05/partner-link/">

   <role name="insuranceService">
      <portType name="ins:ComputeInsurancePremiumPT"/>
   </role>
</partnerLinkType>
```

If we specify only one role, we express willingness to interact with the service, but do not place any additional requirements on the service. In the first example, however, where we have specified two roles, we require that the insurance web service supports the `ComputeInsurancePremiumCallbackPT` port type.

It is important to understand that the partner link types are not part of the BPEL process specification document. This is reasonable, because partner link types belong to the service specification and not the process specification. They can therefore be placed in the WSDL document that describes the partner web service or the BPEL process. Partner link types use the WSDL extensibility mechanism, so they can be a part of a WSDL document.

Shown below is a skeleton of the WSDL document with the `partnerLinkType` section. It specifies types, messages, port types and partner link types. It does not, however, show the bindings and the service sections, because the BPEL execution environment usually automatically generates these:

```
<?xml version="1.0" encoding="UTF-8" ?>
<definitions xmlns:http="http://schemas.xmlsoap.org/wsdl/http/"
             xmlns:soap="http://schemas.xmlsoap.org/wsdl/soap/"
             xmlns:xs="http://www.w3.org/2001/XMLSchema"
             xmlns:soapenc="http://schemas.xmlsoap.org/soap/encoding/"
             xmlns:ins="http://packtpub.com/bpel/insurance/"
             xmlns:com="http://packtpub.com/bpel/company/"
             targetNamespace="http://packtpub.com/bpel/company/"
             xmlns="http://schemas.xmlsoap.org/wsdl/"
             xmlns:plnk=
                    "http://schemas.xmlsoap.org/ws/2003/05/partner-link/" >

  <import ... />
  <types>
    <xs:schema ... >
      ...
    </xs:schema>
  </types>

  <message ... >
    <part ... />
    ...
  </message>

  <portType name="ComputeInsurancePremiumPT">
    <operation name="...">
      <input message="..." />
    </operation>
  </portType>

  <portType name="ComputeInsurancePremiumCallbackPT">
    <operation name="...">
      <input message="..." />
    </operation>
  </portType>
  ...
  <plnk:partnerLinkType name="insuranceLT">
    <plnk:role name="insuranceService">
      <plnk:portType name="ins:ComputeInsurancePremiumPT"/>
    </plnk:role>
    <plnk:role name="insuranceRequester">
      <plnk:portType name="ins:ComputeInsurancePremiumCallbackPT"/>
    </plnk:role>
  </plnk:partnerLinkType>

</definitions>
```

> Sometimes existing web services will not define a partner link type. Then we can wrap the WSDL of the web service and define partner link types ourselves.

Now that we have become familiar with the partner link types and know where to place their declarations, it is time to go back to the BPEL process definition, more specifically to the partner links.

Defining Partner Links

We have already described the role of partner links in BPEL process specifications. However, we have not yet explained how to define partner links, because we first had to get familiar with partner link types.

Partner links are concrete references to services that a BPEL business process interacts with. They are specified near the beginning of the BPEL process definition document, just after the `<process>` tag. Several `<partnerLink>` definitions are nested within the `<partnerLinks>` element:

```
<process ...>

   <partnerLinks>

      <partnerLink ... />
      <partnerLink ... />
      ...

   </partnerLinks>

   <sequence>
      ...
   </sequence>
</process>
```

For each partner link, we have to specify:

- `name`: Serves as a reference for interactions via that partner link
- `partnerLinkType`: Defines the type of the partner link
- `myRole`: Indicates the role of the BPEL process itself
- `partnerRole`: Indicates the role of the partner

We define both roles (`myRole` and `partnerRole`) only if the `partnerLinkType` specifies two roles. If the `partnerLinkType` specifies only one role, the `partnerLink` also has to specify only one role—we omit the one that is not needed.

Let us come back to our previous example, where we have defined the `insuranceLT` partner link type. To define a `partnerLink` called `insurance`, characterized by the `insuranceLT` `partnerLinkType`, we need to specify both roles, because it is an asynchronous relation. The role of the BPEL process (`myRole`) is described as **insurance requester** and the partner role is described as **insurance service**. The definition is shown in the following code excerpt:

```
...
   <partnerLinks>
      <partnerLink name="insurance"
                   partnerLinkType="tns:insuranceLT"
                   myRole="insuranceRequester"
                   partnerRole="insuranceService"/>
   </partnerLinks>
...
```

BPEL Process Tag

Now that we are more familiar with the BPEL, let's focus on the `<process>` tag. This delimits the root element of the BPEL document. The `<process>` tag requires that we specify certain attributes. We have to specify at least the following:

- `name`: Specifies the name of the BPEL business process
- `targetNamespace`: Specifies the target namespace for the business process definition
- `xmlns`: The namespace used by BPEL, `http://schemas.xmlsoap.org/ws/2003/03/business-process/`

Usually we also specify one or more additional namespaces to reference other involved namespaces, for example, those used by web services. Here is a typical process declaration tag:

```
<process name="InsuranceSelectionProcess"
         targetNamespace="http://packtpub.com/bpel/example/"
         xmlns="http://schemas.xmlsoap.org/ws/2003/03/business-process/"
         xmlns:bpws="http://schemas.xmlsoap.org/ws/2003/03/business-process/"
         xmlns:ins="http://packtpub.com/bpel/insurance/"
         xmlns:com="http://packtpub.com/bpel/company/" >
...
```

We can also specify additional attributes for the `<process>` tag, including:

- `queryLanguage`: Specifies which query language is used for node selection in assignments, properties, and other uses. The default is XPath 1.0. However, another language can be specified, such as XPath 2.0 or XQuery. The available options are determined by what is supported by a given BPEL engine.
- `expressionLanguage`: Specifies which expression language is used in the process. The default is XPath 1.0.
- `suppressJoinFailure`: Determines how to handle join failures. Join failures are explained in Chapter 4.
- `enableInstanceCompensation`: Determines whether process instances can be compensated by BPEL execution environments. We discuss this option in Chapter 4.
- `abstractProcess`: Specifies whether the process is abstract or executable. The default for this attribute is `no`, which means executable process. We specify `yes` if we wish to define an abstract process, which is explained in Chapter 4.

Variables

BPEL business processes model the exchange of messages between involved web services. Messages are exchanged as operations are invoked. When the business process invokes an operation and receives the result, we often want to store that result for subsequent invocations, use the result as is, or extract certain data. BPEL provides variables to store and maintain the state.

> Variables are used to store messages that are exchanged between business process partners or to hold data that relates to the state of the process.

Variables can also hold data that relates to the state of the process, but will never be exchanged with partners. Specifically, variables can store WSDL messages, XML Schema elements, or XML Schema simple types. Each variable has to be declared before it can be used. When we declare a variable, we must specify the variable name and type. To specify type we have to specify one of the following attributes:

- `messageType`: A variable that can hold a WSDL message
- `element`: A variable that can hold an XML Schema element
- `type`: A variable that can hold an XML Schema simple type

The declaration of variables is gathered within the `<variables>` element. The following example shows three variable declarations. The first one declares a variable with the name `InsuranceRequest`, which holds WSDL messages of type `ins:InsuranceRequestMessage`. The second declaration defines a variable `PartialInsuranceDescription` that can hold XML elements of type `ins:InsuranceDescription`. The last variable declaration is for variable `LastName`, which can hold XML Schema `string` type data. The first two declarations assume that the corresponding `messageType` and `element` have been declared in the WSDL (these declarations are not shown here):

```
<variables>
   <variable name="InsuranceRequest"
             messageType="ins:InsuranceRequestMessage"/>
   <variable name="PartialInsuranceDescription"
             element="ins:InsuranceDescription"/>
   <variable name="LastName"
             type="xs:string"/>
</variables>
```

You can declare variables globally at the beginning of a BPEL process declaration document or within scopes. Here we focus on globally declared variables and discuss scopes in the next chapter. The following example shows the structure of a BPEL process that uses variables:

```
<process ...>

   <partnerLinks>
      ...
   </partnerLinks>

   <variables>
      <variable ... />
      <variable ... />
      ...
   </variables>

   <sequence>
      ...
   </sequence>
</process>
```

Providing the Interface to BPEL Processes: <invoke>, <receive>, and <reply>

At the beginning of this section we have become familiar with the `<invoke>`, `<receive>`, and `<reply>` activities. With `<invoke>`, the BPEL process invokes operations on other web services, while with `<receive>` it waits for incoming messages (that is operation invocations). With

<receive>, the business process usually waits for the initial message to start the process. Another typical use for <receive> is to wait for callbacks. With <reply> a BPEL process can send a response, if the process is modeled as synchronous.

All three activities use the same three basic attributes:

- partnerLink: Specifies which partner link will be used
- portType: Specifies the used port type
- operation: Specifies the name of the operation to invoke (<invoke>), to wait for being invoked (<receive>), or the name of the operation which has been invoked but is synchronous and requires a reply (<reply>)

<invoke>

The <invoke> operation supports two other important attributes. When the business process invokes an operation on the web service, it sends a set of parameters. These parameters are modeled as input messages with web services. To specify the input message for the invocation, we use the inputVariable attribute and specify a variable of the corresponding type.

If we invoke a synchronous request/response operation, it returns a result. This result is again a message, modeled as an output message. To store it in a variable, <invoke> provides another attribute, called the outputVariable.

The following code excerpt shows an example of the <invoke> clause. We specify that the BPEL process should invoke the synchronous operation ComputeInsurancePremium on port type ins:ComputeInsurancePremiumPT using the insuranceA partner link, providing the input from variable InsuranceRequest and storing output in the InsuranceAResponse variable.

```
<invoke partnerLink="insuranceA"
        portType="ins:ComputeInsurancePremiumPT"
        operation="ComputeInsurancePremium"
        inputVariable="InsuranceRequest"
        outputVariable="InsuranceAResponse" >
</invoke>
```

<receive>

Let us now take a closer look at the <receive> activity. We have said that <receive> waits for the incoming message (operation invocation), either for the initial to start the BPEL process, or for a callback. Usually the business process needs to store the incoming message and it can use the variable attribute to specify a suitable variable.

Another attribute for <receive> activity is the createInstance attribute, which is related to the business process lifecycle and instructs the BPEL engine to create a new instance of the process. Usually we specify the createInstance="yes" attribute with the initial <receive> activity of the process to create a new process instance for each client. We discuss this attribute in more detail in the next chapter.

The following example shows a <receive> that waits for the SelectInsurance operation on port type com:InsuranceSelectionPT using the client partner link. Because this is the initial <receive> activity, the createInstance attribute is used. The client request is stored in the InsuranceRequest variable:

```
<receive partnerLink="client"
         portType="com:InsuranceSelectionPT"
         operation="SelectInsurance"
         variable="InsuranceRequest"
         createInstance="yes" >
</receive>
```

<reply>

Finally let's look at the <reply> clause. As we already know, <reply> is used to return the response for synchronous BPEL processes. <reply> is always related to the initial <receive> through which the BPEL process started. Using <reply> we can return the answer, which is the normal usage, or we can return a fault message. Returning a fault message using <reply> is discussed in Chapter 4.

When we use <reply> to return a response for a synchronous process we have to define only one additional attribute—the name of the variable where the response is stored. The following example shows a reply on an initial receive operation. It uses the `client` partner link and provides a response for the `SelectInsurance` operation on `ins:InsuranceSelectionPT` port type. The return result is stored in the `InsuranceSelectionResponse` variable. Please notice that the same `partnerLink`, `portType`, and operation name have been used in the initial <receive> clause:

```
<reply partnerLink="client"
       portType="com:InsuranceSelectionPT"
       operation="SelectInsurance"
       variable="InsuranceSelectionResponse" >
</reply>
```

The three activities, <invoke>, <receive>, and <reply> support additional functionality. They all support correlations, and <invoke> also supports fault handlers and compensation handlers. We will discuss these in Chapter 4.

Assignments

The variables in the business process hold and maintain the data. We used variables in <invoke>, <receive>, and <reply> to specify the input and output messages for invocation of operations on partner web services. In this section, we get familiar with how to copy data between variables.

To copy data between variables, expressions, and partner link endpoint references BPEL provides the <assign> activity. Within it, we can perform one or more <copy> commands. For each <copy> we have to specify the source (<from>) and the destination (<to>). The syntax of an assignment is presented below:

```
<assign>
  <copy>
    <from ... />
    <to ... />
  </copy>
  <copy>
    <from ... />
    <to ... />
  </copy>
  ...
</assign>
```

There are several choices for the <from> and <to> clauses. To copy values from one variable to the other we have to specify the variable attribute in the <from> and <to> elements. This is shown in the following example, where we have copied a value from the InsuranceAResponse variable to the InsuranceSelectionResponse variable:

```
<assign>
  <copy>
    <from variable="InsuranceAResponse" />
    <to variable="InsuranceSelectionResponse" />
  </copy>
</assign>
```

This copy can be performed only if both variables are of same type, as in our example ins:InsuranceResponseMessage, or if the source type is a subtype of the destination type.

Variables can be of three types:

- WSDL message types
- XML Schema elements
- XML Schema primitive types

If a variable holds a WSDL message, which is common, we can further refine the copy by specifying the part of the message we would like to copy. WSDL messages consist of parts (more on WSDL can be found at http://www.w3.org/TR/wsdl). Presented below is a simple message (defined in the WSDL document) that consists of two parts, the insuredPersonData part and the insuranceDetails part. Both parts are specified with the corresponding XML Schema complex types (not shown here):

```
<message name="InsuranceRequestMessage">
  <part name="insuredPersonData" type="ins:InsuredPersonDataType" />
  <part name="insuranceDetails" type="ins:InsuranceDetailsType" />
</message>
```

Now suppose that we get a variable of type ins:InsuredPersonDataType from invoking another web service, which has the following message declaration in its WSDL and uses the same namespace:

```
...
    <message name="InsuredPersonDataRequestMessage">
      <part name="insuredPersonData" type="ins:InsuredPersonDataType" />
    </message>
...
```

Our BPEL process would declare two variables, InsuranceRequest and InsuredPersonRequest, with the declaration shown below:

```
<variables>
   <variable name="InsuranceRequest"
             messageType="ins:InsuranceRequestMessage"/>
   <variable name="InsuredPersonRequest"
             messageType="ins:InsuredPersonDataRequestMessage"/>
</variables>
```

Now we could perform a copy from the InsuredPersonRequest variable to the insuredPersonData part of the InsuranceRequest variable using the following assignment:

```
<assign>
  <copy>
```

```
        <from variable="InsuredPersonRequest" part="insuredPersonData" />
        <to variable="InsuranceRequest" part="insuredPersonData" />
    </copy>
</assign>
```

We could also perform a copy in the opposite direction. In addition to specifying the part, we can also specify the exact path to the element we require. To specify the path we have to write a query, using the selected query language specified within the <process> tag.

> The default query language is XPath 1.0.

In our previous example, suppose the ins:InsuredPersonDataType is defined as follows:

```
<xs:complexType name="InsuredPersonDataType">
  <xs:sequence>
    <xs:element name="FirstName" type="xs:string" />
    <xs:element name="LastName" type="xs:string" />
    <xs:element name="Address" type="xs:string" />
    <xs:element name="Age" type="xs:int" />
  </xs:sequence>
</xs:complexType>
```

We could perform a copy from the LastName variable to the InsuranceRequest variable, to the message part insuredPersonData, to the last name:

```
<assign>
  <copy>
    <from variable="LastName" />
    <to variable="InsuranceRequest"
        part="insuredPersonData"
        query="/insuredPersonData/ins:LastName" />
  </copy>
</assign>
```

The location path must select exactly one node. In the query attribute, we specify an absolute location path, where the root '/' means the root of the document fragment representing the entire part of the message.

In our examples, we have used the message part name insuredPersonData as the name of the first step (top-level element). This is because we have used RPC-style web services, which use messages defined as XML types. For example, the InsuranceRequest variable is of type InsuranceRequestMessage. This message has been defined with two parts, each defined by an XML type, as shown on the code excerpt below:

```
<message name="InsuranceRequestMessage">
  <part name="insuredPersonData" type="ins:InsuredPersonDataType" />
  <part name="insuranceDetails" type="ins:InsuranceDetailsType" />
</message>
```

If we had used document-style web services, which use messages defined as XML elements, we would have to use a slightly different XPath query expression. Instead of the part name we would use the element name for the first step in the query expression.

We can also use the <assign> activity to copy expressions to variables. Expressions are written in the selected expression language; the default is XPath 1.0. We specify the expression attribute in the <from> element. The following example shows how to copy a constant string to the LastName variable:

```
<assign>
  <copy>
    <from expression="string('Juric')" />
    <to variable="LastName"/>
  </copy>
</assign>
```

We are not restricted to such simple expressions. We can use any valid XPath 1.0 expressions (or the expressions of the selected expression language). For more information, refer to the XPath 1.0 specification: `http://www.w3.org/TR/xpath`.

Another possibility is to copy a constant XML complex element to the `InsuredPersonRequest` variable. In this case, we can specify the source XML directly:

```
<assign>
  <copy>
    <from>
      <insuredPersonData xmlns="http://packtpub.com/bpel/insurance/">
        <FirstName>Matjaz B.</FirstName>
        <LastName>Juric</LastName>
        <Address>Ptuj</Address>
        <Age>30</Age>
      </insuredPersonData>
    </from>
    <to variable="InsuredPersonRequest" part="insuredPersonData" />
  </copy>
</assign>
```

Conditions

We have to get familiar with one more construct before we are ready to start developing our BPEL processes. In a business process specification, we usually have to make choices based on conditions. In BPEL, conditional branches are defined with the `<switch>` activity, where each branch is specified with its own `<case>` element, followed by an `<otherwise>` branch. The latter is optional. The following example shows the structure of the `<switch>` activity:

```
<switch>

  <case condition="boolean-expression">
    <!-- some activity -->
  </case>

  <case condition="boolean-expression">
    <!-- some activity -->
  </case>
  ...
  <otherwise>    <!-- optional -->
    <!-- some activity -->
  </otherwise>

</switch>
```

The Boolean conditions for `<case>` elements are expressed in the selected query language. Since the default query language is XPath 1.0, we can use any valid XPath expression that returns a Boolean value.

Variables are usually used in conditions. BPEL provides several extensions to built-in XPath functions. The extension related to variable data is the `getVariableData` function, which extracts arbitrary values from variables. The function takes up to three parameters. The first, which is required, is the variable name. The second can be the message part name and the third the location path query. The syntax is shown in the following code excerpt:

```
bpws:getVariableData ('variable-name',
                      'part-name',                    <!-- optional -->
                      'location-path')                <!-- optional -->
```

The location path query is written in the selected query language, and must specify the absolute path, where the root is the root of the document fragment.

The usage is straightforward. The following expression returns the `insuredPersonPart` part of the message stored in the `InsuranceRequest` variable:

```
bpws:getVariableData ('InsuranceRequest',
                      'insuredPersonData')
```

The following expression returns the `Age` element (see the XML Schema in the previous section):

```
bpws:getVariableData ('InsuranceRequest',
                      'insuredPersonData',
                      '/insuredPersonData/ins:Age')
```

Let us now define a conditional branch, based on the age of the insured person. Suppose we want to make three different activities, based on the ages from [0, 25], [26, 50], and [51 and above]. The BPEL expression is:

```
<switch>
  <case condition="bpws:getVariableData('InsuranceRequest',
                   'insuredPersonData', '/insuredPersonData/ins:Age') &gt; 50">
    <!-- perform activities for age 51 and over -->
  </case>
  <case condition="bpws:getVariableData('InsuranceRequest',
                   'insuredPersonData', '/insuredPersonData/ins:Age') &gt; 25">
    <!-- perform activities for age 26-50 -->
  </case>
  <otherwise>
    <!-- perform activities for age 25 and under -->
  </otherwise>
</switch>
```

Now we know enough to start writing BPEL business process definitions. In the next section we will write a sample BPEL business process to get familiar with using the core concepts.

BPEL Business Process Example

To demonstrate how business processes are described with BPEL, we will define a simple business process for business travels. Let us consider the business travel process. We describe an oversimplified scenario, where the client invokes the business process, specifying the name of the employee, the destination, the departure date, and the return date. The BPEL business process first checks the employee travel status. We will suppose that a web service exists through which such a check can be made. Then the BPEL process will check the price for the flight ticket with two airlines: American Airlines and Delta Airlines. Again we will suppose that both airline companies provide a web service through which such check can be made. Finally, the BPEL process will select the lower price and return the travel plan to the client.

For the purposes of this example we first build a synchronous BPEL process, to maintain simplicity. This means that the client will wait for the response. Later in this chapter, we modify the example and make the BPEL process asynchronous. We will assume that the web service for checking the employee travel status is synchronous. This is reasonable, because such data can be obtained immediately and returned to the caller.

To acquire the plane ticket prices we use asynchronous invocations. Again, this is reasonable, because it might take a little longer to confirm the plane travel schedule. We assume that both airlines offer a web service and that both web services are identical (provide equal port types and operations). This assumption simplifies our example. In real-world scenarios, you will usually not have the choice about the web services, but will have to use whatever services are provided by your partners. If you have the luxury of designing the web services along with the BPEL process, consider which is the best interface. Usually we use asynchronous services for long-lasting operations and synchronous services for operations that return a result in a relatively short time. If we use asynchronous web services, the BPEL process is usually asynchronous as well.

In our example, we first develop a synchronous BPEL process that invokes two asynchronous airline web services. This is legal, but not recommended in real-world scenarios since the client may have to wait an arbitrarily long time. In the real world, the solution would be to develop an asynchronous BPEL process, which we will do later in this chapter.

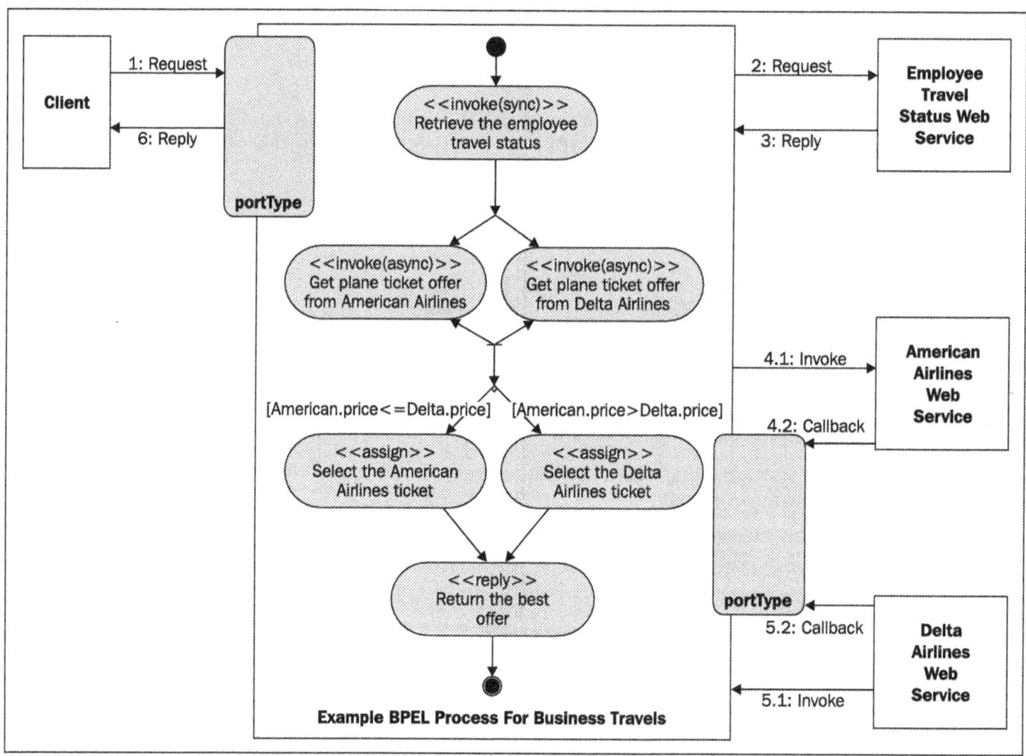

We invoke both airlines' web services concurrently and asynchronously. This means that our BPEL process will have to implement the callback operation (and a port type), through which the airlines will return the flight ticket confirmation.

Finally, the BPEL process returns the best airline ticket to the client. In this example, to maintain simplicity, we will not implement any fault handling, which is crucial in real-world scenarios. This topic is discussed in the next chapter.

Let's start by presenting the BPEL process activities using a UML activity diagram. In each activity, we have used the stereotype to indicate the BPEL operation used:

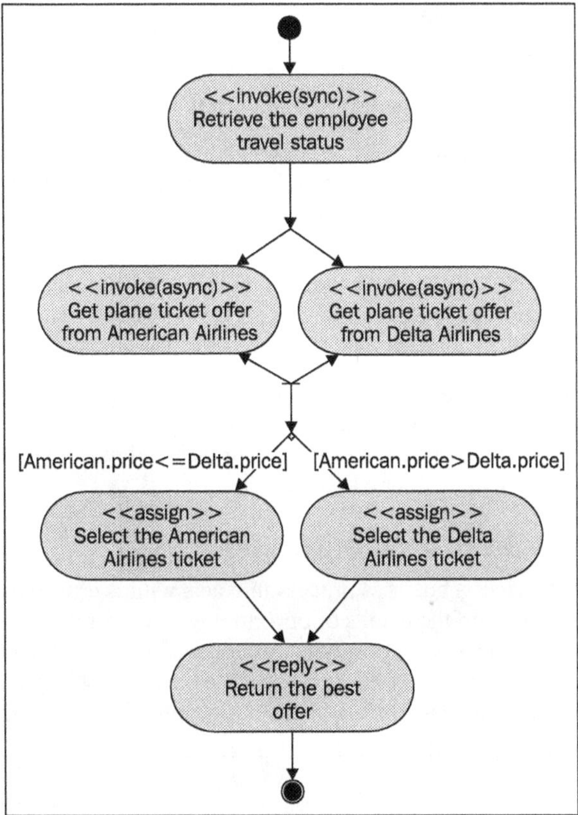

Although the presented process might seem very simple, it will offer a good start for learning BPEL. To develop the BPEL process, we will go through the following steps:

- Get familiar with the involved web services
- Define the WSDL for the BPEL process
- Define partner link types
- Define partner links

- Declare variables
- Write the process logic definition

Involved Web Services

Before we can start writing the BPEL process definition, we have to get familiar with all web services invoked from our business process. These services are sometimes called partner web services. In our example, three web services are involved:

- The Employee Travel Status web service
- The American Airlines web service
- Delta Airlines web service

Note: The two airline services share equal WSDL descriptions.

The web services used in this example are not *real*, so we will have to write WSDLs and even implement them to run the example. In real-world scenarios we would obviously use real web services exposed by partners involved in the business process.

> The web services and the BPEL process example can be downloaded from `http://www.packtpub.com`. The example runs on Oracle BPEL Process Manager.

Web services' descriptions are available through WSDL. WSDL specifies the operations and port types web services offer, the messages they accept, and the types they define. We can also find out whether each web service uses a document or RPC approach and whether it uses literal or SOAP-encoded representation. We will now look at both web services.

Employee Travel Status Web Service

Understanding the web services a business process interacts with is crucial to writing the BPEL process definition. Let's look into the details of our Employee Travel Status web service. It provides the `EmployeeTravelStatusPT` port type through which the employee travel status can be checked using the `EmployeeTravelStatus` operation. The operation will return the travel class an employee can use: economy, business, or first. This is shown in the following figure:

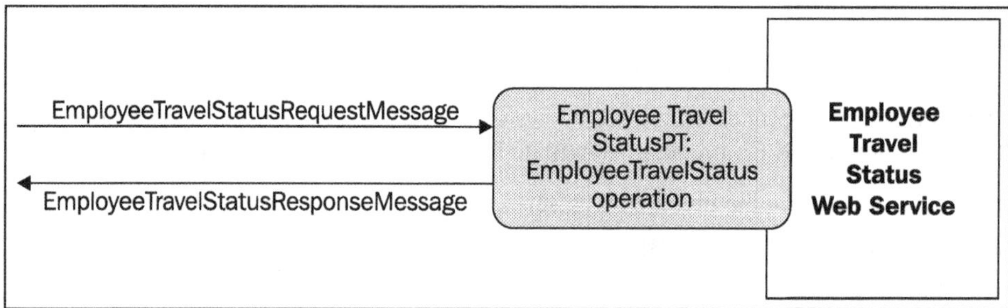

The operation is a synchronous request/response operation as we can see from the WSDL:

```
<?xml version="1.0" encoding="utf-8" ?>
<definitions xmlns:http="http://schemas.xmlsoap.org/wsdl/http/"
             xmlns:soap="http://schemas.xmlsoap.org/wsdl/soap/"
             xmlns:xs="http://www.w3.org/2001/XMLSchema"
             xmlns:soapenc="http://schemas.xmlsoap.org/soap/encoding/"
             xmlns:tns="http://packtpub.com/service/employee/"
             targetNamespace="http://packtpub.com/service/employee/"
             xmlns="http://schemas.xmlsoap.org/wsdl/"
             xmlns:plnk="http://schemas.xmlsoap.org/ws/2003/05/partner-link/">
...
<portType name="EmployeeTravelStatusPT">
  <operation name="EmployeeTravelStatus">
    <input message="tns:EmployeeTravelStatusRequestMessage" />
    <output message="tns:EmployeeTravelStatusResponseMessage" />
  </operation>
</portType>
...
```

The `EmployeeTravelStatus` operation consists of an input and an output message. To maintain simplicity, the fault is not declared. The definitions of input and output messages are also a part of the WSDL:

```
...
<message name="EmployeeTravelStatusRequestMessage">
  <part name="employee" type="tns:EmployeeType" />
</message>

<message name="EmployeeTravelStatusResponseMessage">
  <part name="travelClass" type="tns:TravelClassType" />
</message>
...
```

The `EmployeeTravelStatusRequestMessage` message has a single part, `employee`, of type `EmployeeType`, while the `EmployeeTravelStatusResponseMessage` has a part called `travelClass`, of type `TravelClassType`. The `EmployeeType` and the `TravelClassType` types are defined within the WSDL under the <types> element:

```
...
<types>
  <xs:schema elementFormDefault="qualified"
             targetNamespace="http://packtpub.com/service/employee/">

    <xs:complexType name="EmployeeType">
      <xs:sequence>
        <xs:element name="FirstName" type="xs:string" />
        <xs:element name="LastName" type="xs:string" />
        <xs:element name="Department" type="xs:string" />
      </xs:sequence>
    </xs:complexType>
...
```

`EmployeeType` is a complex type and has three elements: first name, last name, and department name. `TravelClassType` is a simple type that uses the enumeration to list the possible classes:

```
...
    <xs:simpleType name="TravelClassType">
      <xs:restriction base="xs:string">
        <xs:enumeration value="Economy"/>
        <xs:enumeration value="Business"/>
        <xs:enumeration value="First"/>
      </xs:restriction>
```

```
    </xs:simpleType>
  </xs:schema>
</types>
...
```

Now let us look at the airline web service.

Airline Web Service

The Airline web service is an asynchronous web service. Therefore, it specifies *two* port types. The first, `FlightAvailabilityPT`, is used to check the flight availability using the `FlightAvailability` operation. To return the result, the web service specifies the second port type, `FlightCallbackPT`. This port type specifies the `FlightTicketCallback` operation.

Although the Airline web service defines two port types, it only implements the `FlightAvailabilityPT`. `FlightCallbackPT` is implemented by the BPEL process, which is the client of the web service. The architecture of the web service is schematically shown here:

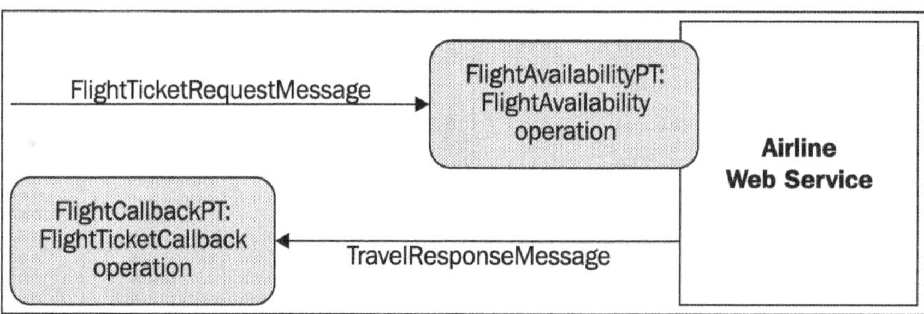

Flight Availability Port Type

`FlightAvailability` is an asynchronous operation, containing only the input message:

```
<?xml version="1.0" encoding="utf-8" ?>
<definitions xmlns:http="http://schemas.xmlsoap.org/wsdl/http/"
             xmlns:soap="http://schemas.xmlsoap.org/wsdl/soap/"
             xmlns:xs="http://www.w3.org/2001/XMLSchema"
             xmlns:soapenc="http://schemas.xmlsoap.org/soap/encoding/"
             xmlns:emp="http://packtpub.com/service/employee/"
             xmlns:tns="http://packtpub.com/service/airline/"
             targetNamespace="http://packtpub.com/service/airline/"
             xmlns="http://schemas.xmlsoap.org/wsdl/"
             xmlns:plnk="http://schemas.xmlsoap.org/ws/2003/05/partner-link/">
...
<portType name="FlightAvailabilityPT">
  <operation name="FlightAvailability">
    <input message="tns:FlightTicketRequestMessage" />
  </operation>
</portType>
...
```

The definition of the input message is shown below. It consists of two parts, the `flightData` part and the `travelClass` part:

```
<message name="FlightTicketRequestMessage">
  <part name="flightData" type="tns:FlightRequestType" />
  <part name="travelClass" type="emp:TravelClassType" />
</message>
```

The `travelClass` part is the same as that used in the Employee Travel Status web service. The `flightData` part is of type `FlightRequestType`, which is defined as follows:

```
...
<types>
  <xs:schema elementFormDefault="qualified"
             targetNamespace="http://packtpub.com/service/airline/">

    <xs:complexType name="FlightRequestType">
      <xs:sequence>
        <xs:element name="OriginFrom" type="xs:string" />
        <xs:element name="DestinationTo" type="xs:string" />
        <xs:element name="DesiredDepartureDate" type="xs:date" />
        <xs:element name="DesiredReturnDate" type="xs:date" />
      </xs:sequence>
    </xs:complexType>
...
```

`FlightRequestType` is a complex type and has four elements, through which we specify the flight origin and destination, the desired departure data, and the desired return date.

Flight Callback Port Type

The Airline web service needs to specify another port type for the callback operation, through which the BPEL process receives the flight ticket response messages. Note that the web service will only specify this port type, which is implemented by the BPEL process.

We define the `FlightCallbackPT` port type with the `FlightTicketCallback` operation, which has the `TravelResponseMessage` input message.

```
...
<portType name="FlightCallbackPT">
  <operation name="FlightTicketCallback">
    <input message="tns:TravelResponseMessage" />
  </operation>
</portType>
...
```

`TravelResponseMessage` consists of a single part called `confirmationData`:

```
...
<message name="TravelResponseMessage">
  <part name="confirmationData" type="tns:FlightConfirmationType" />
</message>
...
```

`FlightConfirmationType` is a complex type used for returning the result. It includes the flight number, travel class, price, departure and arrival date and time, and the approved flag. It is declared as follows:

```
    <xs:complexType name="FlightConfirmationType">
      <xs:sequence>
        <xs:element name="FlightNo" type="xs:string" />
        <xs:element name="TravelClass" type="tns:TravelClassType" />
        <xs:element name="Price" type="xs:float" />
        <xs:element name="DepartureDateTime" type="xs:dateTime" />
        <xs:element name="ReturnDateTime" type="xs:dateTime" />
        <xs:element name="Approved" type="xs:boolean" />
      </xs:sequence>
    </xs:complexType>

  </xs:schema>
</types>
```

Now that we are familiar with both web services types, we can define the BPEL process. Remember that our BPEL process is an actual web service. Therefore, we first have to write the WSDL for the BPEL process.

WSDL for the BPEL Process

The business travel BPEL process is exposed as a web service. We need to define the WSDL for it. The process will have to receive messages from its clients and return results. So it has to expose a port type that will be used by the client to start the process and get the reply. We define the `TravelApprovalPT` port type with the `TravelApproval` operation:

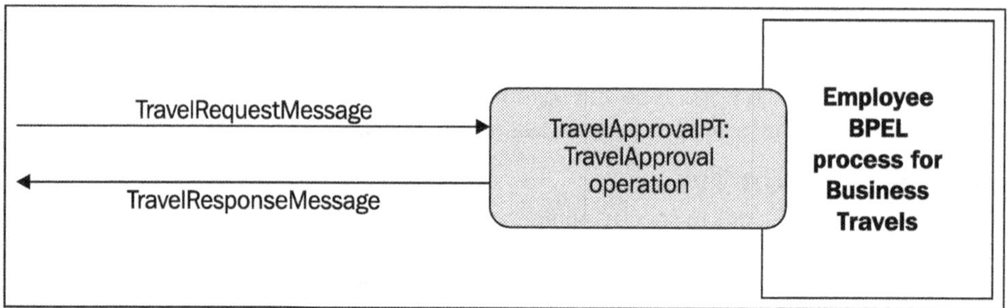

We have already said that the BPEL process is synchronous. The `TravelApproval` operation will be synchronous request/response type:

```
<?xml version="1.0" encoding="utf-8" ?>
<definitions xmlns:http="http://schemas.xmlsoap.org/wsdl/http/"
             xmlns:soap="http://schemas.xmlsoap.org/wsdl/soap/"
             xmlns:xs="http://www.w3.org/2001/XMLSchema"
             xmlns:soapenc="http://schemas.xmlsoap.org/soap/encoding/"
             xmlns:emp="http://packtpub.com/service/employee/"
             xmlns:aln="http://packtpub.com/service/airline/"
             xmlns:tns="http://packtpub.com/bpel/travel/"
             targetNamespace="http://packtpub.com/bpel/travel/"
             xmlns="http://schemas.xmlsoap.org/wsdl/"
             xmlns:plnk="http://schemas.xmlsoap.org/ws/2003/05/partner-link/">
...
<portType name="TravelApprovalPT">
  <operation name="TravelApproval">
    <input message="tns:TravelRequestMessage" />
    <output message="aln:TravelResponseMessage" />
  </operation>
</portType>
...
```

We also have to define messages. The `TravelRequestMessage` consists of two parts:

- `employee`: The employee data, which we reuse from the employee travel status web service definition
- `flightData`: The flight data, which we reuse from the airline web service definition

```
...
<import namespace="http://packtpub.com/service/employee/"
        location="./Employee.wsdl"/>
```

```
<import namespace="http://packtpub.com/service/airline/"
        location="./Airline.wsdl"/>
...
<message name="TravelRequestMessage">
  <part name="employee" type="emp:EmployeeType" />
  <part name="flightData" type="aln:FlightRequestType" />
</message>
...
```

For the output message, we use the same message used to return the flight information from the airline web service: the `TravelResponseMessage` defined in the `aln` namespace. This is reasonable, because the BPEL process will get the `TravelResponseMessage` from both airlines, select the most appropriate (the cheapest) and return the same message to the client. As we have already imported the Airline WSDL, we are done.

When writing the WSDL for the BPEL process we usually do not have to define the bindings (`<binding>`) and the service (`<service>`) sections. These are usually generated by the BPEL execution environment (BPEL server).

Before we can start writing the BPEL process, we still need to define partner link types.

Partner Link Types

Partner link types represent the interaction between a BPEL process and the involved parties, which includes the web services the BPEL process invokes and the client that invokes the BPEL process.

In our example, there are three different partners: the client, the employee travel status service, and the airline service. Ideally, each web service should define the corresponding partner link types (in the WSDL). In real-world scenarios, this may not be the case. Then we can wrap the partner web service with a WSDL that imports the WSDL of the web service and defines the partner link types. Alternatively, we can define all partner links in the WSDL of the BPEL process. However, this is not recommended as it violates the principle of encapsulation.

We define three partner link types, each in the corresponding WSDL of the web service:

- `travelLT`: This is used to describe the interaction between the BPEL process client and the BPEL process itself. This interaction is synchronous. This partner link type is defined in the WSDL of the BPEL process.
- `employeeLT`: This is used to describe the interaction between the BPEL process and the Employee Travel Status web service. This interaction is synchronous too. This partner link type is defined in the WSDL of the Employee web service.
- `flightLT`: This describes the interaction between the BPEL process and the Airline web service. This interaction is asynchronous and the Airline web service invokes a callback on the BPEL process. This partner link type is defined in the WSDL of the Airline web service.

We already know that each partner link type can have one or two roles and for each role we must specify the `portType` it uses. For synchronous operations, there is a single role for each partner link type, because the operation is only invoked in a single direction.

For example, the client invokes the `TravelApproval` operation on the BPEL process. Because it is a synchronous operation, the client waits for completion and gets a response only after the operation is completed.

Note that if `TravelApproval` were an asynchronous callback operation, we would have to specify two roles. The first role would describe the invocation of the `TravelApproval` operation by the client. The second role would describe the invocation of a callback operation. This callback operation would be invoked by the BPEL process and would call the client to return the result. We will make our example process asynchronous later in this chapter. Please remember that there is an asynchronous relation between the BPEL process and the Airline web service.

As we have already figured out, we need three partner link types. The first two have to specify a single role, because they deal with synchronous operations. The third requires us to specify both roles, because it is asynchronous.

Partner link types are defined within a special namespace: `http://schemas.xmlsoap.org/ws/2003/05/partner-link/`. The reference to this namespace has to be included first:

```
<definitions xmlns:http="http://schemas.xmlsoap.org/wsdl/http/"
             xmlns:soap="http://schemas.xmlsoap.org/wsdl/soap/"
             xmlns:xs="http://www.w3.org/2001/XMLSchema"
             xmlns:soapenc="http://schemas.xmlsoap.org/soap/encoding/"
             xmlns:emp="http://packtpub.com/service/employee/"
             xmlns:aln="http://packtpub.com/service/airline/"
             xmlns:tns="http://packtpub.com/bpel/travel/"
             targetNamespace="http://packtpub.com/bpel/travel/"
             xmlns="http://schemas.xmlsoap.org/wsdl/"
             xmlns:plnk="http://schemas.xmlsoap.org/ws/2003/05/
                                                 partner-link/">
...
```

Now we can add the definitions for the partner link types. First, we define the `travelLT` link type in the BPEL process WSDL. This is used by clients to invoke the BPEL process. The only role required is the role of the travel service (our BPEL process). The client uses the `TravelApprovalPT` port type to communicate with the BPEL service:

```
...
<plnk:partnerLinkType name="travelLT">
  <plnk:role name="travelService">
    <plnk:portType name="tns:TravelApprovalPT" />
  </plnk:role>
</plnk:partnerLinkType>
...
```

The second link type is `employeeLT`. It is used to describe the communication between the BPEL process and the Employee Travel Status web service and is defined in the WSDL of the Employee web service. The interaction is synchronous, so we need a single role, called `employeeTravelStatusService`. The BPEL process uses the `EmployeeTravelStatusPT` on the Employee web service:

```
...
<plnk:partnerLinkType name="employeeLT">
  <plnk:role name="employeeTravelStatusService">
    <plnk:portType name="tns:EmployeeTravelStatusPT" />
  </plnk:role>
</plnk:partnerLinkType>
...
```

The last partner link type is `flightLT`, used to describe the communication between the BPEL process and the Airline web service. This communication is asynchronous. The BPEL process invokes an asynchronous operation on the Airline web service. The web service, after it has completed the request, invokes a callback on the BPEL process. Therefore we need two roles:

- The first role describes the role of the Airline web service to the BPEL process, which is the airline service (`airlineService`). The BPEL process uses the `FlightAvailabilityPT` port type to make the asynchronous invocation.
- The second role describes the role of the BPEL process to the Airline web services. For the Airline web service, the BPEL process is an airline customer, thus the role name is `airlineCustomer`. The Airline web service uses the `FlightCallbackPT` port type to make the callback.

This partner link type is defined in the WSDL of the Airline web service:

```
...
<plnk:partnerLinkType name="flightLT">
  <plnk:role name="airlineService">
    <plnk:portType name="tns:FlightAvailabilityPT" />
  </plnk:role>
  <plnk:role name="airlineCustomer">
    <plnk:portType name="tns:FlightCallbackPT" />
  </plnk:role>
</plnk:partnerLinkType>
...
```

Understanding partner link types is crucial for developing a BPEL process specification. Sometimes it helps to make a diagram of all the interactions. Once the partner link types are defined, we have finished the preparation phase and are ready to start writing the business process definition.

Business Process Definition

The BPEL business process definition specifies the order of activities that have to be performed within a business process. Typically, a BPEL process waits for an incoming message, which starts the execution of the business process. This incoming message is usually the client request. Then a series of activities occur, either sequentially or in parallel. These activities include:

- Invoking operations on other web services
- Receiving results from other web services
- Conditional branching, which influences the flow of the business process
- Looping
- Fault handling
- Waiting for certain events to occur

In our example process, we do not cover all these aspects. We will leave loops, faults, and waits for the next chapter. Before we start defining our business process, let's have a quick look at the sequence diagram. It shows the messages exchanged between the involved parties.

The following parties are involved:

- The client that will invoke the BPEL process
- The BPEL process itself
- The Employee Travel Status web service
- Two airline web services: American and Delta

The client initiates the BPEL process through sending an input message: `TravelRequest`. This is a synchronous call. Then the BPEL process invokes the Employee Travel Status web service, sending the `EmployeeTravelStatusRequest` message. Because this is a synchronous invocation, it waits for the `EmployeeTravelStatusResponse` message. Then the BPEL process makes concurrent asynchronous invocations of both airline web services by sending them the `FlightTicketRequest` message. Both airline web services make a callback, sending the `TravelReponse` message. The BPEL process then selects the more appropriate airline and returns the reply message `TravelResponse` to the initial client. See the following sequence diagram:

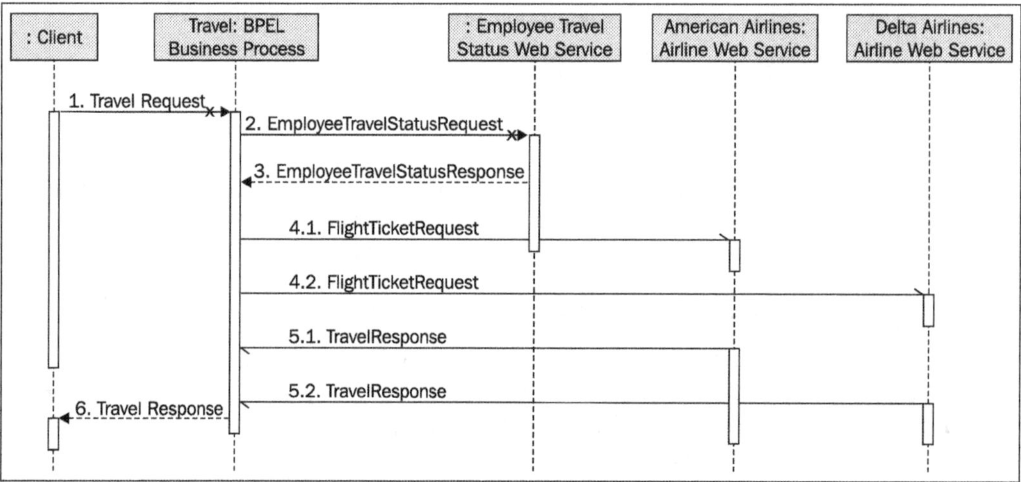

In real-world scenarios, we do not define synchronous BPEL processes that use asynchronous web services since the client may have to wait an arbitrarily long time. We would rather select an asynchronous BPEL process. In this example, we use the synchronous example to maintain simplicity. The next section shows how to define an asynchronous BPEL process.

> Understanding and knowing the exact details of a business process is crucial. Otherwise, we will not be able to specify it using BPEL.

Now we are ready to start writing the BPEL process definition. Each BPEL definition contains at least four main parts:

- The initial `<process>` root element with the declaration of namespaces

- The definition of partner links, using the `<partnerLinks>` element
- The declaration of variables, using the `<variables>` element
- The main body where the actual business process is defined; this is usually a `<sequence>` that specifies the flow of the process

BPEL Process Outline

We start with an empty BPEL process outline that presents the basic structure of each BPEL process definition document:

```
<process name="Travel" ... >

   <partnerLinks>
      <!-- The declaration of partner links -->
   </partnerLinks>

   <variables>
      <!-- The declaration of variables -->
   </variables>

   <sequence>
      <!-- The definition of the BPEL business process main body -->
   </sequence>

</process>
```

Let us first add the required namespaces. Here we have to define the target namespace and the namespaces to access the Employee and Airline WSDLs and the BPEL process WSDL. We also have to declare the namespace for all the BPEL activity tags (here the default namespace so we do not have to qualify each BPEL tag name). The BPEL activity namespace must be `http://schemas.xmlsoap.org/ws/2003/03/business-process/`:

```
<process name="Travel"
         targetNamespace="http://packtpub.com/bpel/travel/"
         xmlns="http://schemas.xmlsoap.org/ws/2003/03/business-process/"
         xmlns:bpws="http://schemas.xmlsoap.org/ws/2003/03/business-process/"
         xmlns:trv="http://packtpub.com/bpel/travel/"
         xmlns:emp="http://packtpub.com/service/employee/"
         xmlns:aln="http://packtpub.com/service/airline/" >
...
```

Partner Links

Next we have to define the partner links. Partner links define different parties that interact with the BPEL process. Each partner link is related to a specific `partnerLinkType` that characterizes it. Each partner link also specifies up to two attributes:

- `myRole`: Indicates the role of the business process itself
- `partnerRole`: Indicates the role of the partner

The partner link can specify a single role, which is usually the case with synchronous request/response operations. In our example, we define four roles. The first partner link is called `client` and is characterized by the `travelLT` partner link type. The `client` invokes the business process. We need to specify the `myRole` attribute to describe the role of the BPEL process. In our case, this is the `travelService`:

```
...
   <partnerLinks>
      <partnerLink name="client"
                   partnerLinkType="trv:travelLT"
                   myRole="travelService"/>
...
```

The second partner link is called `employeeTravelStatus` and is characterized by the `employeeLT` partner link type. It is a synchronous request/response relation between the BPEL process and the web service; we again specify only one role. This time it is the `partnerRole`, because we describe the role of the web service, which is a partner to the BPEL process:

```
...
      <partnerLink name="employeeTravelStatus"
                   partnerLinkType="emp:employeeLT"
                   partnerRole="employeeTravelStatusService"/>
...
```

The last two partner links correspond to the airline web services. Because they use the same type of web service, we specify two partner links based on a single partner link type, `flightLT`. Here we have asynchronous callback communication, therefore we need two roles. The role of the BPEL process (`myRole`) to the airline web service is `airlineCustomer`, while the role of the airline (`partnerRole`) is `airlineService`:

```
...
      <partnerLink name="AmericanAirlines"
                   partnerLinkType="aln:flightLT"
                   myRole="airlineCustomer"
                   partnerRole="airlineService"/>

      <partnerLink name="DeltaAirlines"
                   partnerLinkType="aln:flightLT"
                   myRole="airlineCustomer"
                   partnerRole="airlineService"/>
   </partnerLinks>
```

Variables

Variables are used to store messages and to reformat and transform them. We usually need a variable for every message sent to the partners and received from the partners. Looking at the sequence diagram, this would mean eight variables for our example. However, notice that the messages sent to both airline web services are identical. So, we only need seven variables. Let's call them `TravelRequest`, `EmployeeTravelStatusRequest`, `EmployeeTravelStatusResponse`, `FlightDetails`, `FlightResponseAA`, `FlightResponseDA`, and `TravelResponse`.

For each variable we have to specify the type. We can use a WSDL message type, an XML Schema simple type, or an XML Schema element. In our example we use WSDL message types for all variables:

```
...
   <variables>
      <!-- input for this process -->
      <variable name="TravelRequest"
                messageType="trv:TravelRequestMessage"/>
      <!-- input for the Employee Travel Status web service -->
      <variable name="EmployeeTravelStatusRequest"
                messageType="emp:EmployeeTravelStatusRequestMessage"/>
      <!-- output from the Employee Travel Status web service -->
```

```
        <variable name="EmployeeTravelStatusResponse"
                  messageType="emp:EmployeeTravelStatusResponseMessage"/>
        <!-- input for American and Delta web services -->
        <variable name="FlightDetails"
                  messageType="aln:FlightTicketRequestMessage"/>
        <!-- output from American Airlines -->
        <variable name="FlightResponseAA"
                  messageType="aln:TravelResponseMessage"/>
        <!-- output from Delta Airlines -->
        <variable name="FlightResponseDA"
                  messageType="aln:TravelResponseMessage"/>
        <!-- output from BPEL process -->
        <variable name="TravelResponse"
                  messageType="aln:TravelResponseMessage"/>
    </variables>
...
```

BPEL Process Main Body

The process main body may contain only one top-level activity. Usually this is a <sequence> that allows us to define several activities that will be performed sequentially. Other possibilities for this activity include <flow>, through which several activities can be performed concurrently. We can also specify <while> to indicate loops, or <scope> to define nested activities. However, we usually use <sequence> and nest other activities within the sequence.

Within the sequence, we first specify the input message that starts the business process. We do this with the <receive> construct, which waits for the matching message. In our case this is the `TravelRequest` message. Within the <receive> construct, we do *not* specify the message directly. Rather we specify the partner link, the port type, the operation name, and optionally the variable that holds the received message for consequent operations.

We link the message reception with the client partner, and wait for the `TravelApproval` operation to be invoked on port type `TravelApprovalPT`. We store the received message into the `TravelRequest` variable:

```
...
    <sequence>

        <!-- Receive the initial request for business travel from client -->
        <receive partnerLink="client"
                 portType="trv:TravelApprovalPT"
                 operation="TravelApproval"
                 variable="TravelRequest"
                 createInstance="yes" />
...
```

As already mentioned, <receive> waits for the client to invoke the `TravelApproval` operation and stores the incoming message and parameters about the business trip into the `TravelRequest` variable. Here, the variable name is the same as the message name, but this is not necessary.

Next, we need to invoke the Employee Travel Status web service. Before this, we have to prepare the input for this web service. Looking at the WSDL of the Employee web service, we can see that we have to send a message consisting of the employee part. We can construct such a message by copying the employee part of the message that the client sent. We write the corresponding assignment:

```
...
        <!-- Prepare the input for the Employee Travel Status Web Service -->
        <assign>
          <copy>
            <from variable="TravelRequest" part="employee"/>
            <to variable="EmployeeTravelStatusRequest" part="employee"/>
          </copy>
        </assign>
...
```

Now we can invoke the Employee Travel Status web service. We make a synchronous invocation, for which we use the `<invoke>` activity. We use the `employeeTravelStatus` partner link and invoke the `EmployeeTravelStatus` operation on the `EmployeeTravelStatusPT` port type. We have prepared the input message in the `EmployeeTravelStatusRequest` variable. Because it is a synchronous invocation, the call waits for the reply and stores it in the `EmployeeTravelStatusResponse` variable:

```
...
        <!-- Synchronously invoke the Employee Travel Status Web Service -->
        <invoke partnerLink="employeeTravelStatus"
                portType="emp:EmployeeTravelStatusPT"
                operation="EmployeeTravelStatus"
                inputVariable="EmployeeTravelStatusRequest"
                outputVariable="EmployeeTravelStatusResponse" />
...
```

The next step is to invoke both airline web services. Again we first prepare the required input message (which is equal for both web services). The `FlightTicketRequest` message consists of two parts:

- `flightData`: This is retrieved from the client message (`TravelRequest`).
- `travelClass`: This is retrieved from the `EmployeeTravelStatusResponse` variable.

Therefore, we write an assignment with two copy elements:

```
...
        <!-- Prepare the input for AA and DA -->
        <assign>
          <copy>
            <from variable="TravelRequest" part="flightData"/>
            <to variable="FlightDetails" part="flightData"/>
          </copy>
          <copy>
            <from variable="EmployeeTravelStatusResponse" part="travelClass"/>
            <to variable="FlightDetails" part="travelClass"/>
          </copy>
        </assign>
...
```

The input data includes the data that needs to be passed to the Airline web services. Since it is in the same format, we can pass it directly (using a simple copy). In the real world, we usually need to perform a transformation. We could do that using XPath expressions with `<assign>`, use a transformation service (such as an XSLT engine), or use the transformation capabilities provided by specific BPEL servers.

Now we are ready to invoke both airline web services. We will make concurrent asynchronous invocations. To express concurrency, BPEL provides the `<flow>` activity. The invocation to each web service will consist of two steps:

1. The `<invoke>` activity is used for the asynchronous invocation.
2. The `<receive>` activity is used to wait for the callback.

We use `<sequence>` to group both activities. The two invocations differ only in the partner link name. We use `AmericanAirlines` for one and `DeltaAirlines` for the other. Both invoke the `FlightAvailability` operation on the `FlightAvailabilityPT` port type, sending the message from the `FlightDetails` variable.

The callback is received using the `<receive>` activity. Again, we use both partner link names. `<receive>` waits for the `FlightTicketCallback` operation to be invoked on the `FlightCallbackPT` port type. We store the result message in the `FlightResponseAA` and the `FlightResponseDA` variables respectively:

```
...
        <!-- Make a concurrent invocation to AA in DA -->
        <flow>

          <sequence>
            <!-- Async invoke of the AA web service and wait for the callback-->

            <invoke partnerLink="AmericanAirlines"
                portType="aln:FlightAvailabilityPT"
                operation="FlightAvailability"
                inputVariable="FlightDetails" />

            <receive partnerLink="AmericanAirlines"
                portType="aln:FlightCallbackPT"
                operation="FlightTicketCallback"
                variable="FlightResponseAA" />

          </sequence>

          <sequence>
            <!-- Async invoke of the DA web service and wait for the callback-->

            <invoke partnerLink="DeltaAirlines"
                portType="aln:FlightAvailabilityPT"
                operation="FlightAvailability"
                inputVariable="FlightDetails" />

            <receive partnerLink="DeltaAirlines"
                portType="aln:FlightCallbackPT"
                operation="FlightTicketCallback"
                variable="FlightResponseDA" />

          </sequence>

        </flow>
...
```

In this stage of the process, we have two ticket offers. In the next step, we have to select one. For this, we use the `<switch>` activity.

```
...
        <!-- Select the best offer and construct the TravelResponse -->
        <switch>

          <case condition="bpws:getVariableData('FlightResponseAA',
                           'confirmationData','/confirmationData/aln:Price')
                     &lt;= bpws:getVariableData('FlightResponseDA',
                           'confirmationData','/confirmationData/aln:Price')">
```

```
            <!-- Select American Airlines -->
            <assign>
              <copy>
                <from variable="FlightResponseAA" />
                <to variable="TravelResponse" />
              </copy>
            </assign>
         </case>

         <otherwise>
            <!-- Select Delta Airlines -->
            <assign>
              <copy>
                <from variable="FlightResponseDA" />
                <to variable="TravelResponse" />
              </copy>
            </assign>
         </otherwise>
       </switch>
...
```

In the <case> element, we check whether the offer from American Airlines (FlightResponseAA) is equal or better than the offer from Delta (FlightResponseDA). For this, we use the BPEL function getVariableData and specify the variable name. The price is located inside the confirmationData message part, which is the only message part, but we still have to specify it. We also have to specify the query expression to locate the price element. Here, this is a simple XPath 1.0 expression.

If the American Airlines offer is better than Delta (or equal) we copy the FlightResponseAA variable to the TravelResponse variable (which we finally return to the client). Otherwise we copy the FlightResponseDA variable.

We have come to the final step of the BPEL business process—to return a reply to the client, using the <reply> activity. Here we specify the same partner link as in the initial receive client. We also specify the same port type and operation name. The variable that holds the reply message is TravelResponse:

```
...
       <!-- Send a response to the client -->
       <reply partnerLink="client"
              portType="trv:TravelApprovalPT"
              operation="TravelApproval"
              variable="TravelResponse"/>
    </sequence>

</process>
```

With this, we have concluded our first business process specification in BPEL. You can see that BPEL is not very complicated and allows a relatively easy and natural specification of business processes. The consumption of other web services is also relatively easy if you are familiar with WSDL. In the next section, we modify our BPEL process to make it asynchronous.

Asynchronous BPEL Example

Our first BPEL business process example was synchronous, because this was the easiest case. However, in the real world, we will mostly use asynchronous processes. Most business processes are long running. It makes no sense for client to wait (and be blocked) for the entire duration of the process. A much better alternative is to model the BPEL process as asynchronous. This means that the client invokes the process, and when the process completes, it performs a callback to the client. This has a few consequences:

- For the BPEL process to be able to perform a callback to the client, the client must be a web service and implement a certain port type (usually defined by the BPEL process WSDL).
- The partner link type for the client will have to specify two roles.
- The BPEL process will not `<reply>` to the client. Rather it will `<invoke>` the callback.

Let us now focus on our business process and modify it for asynchronous invocation, presented in the next sequence diagram. We have to perform the following steps:

1. Modify the BPEL process WSDL, where the operation invoked by the client will now have only the input message.
2. Define the client port type and the operation, which the BPEL process will invoke for the callback. We will do this in the WSDL of the BPEL process.
3. Modify the partner link type, where we will add the second role.
4. Modify the BPEL process specification. We have to modify the partner link and replace the `<reply>` activity with an `<invoke>`.

The modified sequence diagram is shown below. It is very similar to the previous example, except that the initial travel request is asynchronous and the final answer is delivered as a callback:

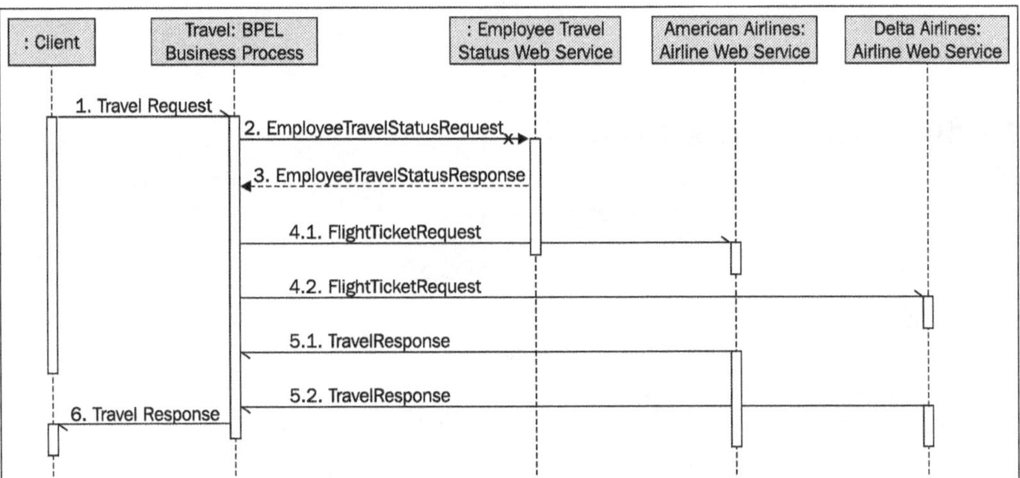

Modify the BPEL Process WSDL

The modified WSDL for the BPEL process will have to specify the `TravelApprovalPT` port type, which will now specify an input message only. It will also have to declare the `ClientCallbackPT` port type, used to return the result to the client (asynchronously, using a callback). This is shown in the following figure:

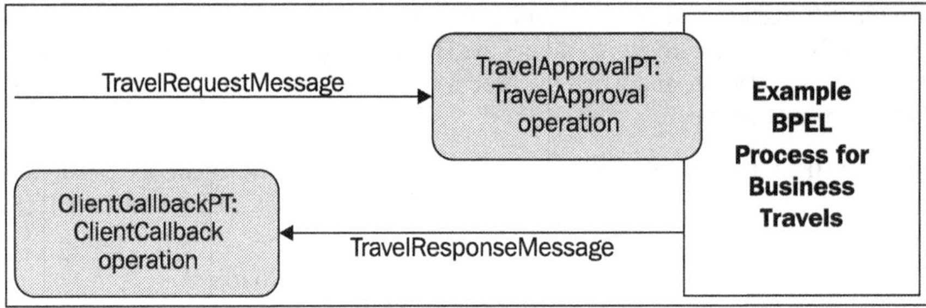

Let us first modify the `TravelApprovalPT` port type used for client interaction, which will now define only the input message:

```
...
<portType name="TravelApprovalPT">
  <operation name="TravelApproval">
    <input message="tns:TravelRequestMessage" />
  </operation>
</portType>
...
```

Next we define the client callback port type (`ClientCallbackPT`) with the `ClientCallback` operation. The response message is `TravelResponseMessage`. Notice that the WSDL only specifies this port type, which is implemented by the client:

```
...
<portType name="ClientCallbackPT">
  <operation name="ClientCallback">
    <input message="aln:TravelResponseMessage" />
  </operation>
</portType>
...
```

Modify Partner Link Types

We need to modify the partner link type for the interaction with the BPEL process, called the `travelLT` link type. We have to add the second role, `travelServiceCustomer`, which characterizes the client to which the BPEL process will perform a callback on the `ClientCallbackPT` port type. This is done in the WSDL of the BPEL process:

```
<plnk:partnerLinkType name="travelLT">
  <plnk:role name="travelService">
    <plnk:portType name="tns:TravelApprovalPT" />
  </plnk:role>
  <plnk:role name="travelServiceCustomer">
    <plnk:portType name="tns:ClientCallbackPT" />
  </plnk:role>
</plnk:partnerLinkType>
```

Modify the BPEL Process Definition

Finally, we modify the BPEL process definition. Here we first have to modify the client partner link, where we have to specify the second role—the `partnerRole`. Here, this is `travelServiceCustomer`, which characterizes the BPEL process client:

```
    <partnerLinks>
       <partnerLink name="client"
                    partnerLinkType="trv:travelLT"
                    myRole="travelService"
                    partnerRole="travelServiceCustomer"/>
...
```

Next, we change the last activity of the BPEL process. We replace the `<reply>` activity with the `<invoke>` callback. For the callback, we use the client partner link and invoke the `ClientCallback` operation on the `ClientCallbackPT` port type. The message signature has not changed, so we use the same variable as before, `TravelResponse`.

```
...
       <!-- Make a callback to the client -->
       <invoke partnerLink="client"
               portType="trv:ClientCallbackPT"
               operation="ClientCallback"
               inputVariable="TravelResponse" />
    </sequence>

</process>
```

Our BPEL process is now asynchronous!

To execute a BPEL process we need a run-time environment. In Chapter 1 we provided an overview of BPEL servers, including Oracle BPEL Process Manager, Microsoft BizTalk, IBM WebSphere Business Integration Server Foundation, etc. Later chapters give a detailed description of the Oracle BPEL Process Manager and Microsoft BizTalk.

> You can download both the synchronous and asynchronous BPEL process examples with the corresponding web services from `http://www.packtpub.com`. They can be deployed to the Oracle BPEL Process Manager using the `obant` command from the top-level directory, which deploys all web services and both BPEL processes. They can be tested using the Oracle BPEL Process Manager Console. For more information on Oracle BPEL Process Manager, refer to Chapter 5 and Chapter 6.

Conclusion

In this chapter, you have become familiar with the basic concepts of web service composition with BPEL. BPEL is an XML-based language for business process definition. Each process has a set of activities and interacts with partner web services. The BPEL process is also a web service.

With BPEL we can define executable and abstract business processes. In this chapter we have focused on executable processes. They exactly define the activities of the processes and can be executed on a BPEL-compliant server. We have overviewed the basic concepts of BPEL, described how to invoke web services synchronously and asynchronously, and discussed the role of WSDL. BPEL processes can be synchronous or asynchronous and we have overviewed both options. Web services with which a BPEL process interacts are called partner services. Therefore we have explained the concepts of partner link types and partner links.

We have overviewed the most important activities for invocation of operations, receiving of messages, and returning replies to clients. We have also become familiar with variables and assignments. With this theoretical knowledge, we defined two example BPEL processes for business travels. We developed a synchronous and then an asynchronous process.

4

Advanced BPEL

In the previous chapter, we covered the basics of BPEL and provided an introduction to the structure of business processes. We are now familiar with defining business processes, invoking web service operations sequentially and in parallel, defining partner links, defining variables, and assigning values. However, using BPEL for complex real-world business processes requires additional functionality. Sometimes the activities of a business process need to be performed in loops. Often activities might have links that would affect the execution order. This is usually the case with concurrent flows. Sometimes we will have to wait either for a message event or an alarm event to occur.

One very important aspect of business process modeling is fault handling. Particularly in business processes that span multiple enterprises and use web services over the Internet, we can assume that faults will occur quite often due to various reasons, including broken connections, unreachable web services, unavailability of services, and so on. If business processes do not finish successfully, we might need a way to undo the partial work. This is called compensation and is one of the features of BPEL.

In this chapter, we will look at these and other advanced BPEL features including:

- BPEL activities not covered in the previous chapter, such as loops, delays, and process termination
- Fault handling
- Scopes and serialization
- Compensation
- Events and event handlers
- Concurrent activities and links
- The business process lifecycle
- Correlations and message properties
- Dynamic partner links
- Abstract business processes
- A model-driven approach for generating BPEL processes from UML activity diagrams

Advanced Activities

In the previous chapter, we familiarized ourselves with important BPEL activities, including invoking web service operations (<invoke>), receiving messages from partners (<receive>), returning results to process clients (<reply>), declaring variables (<variable>), updating variable contents (<assign>), sequential and concurrent structured activities (<sequence> and <flow>), and conditional behavior (<switch>).

However, these activities are not sufficient for complex real-world business processes. Therefore, in the first part of this chapter we will become familiar with the other important activities offered by BPEL, particularly activity names, loops, delays, empty activities, and process termination. We will not discuss concrete use cases where these activities can be used, because they are well known to developers. We will, however, use these activities later in the chapter, where we will present some examples. Let us first look at activity names.

Activity Names

For each BPEL activity, we can specify a name by using the `name` attribute. This attribute is optional and can be used with all basic and structured activities. For instance, the Employee Travel Status web service invocation activity from the example in Chapter 3 could be named `EmployeeTravelStatusSyncInv`; this is shown in the code excerpt below. We will see that naming activities is useful on several occasions; for example, when invoking inline compensation handlers or when synchronizing activities:

```
...
<invoke name="EmployeeTravelStatusSyncInv"
        partnerLink="employeeTravelStatus"
        portType="emp:EmployeeTravelStatusPT"
        operation="EmployeeTravelStatus"
        inputVariable="EmployeeTravelStatusRequest"
        outputVariable="EmployeeTravelStatusResponse" />
...
```

Activity names also improve the readability of BPEL processes.

Loops

When defining business processes we will sometimes want to perform a certain activity or a set of activities in a loop; for example, perform a calculation or invoke a partner web service operation several times, and so on.

BPEL supports loops through the <while> activity. It repeats the enclosed activities until the Boolean condition no longer holds true. The Boolean condition is expressed through the `condition` attribute, using the selected expression language (the default is XPath 1.0). The syntax of the <while> activity is shown in the following code excerpt:

```
<while condition="boolean-expression" >

   <!-- Perform an activity or a set of activities enclosed by <sequence>,
        <flow>, or other structured activity -->

</while>
```

Let us consider a scenario where we need to check flight availability for more than one person. Let us also assume that we need to invoke a web service operation for each person, similar to the example in Chapter 3. In addition to the variables already present in the example, we would need two more: `NoOfPassengers` to hold the number of passengers, and `Counter` to use in the loop. The code excerpt with variable declarations is shown below:

```
<variables>
   ...
   <variable name="NoOfPassengers"
             type="xs:int"/>
   <variable name="Counter"
             type="xs:int"/>
   ...
</variables>
```

We also need to assign values to the variables. The `NoOfPassengers` can be obtained from the Employee Travel web service. In the following code, we initialize both variables with static values:

```
<assign>

  <copy>
    <from expression="number(5)"/>
    <to variable="NoOfPassengers"/>
  </copy>
  <copy>
    <from expression="number(0)"/>
    <to variable="Counter"/>
  </copy>

</assign>
```

The loop to perform the web service invocation is shown in the code excerpt below. Please remember that this excerpt is not complete:

```
<while condition=
  "bpws:getVariableData('Counter') &lt;
   bpws:getVariableData('NoOfPassengers')">

  <sequence>

    <!-- Construct the FlightDetails variable with passenger data -->
    ...

    <!-- Invoke the web service -->
    <invoke partnerLink="AmericanAirlines"
          portType="aln:FlightAvailabilityPT"
          operation="FlightAvailability"
          inputVariable="FlightDetails" />

    <receive partnerLink="AmericanAirlines"
          portType="trv:FlightCallbackPT"
          operation="FlightTicketCallback"
          variable="FlightResponseAA" />

    ...
    <!-- Process the results ... -->
    ...

    <!-- Increment the counter -->
    <assign>
      <copy>
        <from expression="bpws:getVariableData('Counter') + 1"/>
```

```
            <to variable="Counter"/>
          </copy>
        </assign>
      </sequence>
    </while>
```

Loops are helpful when dealing with arrays. In BPEL, arrays can be simulated using XML complex types where one or more elements can occur more than once (using the maxOccurs attribute in the XML Schema definition). To iterate through multiple occurrences of the same element, we can use XPath expressions.

Delays

Sometimes a business process may need to specify a certain delay. In BPEL, we can specify delays either for a specified period of time or until a certain deadline is reached, by using the <wait> activity. Typically, we could specify delays to invoke an operation at a specific time; or wait for some time and then invoke an operation; for example, we could choose to wait before we pool the results of a previously initiated operation or wait between iterations of a loop.

The <wait> activity supports two attributes:

- for: We can specify duration using this attribute; we specify a period of time.

  ```
  <wait for="duration-expression"/>
  ```

- until: We can use this attribute to specify a deadline; we specify a certain date and time.

  ```
  <wait until="deadline-expression"/>
  ```

Deadline and Duration Expressions

To specify deadline and duration expressions, BPEL uses lexical representations of corresponding XML Schema data types. For deadlines, these data types are either dateTime or date. For duration, we use the duration data type. The lexical representation of expressions should conform to the XPath 1.0 (or the selected query language) expressions. The evaluation of such expressions should result in values that are of corresponding XML Schema types: dateTime and date for deadline and duration for duration expressions.

All three data types use lexical representation inspired by the ISO 8601 standard, which can be obtained from the ISO web page http://www.iso.ch. ISO 8601 lexical format uses characters within the date and time information. Characters are appended to the numbers and have the following meaning:

- C represents centuries
- Y represents years
- M represents months
- D represents days
- h represents hours
- m represents minutes

- `s` represents seconds. Seconds can be represented in the format `ss.sss` to increase precision.
- `z` is used to designate Coordinated Universal Time (UTC). It should immediately follow the time of day element.

For the `dateTime` expressions there is another designator:

- `T` is used as time designator to indicate the start of the representation of the time.

Examples of deadline expressions are shown in the code excerpts below:

```
<wait until="'2004-03-18T21:00:00+01:00'"/>
```

```
<wait until="'18:05:30Z'"/>
```

For duration expressions the following characters can also be used:

- `P` is used as the time duration designator. Duration expressions always start with `P`.
- `Y` follows the number of years.
- `M` follows the number of months or minutes.
- `D` follows the number of days.
- `H` follows the number of hours.
- `S` follows the number of seconds.

To specify a duration of 4 hours and 10 minutes, we use the following expression:

```
<wait for="'PT4H10M'"/>
```

To specify the duration of 1 month, 3 days, 4 hours, and 10 minutes, we need to use the following expression:

```
<wait for="'P1M3DT4H10M'"/>
```

The following expression specifies the duration of 1 year, 11 months, 14 days, 4 hours, 10 minutes, and 30 seconds:

```
<wait for="'P1Y11M14DT4H10M30S'"/>
```

Empty Activities

When developing BPEL processes, you may come across instances where you need to specify an activity as per rules, but you do not really want to perform the activity. For example, in `<switch>` activities, we need to specify an activity for each `case`. However, if we do not want to perform any activity for a particular case, we can specify an `<empty>` activity. Not specifying any activity in this case would result in an error, because the BPEL process would not correspond to the BPEL schema. Empty activities are also useful in fault handling, when we need to suppress a fault.

The syntax for the `<empty>` element is rather straightforward:

```
<empty/>
```

Process Termination

BPEL provides the `<terminate>` activity to terminate a business process before it has finished. We can use it to immediately terminate processes that are in execution. Often we use `<terminate>` in switches, where we need to terminate a process when certain conditions are not met.

The `<terminate>` activity terminates the current business process instance and no fault and compensation handling is performed. Process instances, faults, and compensations are discussed later in this chapter.

The syntax is very simple and is shown below:

```
<terminate/>
```

Now that we have become familiar with loops, delays, empty activities, and process termination (which we will use in examples in the rest of this chapter) we will go on to fault handling.

Fault Handling and Signaling

Business processes specified using BPEL will interact with their partners through operation invocations of web services. Web services are based on loosely coupled Service Oriented Architecture (SOA). The communication between web services is done over Internet connections that may or may not be highly reliable. Web services could also raise faults due to logical errors and execution errors arising from defects in the infrastructure. Therefore BPEL business processes will need to handle faults appropriately. BPEL processes may also need to signal faults themselves. Fault handling and signaling is an important aspect of business processes designed using BPEL.

Faults in BPEL can arise in various situations:

- When a BPEL process invokes a synchronous web service operation, the operation might return a WSDL fault message, which results in a BPEL fault.
- A BPEL process can explicitly signal (throw) a fault.
- A fault can be thrown automatically, for example, when a join failure has occurred. We will discuss join failures later in this chapter.
- The BPEL server might encounter error conditions in the run-time environment, network communications, or any other such reason. BPEL defines several standard faults; these are listed in Appendix A.

WSDL Faults

WSDL faults occur due to synchronous operation invocations on partner web services. In WSDL, such faults are denoted with the `<fault>` element within the `<operation>` declaration. In BPEL, WSDL faults are identified by the qualified name of the fault and the target namespace of the corresponding port type used in the operation declaration.

In the Synchronous Business Travel Process example in the previous chapter, we have used the `TravelApproval` operation on the `TravelApprovalPT` port type with input and output messages. This is shown in the WSDL excerpt below:

```
...
<portType name="TravelApprovalPT">
  <operation name="TravelApproval">
    <input message="tns:TravelRequestMessage" />
    <output message="aln:TravelResponseMessage" />
  </operation>
</portType>
...
```

To add fault information to the operation, we first need to define a corresponding message. For simplicity, this message will be of the `xs:string` type:

```
...
<message name="TravelFaultMessage">
  <part name="error" type="xs:string" />
</message>
...
```

Now we will add the fault declaration to the operation signature shown above:

```
...
<portType name="TravelApprovalPT">
  <operation name="TravelApproval">
    <input message="tns:TravelRequestMessage" />
    <output message="aln:TravelResponseMessage" />
    <fault name="fault" message="tns:TravelFaultMessage" />
  </operation>
</portType>
...
```

WSDL does not require that we use unique fault names within the namespace used to define the operation. This implies that faults that have the same name and are defined within the same namespace will be considered as the same fault in BPEL. Keep this in mind when designing web services that can potentially become partners of BPEL business processes because this can lead to conflicts in fault handling during execution. This is a shortcoming of the current WSDL version 1.1 fault model, and should be removed in future versions.

Signaling Faults

A business process may sometimes need to explicitly signal a fault. For such a situation, BPEL provides the `<throw>` activity. It has the following syntax:

```
<throw faultName="name" />
```

BPEL does not require that we define fault names in advance, prior to their use in the `<throw>` activity. This flexible approach can also be error-prone because there is no compile-time checking of fault names. Therefore, a typo could result in a situation where a misspelled fault might not be handled by the designated fault handler.

Faults can also have an associated variable that usually contains data related to the fault. If such a variable is associated with the fault, we need to specify it when throwing the fault. This is done by using the optional `faultVariable` attribute as shown here:

```
<throw faultName="name" faultVariable="variable-name" />
```

The following example shows the most straightforward use of the `<throw>` activity, where a `WrongEmployeeName` fault is thrown—no variable is needed. Remember that fault names are not declared in advance:

```
<throw faultName="WrongEmployeeName" />
```

The faults raised with the <throw> activity have to be handled in the BPEL process. Fault handling is covered later in this chapter. Faults that are not handled will *not* be automatically propagated to the client as is the case in modern programming languages (Java for example). Rather, the BPEL process will terminate abnormally. Sometimes, however, we may want to signal faults to clients.

Signaling Faults to Clients in Synchronous Replies

A BPEL process offers operations to its clients through the <receive> activity. If the process wants to provide a synchronous request/response operation, it sends a <reply> activity in response to the initial <receive>. Remember that the type of the operation is defined in the WSDL document of the BPEL process. A synchronous request/response operation is defined as an operation that has an input and an output message and an optional fault message.

If such an operation has the fault part specified, we can use the <reply> activity to return a fault instead of the output message. The syntax of the <reply> activity in this case is:

```
<reply partnerLink="partner-link-name"
       portType="port-type-name"
       operation="operation-name"
       variable="variable-name"      <!-- optional -->
       faultName="fault-name" >
</reply>
```

When we specify a fault name to be returned through the <reply> activity, the variable name is optional. If we specify a variable name, then the variable has to be of the fault message type as defined in WSDL.

Example

Let's modify the BPEL process definition in the synchronous travel example and signal the fault (TravelFaultMessage) to the client by using the <reply> activity.

First, we need to declare an additional variable that will hold the fault description to return to the client. The variable is of the TravelFaultMessage type:

```
...
<variables>
  ...
  <!-- fault to the BPEL client -->
  <variable name="TravelFault" messageType="trv:TravelFaultMessage"/>

</variables>
...
```

Then we return the fault to the BPEL process client. We will need to check if something went wrong in the travel process. For the purpose of this example, we will check whether the selected flight ticket has been approved. This information is stored in the confirmationData part of the TravelResponse variable in the Approved element (see previous chapter for the complete schema definition). Note that this is an oversimplification but it demonstrates how to return faults. We can use a <switch> activity to determine whether the ticket is approved; then we construct the fault variable and use the <reply> activity to return it to the client. This is shown in the following code:

```
...
<!-- Check if the ticket is approved -->
<switch>
```

```
    <case condition="bpws:getVariableData(
                        'TravelResponse',
                        'confirmationData',
                        '/confirmationData/aln:Approved')='true' ">

          <!-- Send a response to the client -->
          <reply partnerLink="client"
                 portType="trv:TravelApprovalPT"
                 operation="TravelApproval"
                 variable="TravelResponse"/>

    </case>

    <otherwise>
      <sequence>

          <!-- Create the TravelFault variable with fault description -->
          <assign>
             <copy>
               <from expression="string('Ticket not approved')" />
               <to variable="TravelFault" part="error" />
             </copy>
          </assign>

          <!-- Send a fault to the client -->
          <reply partnerLink="client"
                 portType="trv:TravelApprovalPT"
                 operation="TravelApproval"
                 variable="TravelFault"
                 faultName="fault" />
      </sequence>
    </otherwise>
  </switch>
 </sequence>
</process>
```

If the ticket is not approved, the following fault is signaled to the client:

```
<TravelFault>
  <part name="error">
    <error xmlns="http://packtpub.com/bpel/travel/">
       Ticket not approved
    </error>
  </part>
</TravelFault>
```

We have seen that signaling faults in synchronous replies is easy. Let us now discuss signaling faults in asynchronous scenarios.

Signaling Faults to Clients in Asynchronous Scenarios

If an asynchronous BPEL process needs to notify the client about a fault, it cannot use the `<reply>` activity. Remember that in asynchronous scenarios the client does not wait for the reply—rather the process uses a callback. To return a fault in callback scenarios, we usually define additional callback operations on the same port type. Through these callback operations, we can signal that an exceptional situation has prevented normal completion of the process.

To demonstrate how faults can be propagated to the client using a callback operation, we will use the asynchronous travel process example. First, we need to modify the travel BPEL process WSDL and introduce another operation called `ClientCallbackFault`. This operation consists of an input message called `tns:TravelFaultMessage`. The message is of the `string` type (similar to the synchronous example). The declaration of the operation and the message is shown in the following code excerpt:

```
...
<message name="TravelFaultMessage">
  <part name="error" type="xs:string" />
</message>

<portType name="ClientCallbackPT">
  <operation name="ClientCallback">
    <input message="aln:TravelResponseMessage" />
  </operation>

  <operation name="ClientCallbackFault">
    <input message="tns:TravelFaultMessage" />
  </operation>

</portType>
...
```

We can use the <switch> activity to determine whether the ticket has been approved, as in the synchronous example. If the ticket is not approved, however, we <invoke> the ClientCallbackFault operation instead of using the <reply> activity to signal the fault to the client. This is shown in the code excerpt below:

```
      ...
      <!-- Check if the ticket is approved -->
      <switch>

        <case condition="bpws:getVariableData('TravelResponse',
                             'confirmationData',
                             '/confirmationData/aln:Approved')='true' ">

          <!-- Make a callback to the client -->
          <invoke partnerLink="client"
                  portType="trv:ClientCallbackPT"
                  operation="ClientCallback"
                  inputVariable="TravelResponse" />

        </case>

        <otherwise>

          <sequence>
            <!-- Create the TravelFault variable with fault description -->
            <assign>
               <copy>
                 <from expression="string('Ticket not approved')" />
                 <to variable="TravelFault" part="error" />
               </copy>
            </assign>

            <!-- Send a fault to the client -->
            <invoke partnerLink="client"
                    portType="trv:ClientCallbackPT"
                    operation="ClientCallbackFault"
                    inputVariable="TravelFault" />

          </sequence>

        </otherwise>
      </switch>

   </sequence>

</process>
```

In the next section, we will look at how to handle faults thrown in BPEL processes.

Handling Faults

Now that we are familiar with how faults are signaled, let us consider how the business process handles faults. When a fault occurs within a business process (this can be a WSDL fault, a fault thrown by the BPEL process, or any other type of fault), it means that the process may not complete successfully. The process can complete successfully only if the fault is handled within a scope. Scopes are discussed in the next section.

> Business processes handle faults through fault handlers.

A business process can handle a fault through one or more fault handlers. Within a fault handler, the business process defines custom activities that are used to recover from the fault and recover the partial (unsuccessful) work of the activity in which the fault has occurred.

The fault handlers are specified before the first activity of the BPEL process, after the partner links and variables. The overall structure is shown in the following code excerpt:

```
<process ...>

   <partnerLinks>
      ...
   </partnerLinks>

   <variables>
      ...
   </variables>

   <faultHandlers>

      <catch ... >
         <!-- Perform an activity -->
      </catch>
      <catch ... >
         <!-- Perform an activity -->
      </catch>
      ...
      <catchAll>                          <!-- catchAll is optional -->
         <!-- Perform an activity -->
      </catchAll>

   </faultHandlers>

   <sequence>
      ...
   </sequence>
</process>
```

We can see that within the fault handlers we specify several <catch> activities where we indicate the fault that we would like to catch and handle. Within a fault handler, we have to specify at least one <catch> or a <catchAll> activity. Of course, the <catchAll> activity can be specified only once within a fault handler.

Usually we will specify several <catch> activities to handle specific faults and use the <catchAll> to handle all other faults. The <catch> activity has two attributes, of which we have to specify at least one:

- `faultName`: Specifies the name of the fault to be handled
- `faultVariable`: Specifies the variable type used for fault data

The flexibility of `<catch>` activities is high and all the following variations are permissible:

```
<faultHandlers>

   <catch faultName="trv:TicketNotApproved" >
      <!-- First fault handler -->
      <!-- Perform an activity -->
   </catch>

   <catch faultName="trv:TicketNotApproved" faultVariable="TravelFault" >
      <!-- Second fault handler -->
      <!-- Perform an activity -->
   </catch>

   <catch faultVariable="TravelFault" >
      <!-- Third fault handler -->
      <!-- Perform an activity -->
   </catch>

   <catchAll>
      <!-- Perform an activity -->
   </catchAll>

</faultHandlers>
```

We can see that fault handlers in BPEL are very similar to try/catch clauses found in modern programming languages.

Selection of a Fault Handler

Let us consider the fault handlers listed above and discuss the scenarios for which the `<catch>` activities will be selected:

- The first `<catch>` will be selected if the `trv:TicketNotApproved` fault has been thrown and the fault carries no fault data.
- The second `<catch>` will be selected if the `trv:TicketNotApproved` fault has been thrown and carries data of type matching that of the `TravelFault` variable.
- The third `<catch>` will be selected if a fault has been thrown whose fault variable type matches the `TravelFault` variable type and whose name is not `trv:TicketNotApproved`.
- In all other cases the `<catchAll>` will be selected.

We can see that the selection of the `<catch>` activity within fault handlers is quite complicated. It may even happen that a fault matches several `<catch>` activities. Therefore, BPEL specifies exact rules to select the fault handler that will process a fault:

- For faults without associated fault data, the fault name will be matched. The `<catch>` activity with a matching `faultName` will be selected if present; otherwise the default `<catchAll>` handler will be used if present.
- For faults with associated fault data, a `<catch>` activity specifying a matching `faultName` value and `faultVariable` value will be selected, if present. Otherwise, a

<catch> activity with no specified faultName and a matching faultVariable will be selected, if present. Otherwise, the default <catchAll> handler will be used, if present.

> The <catchAll> activity will execute only if no other <catch> activity has been selected.

If no <catch> is selected and <catchAll> is not present, the fault will be re-thrown to the immediately enclosing scope, if present. Otherwise, the process will terminate abnormally. This situation is similar to explicitly terminating the process using the <terminate> activity.

Synchronous Example

Let's go back to the synchronous BPEL travel process example to add a fault handlers section. We need to define a fault handler that will simply signal the fault to the client. In real-world scenarios, a fault handler can perform additional work to try to recover the work done by an activity or retry the activity itself.

To signal the fault to the client, we use the same TravelFaultMessage message that we defined in the previous section. Here is an excerpt from the WSDL:

```
...
<message name="TravelFaultMessage">
  <part name="error" type="xs:string" />
</message>

<portType name="TravelApprovalPT">
  <operation name="TravelApproval">
    <input message="tns:TravelRequestMessage" />
    <output message="aln:TravelResponseMessage" />
    <fault name="fault" message="tns:TravelFaultMessage" />
  </operation>
</portType>
...
```

We define a fault handler and add a <faultHandlers> section immediately after the <variables> definition and before the <sequence> activity, as shown below. The fault handler for the trv:TicketNotApproved fault is defined with the associated TravelFault variable. This handler will use the <reply> activity to signal the fault to the BPEL client. We will also provide a default <catchAll> handler, which will first create a variable and then use the <reply> activity to signal the fault to the client:

```
...
<faultHandlers>

   <catch faultName="trv:TicketNotApproved" faultVariable="TravelFault">

     <reply partnerLink="client"
            portType="trv:TravelApprovalPT"
            operation="TravelApproval"
            variable="TravelFault"
            faultName="fault" />

   </catch>

   <catchAll>
```

```
        <sequence>
            <!-- Create the TravelFault variable -->
            <assign>
              <copy>
                <from expression="string('Other fault')" />
                <to variable="TravelFault" part="error" />
              </copy>
            </assign>

            <reply partnerLink="client"
                   portType="trv:TravelApprovalPT"
                   operation="TravelApproval"
                   variable="TravelFault"
                   faultName="fault" />
        </sequence>

      </catchAll>

   </faultHandlers>
   ...
```

We also have to modify the process itself. Instead of replying to the client (`<reply>`) in the `<switch>` activity if the ticket has not been approved, we will simply throw a fault, which will be caught by the corresponding fault handler. The fault handler will also catch other possible faults:

```
...
<!-- Check if the ticket is approved -->
<switch>

  <case condition="bpws:getVariableData('TravelResponse',
                      'confirmationData',
                      '/confirmationData/aln:Approved')='true' ">

       <!-- Send a response to the client -->
       <reply partnerLink="client"
              portType="trv:TravelApprovalPT"
              operation="TravelApproval"
              variable="TravelResponse"/>

  </case>

  <otherwise>

    <sequence>
       <!-- Create the TravelFault variable with fault description -->
       <assign>
          <copy>
            <from expression="string('Ticket not approved')" />
            <to variable="TravelFault" part="error" />
          </copy>

       </assign>

       <!-- Throw fault -->
       <throw faultName="trv:TicketNotApproved"
              faultVariable="TravelFault" />
    </sequence>

  </otherwise>
</switch>
...
```

Faults that are not handled by the BPEL process result in abnormal termination of the process and are not propagated to the client. In other words, unhandled faults do not cross service boundaries unless explicitly specified using a `<reply>` activity as we did in our example. This differentiates BPEL from Java and other languages where unhandled exceptions are propagated to the client.

Asynchronous Example

In asynchronous BPEL processes, faults are handled in the same way as in synchronous processes by using `<faultHandlers>`. We need to define a fault handler that, in our example, will simply forward the fault to the client. We cannot, however, use the `<reply>` activity to signal the fault to the client. Instead, we need to define an additional callback operation and use the `<invoke>` activity, as we did in our previous example. In this example we will use the same fault callback operation as in the previous asynchronous example:

```
...
<message name="TravelFaultMessage">
  <part name="error" type="xs:string" />
</message>

<portType name="ClientCallbackPT">
  <operation name="ClientCallback">
    <input message="aln:TravelResponseMessage" />
  </operation>

  <operation name="ClientCallbackFault">
    <input message="tns:TravelFaultMessage" />
  </operation>

</portType>
...
```

Now we will define the `<faultHandlers>` section. The difference to the synchronous example will be that we will use the `<invoke>` activity to invoke the newly defined operation instead of the `<reply>` activity to propagate the fault to the client:

```
...
<faultHandlers>

   <catch faultName="trv:TicketNotApproved" faultVariable="TravelFault">

     <!-- Make a callback to the client -->
     <invoke partnerLink="client"
             portType="trv:ClientCallbackPT"
             operation="ClientCallbackFault"
             inputVariable="TravelFault" />
   </catch>

   <catchAll>

     <sequence>
        <!-- Create the TravelFault variable -->
        <assign>
          <copy>
            <from expression="string('Other fault')" />
            <to variable="TravelFault" part="error" />
          </copy>
        </assign>

        <invoke partnerLink="client"
                portType="trv:ClientCallbackPT"
                operation="ClientCallbackFault"
```

```
                    inputVariable="TravelFault" />
      </sequence>

   </catchAll>

</faultHandlers>
...
```

Another important question related to fault handling is how the BPEL process can be notified of faults that occurred in asynchronously invoked partner web service operations. A typical example is the invocation of the American and Delta Airlines web services in our example. To invoke the operation, we used the `<invoke>` activity and then a `<receive>` activity to wait for the callback.

BPEL provides a way to wait for more than just one message (operation call) using the `<pick>` activity, which is described later in this chapter in the *Managing Events* section. By using `<pick>` instead of `<receive>`, our BPEL process can wait for several incoming messages. One of these can be a message for regular callback; others can be messages that signal fault conditions. With `<pick>`, we can even specify a timeout for receiving a callback. For further information on these issues, please see the *Managing Events* section.

Inline Fault Handling

The loosely coupled model of web services and the use of Internet connections for accessing them make the invocation of operations on web services particularly error prone. Numerous situations can prevent a BPEL process from successfully invoking a partner web service operation, such as broken connections, unavailability of web services, changes in the WSDL, and so on.

Such faults can be handled in the general `<faultHandlers>` sections. However, a more efficient way is to handle faults related to the `<invoke>` activity directly and not rely on the general fault handlers. The `<invoke>` activity provides a shortcut to achieve this—inline fault handlers.

> Inline fault handlers can catch WSDL faults for synchronous operations, and also other faults related to the run-time environment, communications, and so on.

The syntax for inline fault handlers in the `<invoke>` activity is similar to the syntax of the `<faultHandlers>` section. As shown in the code excerpt below we can specify zero or more `<catch>` activities and we can also specify a `<catchAll>` handler. The only difference is that in inline `<catch>` activities, we have to specify a fault name. Optionally, we may specify the fault variable:

```
<invoke ... >

   <catch faultName="fault-name" >
      <!-- Perform an activity -->
   </catch>
   ...

   <catch faultName="fault-name" faultVariable="fault-variable" >
      <!-- Perform an activity -->
   </catch>
   ...

   <catchAll>
      <!-- Perform an activity -->
   </catchAll>

</invoke>
```

The following code excerpt shows an inline fault handler for invoking the Employee Travel Status web service from our BPEL travel process example. Please notice that this also requires modifying the Employee Travel Status WSDL and declaring an additional fault message for the operation. Because this code is similar to what we did in previous examples, it is not repeated here again. The following code excerpt demonstrates inline fault handling:

```
<invoke partnerLink="employeeTravelStatus"
        portType="emp:EmployeeTravelStatusPT"
        operation="EmployeeTravelStatus"
        input Variable="EmployeeTravelStatusRequest"
        outputVariable="EmployeeTravelStatusResponse" >

   <catch faultName="emp:WrongEmployeeName" >
      <!-- Perform an activity -->
   </catch>

   <catch faultName="emp:TravelNotAllowed" faultVariable="FaultDesc" >
      <!-- Perform an activity -->
   </catch>

   <catchAll>
      <!-- Perform an activity -->
   </catchAll>

</invoke>
```

This brings us to the thought that it would be useful if we could specify more than one <faultHandlers> section in a BPEL process. It would be great if we could specify different fault handlers sections for different parts of the process, particularly for complex processes. This is possible if we use scopes, described in the next section. We will see that inline fault handling of the <invoke> activity is equal to enclosing the <invoke> activity in a local scope.

Scopes

Scopes provide a way to divide a complex business process into hierarchically organized parts—*scopes*. Scopes provide behavioral contexts for activities. In other words scopes address the problem that we identified in the previous section and allow us to define different fault handlers for different activities (or sets of activities gathered under a common structured activity, such as <sequence> or <flow>). In addition to fault handlers, scopes also provide a way to declare variables that are visible only within the scope. Scopes also allow us to define local correlation sets, compensation handlers, and event handlers. We will discuss these topics later in this chapter.

The code excerpt below shows how scopes are defined in BPEL. We can specify <variables>, <correlationSets>, <faultHandlers>, <compensationHandlers>, and <eventHandlers> locally for the scope:

```
<scope>
   <variables>
     <!-- Variables definitions local to scope -->
   </variables>

   <correlationSets>
     <!-- Correlation sets will be discussed later in this chapter -->
   </correlationSets>

   <faultHandlers>
```

```
      <!-- Fault handlers local to scope -->
    </faultHandlers>

    <compensationHandler>
      <!-- Compensation handlers will be discussed later in this chapter -->
    </compensationHandler>

    <eventHandlers>
      <!-- Event handlers will be discussed later in this chapter -->
    </eventHandlers>

    activity
</scope>
```

Each scope has a primary activity. This is similar to the overall process structure, where we have said that a BPEL process also has a primary activity. The primary activity, often a `<sequence>` or `<flow>`, defines the behavior of a scope for normal execution. Fault handlers and other handlers define the behavior for abnormal execution scenarios.

The primary activity of a scope can be a basic activity such as `<invoke>` or it can be a structured activity such as `<sequence>` or `<flow>`. Enclosing the `<invoke>` activity with a scope and defining the fault handlers is equivalent to using inline fault handlers. The inline fault handler shown in the previous section is equal to the following scope:

```
<scope>

   <faultHandlers>

      <catch faultName="emp:WrongEmployeeName" >
         <!-- Perform an activity -->
      </catch>

      <catch faultName="emp:TravelNotAllowed" faultVariable="Description" >
         <!-- Perform an activity -->
      </catch>

      <catchAll>
         <!-- Perform an activity -->
      </catchAll>

   </faultHandlers>

   <invoke partnerLink="employeeTravelStatus"
           portType="emp:EmployeeTravelStatusPT"
           operation="EmployeeTravelStatus"
           inputVariable="EmployeeTravelStatusRequest"
           outputVariable="EmployeeTravelStatusResponse" >

   </invoke>
</scope>
```

If the primary activity of a scope is a structured activity, it can have many nested activities where the nesting depth is arbitrary. The scope is shared by all nested activities. A scope can also have nested scopes with arbitrary depth.

The variables defined within a scope are only visible within that scope. Fault handlers attached to a scope handle faults of all nested activities of a scope. Faults not caught in a scope are re-thrown to the enclosing scope. Scopes in which faults have occurred are considered to have ended abnormally even if a fault handler has caught the fault and not re-thrown it.

Example

To demonstrate how scopes can be used in BPEL processes, we will rewrite our asynchronous travel process example and introduce three scopes:

- In the first scope we will retrieve the employee travel status (`RetrieveEmployeeTravelStatus`).
- In the second scope we will check the flight availability with both airlines (`CheckFlightAvailability`).
- In the third scope we will call back to the client (`CallbackClient`).

We will also declare those variables that are limited to a scope locally within the scope. This will reduce the number of global variables and make the business process easier to understand. The major benefit of scopes is the capability to define custom fault handlers, which we will also implement. The high-level structure of our travel process will be as follows:

```
<process ...>

   <partnerLinks/>...</partnerLinks>
   <variables>...</variables>

   <faultHandlers>
      <catchAll>...</catchAll>
   </faultHandlers>

   <sequence>
      <!-- Receive the initial request for business travel from client -->
      <receive .../>

      <scope name="RetrieveEmployeeTravelStatus">

        <variables>...</variables>

        <faultHandlers>
          <catchAll>...</catchAll>
        </faultHandlers>

        <sequence>
          <!-- Prepare the input for Employee Travel Status Web Service -->
          <!-- Synchronously invoke the Employee Travel Status Web Service -->
          <!-- Prepare the input for AA and DA -->
        </sequence>
      </scope>

      <scope name="CheckFlightAvailability">

        <variables>...</variables>

        <faultHandlers>
          <catchAll>...</catchAll>
        </faultHandlers>

        <sequence>
          <!-- Make a concurrent invocation to AA and DA -->
          <flow>
            <!-- Async invoke the AA web service and wait for the callback -->
            <!-- Async invoke the DA web service and wait for the callback -->
          </flow>
          <!-- Select the best offer and construct the TravelResponse -->
        </sequence>
      </scope>
```

```
        <scope name="CallbackClient">

          <faultHandlers>...</faultHandlers>

          <!-- Check if the ticket is approved -->
        </scope>

      </sequence>
   </process>
```

To signal faults to the BPEL process client, we will use the `ClientCallbackFault` operation on the client partner link, which we defined in the previous section. This operation has a string message, which we will use to describe the fault. In real-world scenarios the fault message is more complex and includes a fault code and other relevant information.

Let us start with the example. The process declaration and the partner links have not changed:

```
<process name="Travel"
         targetNamespace="http://packtpub.com/bpel/travel/"
         xmlns="http://schemas.xmlsoap.org/ws/2003/03/business-process/"
         xmlns:bpws="http://schemas.xmlsoap.org/ws/2003/03/business-process/"
         xmlns:trv="http://packtpub.com/bpel/travel/"
         xmlns:emp="http://packtpub.com/service/employee/"
         xmlns:aln="http://packtpub.com/service/airline/" >

   <partnerLinks>

      <partnerLink name="client"
                   partnerLinkType="trv:travelLT"
                   myRole="travelService"
                   partnerRole="travelServiceCustomer"/>

      <partnerLink name="employeeTravelStatus"
                   partnerLinkType="emp:employeeLT"
                   partnerRole="employeeTravelStatusService"/>

      <partnerLink name="AmericanAirlines"
                   partnerLinkType="aln:flightLT"
                   myRole="airlineCustomer"
                   partnerRole="airlineService"/>

      <partnerLink name="DeltaAirlines"
                   partnerLinkType="aln:flightLT"
                   myRole="airlineCustomer"
                   partnerRole="airlineService"/>

   </partnerLinks>
   ...
```

The variables section will now define only global variables. These are `TravelRequest`, `FlightDetails`, `TravelResponse`, and `TravelFault`. We have reduced the number of global variables, but we will have to declare other variables within scopes:

```
   ...
   <variables>
      <!-- input for this process -->
      <variable name="TravelRequest"
                messageType="trv:TravelRequestMessage"/>
      <!-- input for the Employee Travel Status web service -->
      <variable name="FlightDetails"
                messageType="aln:FlightTicketRequestMessage"/>
      <!-- output from BPEL process -->
      <variable name="TravelResponse"
                messageType="aln:TravelResponseMessage"/>
```

```
        <!-- fault to the BPEL client -->
        <variable name="TravelFault"
                  messageType="trv:TravelFaultMessage"/>
    </variables>
    ...
```

Next we define the global fault handlers section. Here we use the `<catchAll>` activity, through which we handle all faults not handled within scopes. We will signal the fault to the BPEL client:

```
    ...
    <faultHandlers>

       <catchAll>

         <sequence>
            <!-- Create the TravelFault variable -->
            <assign>
              <copy>
                <from expression="string('Other fault')" />
                <to variable="TravelFault" part="error" />
              </copy>
            </assign>

            <invoke partnerLink="client"
                    portType="trv:ClientCallbackPT"
                    operation="ClientCallbackFault"
                    inputVariable="TravelFault" />
         </sequence>

       </catchAll>

    </faultHandlers>
    ...
```

The main activity of the BPEL process will still be `<sequence>`, and we will also specify the `<receive>` activity to wait for the incoming message from the client:

```
    ...
    <sequence>

       <!-- Receive the initial request for business travel from client -->
       <receive partnerLink="client"
                portType="trv:TravelApprovalPT"
                operation="TravelApproval"
                variable="TravelRequest"
                createInstance="yes" />
    ...
```

First Scope

Now let's define the first scope for retrieving the employee travel status. Here we will first declare two variables needed for the input and output messages for web service operation invocation:

```
    ...
       <scope name="RetrieveEmployeeTravelStatus">

         <variables>
            <!-- input for the Employee Travel Status web service -->
            <variable name="EmployeeTravelStatusRequest"
                      messageType="emp:EmployeeTravelStatusRequestMessage" />
            <!-- output from the Employee Travel Status web service -->
            <variable name="EmployeeTravelStatusResponse"
                      messageType="emp:EmployeeTravelStatusResponseMessage" />
         </variables>
    ...
```

Next we will define the fault handlers section for this scope. We will use the <catchAll> activity to handle all faults, including Employee web service WSDL faults, communication faults, and other run-time faults. We will signal all faults to the client, although in real-world scenarios we could invoke another web service or perform other recovery operations:

```
...
      <faultHandlers>

        <catchAll>

          <sequence>
            <!-- Create the TravelFault variable -->
            <assign>
              <copy>
                <from expression=
                  "string('Unable to retrieve employee travel status')" />
                <to variable="TravelFault" part="error" />
              </copy>
            </assign>

            <invoke partnerLink="client"
                    portType="trv:ClientCallbackPT"
                    operation="ClientCallbackFault"
                    inputVariable="TravelFault" />
            <terminate/>

          </sequence>
        </catchAll>
      </faultHandlers>
...
```

Next we will start a sequence (which is the main activity of the scope) and prepare the input variable, invoke the Employee web service, and prepare the input for both airlines' web services:

```
...
      <sequence>

          <!-- Prepare the input for the
               Employee Travel Status Web Service -->
          <assign>
            <copy>
              <from variable="TravelRequest" part="employee"/>
              <to variable="EmployeeTravelStatusRequest" part="employee"/>
            </copy>
          </assign>

          <!-- Synchronously invoke the
               Employee Travel Status Web Service -->
          <invoke partnerLink="employeeTravelStatus"
                  portType="emp:EmployeeTravelStatusPT"
                  operation="EmployeeTravelStatus"
                  inputVariable="EmployeeTravelStatusRequest"
                  outputVariable="EmployeeTravelStatusResponse" />

          <!-- Prepare the input for AA and DA -->
          <assign>
            <copy>
              <from variable="TravelRequest" part="flightData"/>
              <to variable="FlightDetails" part="flightData"/>
            </copy>
            <copy>
              <from variable="EmployeeTravelStatusResponse"
                    part="travelClass"/>
              <to variable="FlightDetails" part="travelClass"/>
            </copy>
```

```
            </assign>

        </sequence>
      </scope>
...
```

Second Scope

In the second scope we check the flight availability with both airlines' web services. First we declare two variables for storing output from both web service operations:

```
...
   <scope name="CheckFlightAvailability">

      <variables>
        <!-- output from American Airlines -->
        <variable name="FlightResponseAA"
                  messageType="aln:TravelResponseMessage"/>
        <!-- output from Delta Airlines -->
        <variable name="FlightResponseDA"
                  messageType="aln:TravelResponseMessage"/>
      </variables>
...
```

Next we define the fault handlers section, where we use the <catchAll> activity similarly to in the first scope:

```
...
      <faultHandlers>

        <catchAll>

          <sequence>
              <!-- Create the TravelFault variable -->
              <assign>
                <copy>
                  <from expression=
                      "string('Unable to invoke airline web service')" />
                  <to variable="TravelFault" part="error" />
                </copy>
              </assign>

              <invoke partnerLink="client"
                      portType="trv:ClientCallbackPT"
                      operation="ClientCallbackFault"
                      inputVariable="TravelFault" />
              <terminate/>

          </sequence>
        </catchAll>
      </faultHandlers>
...
```

The main activity of the second scope will be a <sequence> in which we will first concurrently invoke both airlines' web services using a <flow> activity and then select the best offer using a <switch> activity:

```
...
      <sequence>

          <!-- Make a concurrent invocation to AA and DA -->
          <flow>

            <sequence>
```

```
          <!-- Async invoke of the AA web service
               and wait for the callback -->

          <invoke partnerLink="AmericanAirlines"
              portType="aln:FlightAvailabilityPT"
              operation="FlightAvailability"
              inputVariable="FlightDetails" />

          <receive partnerLink="AmericanAirlines"
              portType="aln:FlightCallbackPT"
              operation="FlightTicketCallback"
              variable="FlightResponseAA" />

        </sequence>

        <sequence>
          <!-- Async invoke of the DA web service
               and wait for the callback -->

          <invoke partnerLink="DeltaAirlines"
              portType="aln:FlightAvailabilityPT"
              operation="FlightAvailability"
              inputVariable="FlightDetails" />

          <receive partnerLink="DeltaAirlines"
              portType="aln:FlightCallbackPT"
              operation="FlightTicketCallback"
              variable="FlightResponseDA" />

        </sequence>

      </flow>

      <!-- Select the best offer and construct the TravelResponse -->
      <switch>

        <case condition="bpws:getVariableData('FlightResponseAA',
                    'confirmationData','/confirmationData/aln:Price')
                    &lt;= bpws:getVariableData('FlightResponseDA',
                    'confirmationData','/confirmationData/aln:Price')">
           <!-- Select American Airlines -->
           <assign>
             <copy>
               <from variable="FlightResponseAA" />
               <to variable="TravelResponse" />
             </copy>
           </assign>
        </case>

        <otherwise>
           <!-- Select Delta Airlines -->
           <assign>
             <copy>
               <from variable="FlightResponseDA" />
               <to variable="TravelResponse" />
             </copy>
           </assign>
        </otherwise>
      </switch>

   </sequence>
  </scope>
...
```

Third Scope

In the third scope we call back to the BPEL client. For this scope we do not need additional variables. However, we define a fault handler to handle the `TicketNotApproved` fault. Therefore we explicitly specify the fault name and the fault variable. Note that we do not use the `<catchAll>` activity in this fault handlers section, so all unhandled faults will be re-thrown to the main process fault handler:

```
...
   <scope name="CallbackClient">

      <faultHandlers>

        <catch faultName="trv:TicketNotApproved"
               faultVariable="TravelFault">

          <!-- Make a callback to the client -->
          <invoke partnerLink="client"
                  portType="trv:ClientCallbackPT"
                  operation="ClientCallbackFault"
                  inputVariable="TravelFault" />
        </catch>
      </faultHandlers>
...
```

The main activity of this scope is the `<switch>` activity, where we check if the flight ticket has been approved:

```
...
      <!-- Check if the ticket is approved -->
      <switch>

        <case condition="bpws:getVariableData('TravelResponse',
                            'confirmationData',
                            '/confirmationData/aln:Approved')='true' ">

              <!-- Make a callback to the client -->
              <invoke partnerLink="client"
                      portType="trv:ClientCallbackPT"
                      operation="ClientCallback"
                      inputVariable="TravelResponse" />

        </case>

        <otherwise>

          <sequence>
                <!-- Create the TravelFault variable
                     with fault description -->
                <assign>
                   <copy>
                     <from expression="string('Ticket not approved')" />
                     <to variable="TravelFault" part="error" />
                   </copy>

                </assign>

                <!-- Throw fault -->
                <throw faultName="trv:TicketNotApproved"
                       faultVariable="TravelFault" />
          </sequence>

        </otherwise>
```

```
            </switch>
          </scope>
       </sequence>
    </process>
```

Serializable Scopes

For each scope we can specify whether we require concurrency control over shared variables. We will need such control if, in our scenario, more than one instance uses shared variables concurrently. This can occur, for example, if we use an event handler through which we react to an event while the main process is executing. This is discussed later in this chapter.

Scopes that require concurrency control are called **serializable scopes**. In serializable scopes, access to all shared variables is serialized; in other words, concurrency is prohibited. This guarantees that there will be no conflicting situations if several concurrent scopes access the same set of shared variables. Conflicting operations are in this case all read/write and write-only activities, such as assignments, incoming messages stored in variables, etc. The semantics of serializable scopes are similar to the *serializable* transaction isolation level.

We denote a scope as serializable using the optional attribute `variableAccessSerializable` and setting it to `yes`. The default value of this attribute is `no`. Serializable scopes must not contain other serializable scopes (but may contain scopes that are not marked as serializable). The fault handlers associated with the scope also share the serializability. The code excerpt below shows how to declare a scope as serializable:

```
<scope variableAccessSerializable="yes" >
  ...
</scope>
```

At the time of writing this book, not all BPEL severs have supported this feature, so it is wise to check for support before relying on the serializable behavior.

Compensation

Compensation, or undoing steps in the business process that have already completed successfully, is one of the most important concepts in business processes. Let us discuss the compensation on our travel process and suppose that in addition to checking the flight availability, our business process would also have to confirm the flight tickets, make the payments, reserve a hotel room, and make the payment for the hotel room. If the business travel is canceled (for various reasons) the reservation and payment activities would have to be undone—compensated. In business processes, the compensation behavior must be explicitly defined. Therefore, when defining the BPEL process, we would have to explicitly define how to compensate the flight ticket confirmation, how to compensate the flight ticket payment, etc.

> The goal of compensation is to reverse the effects of previous activities that have been carried out as part of a business process that is being abandoned.

Compensation is related to the nature of most business processes, which are long running and use asynchronous communication with loosely coupled partner web services. Business processes are often sensitive in terms of successful completion because the data they manipulate is sensitive. Because they usually span multiple partners (often multiple enterprises) special care has to be taken that business processes either fully complete their work or that the partial (not fully completed) results are undone – compensated.

In enterprise information systems, processes that have not been able to finish all their activities and need to undo the partial work are usually handled with transactions, more exactly with the ACID distributed transaction model, such as X/Open DTP (Distributed Transaction Processing). ACID stands for Atomicity, Consistency, Isolation, and Durability and defines a transaction model that uses data locking and isolation. Such a model works perfectly well in trusted domains within enterprises under the prerequisite that the duration of transactions can be relatively short.

The problem with business processes is that they usually last a long time, sometimes several hours, sometimes even a few days. This is much too long for the ACID model, because we cannot afford to lock certain data for such a long time and to isolate the access to these data.

In business processes compensation is used instead of ACID to reverse the effects of an unfinished process. Compensation requires that an activity specifies a reverse activity, which can be invoked if it is necessary to undo the effect of that activity. BPEL supports the concept of compensation with the ability to define compensation handlers, which are specific to scopes, and calls this feature *Long-Running Transactions* (LRT).

The concept of compensation and LRTs as defined by BPEL is independent of any transaction protocol and can be used with various business transaction protocols. Because BPEL is bound to web services it is, however, reasonable to expect that in most cases the LRTs will be used with the WS-BusinessActivity (WS-Transaction) specification. It has been described in Chapter 2. The BPEL specification even defines a detailed model of BPEL LRTs based on WS-BusinessActivity concepts.

It is very important to understand that compensation differs from fault handling. In fault handling a business process tries to recover from an activity that could not finish normally because an exceptional situation has occurred. The objective of compensation on the other hand is to reverse the effects of a previous activity or a set of activities that have been carried out successfully as part of a business process that is being abandoned. Note that the order in which compensation activities are run is often important. BPEL addresses this aspect with scopes.

Compensation Handlers

To define the compensation activities, BPEL provides compensation handlers. Compensation handlers gather all activities that have to be carried out to compensate another activity. Compensation handlers can be defined:

- For the whole process
- For the scope
- Inline for the `<invoke>` activity

The compensation handler for the whole BPEL process is defined immediately after the fault handlers section and before the main activity of the process, as shown in the next code excerpt:

```
<process ...>

   <partnerLinks>
      ...
   </partnerLinks>

   <variables>
      ...
   </variables>

   <faultHandlers>
      ...
   </faultHandlers>

   <compensationHandler>

     <!-- Compensation activity
          (or several activities within a <sequence>, <flow>,
          or other structured activity) -->

   </compensationHandler>

   main activity
</process>
```

The compensation handler for a scope is also defined after the fault handlers section:

```
<scope>

    <variables>
       ...
    </variables>

    <correlationSets>
      <!-- Correlation sets will be discussed later in this chapter -->
    </correlationSets>

    <faultHandlers>
       ...
    </faultHandlers>

    <compensationHandler>

     <!-- Compensation activity
          (or several activities within a <sequence>, <flow>,
          or other structured activity) -->

    </compensationHandler>

    <eventHandlers>
      <!-- Event handlers will be discussed later in this chapter -->
    </eventHandlers>

    activity

  </scope>
```

Sometimes it is reasonable to define a compensation handler for each `<invoke>` activity. We could define a scope for each `<invoke>`. However, BPEL provides a shortcut where we can inline the compensation handler rather than explicitly using an immediately enclosing scope. This is similar to the inline capability of fault handlers. The syntax is shown below:

```
<invoke ... >

  <compensationHandler>
```

```
    <!-- Compensation activity
         (or several activities within a <sequence>, <flow>,
         or other structured activity) -->

  </compensationHandler>

</invoke>
```

The syntax of the compensation handler is the same for all three cases: we specify the activity that has to be performed for compensation. This can be a basic activity such as `<invoke>` or a structured activity such as `<sequence>` or `<flow>`.

Example

Let us suppose that within a business process we will invoke a web service operation through which we will confirm the flight ticket. The compensation activity would be to cancel the flight ticket. The most obvious way to do this is to define the inline compensation handler for the `<invoke>` activity as shown in the following example:

```
<invoke name="TicketConfirmation"
        partnerLink="AmericanAirlines"
        portType="aln:TicketConfirmationPT"
        operation="ConfirmTicket"
        inputVariable="FlightDetails"
        outputVariable="Confirmation" >

  <compensationHandler>

     <invoke partnerLink="AmericanAirlines"
             portType="aln:TicketConfirmationPT"
             operation="CancelTicket"
             inputVariable="FlightDetails"
             outputVariable="Cancellation" />

  </compensationHandler>

</invoke>
```

Let us now suppose that the business process performs two operations in a sequence. First it confirms the ticket and then makes the payment. To compensate these two activities we could define an inline compensation handler for both `<invoke>` activities. Alternatively, we could also define a scope with a dedicated compensation handler, as shown in the example that follows:

```
<scope name="TicketConfirmationPayment" >

   <compensationHandler>

      <invoke partnerLink="AmericanAirlines"
              portType="aln:TicketConfirmationPT"
              operation="CancelTicket"
              inputVariable="FlightDetails"
              outputVariable="Cancellation" />

      <invoke partnerLink="AmericanAirlines"
              portType="aln:TicketPaymentPT"
              operation="CancelPayment"
              inputVariable="PaymentDetails"
              outputVariable="PaymentCancellation" />

   </compensationHandler>
```

```
        <invoke partnerLink="AmericanAirlines"
                portType="aln:TicketConfirmationPT"
                operation="ConfirmTicket"
                inputVariable="FlightDetails"
                outputVariable="Confirmation" />

        <invoke partnerLink="AmericanAirlines"
                portType="aln:TicketPaymentPT"
                operation="PayTicket"
                inputVariable="PaymentDetails"
                outputVariable="PaymentConfirmation" />

    </scope>
```

Which approach is better depends on the nature of the business process. In most cases we will define inline compensation handlers or compensation handlers within scopes. In the global BPEL process compensation handler, we will usually invoke compensation handlers for specific scopes and thus define the order in which the compensation should perform. Let's have a look at how to invoke a compensation handler.

Invoking Compensation Handlers

Compensation handlers can be invoked only after the activity that is to be compensated has completed normally. If we try to compensate an activity that has completed abnormally, nothing will happen because an `<empty>` activity will be invoked. This is useful because it is not necessary to track the state of activities to know which can be compensated and which cannot.

BPEL provides the `<compensate>` activity to invoke a compensation handler. The syntax is simple and is shown below. The `<compensate>` activity has an optional `scope` attribute through which we can specify which compensation handler should be invoked. We have to specify the name of the scope. To invoke the inline compensation handler, we specify the name of the `<invoke>` activity:

```
<compensate scope="name" />
```

To invoke the compensation handler for the `TicketConfirmationPayment` scope (shown in the previous section) we could simply write:

```
<compensate scope="TicketConfirmationPayment" />
```

To invoke the inline compensation handler for the `TicketConfirmation` `<invoke>` activity (also shown in the previous section) we write:

```
<compensate scope="TicketConfirmation" />
```

If we invoke a compensation handler for a scope that has no compensation handler defined, the default handler invokes the compensation handlers for the immediately enclosed scopes in the reverse order of completion (remember that the order in which compensations are performed is often important). This behavior is also performed if we use the `<compensate>` activity without specifying the scope name.

Compensation handlers can be explicitly invoked only from:

- The fault handler of the scope that immediately encloses the scope for which compensation should be performed
- The compensation handler of the scope that immediately encloses the scope for which compensation should be performed

The compensation handler defined for the whole BPEL process can be invoked only after the process has completed normally. Invoking it is specific to the run-time environment (BPEL server). Usually the environment will provide a command through which the compensation can be invoked. We can control this behavior using the `enableInstanceCompensation` attribute, which can be `yes` or `no`. The default value of this attribute is `no`, which means that the compensation is not allowed.

> When a compensation handler is invoked, it sees a frozen snapshot of all variables as they were when the scope being compensated was completed.

In the compensation we can use the same variables as in regular activities and these variables will have the same values as when the activity being compensated finished. This means that the compensation handler cannot update live data in the variables the BPEL process is using. The compensation handler *cannot* affect the global state of the business process.

In future versions, BPEL will provide two-way communication between the business process and the compensation handler. We expect that compensation handlers will be supplemented with input and output parameters.

Managing Events

A business process may have to react on certain events. We already know that a business process specified in BPEL usually waits for an incoming message using the `<receive>` activity. This incoming message is the event that activates the whole process. A business process also often invokes web service operations asynchronously. For such operations, results are returned using callbacks. The BPEL process often waits for callback messages, which are also events.

Using the `<receive>` activity, we can wait for an exactly specified message on a certain port type. Often, however, it is more useful to wait for more than one message, of which only one will occur. Let us go back to our example, where we invoked the `FlightAvailability` operation and waited for the `FlightTicketCallback` callback. In a real-world scenario, it would be very useful to wait for several messages, `FlightTicketCallback` being one of them. The other messages could include `FlightNotAvaliable`, `TicketNotAvaliable`, etc.

Even more useful would be to specify that we will wait for the callback for a certain period of time (for example, 5 minutes). If no callback is received, we continue the process flow. This is particularly useful in loosely coupled service-oriented architectures, where we cannot rely on web services being available all the time. This way, we could proceed with the process flow even if American Airlines' web service does not return an offer— we would then invoke another airline web service operation.

In most business processes, we will need to react on two types of events:

- **Message events**: These are triggered by incoming messages through operation invocation on port types
- **Alarm events:** These are time related and are triggered either after a certain duration or at a specific time.

Pick Activity

BPEL provides the <pick> activity through which we can specify that the business process awaits the occurrence of one of a set of events. Events can be message events handled using the <onMessage> activity and alarm events handled using the <onAlarm> activity. For each event we then specify an activity or a set of activities that should be performed.

The syntax of the <pick> activity is shown below:

```
<pick>

   <onMessage ...>
      <!-- Perform an activity -->
   </onMessage>

   <onMessage ...>
      <!-- Perform an activity -->
   </onMessage>

   ...

   <onAlarm ...>
      <!-- Perform an activity -->
   </onAlarm>

   ...

</pick>
```

Within <pick> we can specify several <onMessage> elements and several <onAlarm> elements. The <onAlarm> elements are optional (we can specify zero or more), but we have to specify at least one <onMessage> element.

Message Events

Both elements take additional attributes. The <onMessage> element is identical to the <receive> activity, and has the same set of attributes. We have to specify the following attributes:

- partnerLink: Specifies which partner link will be used for the invoke, receive, or reply, respectively
- portType: Specifies the used port type
- operation: Specifies the name of the operation to wait for being invoked
- variable: Specifies the name of the variable used to store the incoming message

The syntax is shown in the code excerpt below:

```
<pick>
   <onMessage partnerLink="name"
              portType="name"
              operation="name"
              variable="name">

      <!-- Perform an activity or a set of activities enclosed by
           <sequence>, <flow>, etc. or throw a fault -->

   </onMessage>

   ...

</pick>
```

Alarm Events

The <onAlarm> element is similar to the <wait> element. We can specify:

- A duration expression using a `for` attribute
- A deadline expression using an `until` attribute

For both expressions we use the same literal format as for the <wait> activity described earlier in this chapter.

Most often we will use the <onAlarm> event to specify duration. A typical example is for a business process to wait for the callback a certain amount of time, for example 15 minutes. If no callback is received the business process invokes another operation or throws a fault. The deadline approach is useful for example if the business process should wait for a callback until an exactly specified time and then throw a fault or perform a backup activity.

The code excerpt below shows examples of both with hard-coded times/dates:

```
<pick>
   <onMessage ...>
      <!-- Perform an activity -->
   </onMessage>
   ...

   <onAlarm for="'PT15M'">

      <!-- Perform an activity or a set of activities enclosed by
           <sequence>, <flow>, etc. or throw a fault -->

   </onAlarm>

</pick>

<pick>
   <onMessage ...>
      <!-- Perform an activity -->
   </onMessage>
   ...

   <onAlarm until="'2004-03-18T21:00:00+01:00'">

      <!-- Perform an activity or a set of activities enclosed by
           <sequence>, <flow>, etc. or throw a fault -->

   </onAlarm>

</pick>
```

Instead of hard-coding the exact date and time or the duration we can use a variable and access the information using the `getVariableData()` function.

Example

Going back to our travel example we could replace the <receive> activity, where the business process waited for the `FlightTicketCallback`, with the <pick> activity, where the business process will also wait for the `FlightNotAvaliable` and `TicketNotAvaliable` operations and throw corresponding faults. The business process will wait no more than 30 minutes, when it will throw a `CallbackTimeout` fault. The code excerpt is shown overleaf:

```
<pick>
    <onMessage partnerLink="AmericanAirlines"
               portType="aln:FlightCallbackPT"
               operation="FlightTicketCallback"
               variable="FlightResponseAA">
       <empty/>
       <!-- Continue with the rest of the process -->
    </onMessage>

    <onMessage partnerLink="AmericanAirlines"
               portType="aln:FlightCallbackPT"
               operation="FlightNotAvaliable"
               variable="FlightFaultAA">
       <throw faultName="trv:FlightNotAvaliable"
              faultVariable="FlightFaultAA"/>
    </onMessage>

    <onMessage partnerLink="AmericanAirlines"
               portType="aln:FlightCallbackPT"
               operation="TicketNotAvaliable"
               variable="FlightFaultAA">
       <throw faultName="trv:TicketNotAvaliable"
              faultVariable="FlightFaultAA"/>
    </onMessage>

    <onAlarm for="'PT30M'">
       <throw faultName="trv:CallbackTimeout" />
    </onAlarm>
</pick>
```

For this example to work, we also need to declare the `FlightFaultAA` variable and to modify the Airline web service WSDL to add the `FlightNotAvaliable` and `TicketNotAvaliable` callback operations. This is not shown here but can be seen from the example, which can be downloaded from Packt's website.

Event Handlers

The `<pick>` activity is very useful when we have to specify that the business process should wait for events. Sometimes, however, we would like to react on events that occur while the business process executes. In other words, we do not want the business process to wait for the event (and do nothing else but wait). Instead the process should execute, and still listen to events and handle them whenever they occur.

For this purpose BPEL provides event handlers. If the corresponding events occur, event handlers are invoked concurrently with the business process. Typical usage of event handlers is to handle a cancellation message from the client. For example, in our travel process we could define an event handler that would allow the BPEL process client to cancel the travel at any time.

We can specify event handlers for the whole BPEL process as well as for each scope. Event handlers for the whole process are specified immediately after the compensation handlers and before the main process activity as shown below:

```
<process ...>
   <partnerLinks>
      ...
   </partnerLinks>
   <variables>
      ...
   </variables>
```

```
    <faultHandlers>
       ...
    </faultHandlers>

    <compensationHandler>
       ...
    </compensationHandler>

    <eventHandlers>

       <onMessage ...>
          <!-- Perform an activity -->
       </onMessage>
       ...

       <onAlarm ...>
          <!-- Perform an activity -->
       </onAlarm>
       ...

    </eventHandlers>

    activity
</process>
```

Event handlers for the scope are also specified after compensation handlers, as shown in the excerpt below:

```
<scope>

    <variables>
       ...
    </variables>

    <correlationSets>
       <!-- Correlation sets will be discussed later in this chapter -->
    </correlationSets>

    <faultHandlers>
       ...
    </faultHandlers>

    <compensationHandler>
       ...
    </compensationHandler>

    <eventHandlers>

       <onMessage ...>
          <!-- Perform an activity -->
       </onMessage>
       ...

       <onAlarm ...>
          <!-- Perform an activity -->
       </onAlarm>
       ...

    </eventHandlers>

    activity

</scope>
```

The syntax of the event handler section is similar to the syntax of the <pick> activity. The only difference is that within the event handler, we can specify zero or more <onMessage> events and/or zero or more <onAlarm> events.

> Message events in event handlers can occur multiple times, even concurrently, while the corresponding scope is active. We have to take care of concurrency and use serializable scopes if necessary.

Example

Let us go back to the example and define the event handler that will allow the BPEL process client to cancel the travel at any time. The difficult part here is to define the appropriate activities to be performed when the client does the cancellation. The simplest solution is to terminate the process, as shown in the example below:

```
<process name="Travel"
         enableInstanceCompensation="yes" ... >

   ...
   <eventHandlers>

      <onMessage partnerLink="client"
                 portType="trv:TravelApprovalPT"
                 operation="CancelTravelApproval"
                 variable="TravelRequest" >

         <terminate/>
      </onMessage>

   </eventHandlers>
   ...
</process>
```

In the real world, we would want to undo some work when a cancellation actually occurs. Since we cannot invoke a compensation handler from an event handler, a better approach is to terminate the process and invoke the compensation handler for the whole process. To enable this, we have to set the enableInstanceCompensation attribute of the <process> tag to yes.

Another possibility would be to specify the alarm event, which would prevent a business process from executing for too long. The following example shows an alarm using a duration expression of 12 hours. We could use variable data to specify the duration instead of hard-coding it.

```
<process name="Travel"
         enableInstanceCompensation="yes" ... >

   ...
   <eventHandlers>

      <onAlarm for="'PT12H'">
         <terminate/>
      </onAlarm>

   </eventHandlers>
   ...
</process>
```

Other usage scenarios depend on the actual business process. Note that the examples shown for the process could also be defined within scopes. Because the code differences are minimal these examples are not shown.

The event handlers associated with the scopes are enabled when the associated scope starts. The event handlers associated with the global BPEL process are enabled as soon as the process instance is created. This brings us to the process lifecycle, which we will discuss in the next section.

Business Process Lifecycle

A business process specified in BPEL has a well-defined structure. It usually waits for the client to invoke the process. This is done using the `<receive>` activity, as we have seen in the previous chapter. A business process can also use the `<pick>` activity to wait for the initial incoming message. Then the business process typically invokes several operations on partner web services and waits for partners to invoke callback operations. The business process also performs some logic, such as comparison and calculation of certain values. The business process terminates after all activities have been performed.

We can see that each BPEL process has a well-defined lifecycle. To communicate with partners BPEL uses web services. Web services provide a stateless model for operation invocation. This means that a web service does not provide a common approach to store client-dependent information between operation invocations. For example, consider a shopping cart where a client uses an `add` operation to add items to the cart. Of course there could be several simultaneous clients using the shopping cart through the web service. We would like each client to have its own cart. To achieve this using web services each client would have to pass its identity for each invocation of the `add` operation. This is because the web services model is a stateless model—a web service does not distinguish between different clients.

For business processes a stateless model is inappropriate. Let us consider the business travel scenario where a client sends a travel order, through which it initiates the business process. The process then communicates with several web services and first sends a ticket approval to the client. Later it sends a hotel approval and an invoice. There are usually several concurrent clients using the business travel process. Also, a single client can start more than one interaction with the business process. The business process has to remember each interaction in order to know to whom to return the results.

> In contrast to stateless web services, BPEL business processes are stateful long-running interactions.

BPEL business processes are stateful and support long-running interactions with a well-defined lifecycle. For each interaction with the process, a **process instance** is created. Therefore we can think of the BPEL process definition as a template for creating process instances. This is similar to the class-object relation where classes represent templates for creating objects at run time.

In BPEL, we do not create instances explicitly as we would in programming languages (there is no `new` command for example). Rather, the creation is implicit and occurs when the process receives the initial message that starts the process. This can happen within the `<receive>` or `<pick>`

Activities, so both activities provide an attribute called `createInstance`. Setting this attribute to `yes` indicates that the occurrence of that activity causes a new instance of the business process to be created.

We usually annotate the initial `<receive>` or `<pick>` of each business process with the `createInstance` attribute. Going back to our business travel example, this is shown in the excerpt below:

```
...
<sequence>

   <!-- Receive the initial request for business travel from client -->
   <receive partnerLink="client"
            portType="trv:TravelApprovalPT"
            operation="TravelApproval"
            variable="TravelRequest"
            createInstance="yes" />
 ...
```

If, however, we would like to specify more than one operation we can use a special form of the `<pick>` activity. Using `<pick>` we can specify several operations and receiving any one of these messages will result in business process instance creation. We specify the `createInstance` attribute for the `<pick>` activity. However, we can only specify `<onMessage>` events; `<onAlarm>` events are not permitted in this specific form.

The following example shows the initial business process activity, which waits for the `TravelApproval` or `TravelCancellation` operations. Receiving one of these messages results in business process instance creation:

```
...
<pick createInstance="yes">

   <onMessage partnerLink="client"
            portType="trv:TravelApprovalPT"
            operation="TravelApproval"
            variable="TravelRequest" >

      <!-- Perform activities -->

   </onMessage>

   <onMessage partnerLink="client"
            portType="trv:TravelCancellationPT"
            operation="TravelCancellation"
            variable="TravelCancel" >

      <!-- Perform activities -->

   </onMessage>

</pick>
```

A business process can be terminated normally or abnormally. **Normal termination** occurs when all business process activities complete. **Abnormal termination** occurs either when a fault occurs within the process scope, or a process instance is terminated explicitly using the `<terminate>` activity.

In more complex business processes more than one start activity could be enabled concurrently. Such start activities are required to use correlation sets.

Correlation and Message Properties

Business processes use a stateful model. When a client starts a business process, a new instance is created. This instance lives for the duration of the business process. Messages sent to the business process (using operations on port types and ports) need to be delivered to the correct instance of the business process. We would expect this to be provided by the run-time environment, such as a BPEL server. This is the case if an appropriate transport mechanism can be used, such as WS-Addressing. However, in some cases where several partners are involved (for example if the BPEL process calls service A, which calls service B, and service B makes a direct callback to the BPEL process), or a lightweight transport mechanism is used that does not provide enough information to explicitly identify instances (such as JMS), manual correlation is required. In such cases we will have to use specific business data, such as flight numbers, social security numbers, chassis number, etc.

BPEL provides a mechanism to use such specific business data to maintain references to specific business process instances and calls this feature **correlation**. Business data used for correlation is contained in the messages exchanged between partners. The exact location usually differs from message to message—for example the flight number in the message from the passenger to the airline might be in a different location than in the confirmation message from the airline to the passenger etc. To specify which data is used for correlation, message properties are used.

Message Properties

Messages exchanged between partner web services in a business process usually contain application-specific data and protocol-specific data. Application-specific data is the data related to the business process. In our example, such data includes the employee name, employee travel status, travel destination, and dates, etc. To actually transfer this data (as SOAP messages, for example) additional protocol-specific data has to be added, such as security context, transaction context, etc. In SOAP, protocol-specific data is usually gathered in the `Header` section and application-specific data in the `Body` section of a SOAP message. However, not all protocols differentiate application- and protocol-specific data.

In business processes we will always need to manipulate application-specific data, and sometimes even protocol-specific data. BPEL provides a notion of **message properties**, which allow us to associate relevant data with names that have greater significance than just the data types used for such data.

For example, a chassis number can be used to identify a motor vehicle in a business process. The chassis number will probably appear in several messages and it will always identify the vehicle. Let us suppose that the chassis number is of type `string`, because a chassis number consists of numbers and characters. Naming it with a global property name `chassisNo` gives this string a greater significance than just the data type `string`.

Examples of such globally significant data are numerous and include social security numbers, tax payer numbers, flight numbers, license plate numbers, etc. These data can be denoted as properties whose significance goes beyond a single business process and can therefore be used for correlation. Other properties will be data significant for a single business process only, such as uniform identifiers, employee numbers, etc.

> Message properties have global significance in business processes and are mapped to multiple messages. So, it makes sense to name them with global property names.

Message properties are defined in WSDL through the WSDL extensibility mechanism, similarly to partner link types. However, in contrast to partner link types, the standard BPEL namespace is used: `http://schemas.xmlsoap.org/ws/2003/03/business-process/`. The syntax is simple and shown below. We have to define a property name and its type:

```
<wsdl:definitions
      xmlns:bpws="http://schemas.xmlsoap.org/ws/2003/03/business-process/"
      ... >
   ...
   <bpws:property name="name" type="type-name" />
   ...
</wsdl:definitions>
```

Let's go back to our travel process example. The flight number is such a significant data element that it makes sense to define it as a property in the Airline web service WSDL:

```
<definitions xmlns:http="http://schemas.xmlsoap.org/wsdl/http/"
        xmlns:soap="http://schemas.xmlsoap.org/wsdl/soap/"
        xmlns:xs="http://www.w3.org/2001/XMLSchema"
        xmlns:soapenc="http://schemas.xmlsoap.org/soap/encoding/"
        xmlns:emp="http://packtpub.com/service/employee/"
        xmlns:tns="http://packtpub.com/service/airline/"
        targetNamespace="http://packtpub.com/service/airline/"
        xmlns="http://schemas.xmlsoap.org/wsdl/"
        xmlns:plnk="http://schemas.xmlsoap.org/ws/2003/05/partner-link/"
        xmlns:bpws="http://schemas.xmlsoap.org/ws/2003/03/business-process/" >
   ...
   <bpws:property name="FlightNo" type="xs:string" />
   ...
</definitions>
```

Mapping Properties to Messages

Properties are parts of messages, usually embedded in the application-specific part of messages. To map a property to a specific element (or even attribute) of the message, BPEL provides **property aliases**. With property aliases, we map a property to a specific element or attribute of the selected message part. We can then use the property name as an alias for the message part and the location. This is particularly useful in abstract business processes where we focus on message exchange description.

Property aliases are defined in WSDL. The syntax is shown below. We have to specify the property name, the message type, message part, and the query expression to point to the specific element or attribute. The query expression is written in the selected query language; the default is XPath 1.0:

```
<wsdl:definitions ...
      xmlns:bpws="http://schemas.xmlsoap.org/ws/2003/03/business-process/"
      ... >
   ...
   <bpws:propertyAlias propertyName="property-name"
                       messageType="message-type-name"
                       part="message-part-name"
                       query="query-string"/>
   ...
</wsdl:definitions>
```

We now define the property alias for the flight number property defined in the previous section. In our travel process example we have defined the `TravelResponseMessage` in the airline WSDL:

```
...
<message name="TravelResponseMessage">
  <part name="confirmationData" type="tns:FlightConfirmationType" />
</message>
...
```

The `FlightConfirmationType` has been defined as a complex type with the `FlightNo` element of type `xs:string` being one of the elements. For the complete WSDL with the type definition please look at Chapter 3. To define the alias we write the following code:

```
<definitions xmlns:http="http://schemas.xmlsoap.org/wsdl/http/"
        xmlns:soap="http://schemas.xmlsoap.org/wsdl/soap/"
        xmlns:xs="http://www.w3.org/2001/XMLSchema"
        xmlns:soapenc="http://schemas.xmlsoap.org/soap/encoding/"
        xmlns:emp="http://packtpub.com/service/employee/"
        xmlns:tns="http://packtpub.com/service/airline/"
        targetNamespace="http://packtpub.com/service/airline/"
        xmlns="http://schemas.xmlsoap.org/wsdl/"
        xmlns:plnk="http://schemas.xmlsoap.org/ws/2003/05/partner-link/"
        xmlns:bpws="http://schemas.xmlsoap.org/ws/2003/03/business-process/" >
   ...

   <bpws:property name="FlightNo" type="xs:string" />
   ...
   <bpws:propertyAlias propertyName="tns:FlightNo"
                       messageType="tns:TravelResponseMessage"
                       part="confirmationData"
                       query="/confirmationData/FlightNo"/>
   ...
</definitions>
```

With this, we have defined a global property `FlightNo` as an alias for the `confirmationData` part of the `FlightConfirmationType` message type on the location specified by the `query`.

Extracting Properties

To extract property values from variables, BPEL defines an extension function called `getVariableProperty`, which is defined in the standard BPEL namespace. The function takes two parameters, the variable name and the property name, and returns the node that represents the property. The syntax is shown below:

```
bpws:getVariableProperty ('variableName', 'propertyName')
```

To extract the `FlightNo` property from the `TravelResponse` variable we write the following:

```
bpws:getVariableProperty ('TravelResponse', 'FlightNo')
```

The use of properties increases flexibility in extracting relevant data from the message compared to the `getVariableData` function. Using properties, we do not have to specify the exact location of the data (such as flight number), but rather use the property name. If the location changes, we only have to modify the property definition.

Properties and Assignments

Properties can also be used in assignments, which is particularly useful in abstract processes. We can copy a property from one variable to another using the `<assign>` activity, as shown in the code excerpt overleaf:

```
<assign>
   <copy>
      <from variable="variable-name" property="property-name"/>
      <to variable="variable-name" property="property-name"/>
   </copy>
</assign>
```

To copy the `FlightNo` property from the `FlightResponseAA` variable to the `TravelResponse` variable we write the following:

```
<assign>
   <copy>
      <from variable="FlightResponseAA" property="FlightNo"/>
      <to variable="TravelResponse" property="FlightNo"/>
   </copy>
</assign>
```

Correlation Sets

Now that we are familiar with properties, let's go back to the problem of correlation of messages. Correlation in BPEL uses the notion of properties to assign global names to relevant data used for correlation messages (such as flight number) and to define aliases through which we specify the location of such data in messages.

> A set of properties shared by messages and used for correlation is called a **correlation set**.

When correlated messages are exchanged between business partners, two roles can be defined. The partner that sends the first message in an operation invocation is the **initiator** and defines the values of the properties in the correlation set. Other partners are **followers** and get the property values for their correlation sets from incoming messages. Both initiator and followers must mark the first activity that binds the correlation sets.

A correlation set is used to associate messages with business process instances. Each correlation set has a name. A message can be related to one or more correlation sets. The initial message is used to initialize the values of a correlation set. The subsequent messages related to this correlation set must have property values identical to the initial correlation set. Correlation sets in BPEL can be declared globally for the whole process or within scopes. The syntax is shown below:

```
<correlationSets>
  <correlationSet name="correlation-set-name"
                  properties="list-of-properties"/>
  <correlationSet name="correlation-set-name"
                  properties="list-of-properties"/>
  ...
</correlationSets>
```

An example of a correlation set definition named `VehicleOrder` that includes two properties `chassisNo` and `engineNo` is shown below:

```
<correlationSets>
  <correlationSet name="VehicleOrder"
                  properties="tns:chassisNo tns:engineNo"/>
</correlationSets>
```

Going back to our example, let's define a correlation set named `TicketOrder` with a single property, `FlightNo`:

```
<process ... >

   <partnerLinks>...</partnerLinks>

   <variables>...</variables>

   <correlationSets>
      <correlationSet name="TicketOrder"
                      properties="aln:FlightNo"/>
   </correlationSets>
   ...
```

Using Correlation Sets

We can use correlation sets in `<invoke>`, `<receive>`, `<reply>`, and the `<onMessage>` parts of `<pick>` activities or event handlers. To specify which correlation sets should be used, we use the `<correlation>` activity nested within any of the above-mentioned activities. The syntax is shown below:

```
<correlations>
   <correlation set="name"
                initiate="yes|no"             <!-- Optional -->
                pattern="in|out|out-in" />    <!-- Used in invoke -->
</correlations>
```

We must specify the name of the correlation set used and indicate whether the correlation set should be initiated. The default value of the `initiate` attribute is `no`. When we use the correlation with the `<invoke>` activity, we must also specify the `pattern` attribute. The `in` value specifies that the correlation applies to inbound messages, `out` to outbound, and `out-in` to both messages.

The following example shows how to use correlation sets in a scenario where the BPEL process first checks the flight availability using an asynchronous `<invoke>` and then waits for the callback. The callback message contains the flight number (`FlightNo`), and is used to initiate the correlation set. Next, the ticket is confirmed using a synchronous `<invoke>`. Here the correlation set is used with the `out-in` pattern. Finally, the result is sent to the BPEL process client using a callback `<invoke>` activity. Here the correlation set is used with the `out` pattern:

```
...
<sequence>
   ...
   <!-- Check the flight avaliablity -->
   <invoke partnerLink="AmericanAirlines"
       portType="aln:FlightAvailabilityPT"
       operation="FlightAvailability"
       inputVariable="FlightDetails" />

   <!-- Wait for the callback -->
   <receive partnerLink="AmericanAirlines"
       portType="aln:FlightCallbackPT"
       operation="FlightTicketCallback"
       variable="TravelResponse" >

       <!-- The callback includes flight no
            therefore initiate correlation set -->
       <correlations>
          <correlation set="TicketOrder"
                       initiate="yes" />
       </correlations>

   </receive>
```

```
...
<!-- Synchrnousy confirm the ticket -->
<invoke partnerLink="AmericanAirlines"
    portType="aln:TicketConfirmationPT"
    operation="ConfirmTicket"
    inputVariable="FlightRespnseAA"
    outputVariable="Confirmation" >

    <!-- Use the correlation set to confirm the ticket -->
    <correlations>
       <correlation set="TicketOrder"
                    pattern="out-in" />
    </correlations>

</invoke>
...
<!-- Make a callback to the client -->
<invoke partnerLink="client"
    portType="trv:ClientCallbackPT"
    operation="ClientCallback"
    inputVariable="TravelResponse" >

    <!-- Use the correlation set to callback the client -->
    <correlations>
       <correlation set="TicketOrder"
                    pattern="out" />
    </correlations>

</invoke>
</sequence>

</process>
```

Concurrent Activities and Links

In business processes activities often occur concurrently. In BPEL, such concurrent activities are modeled using the <flow> activity. Activities within <flow> start concurrently as soon as the <flow> is started. The <flow> completes when all nested activities complete. Gathering nested activities within <flow> is straightforward and very useful for expressing concurrency scenarios that are not too complicated. We have used it in the examples in this and the previous chapter.

To express more complex concurrency scenarios, <flow> provides the ability to express synchronization dependencies between activities. In other words, we can specify which activities can start and when (depending on other activities) and define dependencies that are more complex than those expressed with a combination of <flow> and <sequence> activities. For example, we will often specify that a certain activity or several activities cannot start before another activity or several activities have finished.

We express synchronization dependencies using the <link> construct. For each link we specify a name. Links have to be defined within the <flow> activity. Link definitions are gathered within a <links> element. This is shown in the code excerpt below:

```
<flow>

   <links>
      <link name="TravelStatusToTicketRequest" />
      <link name="TicketRequestToTicketConfirmation" />
   </links>
   ...
</flow>
```

These links can now be used to link activities together. For actual linking we use standard elements that can be used with any BPEL activity.

Sources and Targets

For each BPEL activity, whether basic or structured, we can specify two **standard elements** for linking activities and expressing synchronization dependencies. These two standard elements are nested within the activity:

- `<source>` is used to annotate an activity as being a source of one or more links.
- `<target>` is used to annotate an activity as being a target of one or more links.

Every link declared within `<flow>` must have exactly one activity within the flow as its `<source>`. It must also have exactly one activity within the flow as its `<target>`.

> A link's target activity can be performed only after the source activity has been finished.

The syntax of the `<source>` element is shown below. We have to specify the link name, which has to be defined within the `<flow>` activity. Optionally we can specify the transition condition. We will say more on transition conditions later in this section. If the transition condition is not specified, the default value is `true`.

```
<source linkName="name"
        transitionCondition="boolean-expression" />
```

The syntax of the `<target>` element is even simpler. We only have to specify the link name:

```
<target linkName="name" />
```

Example

Let's now consider the business travel example. There the process had to invoke the Employee Travel Status web service first (synchronous invocation) to get the employee travel class information. Then it asynchronously invoked the American and Delta Airlines' web services to get flight ticket information. Finally, the process selected the best offer and sent the callback to the BPEL client.

In Chapter 3 we used a combination of `<sequence>` and `<flow>` activities to control the execution order. These two activities allowed us to perform basic synchronization, but they are not appropriate for expressing complex synchronization scenarios. In such scenarios, we should use links.

To demonstrate how to use links let's use the business travel example, but keep in mind that the scenario of our example is simple enough to be expressed using a combination of `<flow>` and `<sequence>` activities without the need for links. We will use the example for simplicity reasons. In the real world, we use links only where the scenario is so complex that it cannot be expressed using a combination of `<flow>` and `<sequence>` activities.

We have modified the asynchronous travel example and gathered all activities except the initial `<receive>` and the final `<invoke>` within a single `<flow>` activity. We have also added the `name` attribute to each activity. Although this attribute is optional, we have added it because it simplifies understanding which activities have to be linked:

```
<process name="Travel"
        ... >

   <partnerLinks>
      ...
   </partnerLinks>

   <variables>
      ...
   </variables>

   <sequence>

      <!-- Receive the initial request for business travel from client -->
      <receive name="InitialRequestReceive"
               partnerLink="client"
               portType="trv:TravelApprovalPT"
               operation="TravelApproval"
               variable="TravelRequest"
               createInstance="yes" />

      <flow>

        <!-- Prepare the input for the Employee Travel Status Web Service -->
        <assign name="EmployeeInput">
          <copy>
            <from variable="TravelRequest" part="employee"/>
            <to variable="EmployeeTravelStatusRequest" part="employee"/>
          </copy>
        </assign>

        <!-- Synchronously invoke the Employee Travel Status Web Service -->
        <invoke name="EmployeeTravelStatusSyncInv"
                partnerLink="employeeTravelStatus"
                portType="emp:EmployeeTravelStatusPT"
                operation="EmployeeTravelStatus"
                inputVariable="EmployeeTravelStatusRequest"
                outputVariable="EmployeeTravelStatusResponse" />

        <!-- Prepare the input for AA and DA -->
        <assign name="AirlinesInput">
          <copy>
            <from variable="TravelRequest" part="flightData"/>
            <to variable="FlightDetails" part="flightData"/>
          </copy>
          <copy>
            <from variable="EmployeeTravelStatusResponse" part="travelClass"/>
            <to variable="FlightDetails" part="travelClass"/>
          </copy>
        </assign>

        <!-- Async invoke of the AA web service and wait for the callback -->

        <invoke name="AmericanAirlinesAsyncInv"
                partnerLink="AmericanAirlines"
                portType="aln:FlightAvailabilityPT"
                operation="FlightAvailability"
                inputVariable="FlightDetails" />


        <receive name="AmericanAirlinesCallback"
                 partnerLink="AmericanAirlines"
                 portType="aln:FlightCallbackPT"
                 operation="FlightTicketCallback"
                 variable="FlightResponseAA" />
```

```
            <!-- Async invoke of the DA web service and wait for the callback -->

            <invoke name="DeltaAirlinesAsyncInv"
                    partnerLink="DeltaAirlines"
                    portType="aln:FlightAvailabilityPT"
                    operation="FlightAvailability"
                    inputVariable="FlightDetails" />

            <receive name="DeltaAirlinesCallback"
                     partnerLink="DeltaAirlines"
                     portType="aln:FlightCallbackPT"
                     operation="FlightTicketCallback"
                     variable="FlightResponseDA" />

            <!-- Select the best offer and construct the TravelResponse -->
            <switch name="BestOfferSelect">
              <case condition="bpws:getVariableData('FlightResponseAA',
                                'confirmationData','/confirmationData/aln:Price')
                             &lt;= bpws:getVariableData('FlightResponseDA',
                                'confirmationData','/confirmationData/aln:Price')">

                 <!-- Select American Airlines -->
                 <assign>
                   <copy>
                     <from variable="FlightResponseAA" />
                     <to variable="TravelResponse" />
                   </copy>
                 </assign>
              </case>

              <otherwise>
                 <!-- Select Delta Airlines -->
                 <assign>
                   <copy>
                     <from variable="FlightResponseDA" />
                     <to variable="TravelResponse" />
                   </copy>
                 </assign>
              </otherwise>
            </switch>

          </flow>

          <!-- Make a callback to the client -->
          <invoke name="ClientCallback"
                  partnerLink="client"
                  portType="trv:ClientCallbackPT"
                  operation="ClientCallback"
                  inputVariable="TravelResponse" />

       </sequence>

    </process>
```

Note that all activities gathered within `<flow>` will start concurrently, which is not what we want. We therefore use links to express dependencies. First we identify the dependencies:

- The input for the Employee web service (`EmployeeInput`) has to be prepared before the Employee web service can be invoked (`EmployeeTravelStatusSyncInv`).
- The invocation (`EmployeeTravelStatusSyncInv`) of the Employee web service has to be finished before the input for both airlines' web services can be prepared (`AirlinesInput`).

- The input for both airlines' web services has to be prepared (`AirlinesInput`) before the process can invoke the web services of both airlines (`AmericanAirlinesAsyncInv` and `DeltaAirlinesAsyncInv`).
- The invocation of the American Airlines web service (`AmericanAirlinesAsyncInv`) has to be finished before the callback can be received (`AmericanAirlinesCallback`).
- The invocation of the Delta Airlines web service (`DeltaAirlinesAsyncInv`) has to be finished before the callback can be received (`DeltaAirlinesCallback`).
- Both callbacks (from American and Delta Airlines: `AmericanAirlinesCallback` and `DeltaAirlinesCallback`) have to be received before the best offer can be selected (`BestOfferSelect`).

Let us now name the links. We will need the following eight links:

- The link from the `EmployeeInput` to `EmployeeTravelStatusSyncInv`
- The link from the `EmployeeTravelStatusSyncInv` to the `AirlinesInput` preparation
- Two links form the `AirlinesInput` preparation to `AmericanAirlinesAsyncInv` and `DeltaAirlinesAsyncInv`
- The link from `AmericanAirlinesAsyncInv` to the receive callback `AmericanAirlinesCallback`
- The link from `DeltaAirlinesAsyncInv` to the receive callback `DeltaAirlinesCallback`
- The link from `AmericanAirlinesCallback` to `BestOfferSelect`
- The link from `DeltaAirlinesCallback` to `BestOfferSelect`

We have to define the links within the `<flow>` activity, as shown in the code excerpt below:

```
<flow>

   <links>

     <link name="EmployeeInputToEmployeeTravelStatusSyncInv" />
     <link name="EmployeeTravelStatusSyncInvToAirlinesInput" />
     <link name="AirlinesInputToAmericanAirlinesAsyncInv" />
     <link name="AirlinesInputToDeltaAirlinesAsyncInv" />
     <link name="AmericanAirlinesAsyncInvToAmericanAirlinesCallback" />
     <link name="DeltaAirlinesAsyncInvToDeltaAirlinesCallback" />
     <link name="AmericanAirlinesCallbackToBestOfferSelect" />
     <link name="DeltaAirlinesCallbackToBestOfferSelect" />

   </links>
...
```

The dependency of links and activities is shown in the following activity diagram:

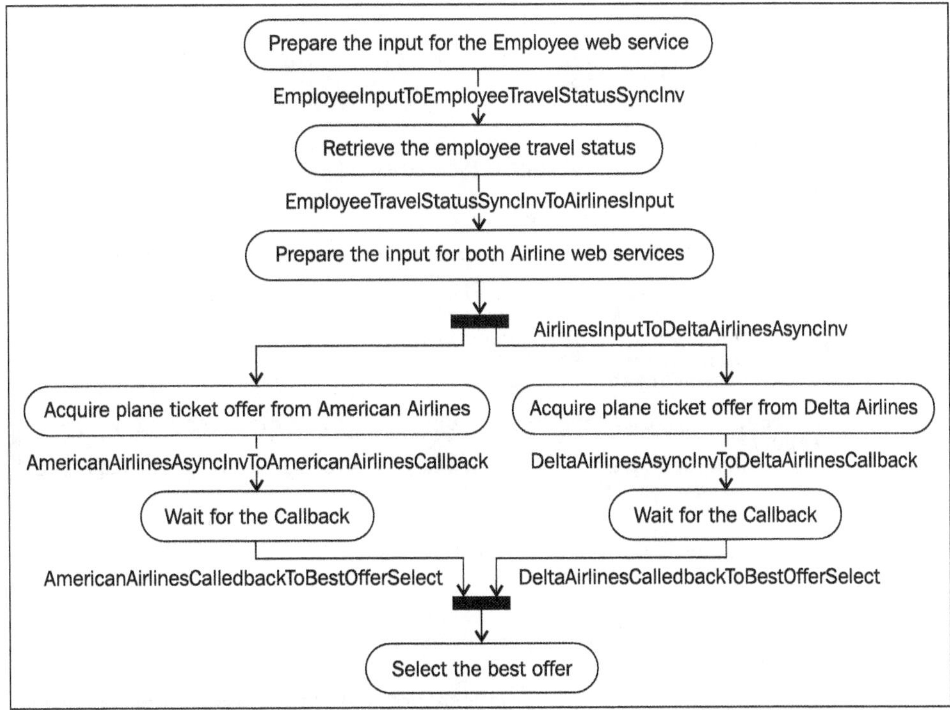

Let us now add the <source> and <target> elements to the BPEL process activities:

```
...
    <!-- Prepare the input for the Employee Travel Status Web Service -->
    <assign name="EmployeeInput">

      <source linkName="EmployeeInputToEmployeeTravelStatusSyncInv" />

      <copy>
        <from variable="TravelRequest" part="employee"/>
        <to variable="EmployeeTravelStatusRequest" part="employee"/>
      </copy>
    </assign>

    <!-- Synchronously invoke the Employee Travel Status Web Service -->
    <invoke name="EmployeeTravelStatusSyncInv"
            partnerLink="employeeTravelStatus"
            portType="emp:EmployeeTravelStatusPT"
            operation="EmployeeTravelStatus"
            inputVariable="EmployeeTravelStatusRequest"
            outputVariable="EmployeeTravelStatusResponse" >

      <target linkName="EmployeeInputToEmployeeTravelStatusSyncInv" />
      <source linkName="EmployeeTravelStatusSyncInvToAirlinesInput" />

    </invoke>

    <!-- Prepare the input for AA and DA -->
    <assign name="AirlinesInput">
```

```
    <target linkName="EmployeeTravelStatusSyncInvToAirlinesInput" />
    <source linkName="AirlinesInputToAmericanAirlinesAsyncInv" />
    <source linkName="AirlinesInputToDeltaAirlinesAsyncInv" />

    <copy>
      <from variable="TravelRequest" part="flightData"/>
      <to variable="FlightDetails" part="flightData"/>
    </copy>
    <copy>
      <from variable="EmployeeTravelStatusResponse" part="travelClass"/>
      <to variable="FlightDetails" part="travelClass"/>
    </copy>
  </assign>

  <!-- Async invoke of the AA web service and wait for the callback -->

  <invoke name="AmericanAirlinesAsyncInv"
          partnerLink="AmericanAirlines"
          portType="aln:FlightAvailabilityPT"
          operation="FlightAvailability"
          inputVariable="FlightDetails" >

    <target linkName="AirlinesInputToAmericanAirlinesAsyncInv" />
    <source
        linkName="AmericanAirlinesAsyncInvToAmericanAirlinesCallback" />

  </invoke>

  <receive name="AmericanAirlinesCallback"
           partnerLink="AmericanAirlines"
           portType="aln:FlightCallbackPT"
           operation="FlightTicketCallback"
           variable="FlightResponseAA" >

    <target
        linkName="AmericanAirlinesAsyncInvToAmericanAirlinesCallback" />
    <source linkName="AmericanAirlinesCallbackToBestOfferSelect" />

  </receive>

  <!-- Async invoke of the DA web service and wait for the callback -->

  <invoke name="DeltaAirlinesAsyncInv"
          partnerLink="DeltaAirlines"
          portType="aln:FlightAvailabilityPT"
          operation="FlightAvailability"
          inputVariable="FlightDetails" >

    <target linkName="AirlinesInputToDeltaAirlinesAsyncInv" />
    <source linkName="DeltaAirlinesAsyncInvToDeltaAirlinesCallback" />

  </invoke>

  <receive name="DeltaAirlinesCallback"
           partnerLink="DeltaAirlines"
           portType="aln:FlightCallbackPT"
           operation="FlightTicketCallback"
           variable="FlightResponseDA" >

    <target linkName="DeltaAirlinesAsyncInvToDeltaAirlinesCallback" />
    <source linkName="DeltaAirlinesCallbackToBestOfferSelect" />

  </receive>

  <!-- Select the best offer and construct the TravelResponse -->
```

```
<switch name="BestOfferSelect">

  <target linkName="AmericanAirlinesCallbackToBestOfferSelect" />
  <target linkName="DeltaAirlinesCallbackToBestOfferSelect" />

  <case condition="bpws:getVariableData('FlightResponseAA',
                'confirmationData','/confirmationData/Price')
              &lt;= bpws:getVariableData('FlightResponseDA',
                'confirmationData','/confirmationData/Price')">

     <!-- Select American Airlines -->
     <assign>
       <copy>
         <from variable="FlightResponseAA" />
         <to variable="TravelResponse" />
       </copy>
     </assign>
  </case>

  <otherwise>
     <!-- Select Delta Airlines -->
     <assign>
       <copy>
         <from variable="FlightResponseDA" />
         <to variable="TravelResponse" />
       </copy>
     </assign>
  </otherwise>
</switch>

</flow>
```

With this we have defined synchronization dependencies between activities. Note that according to the BPEL specification, every link within the <flow> activity must have exactly one activity within the flow as its source and exactly one activity within the flow as its target. This prevents us from using the same link as the source or target of two activities.

Transition Conditions

A <source> element specifies that a certain activity defines an outgoing link. When BPEL processes are executed, outgoing links are evaluated after the activity has finished. Each outgoing link can have a positive or negative status. This status is important when the decision is made to start the linked activity (denoted with <target>).

In our example, the `AmericanAirlinesCallback` <receive> activity defines an outgoing link `AmericanAirlinesCallbackToBestOfferSelect`. This link is the incoming link of the `BestOfferSelect` <switch> activity. The `BestOfferSelect` <switch> activity has another incoming link, `DeltaAirlinesCallbackToBestOfferSelect`, which is the outgoing link of the `DeltaAirlinesCallback` <receive> activity.

After the `AmericanAirlinesCallback` <receive> activity has finished, the outgoing `AmericanAirlinesCallbackToBestOfferSelect` link is evaluated. More precisely, the `transitionCondition` attribute of the outgoing link is evaluated. If the `transitionCondition` is evaluated to `true`, the link status is positive. Otherwise it is negative.

We have already mentioned that the <source> element has an optional attribute called `transitionCondition`. We have also mentioned that if the attribute is omitted, a default value of `true` is used. In our previous example, therefore, the outgoing link status was always `true`.

Let's now modify the example and explicitly add the transition condition. The outgoing link will be positive only if the flight ticket is approved. This is signaled using the `Approved` element of the `FlightConfirmationType` complex type, which is the `confirmationData` part of the `TravelResponseMessage` message, used for the `FlightResponseAA` and `FlightResponseDA` variables (see the previous chapter for corresponding WSDL definitions).

We will use the `getVariableData` function and extract the `Approved` element from the `confirmationData` part of the message stored in the `FlightResponseAA` variable. The code is shown below:

```
...
<!-- Receive the callback -->
<receive name="AmericanAirlinesCallback"
         partnerLink="AmericanAirlines"
         portType="aln:FlightCallbackPT"
         operation="FlightTicketCallback"
         variable="FlightResponseAA" >

  <target
      linkName="AmericanAirlinesAsyncInvToAmericanAirlinesCallback" />
  <source linkName="AmericanAirlinesCallbackToBestOfferSelect"
          transitionCondition="bpws:getVariableData(
                              'FlightResponseAA',
                              'confirmationData',
                              '/confirmationData/aln:Approved')='true'" />
</receive>
...
```

We will do the same for the `DeltaAirlinesCallback` `<receive>` activity:

```
...
<!-- Receive the callback -->
<receive name="DeltaAirlinesCallback"
         partnerLink="DeltaAirlines"
         portType="aln:FlightCallbackPT"
         operation="FlightTicketCallback"
         variable="FlightResponseDA" >

  <target linkName="DeltaAirlinesAsyncInvToDeltaAirlinesCallback" />
  <source linkName="DeltaAirlinesCallbackToBestOfferSelect"
          transitionCondition="bpws:getVariableData(
                              'FlightResponseDA',
                              'confirmationData',
                              '/confirmationData/aln:Approved')='true'" />
</receive>
...
```

Both outgoing links are now evaluated using the transition conditions and statuses can be determined.

Join Conditions and Link Status

The `AmericanAirlinesCallbackToBestOfferSelect` and the `DeltaAirlinesCallbackToBestOfferSelect` are the incoming links for the `BestOfferSelect` `<switch>` activity. In order to start the `BestOfferSelect` activity:

- The status of both incoming links has to be determined. As we already know, the status is determined using the `transitionCondition` expression.
- The join condition for the `BestOfferSelect` activity has to be evaluated.

The join condition is specified using the standard attribute called `joinCondition`. This attribute may be specified for each activity that is the target of a link (has at least one incoming link). If no `joinCondition` is specified, the default (for the default expression language XPath 1.0) is the logical disjunction (logical `or`) of the link status of all incoming links of this activity. In other words, if the `joinCondition` is not explicitly defined, all incoming link statuses are evaluated and the status of at least one incoming link has to be positive. The consequence of evaluating all incoming link statuses is the synchronization of all incoming activities.

In our example, the default (implicit) join condition for the `BestOfferSelect` is therefore a disjunction of both incoming link statuses, the `AmericanAirlinesCallbackToBestOfferSelect` and the `DeltaAirlinesCallbackToBestOfferSelect`. The join condition will be evaluated to `true` if at least one of the airlines has approved the flight tickets. Please notice that the incoming link statuses of both links will be evaluated prior the decision.

Sometimes the default disjunction will not fit our needs and we will want to define our own join condition. To do this we will use the `joinCondition` attribute. We have to specify this attribute for the target link activity. In our example we would define the `joinCondition` for the `BestOfferSelect` `<switch>` activity.

For the `joinCondition` we can specify any valid Boolean expression using the selected expression language (the default is XPath 1.0). Often we will also want to check the status of the incoming links. For these purposes BPEL provides a special function called `getLinkStatus`. This function is defined in the standard BPEL namespace `http://schemas.xmlsoap.org/ws/2003/03/business-process/`. The syntax is straightforward as we only have to provide the name of the incoming link as the parameter. The function returns `true` if the status of the link is positive and `false` if the status of the link is negative. This function can be used only in join conditions:

```
getLinkStatus ( 'link-name' )
```

Suppose instead of the disjunction of link statuses we would rather use a conjunction. Then we would define the following `joinCondition`:

```
...
<!-- Select the best offer and construct the TravelResponse -->
<switch name="BestOfferSelect"
        joinCondition="bpws:getLinkStatus(
                            'AmericanAirlinesCallbackToBestOfferSelect')
                            and
                            bpws:getLinkStatus(
                            'DeltaAirlinesCallbackToBestOfferSelect')" >
...
```

Join Failures

Join conditions are evaluated before the activity is started. In our example the join condition would be evaluated to `true` only if both link statuses (`AmericanAirlinesCallbackToBestOfferSelect` and `DeltaAirlinesCallbackToBestOfferSelect`) are positive. Positive join condition is required for starting the activity.

If a join condition evaluates to `false`, a standard `joinFailure` fault is thrown. A `joinFailure` can be thrown even if a join condition is not explicitly specified. In our previous example (before explicitly specifying the join condition) the default join condition would be used and would be evaluated to `false` if both link statuses were negative. This would be the case if neither American nor Delta Airlines would approve the flight ticket.

Suppressing Join Failures

Sometimes it would be more useful if instead of throwing a `joinFailure` fault the activity would simply not be performed without any fault thrown. BPEL provides an attribute through which we can express this behavior. The attribute is called `suppressJoinFailure` and is a *standard attribute* that can be associated with each activity (basic or structured). The value of the attribute can be either `yes` or `no`. The default is `no`.

In our example we could suppress join failure for the `BestOfferSelect` `<switch>` activity as shown below:

```
...
<!-- Select the best offer and construct the TravelResponse -->
<switch name="BestOfferSelect"
        joinCondition="bpws:getLinkStatus(
                          'AmericanAirlinesCallbackToBestOfferSelect')
                          and
                          bpws:getLinkStatus(
                          'DeltaAirlinesCallbackToBestOfferSelect')"

        suppressJoinFailure="yes" >
...
```

This means that if even one link status is negative, the activity will not be performed and no fault will be thrown—in other words the activity would be silently skipped. Skipping the activity is equivalent to catching the fault locally with an `<empty>` fault handler.

The consequence of skipping an activity is that outgoing links become negative. This way the next activity figures out that the previous activity has been skipped. In our example, the `BestOfferSelect` activity does not have outgoing links.

The default value of the `suppressJoinFailure` attribute is `no`. This is because in simple scenarios without complex graphs such behavior is preferred. In simple scenarios, links without transition conditions are often used. Here the developers often do not think about join conditions. Suppressing join failures would lead to unexpected behavior where activities would be skipped.

In complex scenarios with networks of links, the suppression of join failures can be desirable. If such behavior is desirable for the whole BPEL process, we can set the `suppressJoinFailure` attribute to `yes` in the first process element (often a `<sequence>`). Skipping activities with join conditions evaluated to false and setting the outgoing link statuses to negative is called **dead-path-elimination**. The reason is that in complex networks of links with transition conditions such behavior results in propagating the negative link status along entire paths until a join condition is reached that evaluates to `true`.

With this we have concluded our discussion on concurrent activities, links, and transition conditions. In the next section, we discuss dynamic partner links.

Dynamic Partner Links

So far we have discussed BPEL processes where all partner links have been defined at the design time and related to actual web services. We have used a single partner link for each web service we have communicated with.

In an advanced BPEL process we might want to define the partner link endpoint references at run time. This means that the BPEL process will dynamically determine which actual web service it will use for a certain invocation, based on the variable content. This is particularly useful in scenarios where the BPEL process communicates with several web services that have the same WSDL interface. This has been the case for our travel process example where American and Delta Airline web services shared the same interface.

To understand how we can define partner link endpoint references dynamically at run time, let us look at how endpoint references are represented in BPEL. BPEL uses endpoint references as defined by the WS-Addressing. For each BPEL process instance and for each partner role in a partner link a unique endpoint reference is assigned. We already know that this assignment can take place at deployment or at run time. To make such an assignment at run time we use the `<assign>` activity. There are several ways in which we can use this. We can copy from one partner link to another using the following syntax:

```
<assign>
    <copy>

      <from partnerLink="name" endpointReference="myRole|partnerRole"/>
      <to partnerLink="name"/>

    </copy>
</assign>
```

In the `<from>` activity we have to specify the endpoint role `myRole` or `partnerRole`, while in the `<to>` activity we always copy to the `partnerRole`. We can also copy a partner link to a variable:

```
<assign>
    <copy>

      <from partnerLink="name" endpointReference="myRole|partnerRole"/>
      <to variable="varName"/>

    </copy>
</assign>
```

The most interesting, however, is to copy a variable, expression, or XML literal to a partner link. This way we can store the partner link endpoint reference in a variable and copy it to the partner link at run time, thus selecting the service, which will be invoked dynamically. The syntax for copying a variable to partner link is shown below:

```
<assign>
    <copy>

      <from variable="varNname"/>
      <to partnerLink="name"/>

    </copy>
</assign>
```

The partner link endpoint reference in BPEL is represented as the `wsa:EndpointReference` XML element defined by the WS-Addressing. The `wsa` namespace URL is `http://schemas.xmlsoap.org/`

ws/2003/03/addressing. The wsa:EndpointReference element is of type wsa:EndpointReferenceType and has the following structure:

```
<EndpointReference xmlns="http://schemas.xmlsoap.org/ws/2003/03/addressing">

  <Address>ServiceURL</Address>
  <ReferenceProperties>...</ReferenceProperties>          <!-- optional -->
  <PortType>PortTypeName</PortType>                       <!-- optional -->
  <ServiceName PortName="...">ServiceName</ServiceName>   <!-- optional -->

</EndpointReference>
```

We can see that the endpoint reference <Address> is the only required element. The <Address> should include a valid URL of the partner link service.

To dynamically assign an endpoint reference to a partner link we have to declare a variable of element type wsa:EndpointReference and copy it to the partner link. Alternatively we can hard-code the address into the BPEL process and copy the XML literal to the partner link. This is shown in the following example. It is assumed that a service is available on the specified URL:

```
<assign>
    <copy>

      <from>
        <EndpointReference
            xmlns="http://schemas.xmlsoap.org/ws/2003/03/addressing">
          <Address>
            http://localhost:9700/orabpel/default/AmericanAirline
          </Address>
        </EndpointReference>
      </from>
      <to partnerLink="Airline"/>

    </copy>
</assign>
```

With this we have concluded the discussion on dynamic partner links. Please refer to Chapter 6 for a working demo. In the next section, we discuss abstract business processes.

Abstract Business Processes

Although the BPEL name suggests that this is a language for specifying executable business processes, BPEL supports both executable business processes and abstract business processes. Abstract business processes specify public message exchange between parties only.

The objective of abstract business processes in BPEL is to specify only the externally observable aspects of process behavior (often also called public process behavior) without the exact details of how the process executes. Abstract processes are not executable. An abstract business process should provide a complete description of external behavior relevant to a partner or several partners it interacts with.

The description of the externally observable behavior of a business process may be related to a single web service or a set of web services. It might also describe the behavior of a participant in a business process. In the later case the abstract processes of all partners must be coupled together, usually using a separate global protocol structure description.

We will define abstract processes mainly for two scenarios. First, with an abstract process we can describe the behavior of a web service even though we do not know exactly in which business process it will take part. In this scenario we will use partner links with myRole attributes only. With such an abstract process we can provide a web service behavioral description that does not place any requirements on the partners except that they respect the behavior of the web service.

Second, we can use an abstract process to define collaboration protocols among multiple parties and precisely describe the external behavior of each party. Such abstract processes will usually be defined by large enterprises to define protocols for their partners, or by vertical standards organizations such as RosettaNet, to define business protocols for their domains.

Because abstract processes are not executable, the question is: What are they useful for? The most common scenario is to use abstract processes as a template to define executable processes. Abstract processes can be used to replace sets of rules usually expressed in natural language, which is often ambiguous. This reduces misunderstandings and errors. We also expect tools to generate abstract processes for partner web services based on underlying executable processes.

Abstract processes must specify the abstractProcess attribute of the <process> tag. This attribute should have the value yes:

```
<process name="AbstractBusinessTravelProcess"
         abstractProcess="yes" ... >
   ...
</process>
```

Because abstract processes do not specify the exact process implementation (and are thus not executable), they differ from executable processes in several syntactical details. On one hand, they are not allowed to use certain BPEL constructs. On the other hand, some BPEL constructs can only be used in abstract processes. We will list the most important differences, starting with the functionality not allowed in abstract processes:

- The function getVariableData cannot be used.
- The assignment activity has a special variant that cannot be used in abstract processes. This is the variant where we specify the variable, part, and query expression.
- There is no checking for conflicting receives in abstract processes.
- The <terminate> activity cannot be used.

Important functionality allowed only in abstract processes is:

- The inputVariable and outputVariable attributes for the <invoke> activity and the input attribute for the <receive> and <reply> activities are optional.
- The inputVariable attribute of the <onMessage> activity is optional.
- Variables do not have to be initialized before they are used.
- In abstract processes the type checking is not strictly enforced.
- Property aliases can be used for addressing message parts and locations.
- Abstract processes allow opaque values to be assigned to variables based on non-deterministic choice.

Abstract processes follow the choreography approach of web services composition. However, at the time of writing this book, it seemed that in the majority of cases, BPEL will be used for executable processes.

Model Driven Approach: Generating BPEL from UML Activity Diagrams

Through the chapter we have seen that BPEL is a high-level language for specifying business processes. Because business processes are at such a high level, it is reasonable to think about defining process models using a modeling language and transforming these models to the BPEL code automatically. This is similar to the Model Driven Architecture (MDA) developed by the Object Management Group (OMG). The main objective of MDA is to raise the level of abstraction of development. Business processes are a perfect candidate for this approach.

The MDA approach is not to provide a simple graphical notation and a tool that enables developers to graphically build BPEL processes. The MDA approach is really about:

- Defining a platform-independent model (PIM) of the business process
- Defining exact rules that allow automatic mapping of the PIM to platform-specific models (PSM); these mappings can be done by a tool

In other words, this means that an independent business protocol model could be automatically mapped to several business process specification languages, BPEL being one of them. Such an approach would raise the abstraction level even further and make business process modeling independent of the underlying execution language, thus stimulating companies to invest more in business process modeling.

The fact that the described approach is not a dream has been demonstrated by researchers at IBM/Rational. They have based business process model development on the Unified Modeling Language (UML) and have defined UML extensions (a UML profile) for automated business processes. Based on the profile they have also developed a tool that generates BPEL process definitions and the corresponding WSDL descriptions based on the UML activity diagrams. This tool and the UML profile are part of the IBM Emerging Technologies Toolkit version (ETTK), which can be downloaded from alphaWorks: `http://www.alphaworks.ibm.com/tech/ettk`.

Conclusion

We have seen that BPEL is an efficient language for describing business processes. It provides support for the complexities of real-world business process implementations but is still relatively easy to learn and use. In this chapter we have become familiar with the advanced concepts of BPEL, such as loops, process termination, delays, and deadline and duration expressions. We have addressed fault handling, which is a very important aspect of each business process. Particularly in BPEL processes, which use loosely coupled web services for partner operations, faults can occur quite often. We have discussed scopes, which enable us to break the process into several parts. Each part or scope can have its own variables, correlation sets, fault handlers, compensation handlers, and event handlers. In addition scopes can provide concurrency control through serialization.

Another very important aspect of business processes is compensation. In business processes consistency has to be preserved even if a process is abandoned. Because business processes are often long running and span several partners the usage of ACID transactions is not reasonable. BPEL therefore supports the concept of compensation. The goal of compensation is to reverse the effects of previous activities that have been carried out as part of a business process that is being abandoned. We have become familiar with compensation handlers and how to invoke them. Next we have discussed events and have seen that a business process has to react on message events, which happen when an operation is invoked on the process, and on alarm events, which can occur at a specific time or after certain duration.

We have also addressed complex business processes with many concurrent activities and have seen that BPEL provides links, which enable concurrency control and synchronization using source and target links. Then we have discussed transition and join conditions, and link statuses. We have seen why and when join failures are thrown and how to eliminate dead paths using join failure suppression.

We have discussed the business process lifecycle and process instances and have focused on correlation of messages, another important aspect of BPEL processes. Correlation uses correlation sets to associate messages with business process instances, and is related to message properties. Message properties have global significance in business processes and are mapped to multiple messages. We have become familiar with dynamic partner links. Finally we have discussed abstract business protocols and mentioned the model-driven approach to BPEL process definition. With this we have covered all the advanced aspects of BPEL. The coming chapters discuss important BPEL servers.

5

Oracle BPEL Process Manager and BPEL Designer: Overview

In this chapter, we will get familiar with the Oracle BPEL Process Manager 10g Release 2, a server for deployment, execution, and management of business processes defined in BPEL. Oracle BPEL Process Manager offers several features that make it one of the most powerful BPEL servers at the time of writing this book. We will look at the BPEL Server, command-prompt utilities, and the BPEL Console. We will also look at the BPEL Designer, an integrated graphical development environment. BPEL Designer is available integrated into JDeveloper or as an Eclipse plug-in. BPEL Designer enables BPEL process development using a graphical editor instead of writing BPEL code by hand. It supports debugging, provides several wizards, enables automatic deployment of BPEL processes, and eases the development and maintenance of BPEL processes considerably.

In this chapter, we will discuss the following:

- Architecture of the BPEL Process Manager
- Major features
- Process deployment
- Management and debugging of processes with the BPEL Console
- Graphical development with JDeveloper BPEL Designer
- Graphical development with Eclipse BPEL Designer

Overview and Architecture

The Oracle BPEL Process Manager is a run-time environment for BPEL processes. BPEL Process Manager 10g Release 2 (10.1.2) fully supports BPEL version 1.1 and provides additional tools for deployment, monitoring, and management of BPEL processes. At the time of writing this book, Oracle BPEL Process Manager is one of the most complete BPEL servers available.

BPEL Process Manager has been developed in Java and runs on a Java Enterprise Edition-compliant application server, for example, the Oracle Application Server 10g or OC4J (Oracle Containers for Java). Oracle also provides versions for the open-source JBoss and for the BEA WebLogic Server. With manual installation, Oracle BPEL Process Manager can also be used with IBM and Sun application servers.

Let us look at the architecture of the BPEL Process Manager, shown in the following figure:

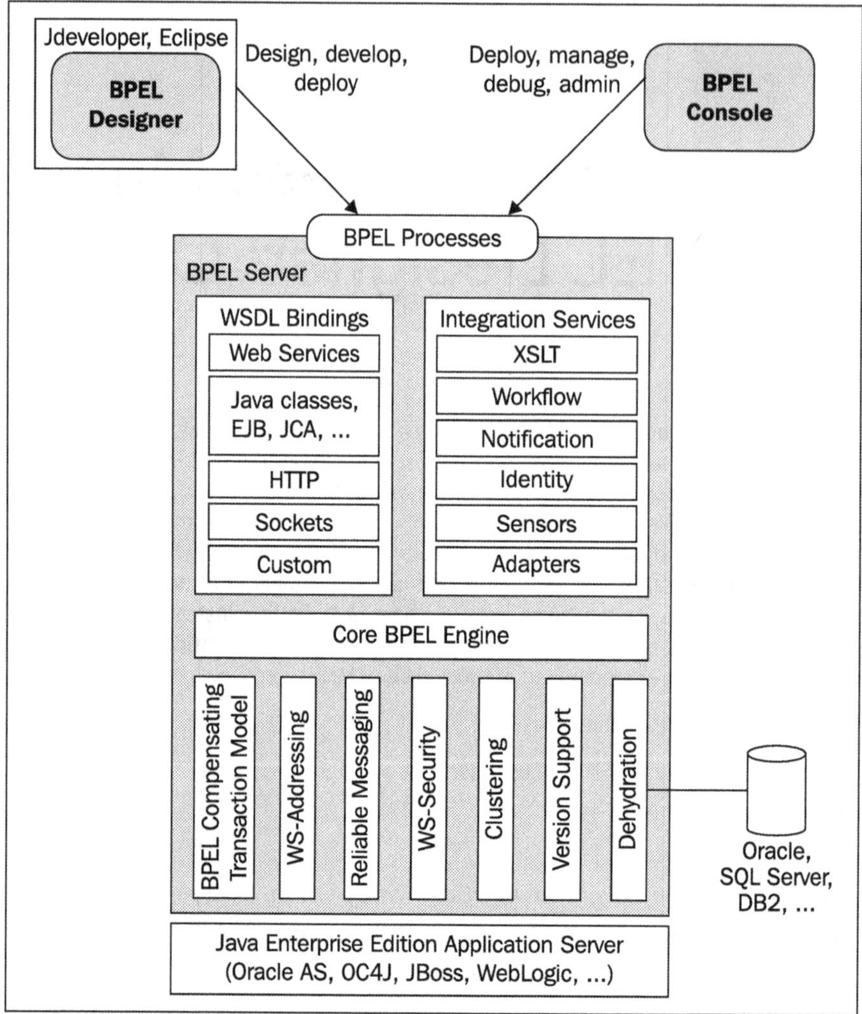

The Oracle BPEL Process Manager has four major parts:

- BPEL Server
- BPEL Console
- BPEL Designer (JDeveloper or Eclipse)
- Database

BPEL Server

BPEL Server runs in a Java Enterprise Edition-compliant application server. It has the following main parts:

- Core BPEL engine
- WSDL bindings
- Integration services

Core BPEL Engine

The core BPEL engine is the run-time environment where BPEL processes are deployed and executed. In addition to full BPEL 1.1 support, this engine provides support for key web services orchestration stack technologies, particularly WS-Addressing, WS Reliable Messaging, WS-Security, and the BPEL compensating transaction model.

The BPEL engine also provides support for version control. This enables development of several versions of a business process, which can be deployed side by side. This feature is important in real-world scenarios because business processes evolve over time. Having effective versioning support simplifies the management.

Another very important feature is **dehydration**. In previous chapters, we have explained that business processes can be long running because the involved partners might not be able to react instantly to the requests. This happens particularly in asynchronous scenarios where a business process invokes a partner web service (using the `<invoke>` activity) and then waits for the response (using the `<receive>` or `<pick>` activities). While waiting for the response the Oracle engine can store the process (and its state) in the database, thus freeing up server resources. This is called dehydration. When the engine receives the response it first restores the process with its state from the database (**hydration**) and then continues with the execution of the process. In real-world scenarios where many business processes might be running side by side, the dehydration capability is important as it reduces the demands on hardware performance.

Oracle BPEL engine also provides support for clustering. **Clustering** increases server reliability because fail-over can be configured on the engine. Clustering also improves scalability with load balancing. These features are very important in real-world usage of the product.

WSDL Bindings

The WSDL binding framework is responsible for communication with the BPEL processes deployed on the server. This includes clients that would like to access a BPEL process and BPEL processes that would like to access other web services (partner links). Although BPEL specification talks only about web services, Oracle BPEL Process Manager enables connectivity using protocols other than SOAP. This is particularly useful in real-world usage scenarios where business processes often have to connect to existing applications or systems. Using the WSDL binding framework, the reach of BPEL is extended to these systems without the need to convert them to web services.

Of particular interest here is connectivity to Java EE artifacts, such as EJBs (Enterprise Java Beans), RMI (Remote Method Invocation), JMS (Java Message Service), JCA (Java Connector

Architecture), and also to email, HTTP GET and POST, and sockets. The integration is achieved through the **WSIF** (Web Services Invocation Framework). All this enables relatively easy and efficient integration of back-end systems, particularly existing and legacy systems, which cannot be simply exposed as web services. Through WSDL bindings BPEL Process Manager provides some features usually offered by ESB (for more ESB features please refer to Oracle Fusion).

Integration Services

Business processes described in BPEL communicate with web services and exchange XML documents. The integration services provide support for transformations (on these XML documents) that go beyond the support of XPath. Oracle BPEL Server provides support for XSLT (Extensible Stylesheet Language for Transformations) transformations and XSQL. It provides engines and the XSLT Mapper, which simplifies the development of stylesheets.

XSLT provides support for complex transformations of XML vocabularies and can be also used to transform XML to other markup formats such as HTML, WML, or VoiceXML for presentation purposes. For more information on XSLT please refer to `http://www.w3.org/TR/xslt`. XSQL, and XQuery, which can also be used, are XML query languages with functionality that goes beyond simple XPath queries. For more information on XSQL please refer to Oracle documentation. For more information on XQuery please refer to `http://www.w3.org/XML/Query`.

Through the Workflow service BPEL Server provides support for human interaction with BPEL process. Human interaction is often required in processes—typical examples include human reviews, confirmations, or decisions before carrying out further steps—but not covered by the BPEL specification. The Workflow service provides a WSDL interface through which human interaction is modeled as partner links. The Workflow service has augmented the User Task service, known from previous versions of BPEL Process Manager.

The Notification service provides a relatively easy-to-use interface through which BPEL processes can send notifications to clients using different (most asynchronous) channels, such as email, short message service (SMS), voice message, fax, etc. The Notification service has augmented the Mail and JMS services, known from previous versions of BPEL Process Manager.

The Identity service provides access to the application server security infrastructure through the web services layer and enables user authentication, authorization, and access to various used properties. The Notification, Workflow, and Identity services are often used together.

BPEL Server also provides **Sensors**, through which access to activities, variables, and faults is provided. These can be monitored during the execution of BPEL processes. Sensors can be useful for reporting, integration with other processes, and for debugging.

To integrate BPEL processes with access to files, FTP servers, database tables and queues, JMS, or Oracle Applications, BPEL Server provides support for technology adapters. Adapters provide access to these resources through WSDL interfaces. They are based on the JCA 1.5 resource adapters and on the WSIF.

BPEL Console

Through the BPEL Console we can deploy, manage, administer, and debug BPEL processes. The most important features of the BPEL Console include:

- Visual process flows
- Audit trails
- Debugging view of processes
- Process history
- Management of BPEL domains and their configuration

Oracle BPEL Console uses a web-based interface, which is basically a set of JSP (Java Server Pages) and servlets that call the BPEL Server API (in Java). Through the API we can extend the functionality of the console or even develop our own console if we need specific handling of BPEL processes.

BPEL Designer

BPEL Designer enables the development of BPEL processes in a graphical environment without having to write BPEL code by hand. Instead of writing code, we drag and drop activities to the process. We can add partner links and locate services. We can also use function and copy wizards, XPath expression builder, and XSLT mapper. BPEL Designer can deploy the developed processes directly to the BPEL Server. This eases the development and maintenance of BPEL processes considerably. BPEL Designer internally uses BPEL as its native format. Because it uses standard BPEL, processes developed by the BPEL Designer can be used with other BPEL servers (and vice-versa) as long as we do not use functionality specific to the Oracle product.

BPEL Designer is available in two versions. It is either integrated with JDeveloper (called JDeveloper BPEL Designer) or a plug-in for the Eclipse platform (Eclipse BPEL Designer). JDeveloper and Eclipse BPEL Designer offer comparable features. JDeveloper BPEL Designer, however, also provides support for some advanced Oracle features, such as sensors and adapters. We will discuss BPEL Designer later in this chapter.

Database

The database is used by BPEL Server to store the BPEL schemas and to provide support for additional features, particularly the dehydration, which stores the process state in the database. BPEL Process Manager provides support for different databases. Usually Oracle Database, or other production-quality DBMS systems such as IBM DB2 or Microsoft SQL Server will be used. The trial version, which can be downloaded from Oracle's website, comes bundled with Oracle Database Lite, which is not appropriate for production use as it offers poor performance and does not support all features.

Process Deployment Example

Let us now show how we deploy a BPEL process on the Oracle BPEL Server. We will assume that Oracle BPEL Process Manager has been successfully installed according to the installation instructions and that it uses the default port 9700. If another port has been selected during installation, the examples have to be modified accordingly.

We will use the Business Travel BPEL process example that we have developed in Chapters 3 and 4. The travel example is a simplified business process that selects the best airline ticket offer. To refresh our memory, let us have a look at the process activity diagram:

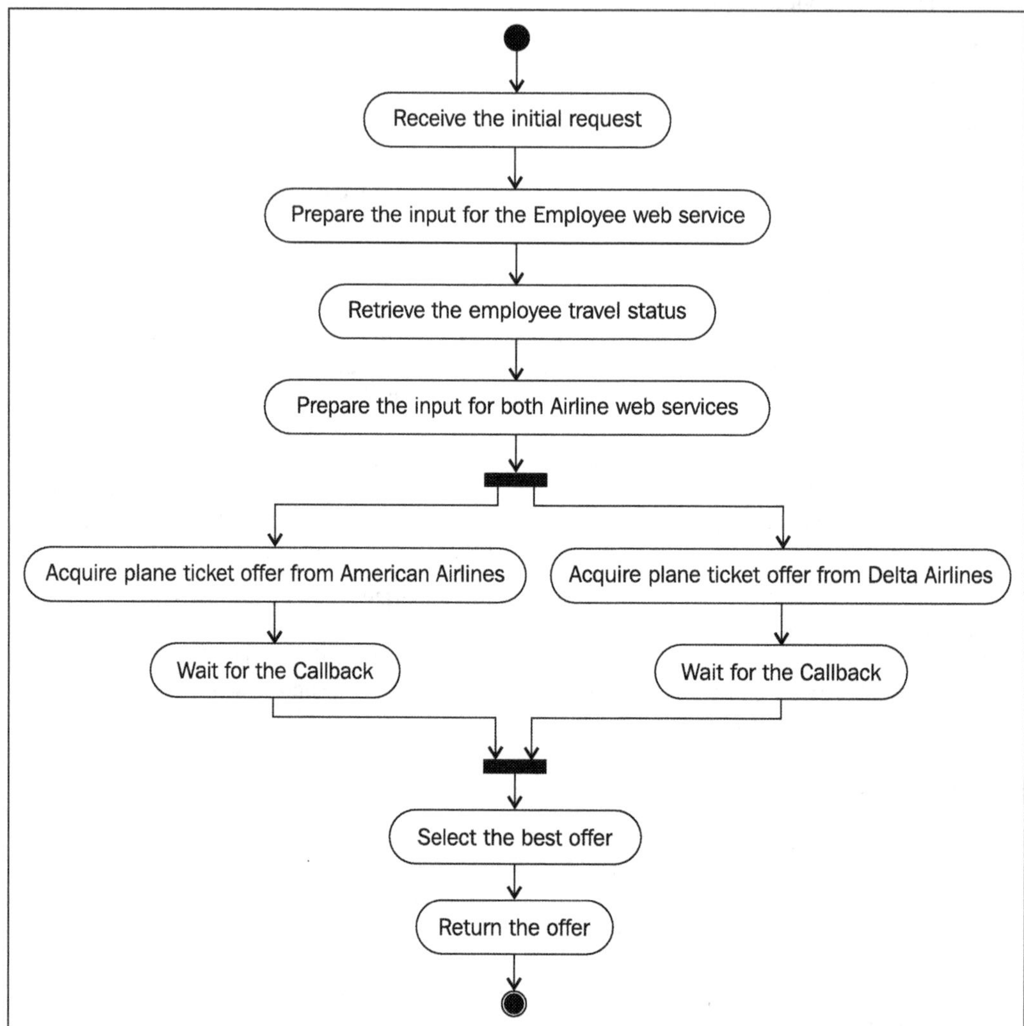

In the previous chapters we developed the BPEL code for the example; this consists of a `Travel.bpel` file with the source code and the `Travel.wsdl` file where the WSDL definitions are stored. We will not show the source of these files here as they have been already shown in previous chapters. They can also be downloaded from `http://www.packtpub.com`.

Process Descriptor

Each BPEL process we deploy to the Oracle BPEL Process Manager requires a process descriptor. This process descriptor is not covered by the BPEL standard and is specific to the BPEL server.

> The deployment process descriptor is the only part of the implementation of a process on a given platform that *must* be rewritten to run the process on a different BPEL server.

The Oracle process descriptor is an XML file specifying the following details about the BPEL process:

- BPEL source file name
- BPEL process name (ID)
- WSDL locations of all partner link web services
- Optional configuration properties

The default file name for the process descriptor is `bpel.xml`, but we can use any other name. Let us now write the process descriptor for our process. First, we have to specify the XML header and the `<BPELSuitcase>` root element. In the `<BPELProcess>` element we specify two attributes, `src`, which denotes the BPEL source file name (`Travel.bpel`), and ID (`id`), which denotes BPEL process name as shown in the BPEL Console (we will use the `TravelProcessCh5` ID):

```
<?xml version="1.0" encoding="UTF-8"?>

<BPELSuitcase>

  <BPELProcess src="Travel.bpel" id="TravelProcessCh5">
...
```

Next, we specify the partner link binding properties for the location of the WSDL for each partner link that we use in the process. In our travel example process we use the following partner links:

- `client`: Used for client interaction with the process
- `employeeTravelStatus`: The link to the Employee web service
- `AmericanAirlines`: The link to the American Airlines web service
- `DeltaAirlines`: The link to the Delta Airlines web service

The WSDL for the `client` partner link is stored locally in the `Travel.wsdl` file. For the location of the other three partner web services' WSDLs, we have to specify the corresponding URLs. Here we have provided simplified implementations of all three web services, which can also be downloaded and deployed on the Oracle BPEL Server. The rest of the process descriptor with the location of the WSDLs is shown below:

```
...
    <partnerLinkBindings>

      <partnerLinkBinding name="client">
        <property name="wsdlLocation">
          Travel.wsdl
        </property>
      </partnerLinkBinding>

      <partnerLinkBinding name="employeeTravelStatus">
        <property name="wsdlLocation">
          http://localhost:9700/orabpel/default/Employee/Employee?wsdl
        </property>
      </partnerLinkBinding>
```

```
    <partnerLinkBinding name="AmericanAirlines">
      <property name="wsdlLocation">
  http://localhost:9700/orabpel/default/AmericanAirline/AmericanAirline?wsdl
      </property>
    </partnerLinkBinding>

    <partnerLinkBinding name="DeltaAirlines">
      <property name="wsdlLocation">
        http://localhost:9700/orabpel/default/DeltaAirline/DeltaAirline?wsdl
      </property>
    </partnerLinkBinding>

  </partnerLinkBindings>
...
```

The only required partner link binding property is `wsdlLocation`. Optionally we can add other partner link binding properties. The most important ones are listed in the table below (for the complete list please refer to Oracle documentation):

Partner link binding property	Description
`wsdlRuntimeLocation`	Specifies the run-time WSDL location of the partner link services (if different from `wsdlLocation`).
`correlation`	Specifies the type of correlation used (correlation is discussed in Chapter 4): • `wsAddressing` for WS-Addressing • `correlationSet` for BPEL correlation sets
`timeout`	Specifies the timeout for partner link invocation calls.
`httpUsername` and `httpPassword`	Specifies the username and password for HTTP authentication.

Configuration Properties

Optionally we can add configuration properties to the deployment descriptor, such as introduction text outputted by the BPEL Console when starting the process and default input data. The introduction text should be included within the `<property>` element with the attribute `name` set to `testIntroduction`:

```
...
  <configurations>

    <property name="testIntroduction">
      The Business Travel Process example.
    </property>
...
```

To add the default input data (also optional) we have to define the `<property>` element with the attribute `name` set to `defaultInput` and provide the input XML message as `CDATA`:

```
...
    <property name="defaultInput">
      <![CDATA[
        <TravelRequest xmlns="http://packtpub.com/bpel/travel/">
          <employee xmlns="http://packtpub.com/service/employee/">
            <FirstName>Matjaz B.</FirstName>
            <LastName>Juric</LastName>
            <Departement>University</Departement>
          </employee>
          <flightData xmlns="http://packtpub.com/service/airline/">
            <OriginFrom>Ptuj</OriginFrom>
```

```
                <DestinationTo>London</DestinationTo>
                <DesiredDepartureDate>2004-04-20</DesiredDepartureDate>
                <DesiredReturnDate>2004-04-24</DesiredReturnDate>
              </flightData>
            </TravelRequest>
          ]]>
        </property>

      </configurations>
    </BPELProcess>
  </BPELSuitcase>
```

Other important optional configuration properties are listed in the table below (for the complete list please refer to Oracle documentation):

Configuration property	Description
`loadSchema`	If this is set to `False`, BPEL processes become typeless because XML schemas are not loaded. Default is `True`.
`relaxTypeChecking`	If this is set to `True`, BPEL compiler does not check types for compatibility in assigns. Default is `False`.
`xpathValidation`	If this is set to `False`, BPEL compiler does not validate XPath expressions. Default is `True`.
`relaxXPathQName`	If this is set to `True`, BPEL compiler does not check name spaces for steps in XPath expressions. Default is `False`.
`transaction`	If this is set to `participate`, faults not handled by fault handlers produce a rollback for transactions in which they are executed.

Setting the Environment

We are now ready to start the BPEL Process Manager. We can do this from the Start menu (if using Windows) or by executing the **`startOraBPEL`** script, which can be found in the `C:\OraBPELPM_1\integration\orabpel\bin` directory (assuming Oracle BPEL Process Manager has been installed in the default directory). It is recommended that we include this directory in the path for easy access.

Next, we will need a command prompt where we have to set the environment variables. We can select the Developer Prompt from the Start menu or execute the **obsetenv** script in the `C:\OraBPELPM_1\integration\orabpel\bin` directory. The script sets several environment variables—we list the most important here:

- `OB_HOME` specifies the path to the Oracle BPEL installation directory.
- `OB_PLATFORM` specifies the application server (`oc4j_10g` if using Oracle OC4J).
- `MY_CLASSPATH` and `MY_CLASSES_DIR` specify the class path for Oracle BPEL Server.
- `JAVA_HOME` points to the Java SDK home directory.
- `J2EE_APPLICATIONS` specifies the application server directory where J2EE applications can be deployed.

Setting the environment variables is essential for successful deployment of BPEL processes.

BPEL Compiler and Revision Numbers

After we have written the process descriptor and set the environment, we are ready to deploy the BPEL process. For this, Oracle BPEL Process Manager provides the **BPEL Complier**, which can be started with the **bpelc** command from the command line. **bpelc** compiles the BPEL process source files and creates the BPEL process archive JAR file. It can also automatically deploy the process to the Oracle BPEL Server. This is discussed in the next section.

The BPEL compiler has the following syntax:

```
> bpelc [options] process_descriptor_name.xml
```

The default for process_descriptor_name.xml is bpel.xml. The most important options are:

- -rev <revision_tag>: This specifies the revision (version) number for the deployed BPEL process.
- -force: This directs the compiler not to check the timestamps of the .bpel, .wsdl, and .xml files.

> Revision numbers are used to deploy different versions of the same BPEL process on the Oracle BPEL Process Manger and run them simultaneously.

Revision numbers are most useful in production environments, where it is more appropriate to deploy new version of a process under a new revision number than to override an existing revision number. In the latter case, all existing process instances get stalled and cannot be accessed anymore. If we use a new revision number, we can mark older process revisions as retired but retain access to already created instances. We will explain how to mark processes as retired later in this chapter.

We can use the following command to generate the BPEL process JAR archive with the revision number 1.0 for our travel example:

```
> bpelc -rev 1.0
```

This command generates the bpel_TravelProcessCh5_1.0.jar archive file, as shown:

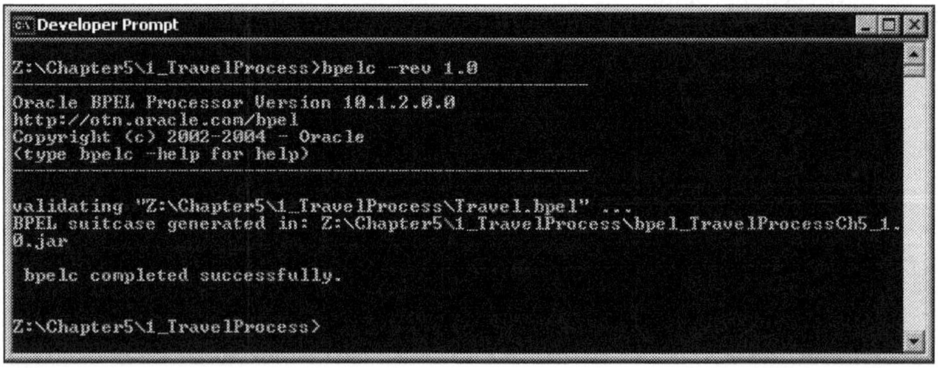

```
Developer Prompt
Z:\Chapter5\1_TravelProcess>bpelc -rev 1.0
Oracle BPEL Processor Version 10.1.2.0.0
http://otn.oracle.com/bpel
Copyright (c) 2002-2004 - Oracle
(type bpelc -help for help)

validating "Z:\Chapter5\1_TravelProcess\Travel.bpel" ...
BPEL suitcase generated in: Z:\Chapter5\1_TravelProcess\bpel_TravelProcessCh5_1.
0.jar
 bpelc completed successfully.

Z:\Chapter5\1_TravelProcess>
```

The generated archive includes the BPEL source and the related WSDL and XML files. It also includes the process model file (in our example called `TravelModel.xml`) which is a normalized BPEL representation with an added `id` for each activity.

Deployment and Domains

To deploy our travel process we have several options:

- Copy the BPEL archive to the server domain manually
- Use **`bpelc`** to deploy the process
- Use the **`obant`** utility to do the deployment
- Use the BPEL Console to deploy the BPEL process archive

Before we deploy, let's discuss the Oracle BPEL Server architecture. Each Oracle BPEL Server installation can be logically partitioned into several domains. The default domain is created automatically by the installation (called `default`). Additional domains can be created using the BPEL Console; this is discussed later in the chapter. The domains are located in the `C:\OraBPELPM_1\integration\orabpel\domains` directory.

To manually deploy a BPEL process we simply copy the JAR archive to the corresponding directory. In our case this is `C:\OraBPELPM_1\integration\orabpel\domains\default\deploy`. The BPEL Server will automatically pick up the process.

Using **`bpelc`** to deploy the process requires us to use the `-deploy <domain_id>` option, which directs the compiler to automatically deploy the archive to the specified domain. The domain to which the deployment is done must be accessible via the file system. To deploy our travel example using **`bpelc`** we need to use the following command:

```
> bpelc -rev 1.0 -deploy default
```

The following screenshot shows the output:

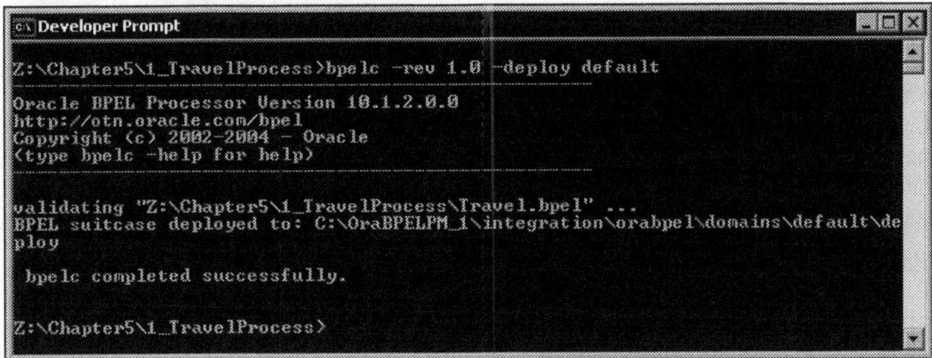

Ant Utility

The Oracle BPEL Process Manager provides the Ant utility called **`obant`**. This can be used to configure complex compilation and deployment scenarios. **`obant`** is just a wrapper around standard

Ant, which sets the environment and then invokes the standard Ant Java task. To use it we have to prepare the corresponding project file, usually called `build.xml`. The project file for our travel example process is shown below:

```
<?xml version="1.0"?>
<project name="TravelProcessCh5" default="main" basedir=".">

    <property name="deploy" value="default"/>
    <property name="rev" value="1.0"/>

    <target name="main">
        <bpelc home="${home}" rev="${rev}" deploy="${deploy}"/>
    </target>

</project>
```

For more information on Ant, visit `http://ant.apache.org/`.

To compile and deploy our BPEL process we simply start **obant** from the command line. The output is shown in the following screenshot:

```
Developer Prompt

Z:\Chapter5\1_TravelProcess>obant

Z:\Chapter5\1_TravelProcess>SETLOCAL
Buildfile: build.xml

main:
    [bpelc] validating "Z:\Chapter5\1_TravelProcess\Travel.bpel" ...
    [bpelc] BPEL suitcase deployed to: C:\OraBPELPM_1\integration\orabpel\domain
s\default\deploy

BUILD SUCCESSFUL
Total time: 9 seconds

Z:\Chapter5\1_TravelProcess>ENDLOCAL

Z:\Chapter5\1_TravelProcess>
```

Process Management with the BPEL Console

Now that we have successfully deployed a BPEL process on the Oracle BPEL Server, let's execute it. In Chapter 3 we mentioned that each BPEL process is a web service. Therefore, to start the BPEL process we need to invoke it just like any other web service. This requires writing a web services client based on the WSDL. Because web services are not bound to a particular platform or programming language, we can do this using most languages (Java, C#, VB.NET, Delphi, etc.), applications (SAP, Navision, even Microsoft Office), tools (XML Spy), or other BPEL processes.

In addition to these options, Oracle BPEL Process Manager provides a BPEL Console through which we can execute, monitor, manage, and debug BPEL processes on a BPEL Server domain. The BPEL Console is accessible at `http://localhost:9700/BPELConsole/`. Of course we can replace `localhost` with the valid computer name URL. Once we enter the domain password, we can start our travel process and create a new process instance by clicking the process name (TravelProcessCh5) on the BPEL Console dashboard, as shown in the following screenshot:

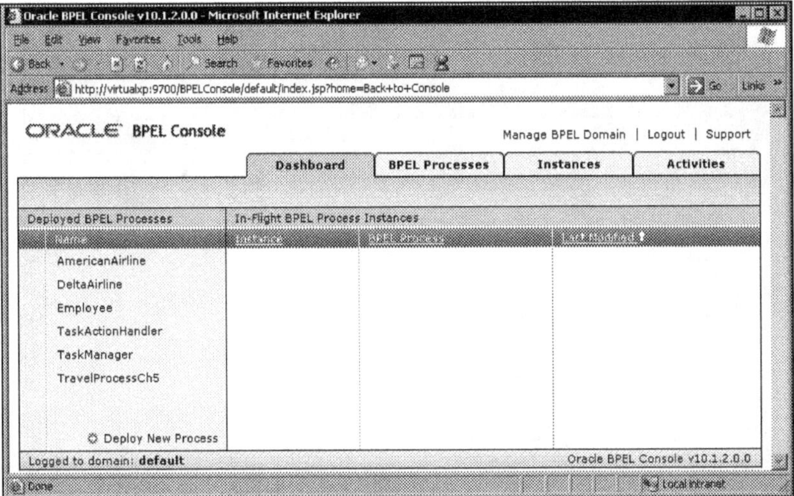

Note that in addition to the Travel Process, the Employee, American Airline, and Delta Airline web services have to be deployed as well. After clicking TravelProcessCh5 we have to enter the input XML message (the default from the process descriptor is shown) and click the Post XML Message button:

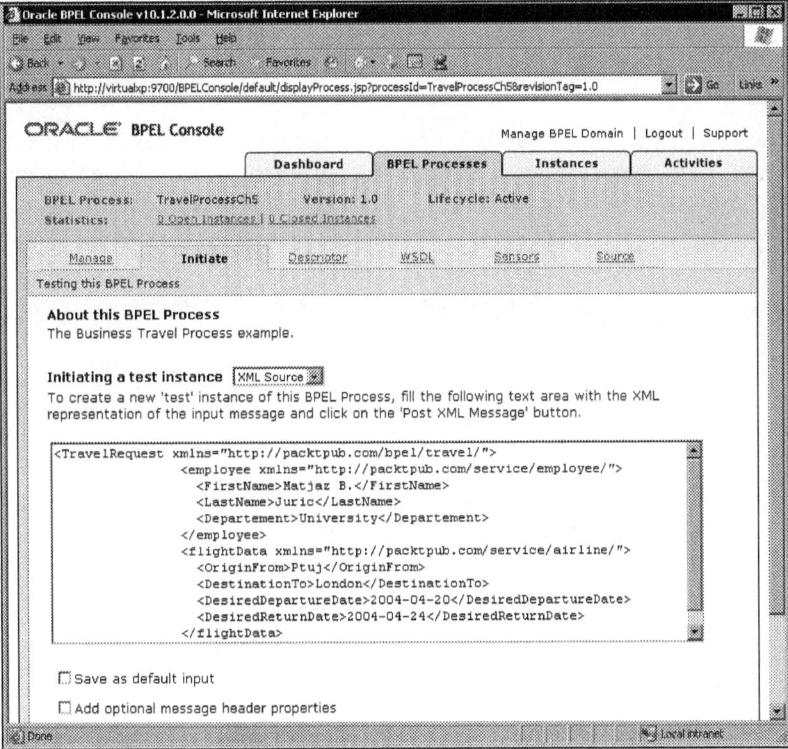

We can also switch to the HTML form and enter the necessary fields:

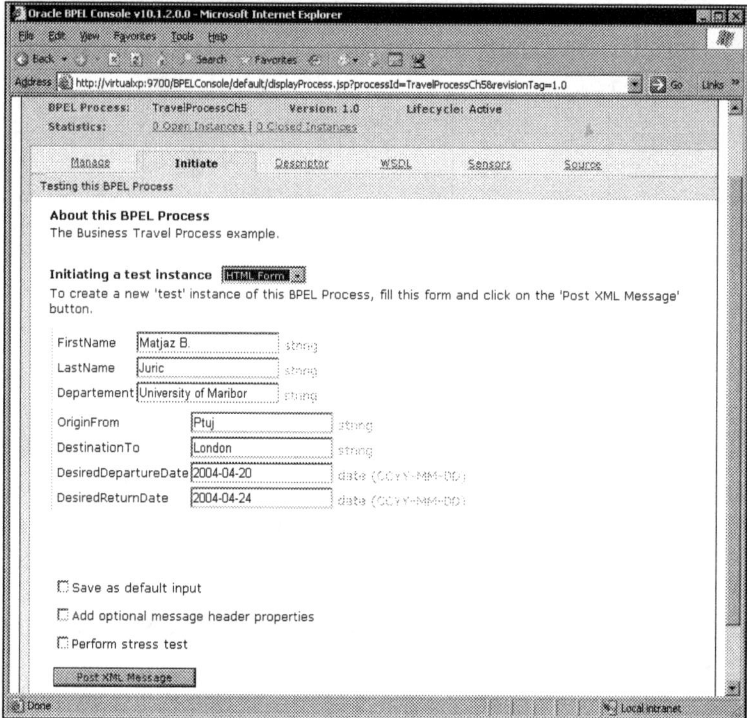

Next, we see a screen notifying us that the process instance is being processed asynchronously, because this is an asynchronous process. If this was a synchronous process, we would see the final result (returned through the `<reply>` activity) immediately. The screen is shown below:

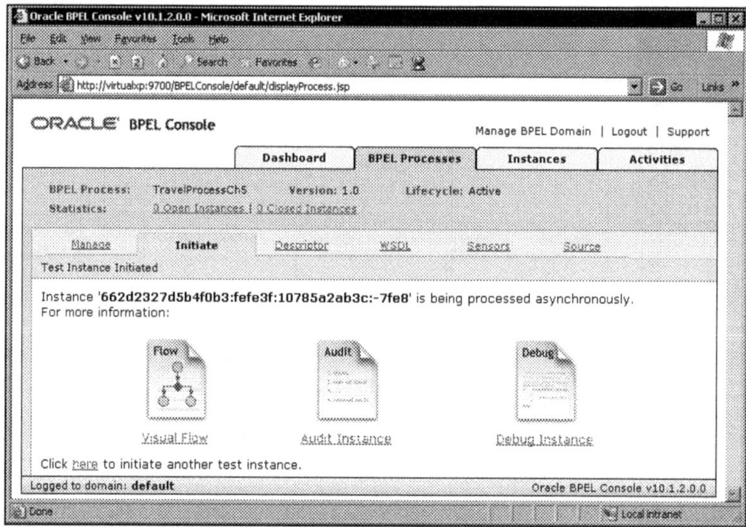

Visual Flow

In the next step, we can select the visual flow of the execution, instance auditing, or instance debugging. The visual flow of the instance graphically shows the execution of a BPEL process instance. We can monitor the execution of the process and its state (running, completed, canceled, or stale):

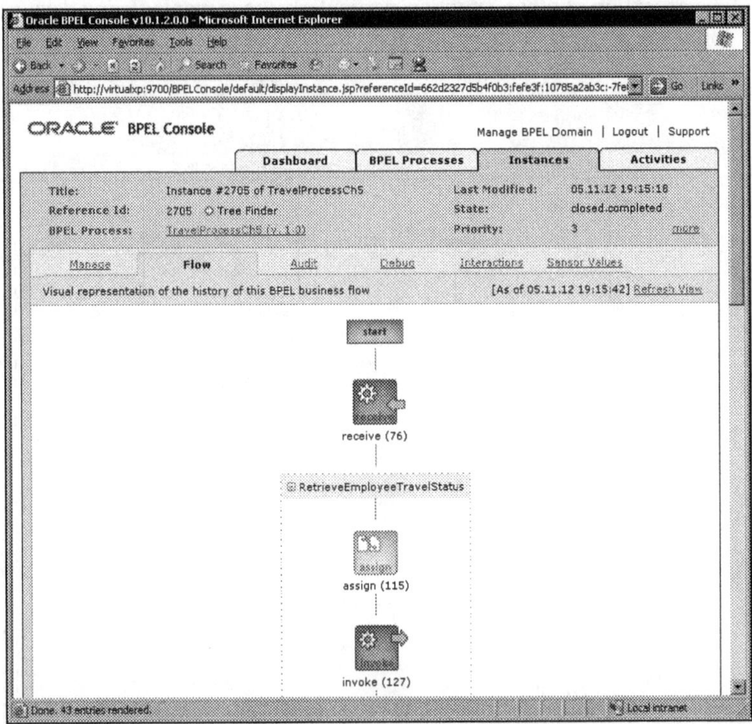

The important thing is that we can click on each activity symbol (such as `<receive>`, `<assign>`, etc.) and we will see the corresponding XML input and output. This enables us to verify the processing of each activity. Clicking on the first `<receive>` activity (client `TravelApproval`) would open this screen, showing the received message, `TravelRequest`:

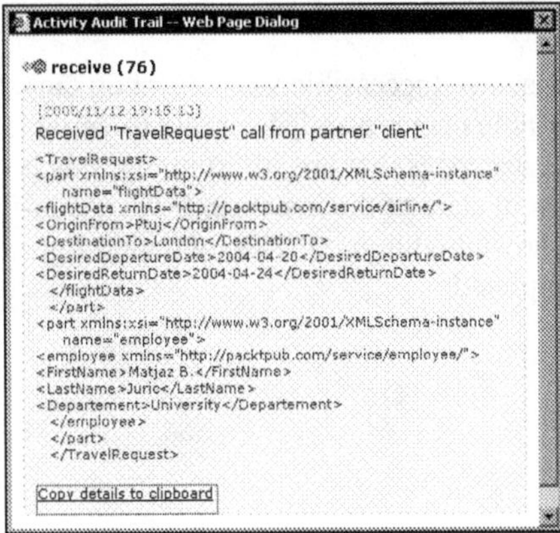

Instance Auditing

The audit view of the process instance, which we can activate by selecting the Audit tag, shows a complete BPEL process with the received and sent messages. Clicking on the More... link reveals the complete XML of messages exchanged. This view is useful for auditing the messages exchanged by the process and the execution of other activities, particularly those manipulating data, such as `<assign>`. The following screenshot shows the audit trail of our travel example process:

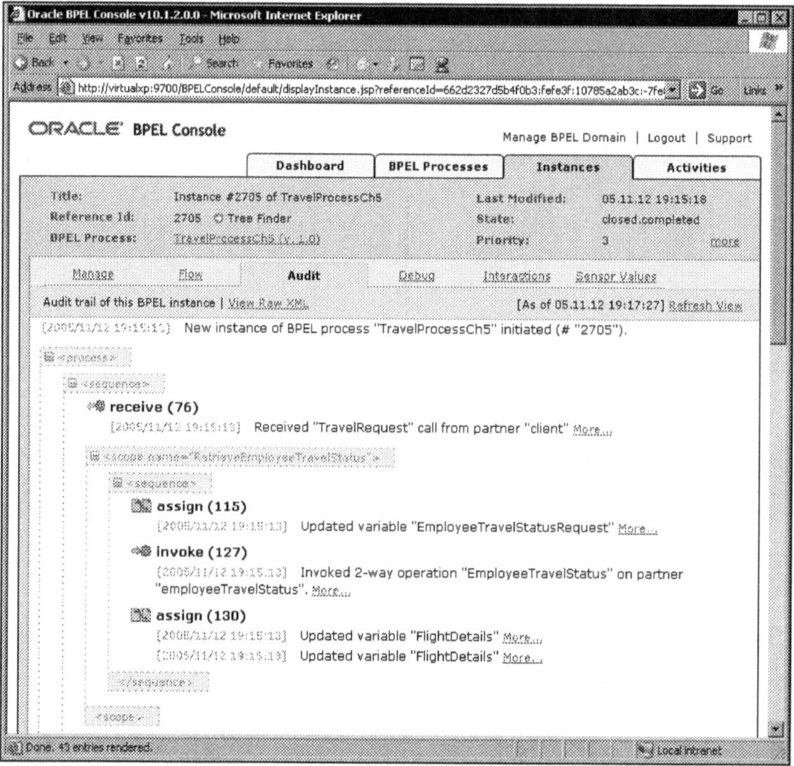

Debugging

The debug view of a process instance (accessible via the Debug tag) shows the BPEL source code. Clicking on the underlined variable names provides access to variable content. We can debug already completed instances or instances that are still running; this is called **in-flight debugging**. The debug view shows the current state of the instance. If we use in-flight debugging, the point where execution is paused is shown highlighted. The following figure shows the debug view of our process instance, once completed:

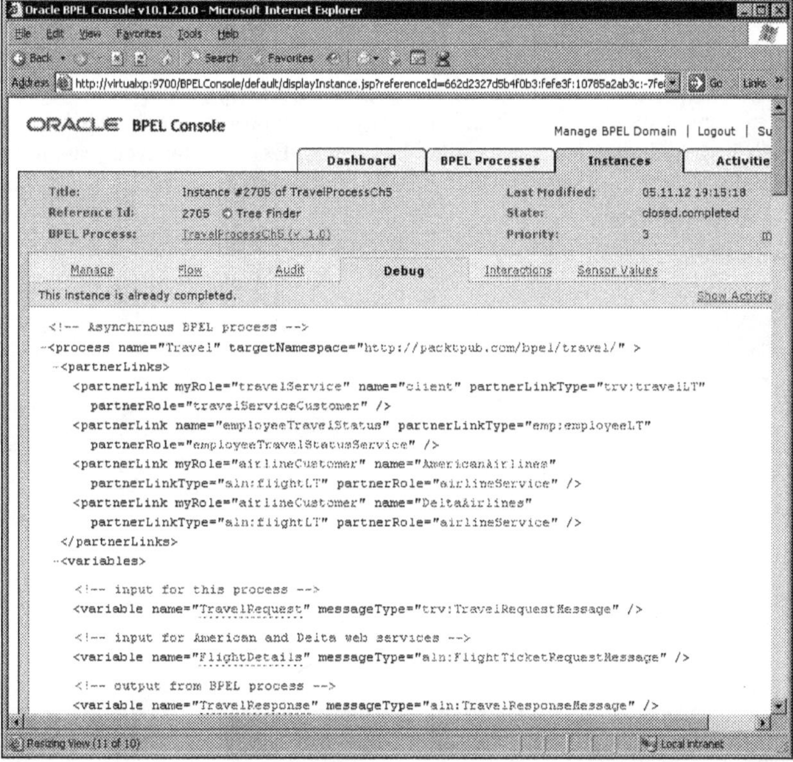

Clicking on the `TravelResponse` variable, for example, gives us the following output:

```
XML Watch Window -- Web Page Dialog
variable: TravelResponse                     Copy to clipboard
<confirmationData >
  <confirmationData >
    <FlightNo xmlns = "http://packtpub.com/service/airline/" >
      123
    </FlightNo>
    <TravelClass xmlns = "http://packtpub.com/service/airline/" >
      Economy
    </TravelClass>
    <Price xmlns = "http://packtpub.com/service/airline/" >
      120
    </Price>
    <DepartureDateTime xmlns =
    "http://packtpub.com/service/airline/" >
      2004-01-01
    </DepartureDateTime>
    <ReturnDateTime xmlns = "http://packtpub.com/service/airline/" >
      2004-01-05
    </ReturnDateTime>
    <Approved xmlns = "http://packtpub.com/service/airline/" >
      true
    </Approved>
  </confirmationData>
</confirmationData>
                                             Close Watch Window
```

Overview of Other BPEL Console Functions

Using the BPEL Processes tab, we can manage the process lifecycle and process state. The state of a process can be *on* or *off*. When the state of a process is off, new instances cannot be created and access to existing instances is blocked. The lifecycle of a process can be *active* or *retired*. When a process is retired, new instances cannot be created. Existing instances can, however, complete normally. The retired state is usually used for process revisions that have been superseded by newer revisions:

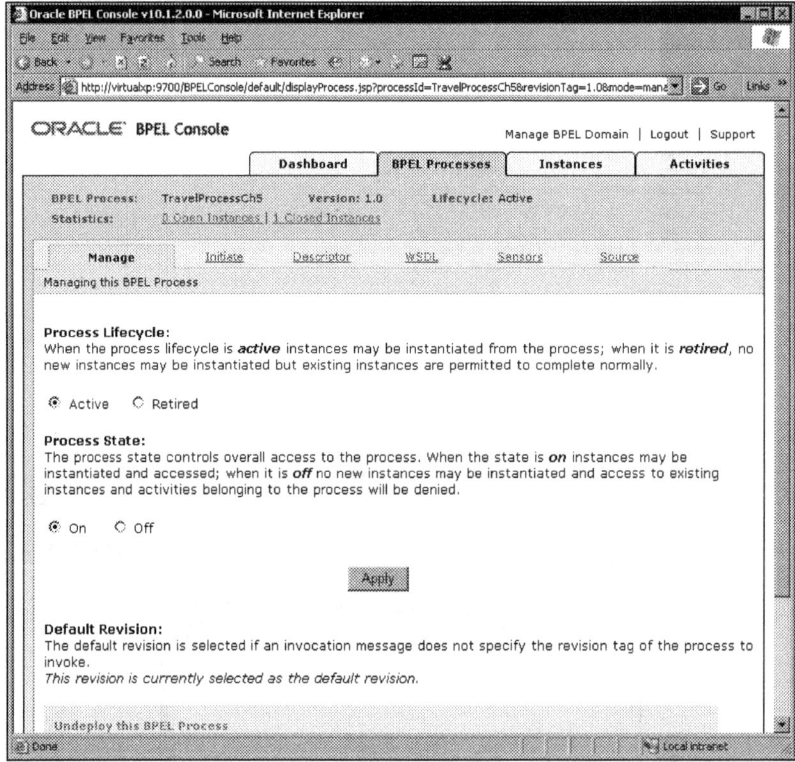

From this view we can navigate to the following:

- Initiate: Initiate new instances of the process (described in previous section)
- Descriptor: Look at the properties defined in the BPEL process descriptor (`bpel.xml`)
- WSDL: Get the WSDL location and the BPEL process endpoint location
- Sensors: Get an overview of the sensors defined for the process
- Source: Look at the process source code

Under the **Instances** tab we can overview process instances. We can archive and purge instances, remove completed process instances, and supervise those that have not completed yet. A BPEL process instance can have the following states:

- Running
- Completed
- Canceled
- Stale

For our example, we can see that four instances have completed successfully:

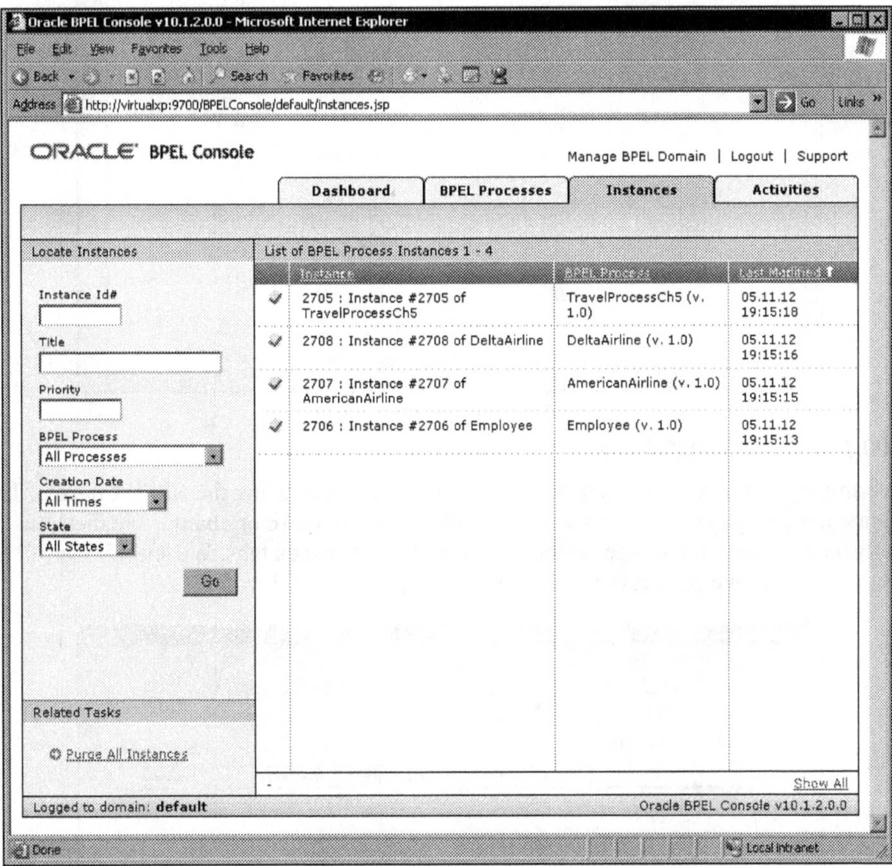

Under the **Activities** tab we can locate activities by name and find relations to instances and processes. An activity can also have four states: open, completed, canceled, or stale:

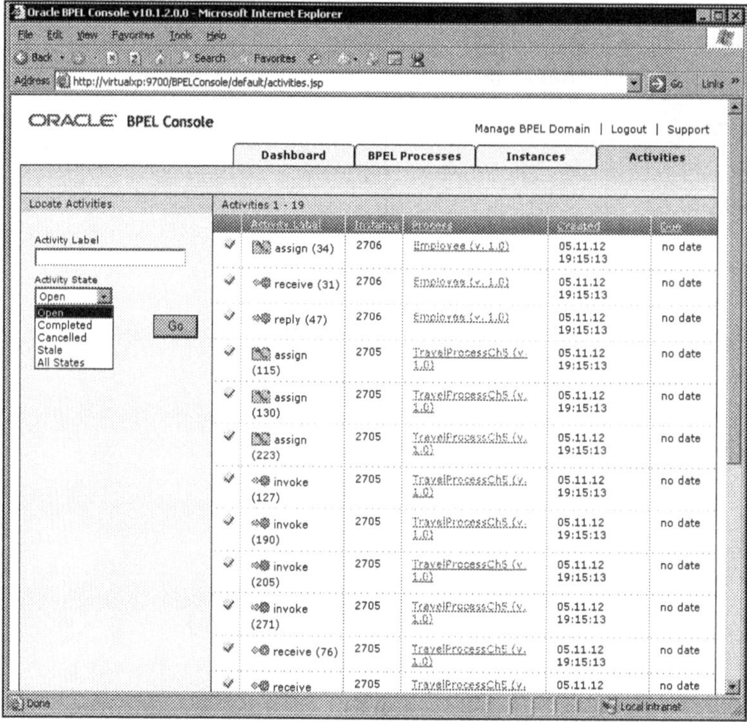

Deploying Processes

We have already mentioned that new processes can be deployed using the BPEL Console. To do this we first have to generate the process JAR archive (using **`bpelc`** or **`obant`**). We then click the Deploy New Processes link on the Dashboard or BPEL Processes tabs. We specify the full path to the process JAR archive and press the Deploy button, as shown below:

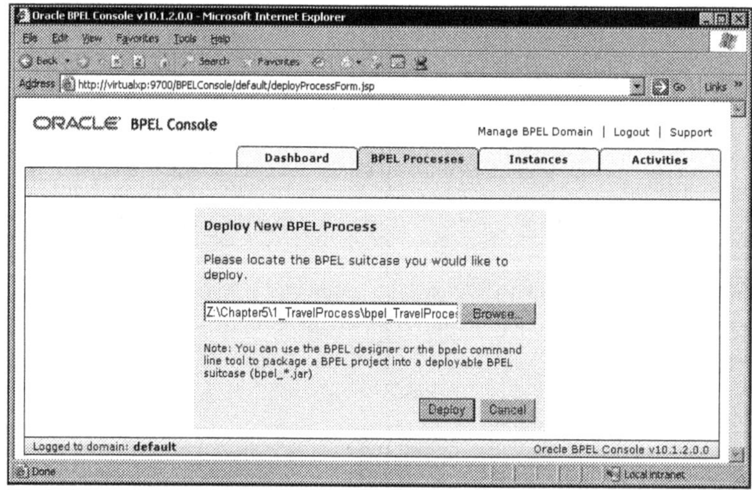

Management

The BPEL Console also provides tools for BPEL domain management. These can be accessed by pressing the Manage BPEL Domain link in the upper right corner of the screen, which brings us to the following screen:

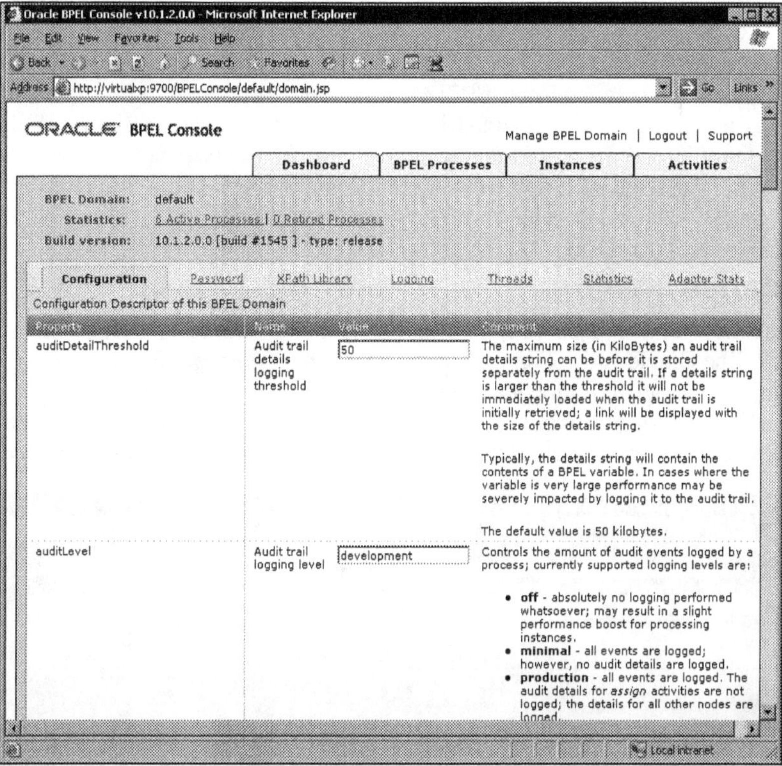

The management console has the following important options:

- Configuration descriptor (Configuration)
- Setting the password (Password)
- List of XPath extension functions for the domain (XPath Library)
- Setting the logging configuration (Logging)
- Thread allocation statistics (Threads)
- Runtime performance statistics (Statistics)
- Adapter statistics (Adapter Stats)

The configuration descriptor enables us to set various important parameters that affect the BPEL Server operation. These parameters include:

- Process instance stale check interval (specified in seconds)
- Allocation of invocation threads and load factor

- Instance cache size (minimum and maximum)
- Persistence and database parameters
- Management of large XML documents
- Recovery agent settings
- Audit trail and other settings

We can also set a parameter that defines the behavior of the server when performing the `<assign>` activity. This parameter is called **Relax BPEL4WS1.1 spec assign rules**. BPEL specification sets certain rules by assignments (discussed in Chapter 4). For example, null assignments are not allowed by default. If these rules are too restrictive for us, we can change the behavior by setting this parameter to `true`. However, doing this is not recommended because it can hinder portability of BPEL processes. The default value of this parameter is `false`.

Performance Tuning

The above-mentioned parameters on stale check, threads and load factor, cache size, etc. affect the performance of the Oracle BPEL Server. Together with the runtime performance statistics (**Statistics** tab) and thread allocation statistics (**Threads** tab), they can be used to tune the performance. The runtime performance statistics provide comprehensive data about the execution time of processes and a breakdown of times by activities, as shown in the following screenshot:

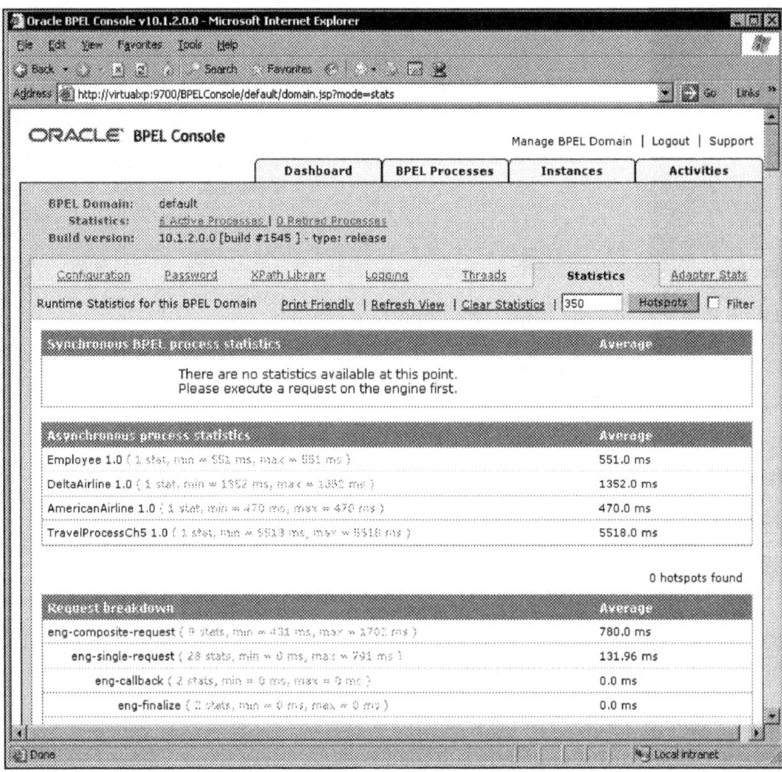

The thread allocation statistics provide information on the usage of threads and their allocation, and on the number of requests on BPEL processes, as shown in the next screenshot:

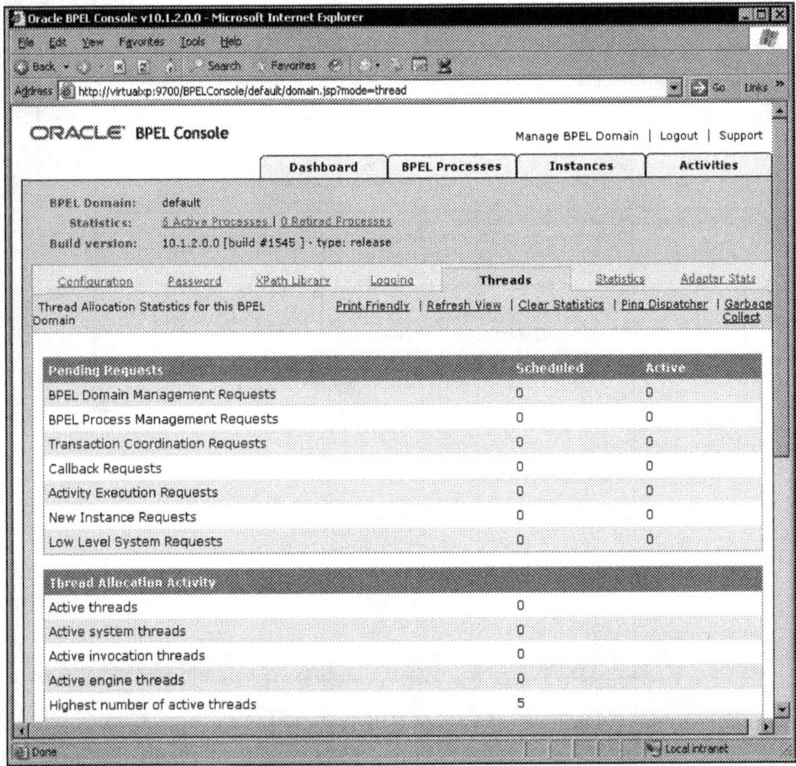

When creating a BPEL process test instance, the Oracle BPEL Server provides an option through which we can perform stress tests. Stress tests enable us to monitor the performance and to do load testing of processes. With the performance statistics, we can identify the possible bottlenecks and optimize the performance. To perform a stress test we simply select the **Perform stress test** option in the **BPEL Processes/Initiate** tab, as shown in the following screenshot. We then have to specify the number of concurrent threads allocated to the process, number of loops for the test, and the delay between invocations. We also have to select whether to clear statistics before running the stress test. In this way we can identify the most appropriate number of threads:

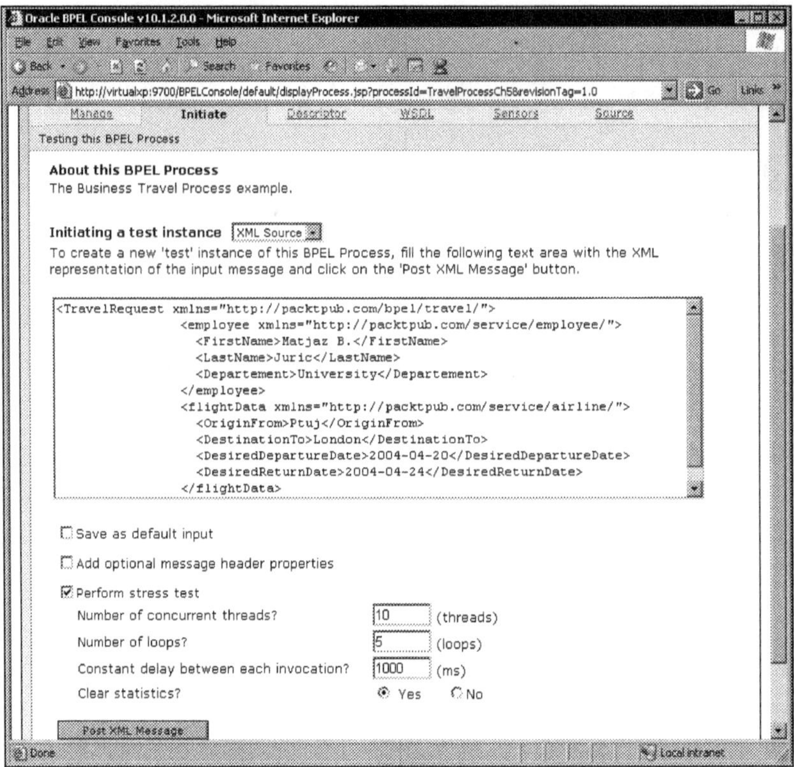

Note that the default download edition of Oracle BPEL Process Manager on Windows platform bundles Oracle Lite as the database, which will not yield meaningful results for a stress test. The BPEL Server should be configured to use a production-quality database (Oracle, SQL Server, or DB2) before doing stress testing. Please refer to Oracle documentation and to `http://otn.oracle.com/bpel` for description how to configure the Oracle BPEL Process Manager for a database server other than Oracle Lite.

Domains and Administration

BPEL Console can also be used for server administration. The BPEL administration can be accessed if we follow the Goto BPEL Admin link on the main logon page or go to the URL `http://localhost:9700/BPELAdmin/`. We have to supply the administration password, which is initially `oracle`. The BPEL Admin has three major functions:

- Administration of server-related parameters and administration passwords (Server)
- Managing BPEL domains (BPEL Domains)
- Threads statistics (Threads)

Administration of Server-Related Parameters

The administration of server-related parameters includes four tabs: Configuration, Password, Logging, and WSIF:

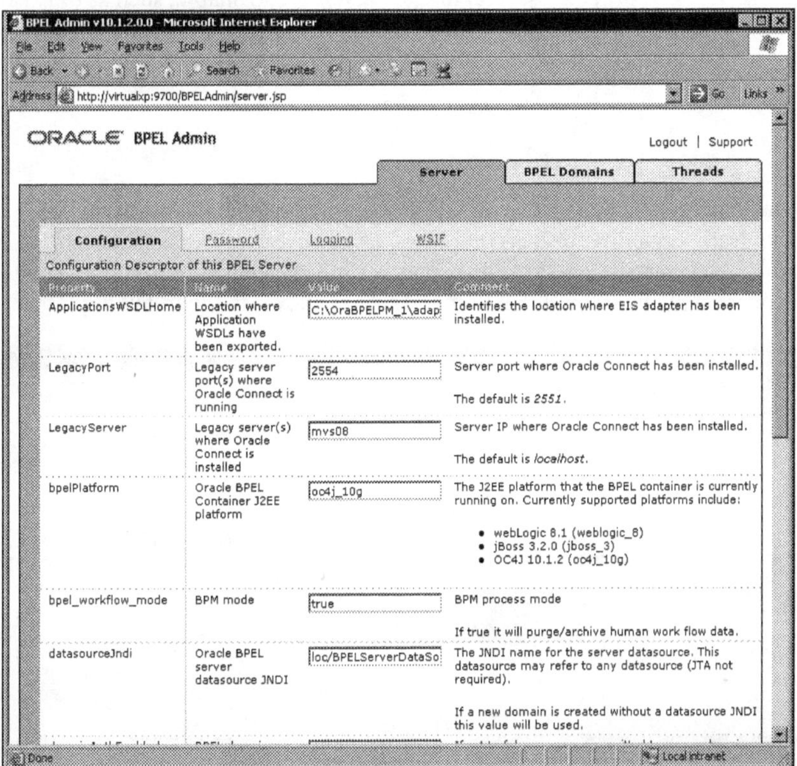

Within Configuration we can modify various server parameters, including the location of WSDLs, ports of legacy servers accessed through Connect, J2EE container platform (OC4J, JBoss, or WebLogic), workflow mode, which specifies how human interactions are archived, authentication parameter, data sources, BPEL SOAP server URL, and a list of WSIF providers. We can also specify whether users need to supply a password when they log on to a BPEL domain and whether they can see a list of available domains.

Here we can also change the BPEL Server mode from production to development. In production mode, if we try to redeploy a process with the same name and revision tag, the server asks whether we would like to replace an existing version or use a different revision number. In development mode, a process is redeployed without any questions asked. The server mode can be changed by modifying the `productionServer` property. The default is `true`, which is used for production mode. For development mode it should be changed to `false`.

Under the Password tab, we can change the administrator password. This should be done immediately after the installation.

The Logging tab enables us to set the logging level for various server components, such as infrastructure, services, WSIF, etc. Several logging levels are available, such as `off`, `fatal`, `error`, `warn`, `info`, `debug`, and `all`.

The WSIF tab shows the supported WSIF bindings. We will say more on WSIF bindings in Chapter 6.

Managing BPEL Domains

We have already mentioned that Oracle BPEL Server is organized into domains. Since domains enable us to logically organize business processes, using several domains is recommended in real-world scenarios. After installation, the `default` domain is created automatically. Additional domains can be created under the BPEL Domains tab, as shown in the following screenshot:

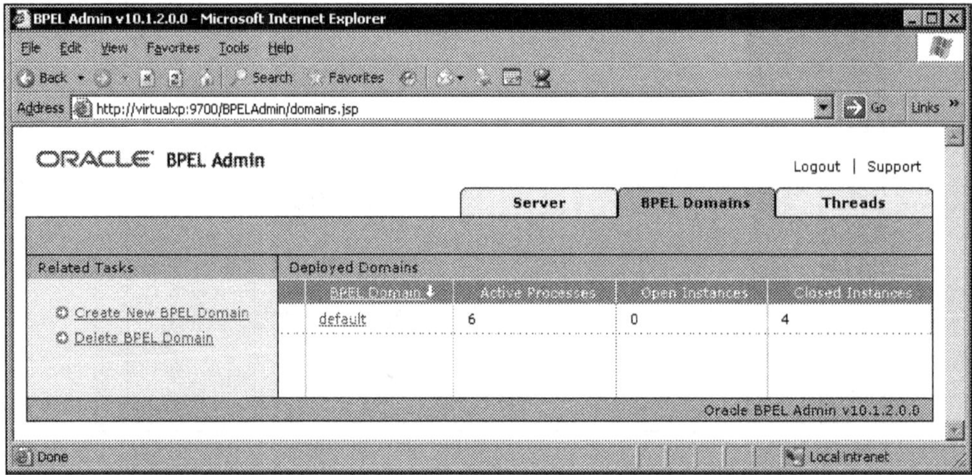

If we follow the Create New BPEL Domain link, we can create new domains. We have to specify the domain ID, password, and JNDI (Java Naming and Directory Interface) addresses for regular and transactional data sources:

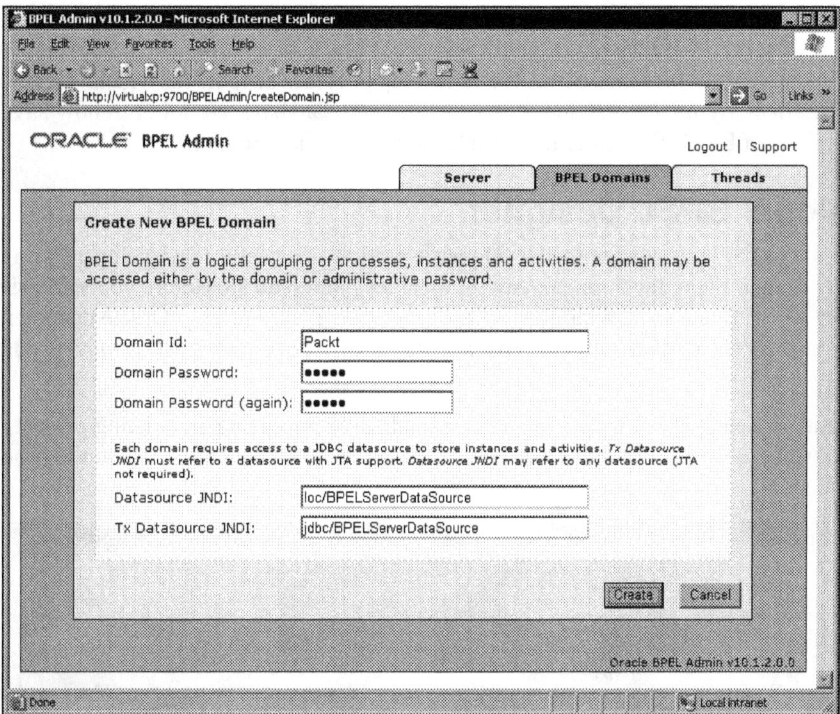

With this, we have concluded our review of the BPEL Console. In the next section, we look at the BPEL Designer.

Graphical Development with BPEL Designer

Writing BPEL processes by hand, as we have done in previous chapters, can become time consuming and complex. Therefore, Oracle has developed the BPEL Designer, which enables graphical development of BPEL processes. Instead of writing BPEL code we can develop processes in a graphical environment where we can add activities using drag-and-drop. BPEL Designer simplifies development and makes it faster. In addition to drag-and-drop modeling it provides a browser through which we can locate web services. It also provides a copy assistant, an XPath editor, the ability to compile and deploy a process on the BPEL Server with one mouse click, and several other useful tools. Oracle BPEL Designer natively supports BPEL version 1.1, so we can also use it for developing BPEL processes that will be deployed to any other BPEL server.

BPEL Designer is available for two environments:

- JDeveloper BPEL Designer, integrated with Oracle JDeveloper
- Eclipse BPEL Designer, a plug-in for the Eclipse platform

Both versions of BPEL Designer offer comparable functionality, but differ in several details. Some of the differences are based on the differences of the host environments, JDeveloper and Eclipse respectively. JDeveloper BPEL Designer also provides support for Oracle-specific functions, particularly for sensors and adapters (file, FTP, database, etc.). Let us now have a look at both versions of BPEL Designer, first at JDeveloper and then Eclipse.

JDeveloper BPEL Designer

The BPEL Designer integrated with JDeveloper is particularly useful for developers who use JDeveloper as their main development environment, or plan to do so. Before you start using JDeveloper BPEL Designer, get familiar with JDeveloper. Please refer to Oracle documentation on JDeveloper for more information or visit `http://www.oracle.com/technology/products/jdev/index.html`.

After creating a new BPEL Process project, or loading or importing an existing project, we see the JDeveloper BPEL Designer window. It shows the graphical structure of the process and partner links:

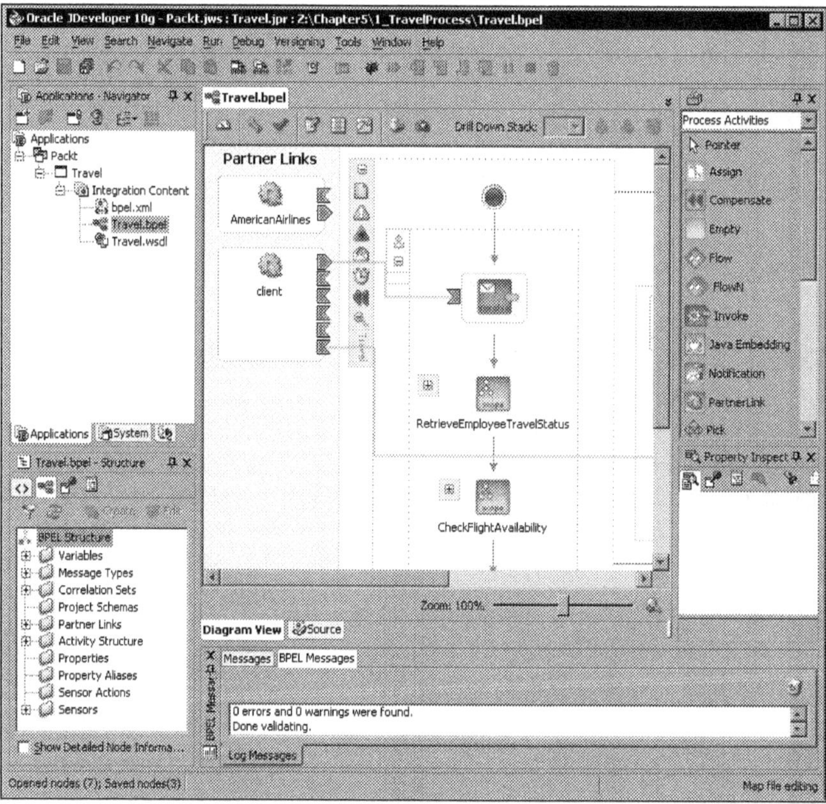

BPEL Designer also provides the source-code view where we can edit the BPEL code directly. Changes made in source view are reflected immediately in the BPEL Designer visual representation, and vice versa.

Please notice that it is not the intention of this section to provide in-depth instructions on using JDeveloper BPEL Designer. Rather we will highlight the most important features including importing existing BPEL processes, adding partner links, creating variables, adding activities, copying variables, entering XPath functions, and using XSLT Mapper and Validation Browser. For detailed instructions on using JDeveloper please refer to Oracle documentation.

Importing Existing BPEL Processes

First, let us look at how we can import existing BPEL processes into JDeveloper. After selecting the workspace in Applications – Navigator we choose Import from the File menu. In the Import dialog window we select BPEL Process. Next, we have to enter the source file name and path and the project name. Optionally we can select the project directory:

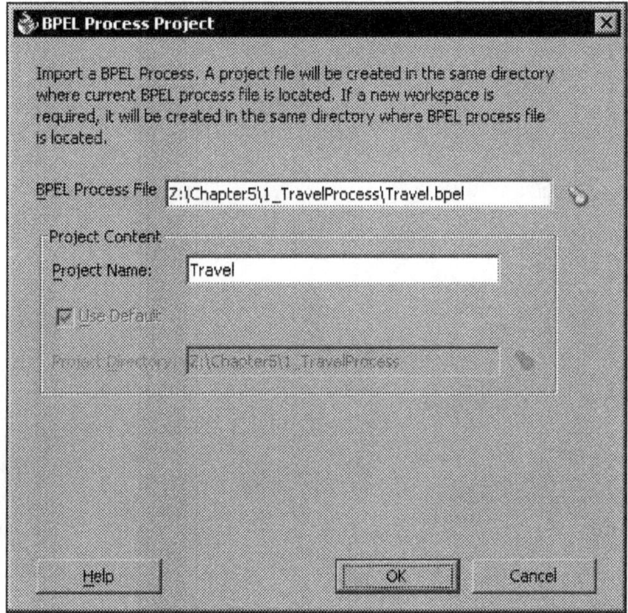

After clicking OK, the project is imported into the selected workspace and validated. JDeveloper BPEL Designer in version 10.1.2 requires that the process name specified in the `name` attribute of the `<process>` root element is equal to the name of the file in which the source is stored. If the names are not equal we have to manually add the BPEL and WSDL files to the project.

Partner Links and Web Services

To add partner links we have to select the Process Activities in the Component Palette (upper right side of the screen). From there we select the PartnerLink and drag-and-drop it to the Partner Links section of the main design window. Alternatively, we can right-click in the main design window and use the context menu. A dialog window opens where we have to enter the partner link name and the details, including the WSDL location, partner link type, and both roles:

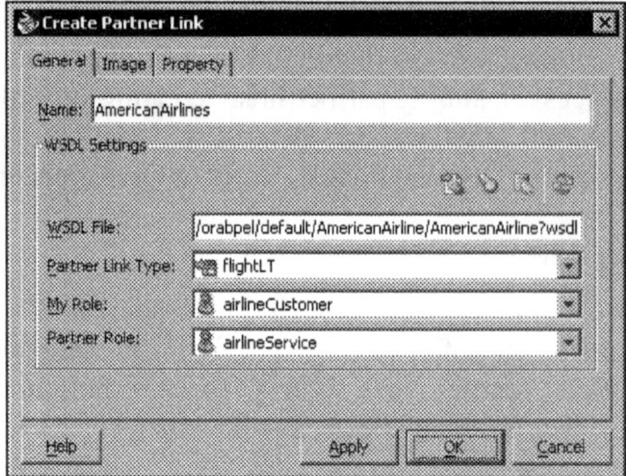

If we do not know the exact location of the WSDL, we can use WSDL Chooser by clicking on the flashlight icon (second from the left). The WSDL Chooser uses UDDI and WSIL (Web Services Inspection Language) for locating web services. The following screenshot shows the selected web service on the local BPEL server:

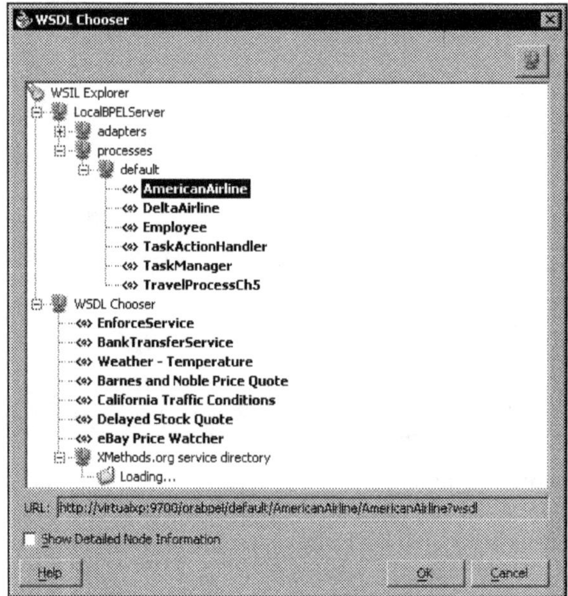

Variables

To add variables to the BPEL process we have two choices. We can add them manually, as we will show in this section, or we can use automatic variable creation, as we will see in the next section. Let us look at how to add variables manually or edit existing variables. In the BPEL Structure navigator window (lower left side of the screen) we navigate to the variables. Then we either click an existing variable or right-click to create a new variable. A dialog window opens where we have to specify the variable name and type:

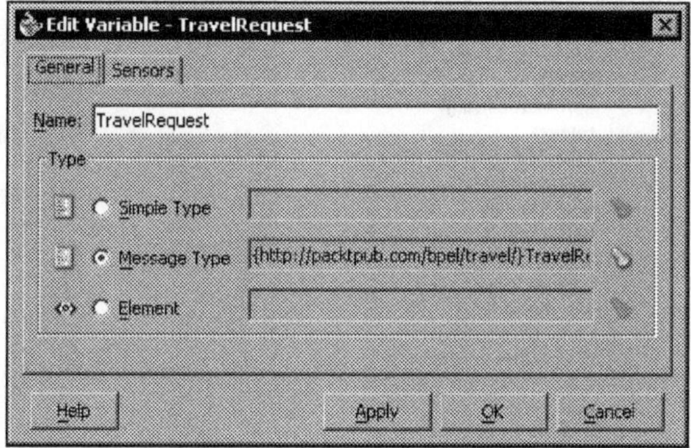

To select the variable type we can use the **Type Chooser** by clicking the flashlight icon. Here we can navigate through message types in partner links or project WSDL files and select the appropriate type:

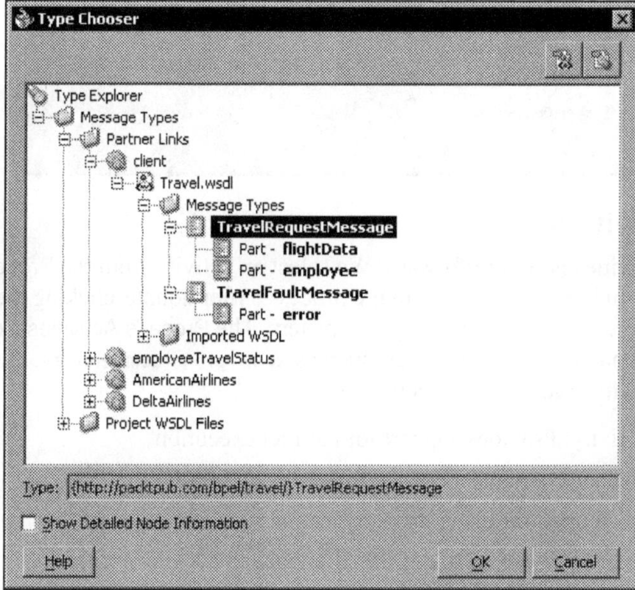

If we are using a simple type, we can choose from the predefined XML types:

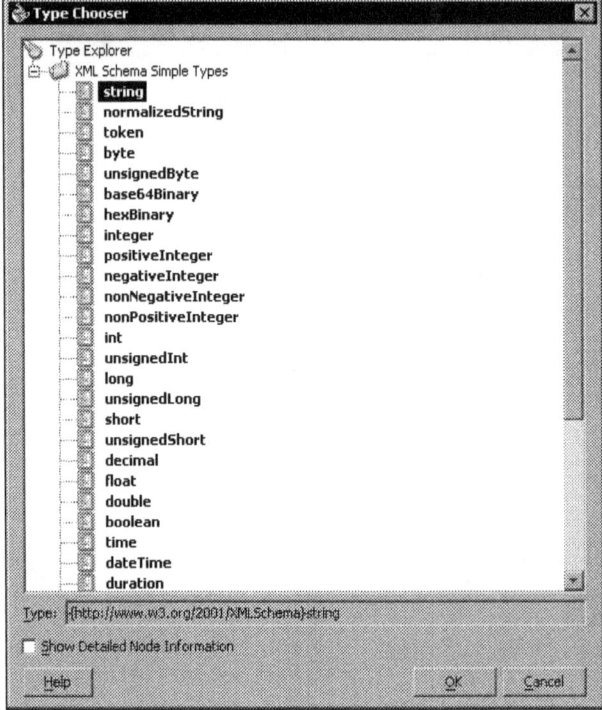

Process Activities

Adding process activities is straightforward. We select an activity from the Process Activities Component Palette and drag-and-drop it to the process. After double-clicking the activity a dialog windows opens where we enter the activity parameters. The Process Activities Component Palette provides access to standard BPEL activities, such as `<assign>`, `<compensate>`, `<empty>`, etc. It also provides access to Oracle-specific activities:

- `<flowN>` activity: Provides support for parallel execution
- Java Embedding: Enables inclusion of Java code into BPEL
- Notification: Wizard for using the Notification service
- Transform: Enables access to the XSLT engine and XSLT Mapper
- User Task: Wizard for using the Workflow service

We will explain these Oracle-specific activities in Chapter 6.

Now we will show how to add an `<assign>` activity. First, we select the Assign process activity from the Component Palette and drag-and-drop it to the process. Then a dialog window opens, where we have to specify the copy rules, as shown on the screenshot opposite. Here we can edit existing copy rules or add new rules:

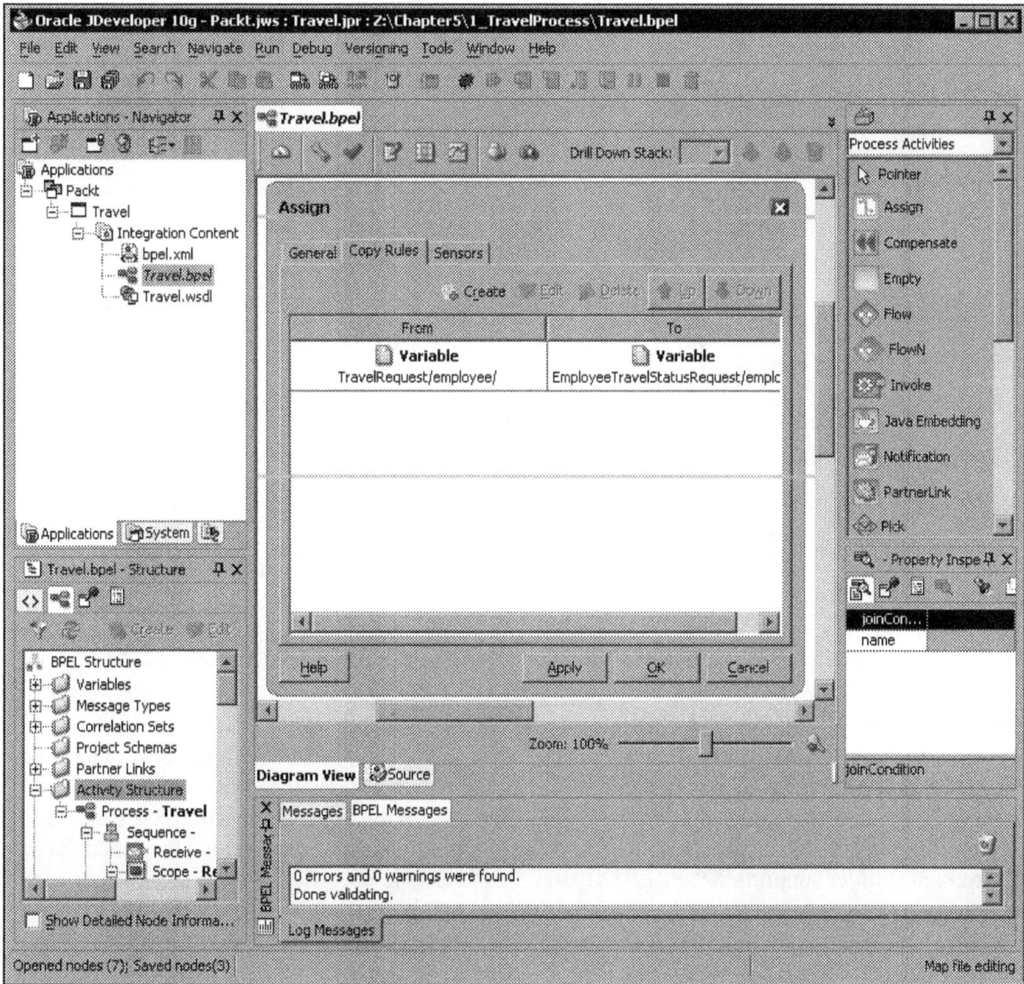

Copy Rule Editor

For adding new copy rules in the <assign> activities or editing existing rules, we can use the Copy Rule editor, which simplifies the procedure. Using this editor we can create the <from> and <to> expressions by navigating through the variables trees. The Copy Rule editor supports all forms of <assigns> with a variable, expression, XML fragment, or partner link being the source and/or the destination of the assignment. When copying variables we can navigate thorough the variables tree, as shown on the screenshot overleaf. We can also enter expressions using XPath Expression Builder (shown in the next section), enter XML, or edit/create a new partner link:

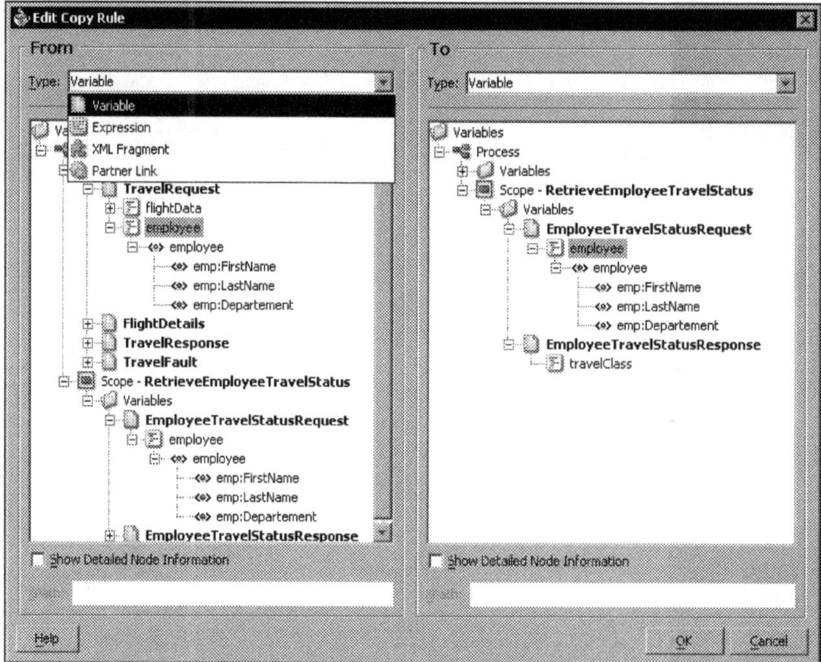

XPath Expression Builder

To simplify the creation or editing of XPath expressions JDeveloper BPEL Designer provides the XPath Expression Builder. It is accessible from all dialogs where XPath expressions need to be entered by pressing on the XPath Expression Builder icon. In the upper-left section, we can navigate through BPEL variables. In the lower-left section, we can select various functions. XPath Expression Builder supports XPath 1.0, XPath 2.0, and Oracle-specific XPath extensions functions, which are covered in Chapter 6. In the lower-right section, we can access operators. Pressing Ctrl-Space in the Expression Body window we get context-sensitive help. The screenshot opposite shows how we can create XPath expressions using the builder:

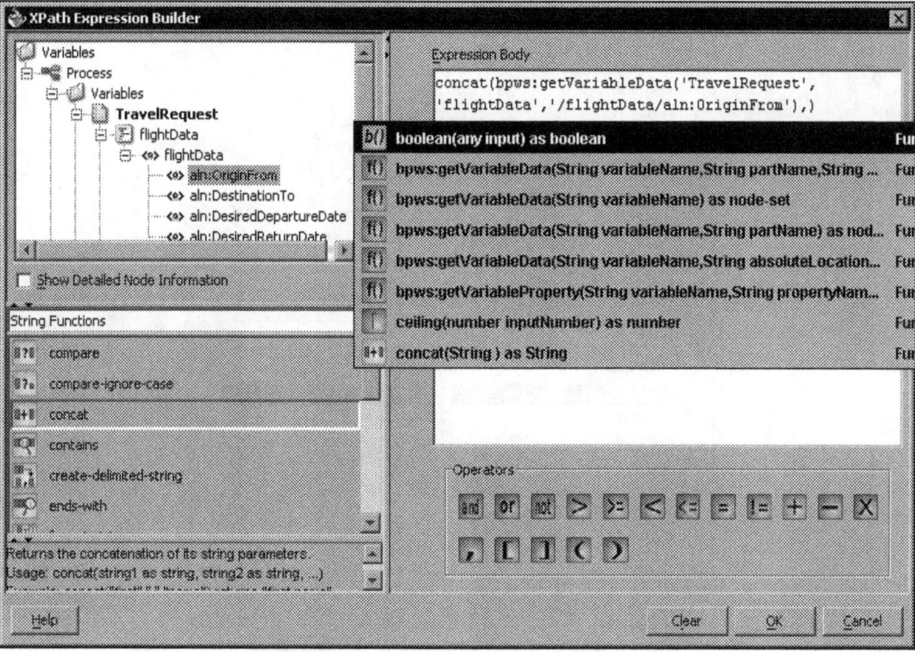

XSLT Mapper

In BPEL processes we often need to transform XML (stored in variables). For example, we have to modify the vocabulary to adapt the output of one service to the input of another. We might also want to transform XML to other markup languages. Instead of using XPath, Oracle BPEL Process Manager provides a built-in XSLT engine. To compose XSLT stylesheets JDeveloper BPEL Designer provides a built-in XSLT Mapper, which simplifies the mapping definition considerably.

To activate the XSLT engine from a BPEL process we need to add the transformation activity to the process. We do this by dragging-and-dropping the Transform activity from the Process Activities Component Palette to the process. This activity simply calls the built-in XSLT engine, explained in the *Extension Functions and Activities* section in Chapter 6.

After double-clicking the activity, a Transform window appears. Here we select the source and the target variable name along with the corresponding parts. Then we enter the XSLT file name:

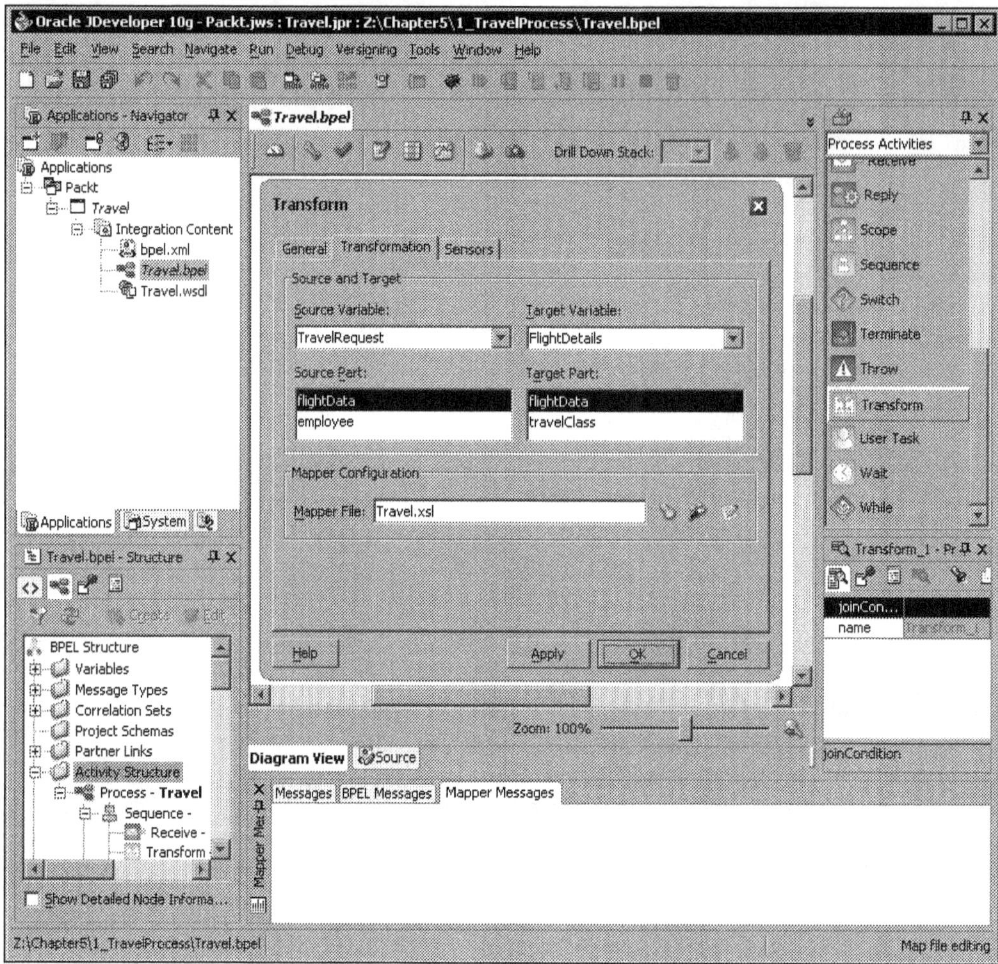

After pressing the icon to create a mapping (second from the left) the XSLT Mapper window opens. We can drag-and-drop the elements from the left side to the right side. We can also use XPath functions, which we can select from the Component Palette in the upper right side of the window (Oracle provides support for XPath 1.0, some XPath 2.0, and Oracle-specific functions). As the result, an XSLT stylesheet is generated, which takes care for the transformation:

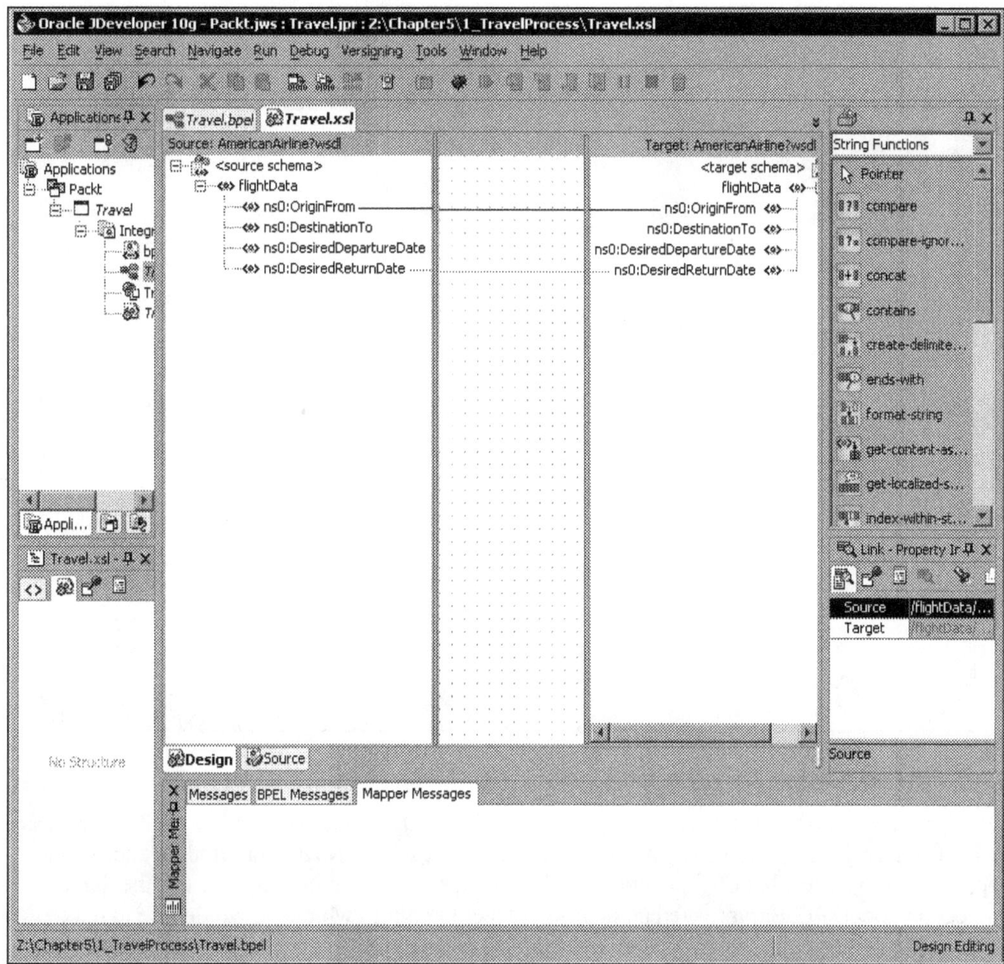

With XSLT Mapper we use several functions that influence the mapping and also transform the source data. We can also use an Auto Map feature, which tries to map attributes automatically. In this way we can develop XSLT transformations easily without being familiar with the XSLT language. From more information on XSLT please refer to `http://www.w3.org/TR/xslt`. For more information on XSLT Mapper please refer to Oracle documentation.

BPEL Validation Browser

To simplify finding and correcting errors and warnings JDeveloper provides a BPEL Validation Browser. We can access it by clicking the tool icon (second from the left) in the main design window. The BPEL Validation Browser window opens. In the screenshot, we can see that there is one error in the BPEL process, related to the assign activity where no copy rules are specified. The browser also suggests the solution:

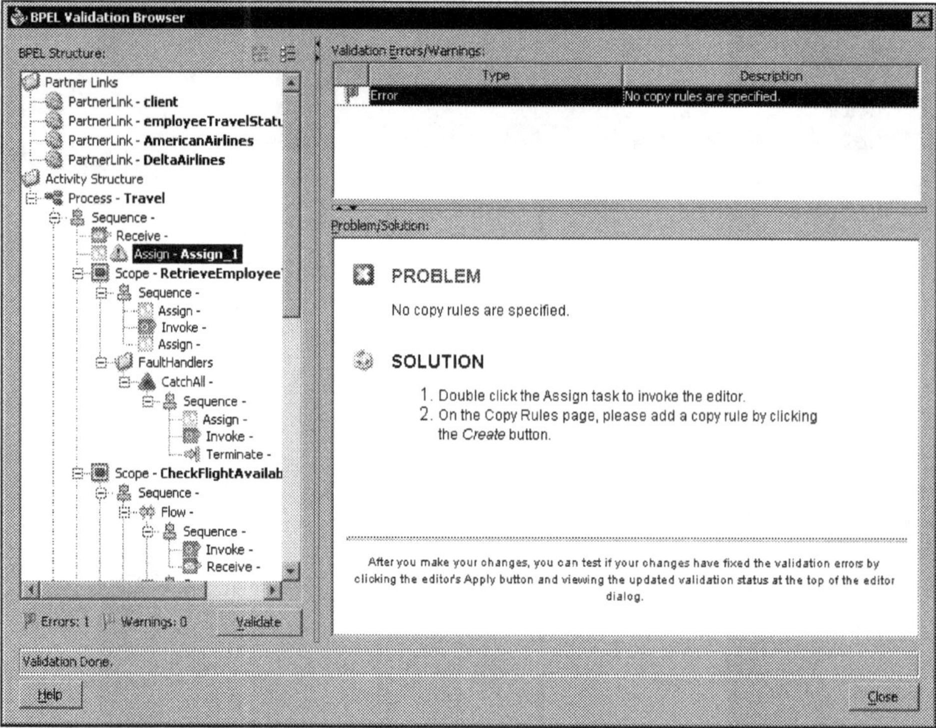

Building and Deploying

BPEL processes can be built and deployed directly from JDeveloper. To deploy a BPEL process we have to right-click on the Integration Content in the System – Navigator window and select Deploy. Next, we see a list of connections to the BPEL servers—in our case we use the default connection LocalBPELServer. We can then select the domain to which we would like to make the deployment, as shown in the screenshot below. To start the deployment we have to enter the password for the domain:

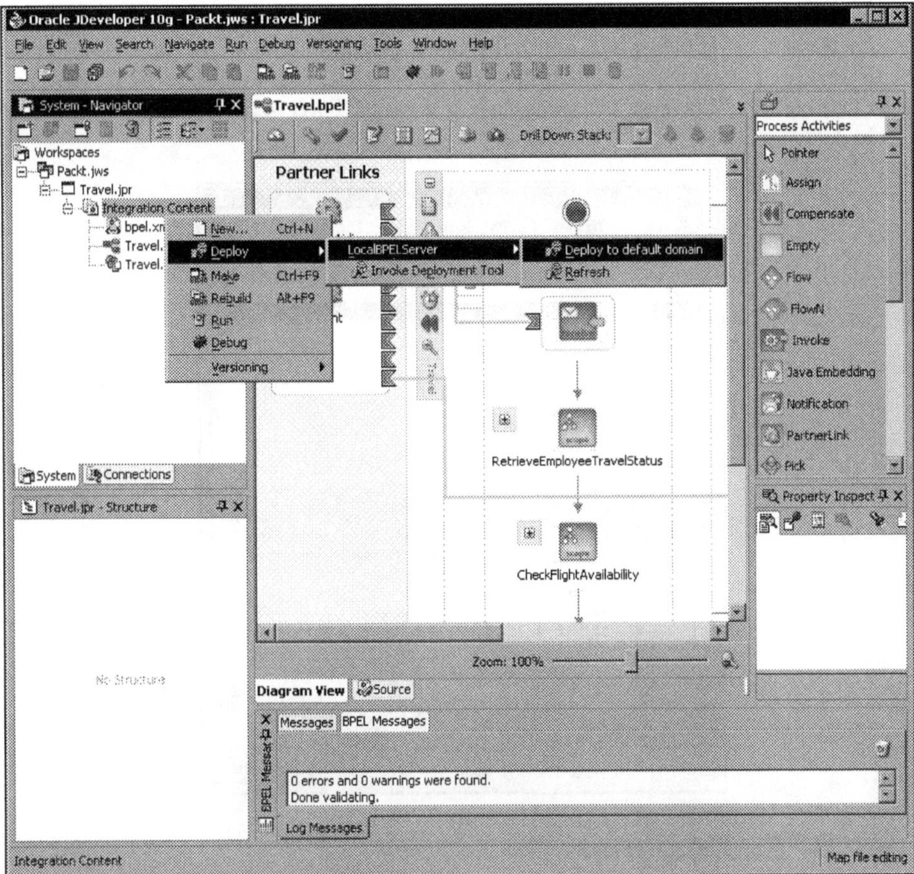

Alternatively, we can select the Invoke Deployment Tool. Then a dialog window appears where we have to select the connection to the server, the address, domain name and password, and version:

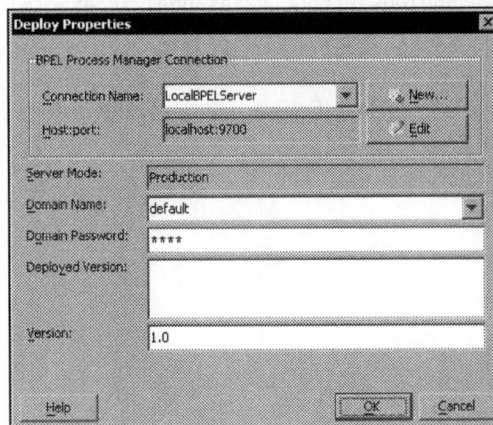

Deploy Properties

BPEL Process Manager Connection

Connection Name: LocalBPELServer New...

Host:port: localhost:9700 Edit

Server Mode: Production

Domain Name: default

Domain Password: ****

Deployed Version:

Version: 1.0

Help OK Cancel

From JDeveloper we can access the **Deployment Descriptor Properties** window, where we can set various deployment properties, which is usually easier than editing `bpel.xml` manually. Please refer to the *Process Descriptor* section of this chapter for more information on `bpel.xml`. To access the **Deployment Descriptor Properties** window we have to click the icon (first from the left in the main design window):

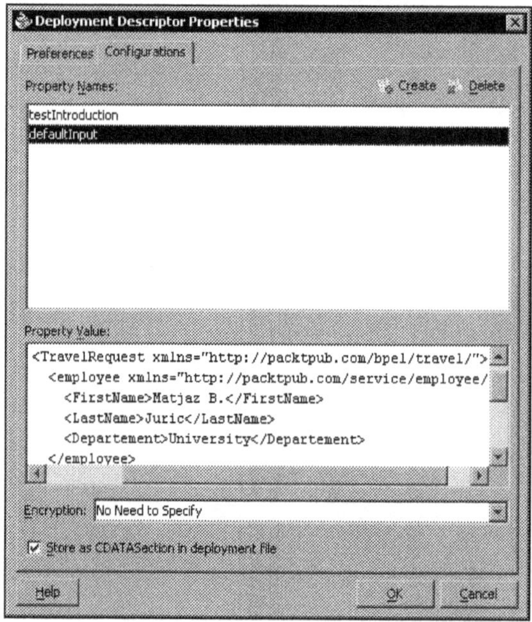

Eclipse BPEL Designer

The Eclipse BPEL Designer is an Eclipse plug-in. Therefore, we should get familiar with the basics of the Eclipse platform (`http://www.eclipse.org/`). For detailed installation instructions please refer to Oracle documentation and tutorials, which can be downloaded from `http://www.oracle.com/technology/products/ias/bpel/index.html`.

The following screenshot shows the main Eclipse BPEL Designer screen with the opened Travel process. The main window shows the overview of the process with partner links and global XML variables exposed. This view is specific to Eclipse and not found in JDeveloper:

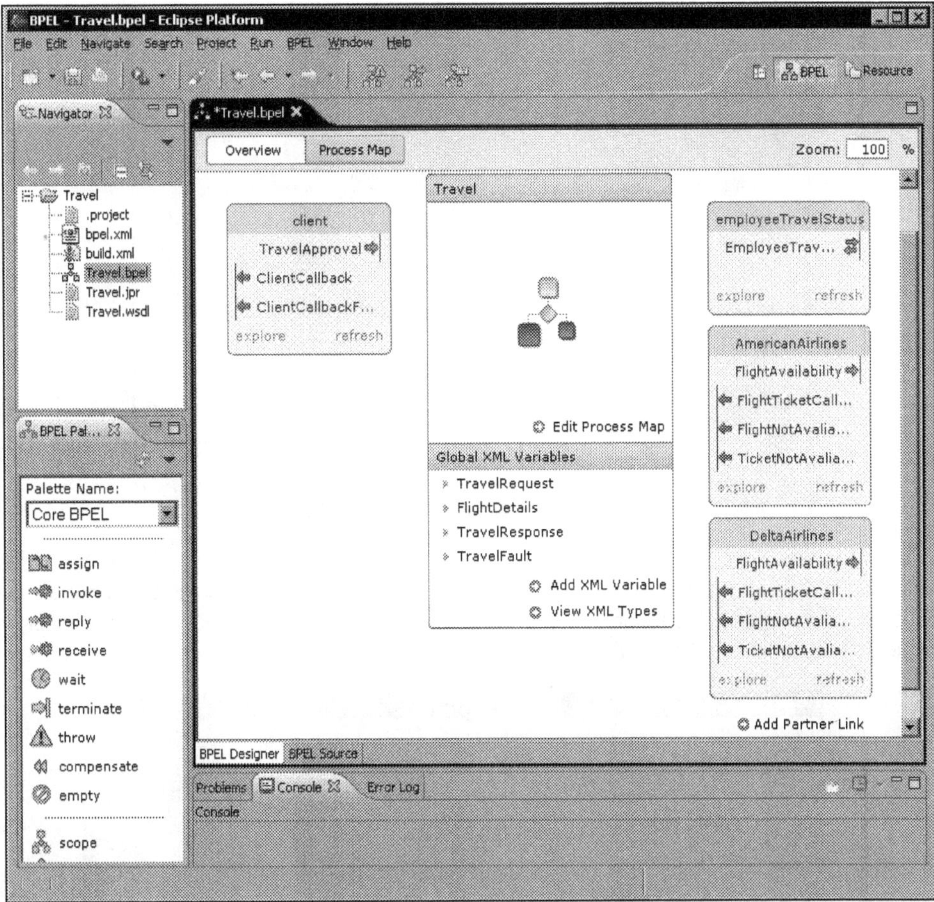

From this view we can add partner links and variables to our process. BPEL Designer also provides the source-code view where we can edit the BPEL code directly. Changes made in source view are reflected immediately in the BPEL Designer visual representation, and vice versa.

Partner Links and Web Services

To add a partner link to the process, we simply click Add Partner Link, located in the lower right corner of the main window. After entering the partner link name and WSDL location, the designer will help us in selecting the partner link types and roles. This is shown in the following screenshot:

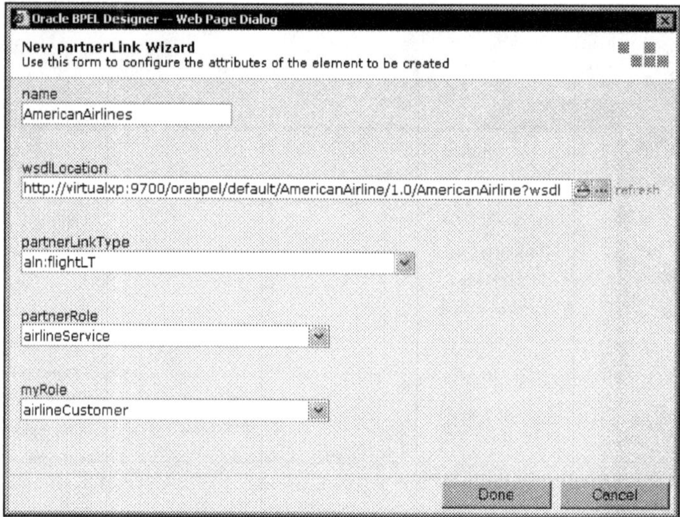

If we do not know the exact location of the WSDL, we can use the UDDI browser, through which we can locate and select the appropriate web service. The web services can be located on the local BPEL server or on remote BPEL servers. We can use the WSIL interface or use the built-in services, which we will discuss later. The following screenshot shows the view of the root WSIL document:

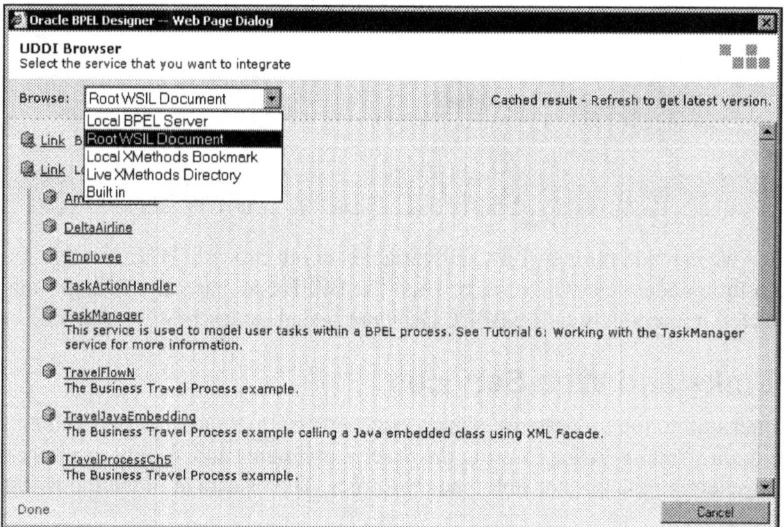

Variables

By following the Add XML Variable link, we can add a global variable to the process. Variables in BPEL processes can be defined globally or within scopes. Adding them with the Variable Wizard requires us to fill out the following form:

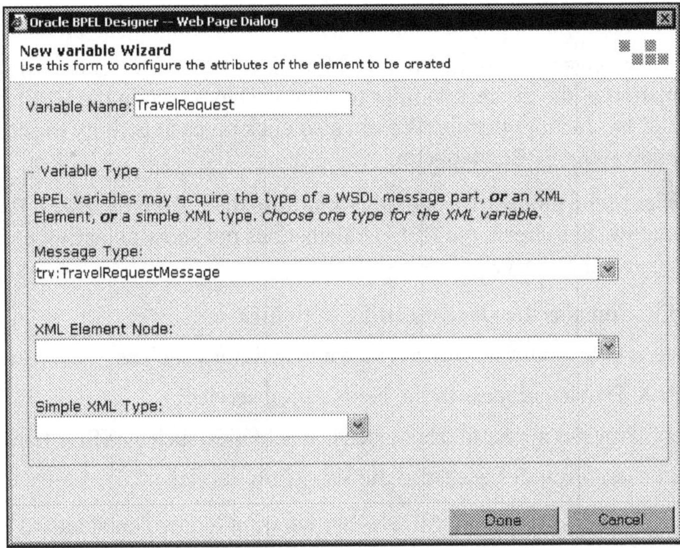

We have to enter the variable name and type, which can be a message type, element, or XML Schema type. We can select the available types from the drop-down list.

XML Type Browser

From the overview process window we can access the XML Schema Type Browser by clicking the View XML Types link. The XML Schema Type Browser allows us to browse schemas in different namespaces. It also shows the XPath expressions, which are particularly useful for `<assign>` activities and complex schemas:

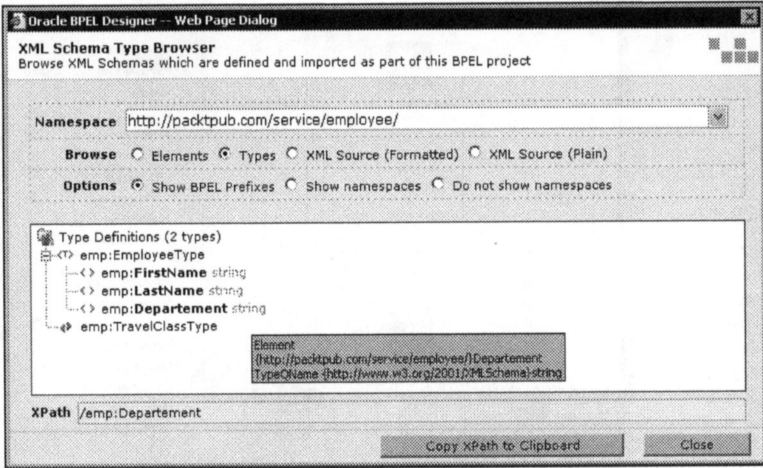

Process Map

Let us now switch from **Overview** to the **Process Map** view. BPEL Designer will show the graphical representation of the process, similar to what we have seen in the BPEL Console. We can expand activities to see more details. We can also click on each activity to see the details in the right-hand window—the **BPEL Inspector**.

To add new activities to the process we can drag-and-drop them from the **BPEL Palette** in the lower left-hand window. In Eclipse, the BPEL Palette does not show all activities in one pane. Rather, they are organized into five groups:

- **Core BPEL**: Contains the standard BPEL activities
- **BPEL Extensions**: Contains Oracle extension activities such as `<flowN>` and `<exec>`
- **Notifications**: Provides access to the Notification service
- **Experiment**: Provides access to other extension activities, such as XSLT transformations
- **User Interaction**: Provides access to the Workflow service

The Process Map view allows us to control whether we want to develop standard BPEL processes or include specific extensions. The screenshot below shows the **Process Map** view with opened **BPEL Palette**:

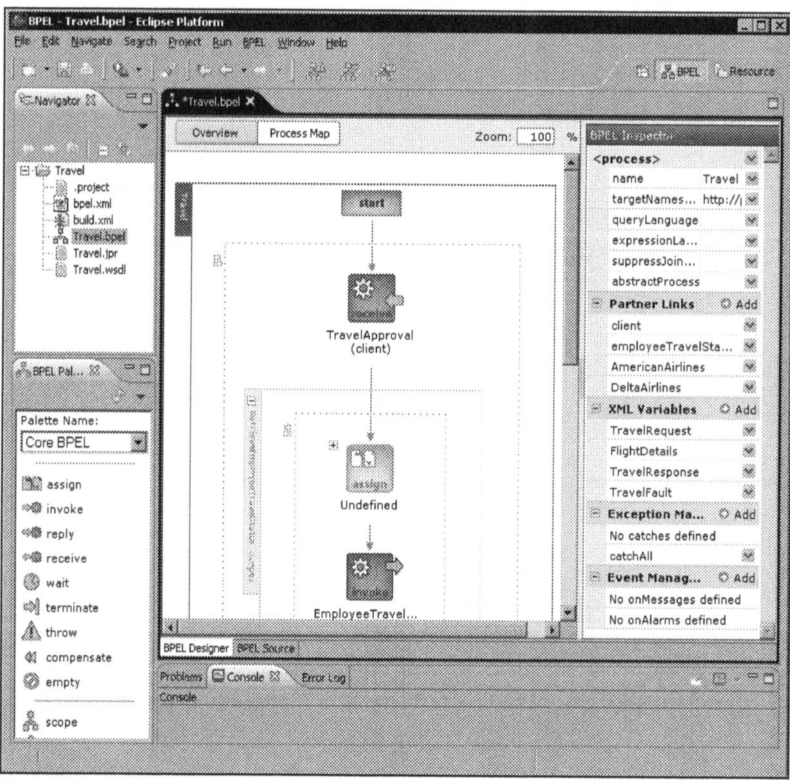

Copy Rule Editor

Similar to JDeveloper, Eclipse also provides the Copy Rule editor, which simplifies adding new copy rules in the `<assign>` activities or editing existing rules. Using the editor we can create the `<from>` and `<to>` expressions by navigating through the variable trees. The Copy Rule editor supports `<assigns>` with a variable, expression, or XML fragment as the source. We can use the Variable & Query Picker to navigate to the variable, part, and query:

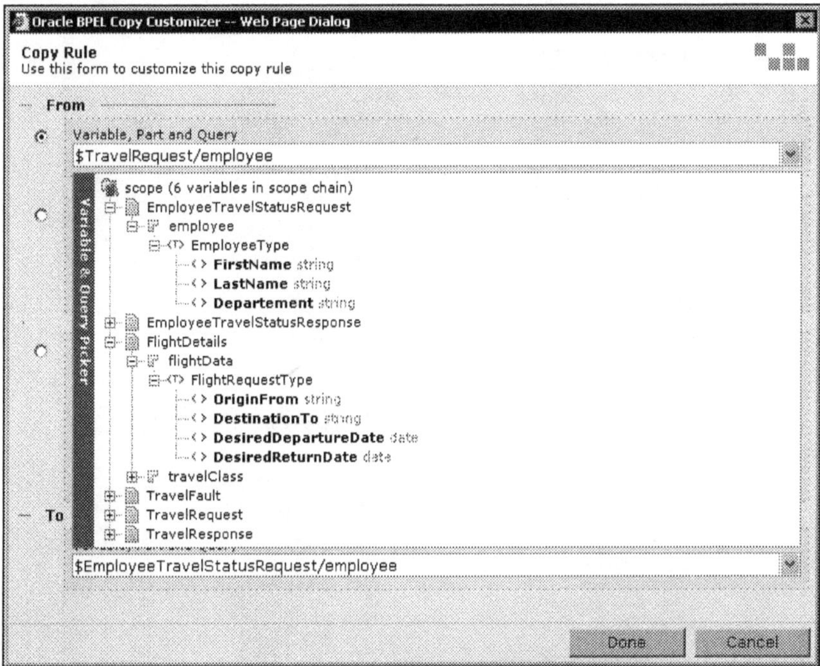

Function Wizard

To enter an expression we can open the BPEL Function Wizard. This wizard helps us to compose XPath expressions. In the first step, we have to select a function from the list of available functions. Note that it also offers some Oracle-specific functions (with namespace prefixes other than bpws), which are discussed in Chapter 6:

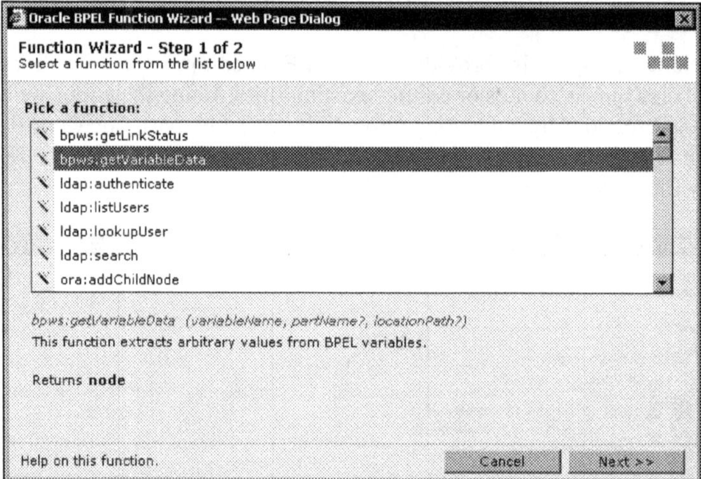

After selecting the function, we have to fill in the required parameters. In our case we have selected the `bpws:getVariableData()` function and have to specify the variable, part, and query in the second step:

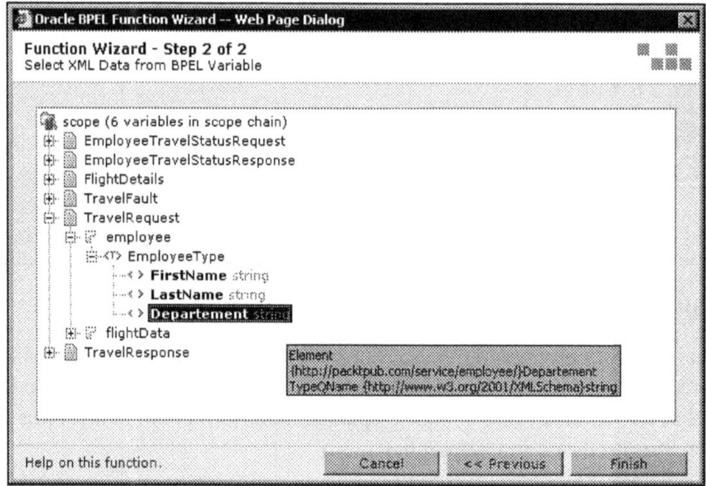

Building and Deploying

Eclipse BPEL Designer offers direct compilation and deployment on the Oracle BPEL Server. This can be done from the toolbar or from the BPEL menu. In addition to building and deploying, we can also validate our project and open the BPEL Console:

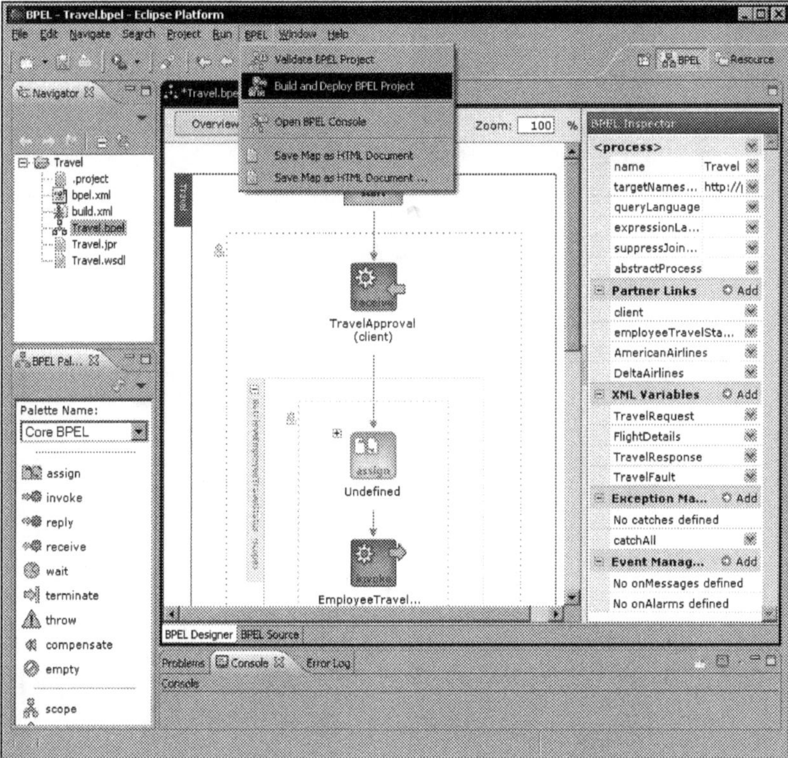

For more information on the Eclipse and JDeveloper BPEL Designer please refer to Oracle and Eclipse documentation.

Summary

In this chapter, we have become familiar with the Oracle BPEL Process Manager 10g. We have seen that Oracle BPEL Process Manager is a Java-based BPEL server that provides comprehensive support for BPEL. We have provided an overview of BPEL Process Manager architecture and reviewed the major features, such as dehydration, version control, and clustering. We have become familiar with how processes can be deployed, with the deployment descriptor, and with the BPEL Console. Using the BPEL Console we can deploy, test, manage, and debug BPEL processes. We have also become familiar with domains.

For BPEL development, Oracle provides an integrated graphical development environment called BPEL Designer in two versions: JDeveloper BPEL Designer and Eclipse BPEL Designer. BPEL Designer offers several tools that simplify development, such as the Copy Rule editor, XPath Expression builder, XSLT Mapper, and BPEL Validation browser.

In the next chapter, we will look at the advanced features of Oracle BPEL Process Manager.

6

Oracle BPEL Process Manager: Advanced Features

In this chapter, we will discuss the advanced features provided by the Oracle BPEL Process Manager 10g Release 2. We will overview the extension functions and activities provided by the BPEL Process Manager. We will take a detailed look at dynamic parallel flows and dynamic partner links. We will explain and demonstrate how BPEL processes can be integrated with resources other then web services using Web Services Invocation Framework. We will also look at Java embedding. Finally we will overview three important services provided by Oracle BPEL Process Manager: the Notification service for sending and receiving asynchronous notifications using email and other channels, the Workflow service for including human interaction into BPEL processes, and the Identity service for user authentication and authorization.

In this chapter, we will discuss the following:

- Extension functions and activities provided by BPEL Process Manager
- Dynamic parallel flow activity
- Web Services Invocation Framework
- Java embedding
- Notification service
- Workflow service
- Identity service
- Oracle BPEL Server APIs

Extension Functions and Activities

In Chapters 3 and 4 we saw that BPEL is very flexible with respect to the expression and query language used. By default XPath 1.0 is used; however, any other language supported by the BPEL server can also be used. The idea behind this flexibility is to open up BPEL for future versions of XPath and XQuery.

XPath 1.0 does not provide all functions necessary to develop BPEL processes. Therefore, the BPEL specification defines additional functions such as `getVariableData()`, `getVariableProperty()`, and `getLinkStatus()`. Oracle BPEL Process Manager provides additional extension functions and activities to simplify development.

> Using functions and activities described in this section limits the portability of BPEL processes, because these will not be available on other BPEL servers.

Oracle BPEL Process Manager provides the following extension functions and activities:

- **Oracle-specific BPEL activities**: These include activities for data/array manipulation, Java embedding, parallel dynamic flows, etc. They are defined in the `http://schemas.oracle.com/bpel/extension` namespace, for which the `bpelx` prefix is used. Examples include `<bpelx:append>`, `<bpelx:insertBefore>`, `<bpelx:copyList>`, but also `<bpelx:exec>`, and `<bpelx:flowN>`. These activities will be explained later in this chapter.
- **XPath 2.0 functions**: These functions are not Oracle specific, and taken strictly are not part of XPath 1.0, which is the default query language. They are used for data manipulation and are defined in the `http://www.oracle.com/XSL/Transform/java/oracle.tip.pc.services.functions.Xpath20` namespace, for which the prefix `xp20` is used. Examples include `xp20:compare()`, `xp20:current-date()`, `xp20:lower-case()`, etc. For more information on XPath 2.0 please visit `http://www.w3.org/TR/xpath20/`.
- **Oracle-specific XPath extension functions**: These are used primarily for data manipulation and are defined in the `http://schemas.oracle.com/xpath/extension` namespace. Usually the `ora` prefix is used. These functions are described later in this section.
- **XPath extension functions for LDAP access and user authentication**: These functions are defined in the `http://schemas.oracle.com/xpath/extension/ldap` namespace with `ldap` prefix. Examples include `ldap:listUsers()` and `ldap:search()`.
- **Oracle-specific XSLT transformation extension functions**: These are helpful in stylesheet transformations. The namespace is `http://www.oracle.com/XSL/Transform/java/oracle.tip.pc.services.functions.ExtFunc`, for which the `orcl` prefix is usually used. Example functions: `orcl:square-root()` and `orcl:right-trim()`.

> All Oracle-specific functions and activities can be accessed from BPEL Designer.

We will look at the most important extension functions and activities based on their functionality:

- Transformation and query support
- Data and array manipulation

- XML manipulation
- Date and time expressions
- Process identification
- LDAP access and user management

Later in this chapter, we will also take a detailed look at the important extension activities, such as `<flowN>` and `<exec>`.

Transformation and Query Support

In real-world business processes we often have to match the schema of our XML document to the schema required by the partner web service. Consider our travel process example. Here we designed both the process and the partner web services, so we only had to perform minimal transformations for calling the Employee or Airlines web services. In real-world scenarios this will often not be the case and we will have to make more complex transformations.

To perform the transformations, we can use the BPEL `<assign>` activity. As this can be time consuming, Oracle provides an XSLT engine and an extension function through which we can activate the XSLT engine. This enables us to use XSLT to perform complex data transformations. Using XSLT is more appropriate than using `<assign>` because XSLT is the standard transformation language for XML. Also, sometimes we already have the stylesheets for the transformations. This way we can easily integrate them into BPEL processes.

To activate the XSLT engine we use the `ora:processXSLT()` function. The function requires two parameters—the XSLT stylesheet and the XML input on which the transformation should be made. The result of the function is the transformed XML. The syntax is:

```
ora:processXSLT('stlyesheet','XML_input')
```

Note that the same function is defined in the `http://schemas.oracle.com/bpel/extension/xpath/function/xdk` namespace as well. We can use either.

Usually we use this function within the `<assign>` activity, in the `<from>` clause. For example, to modify our travel process and make a more complex transformation to prepare the input for the Employee web service, we could use the XSLT engine, as shown in the following code excerpt:

```
<assign>
  <copy>

    <from expression="ora:processXSLT('employee.xslt',
                      bpws:getVariableData('TravelRequest','employee') )"/>

    <to variable="EmployeeTravelStatusRequest" part="employee"/>

  </copy>
</assign>
```

For this code to work we must create the `employee.xslt` stylesheet and deploy it with the process. For more information on XSLT, please refer to `http://www.w3.org/TR/xslt`.

> The `ora:processXSLT()` function can be accessed from BPEL Designer, which provides a graphical tool for creating stylesheets. Please refer to the *XSLT Mapper* section of Chapter 5.

In addition to the XSLT engine, Oracle BPEL Process Manager also provides an XSQL engine, which can be used in a similar way to the XSLT engine. It can be activated using the `ora:processXSQL()` function. We have to provide the XSQL template and the input XML on which the query should be performed:

```
ora:processXSQL('query_template','XML_input')
```

To use the XSQL engine the `XSQLConfig.xml` file should be updated. It is located in the `C:\OraBPELPM_1\integration\orabpel\system\classes` directory.

Data and Array Manipulation

Data manipulation in BPEL is done with the `<assign>` activity, where we can use XPath and BPEL functions in the `<from>` and `<to>` clauses. In addition, Oracle provides several custom functions that ease data manipulation considerably.

A very important aspect in data manipulation is arrays. In Chapter 4 we mentioned that arrays in BPEL are realized with XML elements that can occur more than once. In XML schema they are identified with the `maxOccurs` attribute, which can be set to a specific value or can be unbounded (`maxOccurs="unbounded"`). The items are addressed with the XPath `position()` function, as shown in the following example:

```
<assign>
  <copy>
    <from variable="TicketOffer"
          part="ticket"
          query="/item[position()=1]"/>
    <to variable="FirstOffer" part="ticket"/>
  </copy>
</assign>
```

The short notation is:

```
<assign>
  <copy>
    <from variable="TicketOffer"
          part="ticket"
          query="/item[1]"/>
    <to variable="FirstOffer" part="ticket"/>
  </copy>
</assign>
```

Often we need to dynamically address the items. Instead of hard-coding the index we can use a variable, such as:

```
<variable name="position" type="xs:int"/>
```

We could then create the XPath query expression, store it in a variable, and then use this variable to address the desired item, as shown in the following example:

```
<assign>
  <copy>
```

```
      <from expression="concat('/item[',
                        bpws:getVariableData('position'), ']')"/>
      <to variable="itemAddress"/>
    </copy>
    <copy>
      <from expression="bpws:getVariableData('TicketOffer', 'ticket',
                        bpws:getVariableData('itemAddress'))"/>
      <to variable="SelectedOffer" part="ticket"/>
    </copy>
  </assign>
```

Alternatively we can use an Oracle-specific function called `ora:getElement()`. The function takes four parameters: variable name, part name, query path, and element index:

```
ora:getElement('variable_name', 'part_name', 'query', index)
```

Using this function, the previous example would look like this:

```
<assign>
  <copy>
    <from expression="ora:getElement('TicketOffer', 'ticket', '/item',
                                     bpws:getVariableData('position'))"/>
    <to variable="SelectedOffer" part="ticket"/>
  </copy>
</assign>
```

We usually dynamically address items in loops using the `<while>` activity. To determine the number of items (array size), we can use the Oracle-specific function `ora:countNodes()`. The function returns the number of items as an integer and takes three parameters: variable name, part name, and query path (the last two parameters are optional):

```
ora:countNodes('variable_name', 'part_name', 'query')
```

To count the number of ticket offers in our example we could use the following code:

```
<assign>
  <copy>
    <from expression="ora:countNodes('TicketOffer',
                                     'ticket',
                                     '/item')"/>
    <to variable="NoOfOffers"/>
  </copy>
</assign>
```

To append a variable to the existing variable (array) we can use the Oracle-specific activity `<bpelx:append>`. This activity can be used within the `<assign>` activity. To add a new ticket offer to the existing offers we can use the following code:

```
<assign>
  <bpelx:append>

    <bpelx:from variable="NewOffer" part="ticket" />
    <bpelx:to variable="TicketOffer" part="ticket" />

  </bpelx:append>
</assign>
```

In a similar way we can use other extension activities, including `<bpelx:insertBefore>` and `<bpelx:copyList>`.

We have seen that Oracle-specific functions and activities simplify data and array management considerably. Next, we look at functions related to XML manipulation.

XML Manipulation

In some cases our BPEL processes will invoke web services that return strings. The content of these strings is XML. This approach is used by some developers, particularly on the .NET platform. Using such web services with BPEL is problematic because no function exists to parse string content to XML. In programming languages such as Java and C# we use XML parser functions or XML serialization (JAXB in Java).

Oracle therefore provides a custom function called `ora:parseEscapedXML()`. This function takes a string as a parameter and returns structured XML data:

```
ora:parseEscapedXML(string)
```

Let us suppose that the Employee web service returns a string instead of XML. We can parse it using the `ora:parseEscapedXML()` function:

```
<!-- Synchronously invoke the Employee Travel Status Web Service -->
<invoke partnerLink="employeeTravelStatus"
        portType="emp:EmployeeTravelStatusPT"
        operation="EmployeeTravelStatus"
        inputVariable="EmployeeTravelStatusRequest"
        outputVariable="EmployeeTravelStatusResponseString" />

<assign>
  <copy>
    <from expression="ora:parseEscapedXML(
          bpws:getVariableData('EmployeeTravelStatusResponseString'))"/>
    <to variable="EmployeeTravelStatusRespose" part="employee"/>
  </copy>
</assign>
```

To perform an inverse operation—convert structured XML to a string—we can use the `ora:getContentAsString()` function. It takes structured XML data as a parameter and returns a string:

```
ora:getContentAsString(XMLElement)
```

To get the node value as an integer instead of a string we can use the `ora:integer()` function:

```
ora:integer(node)
```

To add single quotes to a string we can use the `ora:addQuotes()` function:

```
ora:addQuotes(string)
```

Oracle even provides a function to read the content of a file. The function is called `ora:readFile()` and is often used together with the `ora:parseEscapedXML()` function, which converts the file content to structured XML (if the file content is XML). The syntax of the `ora:readFile()` function is:

```
ora:readFile('file_name')
```

Next, we look at the expressions related to date and time.

Date and Time Expressions

Sometimes in our BPEL processes we need the current date and/or time, for example, to time-stamp certain data. For this, we can use the Oracle-specific functions. The most important are:

- `ora:getCurrentDate()`: Get current date
- `ora:getCurrentTime()`: Get current time
- `ora:getCurrentDateTime()`: Get current date and time

Note that all three functions return strings (and not the date or date/time types). All three functions also take an optional parameter that specifies the date/time format. The format is specified according to `java.text.SimpleDateFormat`. For details, refer to Java API documentation at `http://java.sun.com/j2se/1.4.2/docs/api/java/text/SimpleDateFormat.html`).

To format an XML Schema `date` or `dateTime` to a string representation, which is more suitable for output, Oracle provides the `ora:formatDate()` function. The syntax of the function that returns a string is:

```
ora:formatDate('dateTime', 'format')
```

Once again, the format is specified according to `java.text.SimpleDateFormat` format.

A similar function is provided in the `xp20` namespace:

```
xp20:format-dateTime('dateTime', 'format')
```

Next, let us look at functions related to process identification.

Process Identification

Oracle provides several functions related to process identification. With these functions we can get process IDs, URLs, and more. These functions are:

- `ora:getProcessId()`: Returns the ID of the current BPEL process
- `ora:getProcessURL()`: Returns the root URL of the current BPEL process
- `ora:getInstanceId()`: Returns the process instance ID
- `ora:getConversationId()`: Returns the conversation ID used in asynchronous conversations
- `ora:getCreator()`: Returns the process instance creator
- `ora:generateGUID()`: Generates a unique GUID (Globally Unique ID)

LDAP Access and User Management

XPath extension functions for LDAP access and user authentication are defined in the `http://schemas.oracle.com/xpath/extension/ldap` namespace with `ldap` prefix. These functions are:

- `ldap:listUsers('properties','filter')`
- `ldap:search('properties','filter','scope'?)`
- `ldap:authenticate('properties','userId','password')`

With this, we have concluded the overview of extension functions provided by BPEL Process Manager. In the next section, we will take a look at the dynamic parallel flow activity.

Dynamic Parallel Flow

In Chapter 3 we became familiar with the `<flow>` activity, which enables to start several parallel activities. In our Travel process example we used `<flow>` activity to start two parallel sequences that acquired plane ticket offers from American and Delta Airline web services. As the operation invocations for the ticket offers were asynchronous, we had to use `<receive>` activities to wait for the callbacks.

The problem with the `<flow>` activity is that we need to know in advance how many parallel activities are required. The number of parallel activities is specified by the BPEL code. In several real-world use cases this is limiting, because the number of required parallel branches can depend on the information stored in a variable or received from the partner web service. In such cases, the `<flow>` activity is inadequate.

Oracle BPEL Process Manager therefore provides `<flowN>` activity, which can create multiple parallel activities at run time. The number of parallel activities is specified by a variable. The parallel branches created by `<flowN>` perform the same operations but use different data (variables). Each branch gets a unique index number, which can be used to acquire the data (for example using XPath expressions and XML sequences that mimic arrays).

> `<flowN>` functionality is very similar to the forthcoming BPEL 2.0 `<forEach>` activity.

The `<flowN>` activity is defined in the `http://schemas.oracle.com/bpel/extension` namespace, for which the `bpelx` prefix is used. The syntax is shown below:

```
<bpelx:flowN N="number-of-parallel-flows"
             indexVariable="variable-name-for-index">

   activity

</bpelx:flowN>
```

We have to specify the number of parallel flows that need to be created—for this the attribute `N` is used. Usually we will use an expression to get the number of parallel flows from a variable (using `bpws:getVariableData()`) or to count the number of parameters of array items (using `ora:countNodes()` for example). We also have to specify the name of the variable used for the index (the number of the parallel flow) that has been created. This variable should be of type `xs:int` or similar. We will use the variable to extract appropriate data, for example from an array. The parallel branches created by `<flowN>` execute the same activities, but they usually use different data, for which the index variable is used to reference an array or XML sequence.

At first glance, the `<while>` activity looks similar to the `<flowN>` activity. However, there is a huge difference between them. `<while>` creates a loop that is executed several times sequentially. `<flowN>` creates several branches that are executed in parallel.

> `<flowN>` activity is accessible from BPEL Designer.

As the code within the `<flowN>` activity is executed in parallel, we must take care while providing parallel access to variables and other resources (for example partner links). If variables are updated within `<flowN>` we should make sure that we do not use the same variable instance in multiple branches. We should also not use the same partner link in parallel branches. Usually it is appropriate to include the activities within `<flowN>` in a scope. For more information on scopes and serializable access to variables, please refer to Chapter 4.

Within `<flowN>` we might want to use different data for each parallel branch, or store several responses from partner links. The most appropriate way to achieve this is to use arrays—or XML sequences where the maximal occurrence of an element is unbounded. Therefore we should be familiar with XPath and also with Oracle-specific functions for management of data and arrays. We have covered these earlier in this chapter.

Finally, we will often want different parallel branches to invoke operations of different partner web services. To achieve this we will have to use dynamic partner links. We have explained dynamic partner links in Chapter 4.

Dynamic Flow Example

To demonstrate how we can use the `<flowN>` activity let us modify our travel process example. So far, our example has invoked two airline web services in parallel using the `<flow>` activity (American and Delta Airlines). We will extend the example so that it will invoke several web services. The list of web services (actually their addresses) will be provided as the input parameter. In real-world use cases this information could be retrieved from a service, database, etc.

The output from the airline web services will be stored in an array. We will also modify how the best offer is selected. So far, we have used a simple `<switch>` activity that had to select between two offers. Now we will write a `<while>` loop that will select the lowest offer from all offers stored in the array.

Besides the `<flowN>` activity, this example will demonstrate how to use dynamic partner links, array, and loops. Our travel process will require several modifications:

- First, we will have to supplement the input message from the client, which will now include the list of partner links (airline web services) our process should invoke to get an airline ticket offer. We will have to modify the process WSDL to achieve this.
- Then, we will need to modify the part of the process that makes parallel invocations to airline web services. Here we will use the `<flowN>` activity and use an array to store the results.
- Next, we will use dynamic partner links to invoke airline web services in parallel.
- Finally, we will modify the code that selects the best offer. We will use a `<while>` loop to make the selection and access the results from airline web services to compare the prices.

In this example, we assume that all airline web services provide the same WSDL interface. Let's start with modifying the WSDL.

Providing a List of Partner Links

To provide a list of airline web services that our process should invoke to get airline ticket offers we will modify the WSDL of the process. In Chapter 4 we explained that the partner link endpoint references in BPEL are stored as `wsa:EndpointReferences` as defined by WS-Addressing. We will use this XML element in the client message to specify the addresses of airline web services.

To achieve this we add a part to the `TravelRequestMessage`. The part `airlineData` will be of type `AirlineDataType`:

```
<message name="TravelRequestMessage">

  <part name="employee" type="emp:EmployeeType" />
  <part name="flightData" type="aln:FlightRequestType" />
  <part name="airlineData" type="tns:AirlineDataType" />

</message>
```

We define the `AirlineDataType` as a sequence of `wsa:EndpointReferences`. To use the `wsa:EndpointReference` element in our schema we have to import the WS-Addressing schema. It is provided by the BPEL Process Manager on the following URL: `http://localhost:9700/orabpel/xmllib/ws-addressing.xsd`. We write the following schema (as part of the WSDL):

```
<xs:schema elementFormDefault="qualified"
           targetNamespace="http://packtpub.com/bpel/travel/">

  <xs:import namespace="http://schemas.xmlsoap.org/ws/2003/03/addressing"
   schemaLocation="http://localhost:9700/orabpel/xmllib/ws-addressing.xsd" />

  <xs:complexType name="AirlineDataType">

    <xs:sequence>
      <xs:element name="AirlineLink" maxOccurs="unbounded">
        <xs:complexType>

          <xs:sequence>
            <xs:element ref="wsa:EndpointReference" />
          </xs:sequence>

        </xs:complexType>
      </xs:element>
    </xs:sequence>

  </xs:complexType>
</xs:schema>
```

Dynamic Parallel Invocation of Airline Services

Next, we will modify the part of the travel process that makes parallel invocations to airline web services. We will use the `<flowN>` activity to make as many parallel invocations as there are addresses provided in the input message from the client. We will also store the results of each airline web service in an array.

Next we modify the `CheckFlightAvailability` scope. First, we declare the variables. We declare the index variable `index` of type `xs:int`. We also declare a `CombinedFlightResponse` variable where we will store the output of each airline web service:

```
<variables>

  <!-- output from all Airlines -->
  <variable name="CombinedFlightResponse"
          messageType="aln:TravelResponseMessage"/>

  <!-- counter for flowN -->
  <variable name="index" type="xsd:int"/>
</variables>
```

Next, we replace the `<flow>` activity with `<flowN>`. We will use the index as the `indexVariable`. The `<flowN>` should start as many parallel branches as there are addresses in the input message from the client. We use the `ora:countNodes()` function to count the number of airline web service addresses:

```
<bpelx:flowN N="ora:countNodes('TravelRequest',
                               'airlineData',
                               '/airlineData/trv:AirlineLink')"
        indexVariable="index">
```

Dynamic Partner Links

We have already mentioned that we will invoke airline web services in parallel branches, created by `<flowN>`. As the addresses of web services are provided in the message from the client, we will need to create a dynamic partner link in each branch. The parallel branches will execute the same activities (including the `<invoke>` for operation invocation and `<receive>` for callback). This means that the same variable will store the result from the callback. To shield the parallel branches we use a local scope for each branch.

In the scope we will declare a partner link, called `Airline`. We will also declare a variable to store the result from the callback (`FlightResponse`):

```
<scope name="LocalScopeFlowN">

  <partnerLinks>

    <partnerLink name="Airline"
             partnerLinkType="aln:flightLT"
             myRole="airlineCustomer"
             partnerRole="airlineService"/>

  </partnerLinks>

  <variables>

    <!-- output from Airline -->
    <variable name="FlightResponse"
              messageType="aln:TravelResponseMessage"/>

  </variables>
```

Next we define a sequence (remember that it will be started in parallel branches). Within the sequence, we first copy the airline web service endpoint reference (address) to the partner link. Then we invoke the web service and wait for the callback:

```
<sequence>

  <!-- Create the partner link  -->
     <assign>
     <copy>
      <from expression="bpws:getVariableData('TravelRequest',
                     'airlineData',
```

```
                     concat('/airlineData/trv:AirlineLink[',
                     bpws:getVariableData('index'),
                     ']/wsa:EndpointReference'))"/>
        <to partnerLink="Airline"/>
      </copy>
    </assign>

    <!-- Invoke the airline web service -->
    <invoke partnerLink="Airline"
         portType="aln:FlightAvailabilityPT"
         operation="FlightAvailability"
         inputVariable="FlightDetails" />

    <receive partnerLink="Airline"
         portType="aln:FlightCallbackPT"
         operation="FlightTicketCallback"
         variable="FlightResponse" />
```

Finally, we store the result in the array called `CombinedFlightResponse`. We use the Oracle-specific `<bpelx:append>` activity to achieve this:

```
    <!-- Store the result -->
    <assign>
      <bpelx:append>
        <bpelx:from variable="FlightResponse"
                      part="confirmationData" />
        <bpelx:to variable="CombinedFlightResponse"
                    part="confirmationData" />
      </bpelx:append>
    </assign>

  </sequence>
</scope>

</bpelx:flowN>
```

Offer Selection Loop

The final step is to modify the code that selects the best offer. We replace the simple `<switch>` activity with a `<while>` loop where we iterate through all offers and compare them by price. We store the final result in the `TravelResponse` variable. We also need a variable to store the temporary result from the airline that we compare to the best offer. We name this variable `TempResponse`:

```
<variables>
  <variable name="TempResponse"
            messageType="aln:TravelResponseMessage"/>
</variables>
```

The `<while>` loop makes as many iterations as there are airline web services that have been invoked. We get this number by counting the airline web service addresses using `ora:countNodes()` function. To access the array data we use the `ora:getElement()` function. The code is shown below:

```
<assign>
  <copy>
    <from expression="0"/>
    <to variable="index"/>
  </copy>
  <copy>
    <from expression="ora:getElement('CombinedFlightResponse',
                               'confirmationData',
```

```
                         '/confirmationData/confirmationData','1')" />
      <to variable="TravelResponse" part="confirmationData" />
    </copy>
  </assign>

  <while condition="bpws:getVariableData('index') &lt;
                  ora:countNodes('TravelRequest',
                      'airlineData','/airlineData/trv:AirlineLink')">

    <sequence>
      <assign>
         <copy>
           <from expression="bpws:getVariableData('index') + 1"/>
           <to variable="index"/>
         </copy>
         <copy>
           <from expression="ora:getElement('CombinedFlightResponse',
                                'confirmationData',
                                '/confirmationData/confirmationData',
                                bpws:getVariableData('index'))" />
           <to variable="TempResponse" part="confirmationData" />
         </copy>
      </assign>

      <switch>
        <case condition="bpws:getVariableData('TempResponse',
                           'confirmationData','/confirmationData/aln:Price')
                    &lt; bpws:getVariableData('TravelResponse',
                           'confirmationData','/confirmationData/aln:Price')">
           <assign>
             <copy>
               <from variable="TempResponse" />
               <to variable="TravelResponse" />
             </copy>
           </assign>
        </case>

      </switch>
    </sequence>

  </while>
```

Deploying and Testing the Example

We are now ready to deploy the example to the BPEL Server and to test it. To deploy the example we use the **obant** utility. Note that we could also develop and deploy this example from JDeveloper or Eclipse BPEL Designer. After starting **obant** we should see the following output:

```
Developer Prompt

Z:\Chapter6\1_FlowN>obant

Z:\Chapter6\1_FlowN>SETLOCAL
Buildfile: build.xml

main:
    [bpelc] validating "Z:\Chapter6\1_FlowN\Travel.bpel" ...
    [bpelc] BPEL suitcase deployed to: C:\OraBPELPM_1\integration\orabpel\domain
s\default\deploy

BUILD SUCCESSFUL
Total time: 17 seconds

Z:\Chapter6\1_FlowN>ENDLOCAL

Z:\Chapter6\1_FlowN>
```

We use BPEL Console to start the process. In the visual flow representation, we can observe how many parallel branches have been started and how many times the loop has executed:

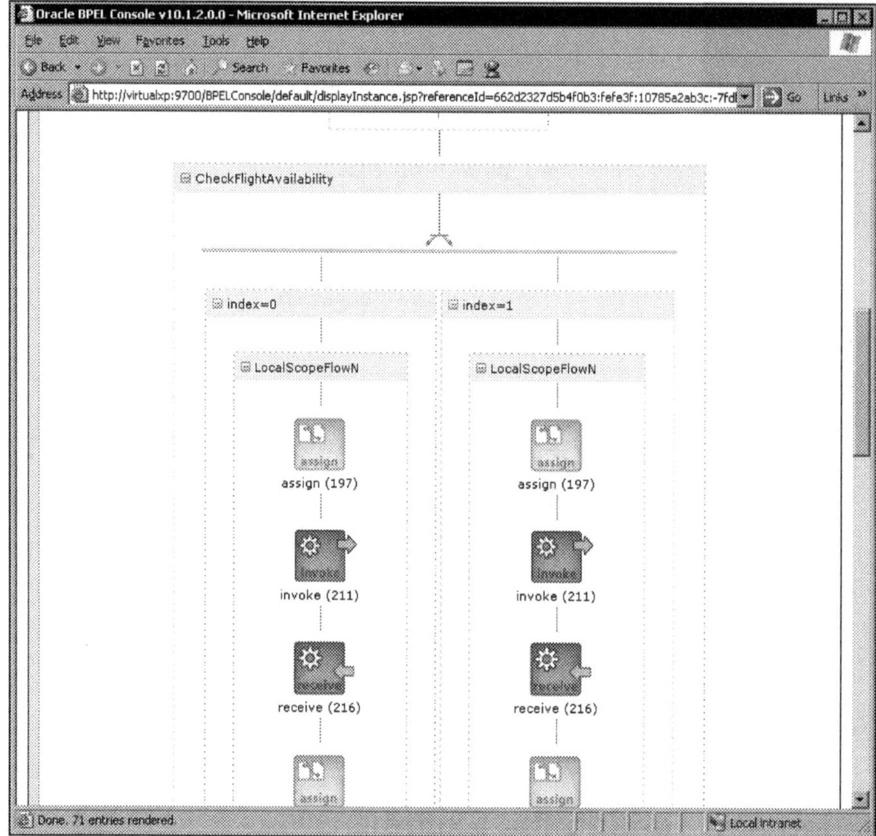

This concludes the example. Through it, we have demonstrated dynamic parallel flows, dynamic partner links, arrays, and loops. In the next section, we will discuss the Web Services Invocation Framework.

Web Services Invocation Framework

In real-world scenarios, a business process will often have to invoke operations on services that have not been implemented as web services. Enterprises usually have several applications and systems that incorporate valuable business logic. Not all this logic has been exposed as web services. Although exposing functionality as web services is quite straightforward, there are several reasons why we might prefer not using web services and instead access resources directly. Converting existing resources to web services is time consuming and requires additional resources on the server. Web services have to be secured adequately as they are accessible from everywhere, even outside the firewall. Web services usually also perform slower than native resources and do not provide automatic propagation of transaction contexts.

In this section, we will overview the Web Services Invocation Framework (WSIF). It allows connectivity of BPEL processes with resources other than web services and achieves this without the need to modify BPEL code or include any vendor-specific extensions in the BPEL code. WSIF extends the web services model. It allows us to describe each service in WSDL, even if it is not a web service that communicates through SOAP. It also allows us to map such a service to the actual implementation and protocol. WSIF is an Apache technology that was originally developed by IBM alphaWorks as a part of WSTK (Web Services Toolkit). For more information about WSIF, visit `http://ws.apache.org/wsif/`.

> Web Services Invocation Framework provides connectivity of BPEL processes with resources other than web services without BPEL code modifications and without any vendor-specific BPEL extensions. Only a WSDL binding has to be provided.

Oracle BPEL Process Manager provides support for WSIF. As BPEL Process Manager uses a Java Enterprise Edition application server underneath we are most interested in connectivity with Java resources, such as Java classes, EJBs (Enterprise Java Beans), JMS (Java Message Service), ERP systems accessible through JCA (Java Connector Architecture), JDBC databases, etc. WSIF included with BPEL Process Manager provides bindings for the following resources:

- Java classes
- Enterprise Java Beans (EJB)
- Java Connector Architecture (JCA)
- HTTP GET and POST
- Sockets

Support for other resources, such as JMS, will follow. It is also possible to write our own binding.

Advantages of WSIF

To incorporate resources for which a WSIF binding exists into BPEL processes we only need to modify the service binding (WSDL). For example, to use a Java class instead of the Employee Travel Status web service we only have to modify the WSDL of the Employee web service. In other words, we can bind the abstract description of the Employee web service (the port types) to a SOAP-based implementation, to a Java class, to an EJB, or any other supported resource simply by modifying the WSDL binding. No code changes in the BPEL process are necessary. We will show how to achieve this later in this section.

This approach is suitable for real-world scenarios and makes BPEL very useful for EAI as well as B2B. Enterprise information systems usually consist of a large number of different software pieces, such as legacy applications accessible though JCA, EJBs, messaging infrastructure, web services developed on different platforms, etc. To integrate all these pieces we have to deal with different protocols. If we migrate the software used to a different server or upgrade it to use a new technology, we have to upgrade the integration code—unless we use WSIF. WSIF allows us to describe all these services with WSDL and then bind them to the actual software through providers. It actually separates the interface and the protocol. This gives us the flexibility to change the protocol (and implementation technology) without the need to modify (or even recompile) the BPEL code.

In addition to this flexibility, using WSIF we also gain other important benefits:

- The performance when invoking web service operations is several orders of magnitude slower than the performance when invoking native Java classes, and an order of magnitude slower than invoking EJBs, or other native Java resources. Invoking services through WSIF **maintains the performance** of native protocols. Thus, when invoking Java resources, native Java classes, EJBs, or any other resources, we do not have to pay the performance penalty of web services.
- Web services invocations do not have the ability to propagate contexts; particularly the transaction context is important and it is not propagated automatically between web services. WSIF enables automatic propagation of transaction contexts between invoked transaction-aware Java resources using JTA/JTS (Java Transaction API/Service), such as EJBs or JCA. In this way, Java resources can participate in distributed transactions.

To demonstrate how WSIF works we will modify our travel process. We will demonstrate how to invoke the following resources over WSIF:

- Java class
- EJB

First, we will show how to invoke a Java class instead of the Employee web service. We will also explain how exceptions can be propagated between Java and BPEL. Later, we will extend our process and add an Airline Rating service. We will invoke this service like any other web service (using the `<invoke>` activity), but actually implement it as an EJB (session bean) and use WSIF to access it.

Let us now concentrate on replacing the Employee web service with a Java class. The contract between the BPEL process and the web services has already been defined as a WSDL definition. To replace the web service our Java class has to provide the same interface, so we will first write such a Java class. The other possibility would be to adapt the WSDL to an existing Java class (or other resource), but this would require modifications in BPEL because of the changed interface. The first approach is better, because it is a contract-first approach. This way the interface of the service is adapted to the needs of the BPEL process and not vice versa.

Java to XML Bindings

To invoke any Java resource from BPEL we need to access data from BPEL variables sent as input parameters from Java, and send responses back to BPEL. Because BPEL variables are XML and Java variables are not, we need a mapping between XML and Java.

To handle XML data from Java we have several options:

- We can handle XML manually through the DOM (Document Object Model) API. This way the input and output parameters of the corresponding Java methods are of type `Element` from the W3C DOM API for Java. We need to use DOM methods to manipulate XML directly.

- We can use automated Java to XML bindings. Java to XML binding enables automatic conversion of XML Schema types to Java types. To achieve this, interfaces and a set of Java classes are generated through which we manipulate the XML. This way the XML is hidden and we can use it though interfaces (like JavaBeans). Here we have two options:
    - We can use XML façades. Oracle BPEL Server supports default Java to XML bindings using XML façades.
    - We can use custom Java serializers. Oracle already provides custom serializers that support JAXB (Java API for XML Bindings), XML Beans, and Axis Beans. We can also write our own serializers.

In the next section, we will look at the XML façades.

XML Façades

XML façades are the default Oracle BPEL Process Manager Java to XML binding for WSIF and are an integral part of the product. XML façades are a set of Java interfaces and classes through which we can access and modify XML data stored in BPEL variables in a relatively easy way using get/set methods. This way we are not required to manipulate XML directly from the Java code. More importantly, the XML is hidden behind the façade and we manipulate the data through regular Java interfaces. This concept is known as **XML serialization**. The idea behind XML façades is to provide support for basic data types through mapping them to built-in types and to generate Java classes from XML Schemas for complex types. XML façades are a lightweight alternative to JAXB.

Basic data types are automatically mapped between XML Schema and Java. Most of the simple types can be mapped to either primitive or object types. This is useful as we can adapt the mapping to the actual types used in our Java code. The following table shows the mappings:

XML Schema Type	Java Type
`xs:string`	`java.lang.String` or `char` or `java.lang.Character`
`xs:int`, `xs:integer`	`int` or `java.lang.Integer` or `java.math.BigInteger`
`xs:long`	`long` or `java.lang.Long`
`xs:short`	`short` or `java.lang.Short`
`xs:float`	`float` or `java.lang.Float`
`xs:double`	`double` or `java.lang.Double` or `java.math.BigDecimal`
`xs:byte`	`byte` or `java.lang.Byte`
`xs:Boolean`	`boolean` or `java.lang.Boolean`
`xs:dateTime`	`java.util.Calendar`
`xs:date`	`java.util.Date`

Complex XML types, defined in the `<types>` section of the WSDL or in the external XML Schemas (XSD) files, also need to be mapped to Java. For example in our Employee web service

WSDL, we can see that it provides an operation that takes as input the `EmployeeTravelStatusRequestMessage`, which is of type `EmployeeType`. Let us look at the WSDL description of the Employee web service in the `Employee.wsdl` file. In the WSDL the `EmployeeType` complex XML type is defined, which is used for the above message and for the corresponding `EmployeeTravelStatusRequest` BPEL variable:

```
<xs:complexType name="EmployeeType">
   <xs:sequence>
      <xs:element name="FirstName" type="xs:string" />
      <xs:element name="LastName" type="xs:string" />
      <xs:element name="Department" type="xs:string" />
   </xs:sequence>
</xs:complexType>
```

The XML façade for this complex XML type provides an interface and a class through which we can access the elements (first name, last name, department) using Java getter methods. The XML façade also allows us to modify the element data using setter methods. It consists of an interface (`IEmployeeType`) and a class (`EmployeeType`), which provides the following methods:

- `getFirstName()` and `setFirstName()`
- `getLastName()` and `setLastName()`
- `getDepartment()` and `setDepartment()`

There is also a factory class (`EmployeeTypeFactory`) through which we can create the `IEmployeeType` using the `createFacade()` method. The XML façade makes the code simpler and easier to maintain; this is particularly true for larger variables with many member fields.

To generate mappings Oracle BPEL Process Manager provides a schema compiler utility called **schemac**. To generate the XML façade for `Employee.wsdl` we can use the following command:

`schemac Employee.wsdl`

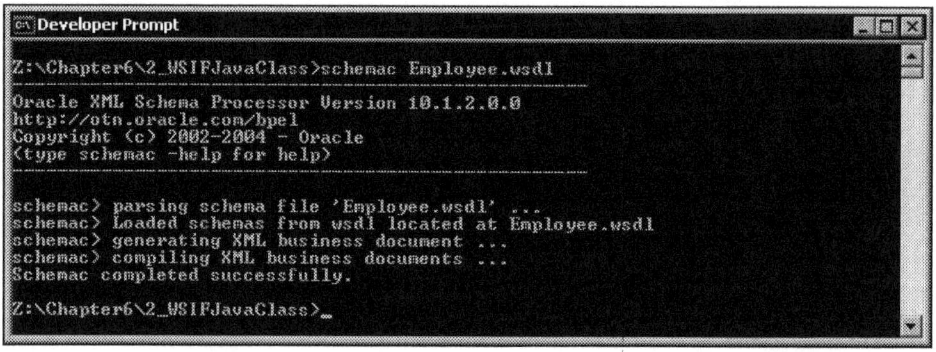

```
Developer Prompt

Z:\Chapter6\2_WSIFJavaClass>schemac Employee.wsdl

Oracle XML Schema Processor Version 10.1.2.0.0
http://otn.oracle.com/bpel
Copyright (c) 2002-2004 - Oracle
(type schemac -help for help)

schemac> parsing schema file 'Employee.wsdl' ...
schemac> Loaded schemas from wsdl located at Employee.wsdl
schemac> generating XML business document ...
schemac> compiling XML business documents ...
Schemac completed successfully.

Z:\Chapter6\2_WSIFJavaClass>_
```

To use these classes from Java resources we will need to compile them into the following directory where the BPEL server can access them: `C:\OraBPELPM_1\integration\orabpel\system\classes`.

The `schemac` utility has several options. We can use the `-d` switch to define the directory where the generated façade classes should be stored. To see the façade source code we can use the `-trace` option. The **`schemac`** utility can also be used to generate XML Schemas from Java classes.

This is useful if we would like to adapt the service interface to an existing Java resource. We have to use the `-R` switch and provide the Java class name without the extension.

Invoking a Java Class through WSIF

To replace the Employee web service with a Java class without modifying BPEL we need a Java class that has the same interface (contract) as the original web service. This means that the Java class has to provide the operations with identical functionality. The operations have to accept the same parameters and return the same result type. The operation name, however, does not need to be identical. Looking at the original WSDL we can see that the Employee web service provides a synchronous operation called `EmployeeTravelStatus` (the WSDL is shown in Chapter 3).

The input parameter of the operation is of type `EmployeeType`. To map it to Java we will use the XML façade that we generated earlier using the **schemac** tool. The return type of the operation is of type `TravelClassType`, which is a restriction of `xs:string`. Therefore, we will map this type to `java.lang.String`.

We are now ready to write the Java equivalent class for the Employee web service. We will call the new Java class `EmployeeStatusJava`, which will have a single method called `getTravelStatus`. The method body will be oversimplified—we will print a notification to the server console (to verify that the class has actually been called) and return the status Economy. In a real-world example, we would access a database or retrieve the status from an application. The code is shown below. We have imported the XML façade classes and used the getter methods to access the first and the last name of the employee:

```
package com.packtpub;

import com.packtpub.service.employee.*;

public class EmployeeStatusJava {

  public String getTravelStatus (EmployeeType emp) {

    System.out.println("Java employee status for "+emp.getFirstName()+
                       " "+emp.getLastName()+": Economy.");

    return "Economy";

  }
}
```

Defining WSIF Bindings in WSDL

To persuade the BPEL process to use the Java class instead of the web service we have to define the WSIF binding to the Java class. We do this in the Employee WSDL, where we will add the binding section. Each WSIF binding consists of two parts. First, we have to define the actual binding, where we specify the following:

- Type of binding we use (Java class, EJB, JCA, ...)
- Mapping of types: We specify the mapping of XML types to the destination types (for Java resources these are Java types). We have to define the mapping for all complex types; simple types are mapped automatically based on the table presented earlier in this section.

- Mapping of operations: For each WSDL operation we specify the corresponding operation in the destination resource (in our example we specify the method name used by the Java class).

Second, we have to specify the service that we will be using. We specify the exact name of the resource—for the Java class we specify the full name of the Java class including the package name.

In a real-world scenario, it may happen that we will have a resource, such as a Java class or an EJB, for which a WSDL does not exist. Then we have to go through the following steps:

1. Define the Java to XML bindings, where we select how to map input parameters and return values to XML. We can use XML façades and simplify the work using the `schemac` tool with the `-R` switch, which will generate an XML Schema based on a Java class.
2. Define signatures for each operation and the corresponding input and output messages. Later in this section, we will also show how to handle faults.
3. Add the WSIF binding.
4. Add the `<partnerLinkType>` declaration in order to use the WSDL from the BPEL process.

Particularly in the first two steps, we can use a tool or a wizard for automatic conversion of resources to web services. Such tools are available for most environments. Of course, we do not actually convert the resource to a web service, but make use of the generated WSDL (with additional modifications). Later we will show how we can use JDeveloper version 10.1.3 (or later) for automatic generation of WSIF bindings.

WSIF Bindings for Java Classes

Let us now define the WSIF binding for the Employee Java class. We start by defining the two namespaces used by WSIF providers in the root element of the WSDL document, the `<definitions>` tag. The `format` namespace is used to define the type mappings and the `java` namespace to define the operation mappings and the full name of the Java class:

```
<?xml version="1.0" encoding="utf-8" ?>
<definitions xmlns:xs="http://www.w3.org/2001/XMLSchema"
             xmlns:tns="http://packtpub.com/service/employee/"
             targetNamespace="http://packtpub.com/service/employee/"
             xmlns="http://schemas.xmlsoap.org/wsdl/"
             xmlns:plnk="http://schemas.xmlsoap.org/ws/2003/05/partner-link/"
             xmlns:format="http://schemas.xmlsoap.org/wsdl/formatbinding/"
             xmlns:java="http://schemas.xmlsoap.org/wsdl/java/" >
...
```

Next, we add the binding section. This section is usually located after port type declarations and before partner link types. Here we define a Java binding for the `EmployeeTravelStatusPT` port type:

- We define the type mapping from XML to Java. The input parameter XML type `EmployeeType` is mapped to the `com.packtpub.service.employee.EmployeeType` Java class. The output parameter `TravelClassType` is mapped to the `java.lang.String`.

- We also define that the WSDL operation `EmployeeTravelStatus` is mapped to the Java method `getTravelStatus()`. Notice that the name of the WSDL operation and the method name of the Java class do not need to be equal, but the types of input and return parameters have to be equal:

```
...
  <binding name="JavaBinding" type="tns:EmployeeTravelStatusPT">

    <java:binding/>
    <format:typeMapping encoding="Java" style="Java">

      <format:typeMap typeName="tns:EmployeeType"
              formatType="com.packtpub.service.employee.EmployeeType" />
      <format:typeMap typeName="tns:TravelClassType"
              formatType="java.lang.String" />

    </format:typeMapping>

    <operation name="EmployeeTravelStatus">
      <java:operation methodName="getTravelStatus"/>
      <input/>
      <output/>
    </operation>

  </binding>
...
```

Next, we have to specify the service used. We define that the service is provided by the Java class. The Employee service will use the `com.packtpub.EmployeeStatusJava` Java class:

```
...
  <service name="Employee">
    <documentation>Employee</documentation>

    <port name="JavaPort" binding="tns:JavaBinding">
      <java:address className="com.packtpub.EmployeeStatusJava"/>
    </port>

  </service>
```

The rest of the Employee WSDL including partner link types has not been changed.

Testing the Example

We are almost ready to test the example and to ensure that the BPEL process uses the Java class instead of the original web service. Remember that we have only modified the WSDL. We have not made any changes to the BPEL process code. We use the original BPEL code and the same partner link and invoke the `EmployeeStatusJava` Java class with the usual `<invoke>` activity used for invoking the web service.

Before we can run the example, we have to do a few "book-keeping" activities. First, we have to ensure that the BPEL process uses the modified WSDL. For this, we have to modify the `bpel.xml` file and specify that the `Employee.wsdl` file should be taken from the current directory and not from the web service itself:

```
...
      <partnerLinkBinding name="employeeTravelStatus">
        <property name="wsdlLocation">
          Employee.wsdl
        </property>
      </partnerLinkBinding>
...
```

Then we must generate the XML façade using the **schemac** utility and compile the `EmployeeStatusJava` class. We have to deploy the XML façade and the Java class to the `C:\OraBPELPM_1\integration\bpelpm\orabpel\system\classes` directory, where the BPEL server can locate and use them. The easiest way to do this is to modify `build.xml`, which should invoke the scemac compiler, the javac compiler, and the bpelc compiler. After starting the obant utility, we should get the following output:

```
Developer Prompt

Z:\Chapter6\2_WSIFJavaClass>obant

Z:\Chapter6\2_WSIFJavaClass>SETLOCAL
Buildfile: build.xml

CompileJava:
   [schemac] schemac> parsing schema file 'Z:\Chapter6\2_WSIFJavaClass/Employee.w
sdl' ...
   [schemac] schemac> Loaded schemas from wsdl located at Z:\Chapter6\2_WSIFJavaC
lass/Employee.wsdl
   [schemac] schemac> generating XML business document ...
   [schemac] schemac> compiling XML business documents ...
     [javac] Compiling 1 source file to C:\OraBPELPM_1\integration\orabpel\system
\classes

main:
     [bpelc] validating "Z:\Chapter6\2_WSIFJavaClass\Travel.bpel" ...
     [bpelc] BPEL suitcase deployed to: C:\OraBPELPM_1\integration\orabpel\domain
s\default\deploy

all:

BUILD SUCCESSFUL
Total time: 15 seconds

Z:\Chapter6\2_WSIFJavaClass>ENDLOCAL

Z:\Chapter6\2_WSIFJavaClass>_
```

Next, we use the BPEL Console to start the process. In the visual flow window we can observe the execution of the process. We can see that the Employee service has been invoked and that it has returned the status Economy:

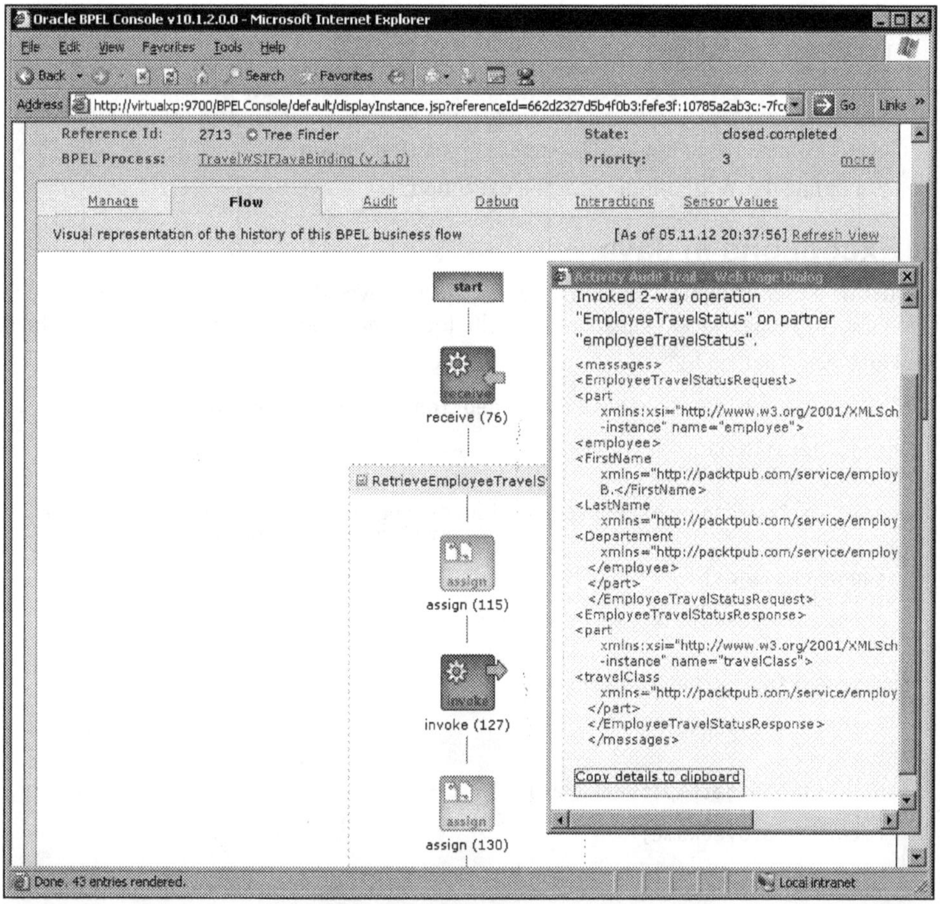

To verify that the BPEL Process Manager has invoked the Java class, the BPEL Process Manager console window should show the following output:

Exception Handling

When invoking Java resources from BPEL we need a way to propagate Java exceptions to BPEL. With WSIF we can map Java exceptions to WSDL faults and handle them using BPEL fault handlers. The exception serializer is responsible for this mapping. Oracle BPEL Process Manager provides a default exception serializer and we can also write our own custom exception serializer. To demonstrate how Java exceptions can be propagated to BPEL we will extend our example. First, we will use the default serializer. Then, we will extend the example with a custom serializer. For using the default serializer we go through the following steps:

1. We define a user exception in Java and modify the `EmployeeStatusJava` Java class to throw the exception.
2. We define the corresponding fault in the WSDL. This includes the definition of XML Schema type for the fault message, the fault message, and addition of the `<fault>` message to the WSDL `<operation>` description.
3. We define the WSIF binding for the exception.

User Exceptions in Java

We will define a user exception for signaling that an employee does not exist. We will name the exception `EmployeeDoesNotExistException`. The following code shows the exception in Java:

```
package com.packtpub;

public class EmployeeDoesNotExistException extends Exception
{
  String detailDesc;
  String employeeName;

  public EmployeeDoesNotExistException(String message, String detailDesc,
                                        String employeeName)
  {
    super(message);
    this.detailDesc = detailDesc;
    this.employeeName = employeeName;
  }

  public String getDetailDesc()
  {
    return detailDesc;
  }

  public String getEmployeeName()
  {
    return employeeName;
  }
}
```

Next, we will modify the `EmployeeStatusJava` Java class. We will throw the exception if the last name of the employee equals "Juric". This modification of code is straightforward therefore we do not show it here.

Defining Faults in WSDL

In the next step, we will define the corresponding fault in WSDL. The Java exception will be propagated to this fault. To use the default exception serializer we have to use a specific complex type for the exception, which has two elements: `faultstring` and `detail`. We will add this complex type to the `<types>` section of the Employee WSDL:

```
<xs:complexType name="EmployeeDoesNotExistExceptionType">
  <xs:sequence>
    <xs:element name="faultstring" type="xs:string" />
    <xs:element name="detail" type="xs:string" />
  </xs:sequence>
</xs:complexType>
```

Next, we will define the corresponding message:

```
<message name="EmployeeDoesNotExistException">
  <part name="exception" type="tns:EmployeeDoesNotExistExceptionType" />
</message>
```

Finally, we will add the fault message to the `EmployeeTravelStatus` operation signature:

```
<portType name="EmployeeTravelStatusPT">
  <operation name="EmployeeTravelStatus">
    <input message="tns:EmployeeTravelStatusRequestMessage" />
    <output message="tns:EmployeeTravelStatusResponseMessage" />
    <fault name="EmployeeDoesNotExistException"
           message="tns:EmployeeDoesNotExistException" />
  </operation>
</portType>
```

The default exception serializer will create the fault element and fill the `faultstring` with the content returned by `Exception.getMessage()` and the `detail` element with the content returned by `Exception.toString()`.

Defining WSIF Binding for an Exception

Now we are ready to add the exception to the WSIF binding. We have to define the type mapping for the `EmployeeDoesNotExistExceptionType` XML type, which in our case will map to the corresponding Java exception class—to the `com.packtpub.EmployeeDoesNotExistException`. We also have to add the fault message name (`EmployeeDoesNotExistException`) to the operation mapping part:

```
<binding name="JavaBinding" type="tns:EmployeeTravelStatusPT">
  <java:binding/>
  <format:typeMapping encoding="Java" style="Java">
    <format:typeMap typeName="tns:EmployeeType"
            formatType="com.packtpub.service.employee.EmployeeType" />
    <format:typeMap typeName="tns:TravelClassType"
            formatType="java.lang.String" />
    <format:typeMap typeName="tns:EmployeeDoesNotExistExceptionType"
            formatType="com.packtpub.EmployeeDoesNotExistException" />
  </format:typeMapping>
  <operation name="EmployeeTravelStatus">
    <java:operation methodName="getTravelStatus"/>
    <input/>
    <output/>
    <fault name="EmployeeDoesNotExistException"/>
  </operation>
</binding>
```

We have to compile the Java classes and deploy them to the `C:\OraBPELPM_1\integration\orabpel\system\classes` directory, where the BPEL server can access them. The easiest way is to use the **obant** utility:

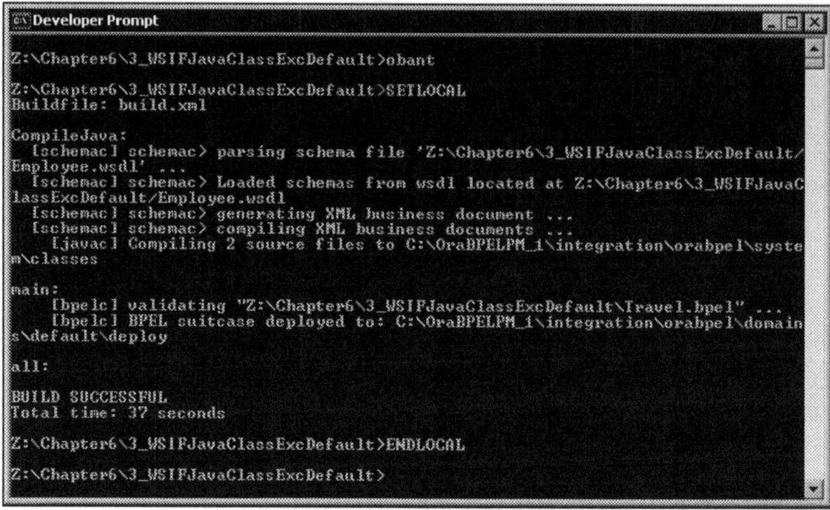

Next, let us create a test instance of the process using the BPEL Console. If we use "Juric" as the employee last name, we get the exception on the `<invoke>` activity:

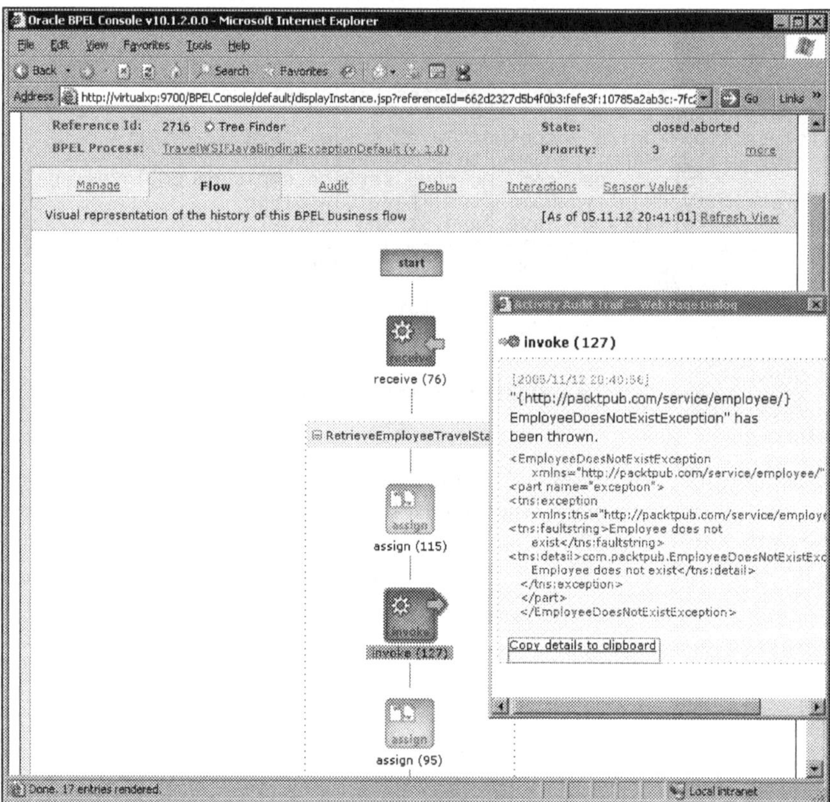

Custom Exception Serializers

In case we are not happy with the structure of the default WSDL fault or we would prefer to have more control over the mapping of Java exceptions to WSDL faults, we can use custom exception serializers. A custom exception serializer is a Java class that maps the exception and its attributes to the complex type used for the WSDL fault. To demonstrate how a custom serializer is developed we will go through the following steps:

1. Define a custom complex type used for the WSDL fault message.
2. Write a custom exception serializer to propagate the Java exception as a WSDL fault.
3. Register the custom exception serializer.

Defining Custom Fault Type in WSDL

First, let us define the XML Schema custom complex type to represent the Java exception, which will include three exception attributes: message, detail description, and passenger name. We will replace the default complex type with this type in the `<types>` section of the Employee WSDL:

```
<xs:complexType name="EmployeeDoesNotExistExceptionType">
  <xs:sequence>
    <xs:element name="message" type="xs:string" />
    <xs:element name="detailDesc" type="xs:string" />
    <xs:element name="employeeName" type="xs:string" />
  </xs:sequence>
</xs:complexType>
```

Writing the Custom Exception Serializer

The custom exception serializer is a Java class that defines how the Java exception maps to the WSDL fault complex type. The exception serializer has to map the Java exception attributes to the corresponding XML elements of the fault message, and implement the following interface:

```
public interface IExceptionSerializer {

    public Element serialize(Throwable ex,
                             String messageName,
                             String namespaceURI);
}
```

For our example, we will name the custom exception serializer `EmployeeDoesNotExistExceptionSerializer` and extend the existing `ExceptionSerializer` class. Using the DOM API we will map the three attributes of the Java exception (message, detail description, employee name) to the above presented XML Schema type (`EmployeeDoesNotExistExceptionType`):

```
package com.packtpub;

import org.w3c.dom.Element;

import com.collaxa.xml.XMLHelper;
import com.oracle.bpel.xml.util.ExceptionSerializer;
import com.oracle.bpel.xml.util.IExceptionSerializer;


public class EmployeeDoesNotExistExceptionSerializer extends
ExceptionSerializer
        implements IExceptionSerializer {
```

```
    public Element serialize(Throwable ex, String messageName,
                                           String namespaceURI) {

        if(ex instanceof EmployeeDoesNotExistException)
        {
            EmployeeDoesNotExistException emEx =
                                (EmployeeDoesNotExistException)ex;
            Element exceptionElement = XMLHelper.createRootElement(messageName,
                                  namespaceURI,"tns");

            Element messageElement = XMLHelper.createElement("message",
                                          "tns",namespaceURI);
            messageElement.setNodeValue(emEx.getMessage());
            exceptionElement.appendChild(messageElement);

            Element detailElement = XMLHelper.createElement("detailDesc",
                                         "tns",namespaceURI);
            detailElement.setNodeValue(emEx.getDetailDesc());
            exceptionElement.appendChild(detailElement);

            Element employeeElement = XMLHelper.createElement("employeeName",
                                            "tns",namespaceURI);
            employeeElement.setNodeValue(emEx.getEmployeeName());
            exceptionElement.appendChild(employeeElement);

            return exceptionElement;

        }
        return super.serialize(ex, messageName, namespaceURI);
    }
}
```

Registering the Custom Exception Serializer

The final step is to register the custom exception serializer with the Oracle BPEL Process Manager. This will instruct the BPEL Process Manager to use our serializer class instead of the default serializer class. To achieve this we have to define the `exceptionSerializer` property in the `bpel.xml` deployment descriptor:

```
<partnerLinkBinding name="employeeTravelStatus">
  <property name="wsdlLocation">
    Employee.wsdl
  </property>
  <property name="exceptionSerializer">
      com.packtpub.EmployeeDoesNotExistExceptionSerializer
  </property>
</partnerLinkBinding>
```

As in the previous example, we have to compile Java classes and deploy the example. After starting **obant** we should see the following:

```
Developer Prompt

Z:\Chapter6\4_WSIFJavaClassExcCustom>obant

Z:\Chapter6\4_WSIFJavaClassExcCustom>SETLOCAL
Buildfile: build.xml

CompileJava:
  [schemac] schemac> parsing schema file 'Z:\Chapter6\4_WSIFJavaClassExcCustom/E
mployee.wsdl' ...
  [schemac] schemac> Loaded schemas from wsdl located at Z:\Chapter6\4_WSIFJavaC
lassExcCustom/Employee.wsdl
  [schemac] schemac> generating XML business document ...
  [schemac] schemac> compiling XML business documents ...
    [javac] Compiling 3 source files to C:\OraBPELPM_1\integration\orabpel\syste
m\classes

main:
    [bpelc] validating "Z:\Chapter6\4_WSIFJavaClassExcCustom\Travel.bpel" ...
    [bpelc] BPEL suitcase deployed to: C:\OraBPELPM_1\integration\orabpel\domain
s\default\deploy

all:

BUILD SUCCESSFUL
Total time: 37 seconds

Z:\Chapter6\4_WSIFJavaClassExcCustom>ENDLOCAL

Z:\Chapter6\4_WSIFJavaClassExcCustom>
```

After starting the process from the BPEL console and using "Juric" as the employee last name, an exception should be generated on the <invoke> activity for the Employee service. The structure of the exception will, however, differ from the previous example:

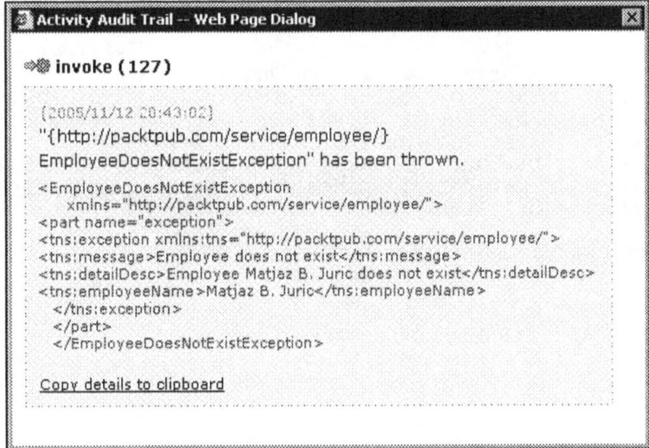

Invoking EJB through WSIF

So far we have seen how to use a Java class instead of a web service through WSIF bindings. In a very similar way, we can use Enterprise Java Beans—stateless session beans. To demonstrate the WSIF EJB binding we will extend our example. We will include an additional service (partner link) in our Travel BPEL process—the Airline Rating service. This service will be invoked for each airline before the ticket offer is acquired.

We use a session bean instead of a web service for the Airline Rating. This time we assume that the session bean already exists and use the remote interface provided by the session bean without modifications. In other words, the BPEL process will adapt to the interface of the bean, which will not be a problem, as we will add an `<invoke>` activity to the process in order to use the service. We will go through the following steps:

1. Define the WSDL for the Airline Rating session bean and add the partner link type.
2. Add the WSIF binding for the EJB to the Airline Rating WSDL.

WSDL for Session Bean

The session bean that we use provides a method called `getAirlineRating()`, which takes a string as input and returns an integer. The remote component interface is shown below. We will not show the home interface, the implementation class, and the deployment descriptors here (see the source code for this example):

```
package com.packtpub.ratingSB;

import java.rmi.RemoteException;
import javax.ejb.EJBObject;

public interface AirlineRating extends EJBObject
{
    public int getAirlineRating(String name) throws RemoteException;
}
```

Let us now define the corresponding WSDL document, which is very simple and defines two messages (`PubRatingRequestMessage` and `PubRatingResponseMessage`). They are used in the operation `PubRating` as input and output. The operation is declared within the `PubRatingPT` port type:

```
<?xml version="1.0"?>
<definitions xmlns:xs="http://www.w3.org/2001/XMLSchema"
             xmlns:tns="http://packtpub.com/service/airlineRating/"
             targetNamespace="http://packtpub.com/service/airlineRating/"
             xmlns="http://schemas.xmlsoap.org/wsdl/"
             xmlns:plnk="http://schemas.xmlsoap.org/ws/2003/05/partner-link/"
             xmlns:format="http://schemas.xmlsoap.org/wsdl/formatbinding/"
             xmlns:ejb="http://schemas.xmlsoap.org/wsdl/ejb/" >

  <message name="AirlineRatingRequestMessage">
    <part name="name" type="xs:string" />
  </message>

  <message name="AirlineRatingResponseMessage">
    <part name="rating" type="xs:int" />
  </message>

  <portType name="AirlineRatingPT">
    <operation name="AirlineRating">
      <input name="AirlineRatingRequest"
             message="tns:AirlineRatingRequestMessage" />
      <output name="AirlineRatingResponse"
              message="tns:AirlineRatingResponseMessage" />
    </operation>
  </portType>
```

For the BPEL process we have to add the partner link type. The operation is synchronous therefore we need only one role:

```
  <plnk:partnerLinkType name="AirlineRatingLT">
    <plnk:role name="AirlineRatingService">
```

```
      <plnk:portType name="tns:AirlineRatingPT" />
    </plnk:role>
  </plnk:partnerLinkType>
```

WSIF Binding for EJB

We are ready to define the WSIF binding for the EJB. WSIF EJB binding is similar to the Java class binding that we demonstrated earlier. The major difference is that we have to specify the details regarding the mapping of WSDL operations to EJB methods. Shown below is the WSIF EJB binding excerpt from the Airline Rating service WSDL file. We have first defined the type mapping and then specified which method should be used for the `AirlineRating` operation (`getAirlineRating()`). Please notice that we have specified the message part names for parameters (`name`) and for return (`rating`). We have also specified the input and output message names (`AirlineRatingRequest` and `AirlineRatingResponse` respectively):

```
<binding name="EJBBinding" type="tns:AirlineRatingPT">
  <ejb:binding/>
  <format:typeMapping encoding="Java" style="Java">
    <format:typeMap typeName="xs:string" formatType="java.lang.String" />
    <format:typeMap typeName="xs:int" formatType="int" />
  </format:typeMapping>
  <operation name="AirlineRating">
    <ejb:operation
       methodName="getAirlineRating"
       parameterOrder="name"
       interface="remote"
       returnPart="rating" />
    <input name="AirlineRatingRequest"/>
    <output name="AirlineRatingResponse"/>
  </operation>
</binding>
```

In the services binding we have to specify additional details of the EJB such as JNDI name, JNDI provider URL, and initial context factory. The JNDI provider URL is specific for each deployment. In our case it would be `ormi://localhost/SessionBean`. We can use the `obant` utility to replace the `[jndiProviderURL]` with the actual address at the time of deployment (please look in the `build.xml` file for details):

```
<service name="AirlineRatingPT">
  <port name="EJBPort" binding="tns:EJBBinding">
      <ejb:address className="com.packtpub.ratingSB.AirlineRatingHome"
            jndiName="ejb/session/AirlineRating"
            initialContextFactory=
                    "com.evermind.server.rmi.RMIInitialContextFactory"
            jndiProviderURL="[jndiProviderURL]"/>
  </port>
</service>
```

Now we are almost ready to deploy the example and test it. We must not forget to add the `wsdlLocation` property to the `bpel.xml` deployment descriptor to link the partner link with the corresponding WSDL file. In the deployment descriptor we could also specify additional properties required by the EJB, such as `java.naming.security.principal` and `java.naming.security.credentials` if our EJB requires authentication and authorization:

```
<partnerLinkBinding name="airlineRating">
  <property name="wsdlLocation">AirlineRatingBinded.wsdl</property>
  <property name="java.naming.security.principal">admin</property>
  <property name="java.naming.security.credentials">welcome</property>
</partnerLinkBinding>
```

To test the example we first have to deploy the session bean and then the BPEL process. Again, we can use **obant**, which automates the procedure:

```
Developer Prompt

Z:\Chapter6\5_WSIF-EJB>obant

Z:\Chapter6\5_WSIF-EJB>SETLOCAL
Buildfile: build.xml

deploySessionBean:

build_ear:

deployIas:

deployOc4j:
     [java] Notification ==> Application Deployer for SessionBean STARTS [ 2005-
11-12T20:45:20.443CET ]
     [java] Notification ==> Undeploy previous deployment
     [java] Notification ==> Copy the archive to C:\OraBPELPM_1\integration\orab
pel\system\appserver\oc4j\j2ee\home\applications\SessionBean.ear
     [java] Notification ==> Unpack SessionBean.ear begins...
     [java] Notification ==> Unpack SessionBean.ear ends...
     [java] Notification ==> Initialize SessionBean.ear begins...
     [java] Notification ==> Initialize SessionBean.ear ends...
     [java] Notification ==> Application Deployer for SessionBean COMPLETES [ 20
05-11-12T20:45:41.685CET ]


bindingWsdl:
     [copy] Copying 1 file to Z:\Chapter6\5_WSIF-EJB

setJndiUrlOrclej2ee:

setJndiUrlIas:

setJndiUrlOc4j:
     [echo] Replacing token [jndiProviderURL] by ormi://virtualxp/SessionBean in
 Z:\Chapter6\5_WSIF-EJB/AirlineRatingBinded.wsdl

main:
    [bpelc] validating "Z:\Chapter6\5_WSIF-EJB\Travel.bpel" ...
    [bpelc] BPEL suitcase deployed to: C:\OraBPELPM_1\integration\orabpel\domain
s\default\deploy

all:

BUILD SUCCESSFUL
Total time: 39 seconds

Z:\Chapter6\5_WSIF-EJB>ENDLOCAL

Z:\Chapter6\5_WSIF-EJB>_
```

After starting the BPEL process from the console, we should see that the Airline Rating service has been invoked:

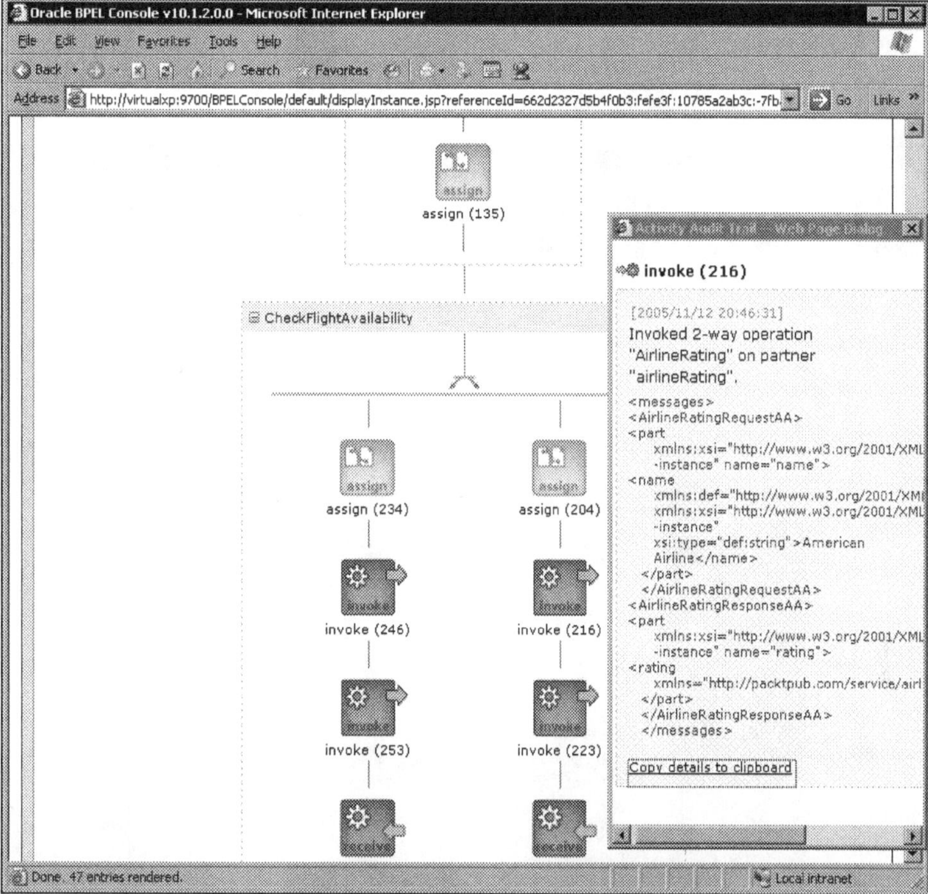

To be absolutely sure that the EJB has been invoked we can look at the BPEL server console window where we should see the following output:

```
Start BPEL PM Server
Process "TravelWSIFEJBBinding" (revision "1.0") successfully compiled.
<2005-11-12 20:46:03,486> <INFO> <default.collaxa.cube.engine.deployment> Proces
s "TravelWSIFEJBBinding" (revision "1.0") successfully loaded.
05/11/12 20:46:31 Airline rating for Delta Airline: 5.
05/11/12 20:46:31 Airline rating for American Airline: 5.
```

Generating WSIF Bindings from JDeveloper

Writing WSIF bindings "by hand" can be quite complicated, so Oracle JDeveloper 10.1.3 (or higher) provides a wizard for automatic generation of WSDL and WSIF for existing Java resources, such as Java classes and EJBs. This greatly reduces the effort to invoke Java resources from BPEL and makes BPEL even more attractive for integration.

WSIF bindings are generated by the web services creation wizard. To use it we have to start the wizard from the **File | New | Business Tier | Web Services** menu and select **Java Web Service**. We select the **J2EE 1.4 (JAX-RPC) Web Service**. Then we specify the web service name, and select the component to publish. Please be sure to check the **WSIF Binding** checkbox:

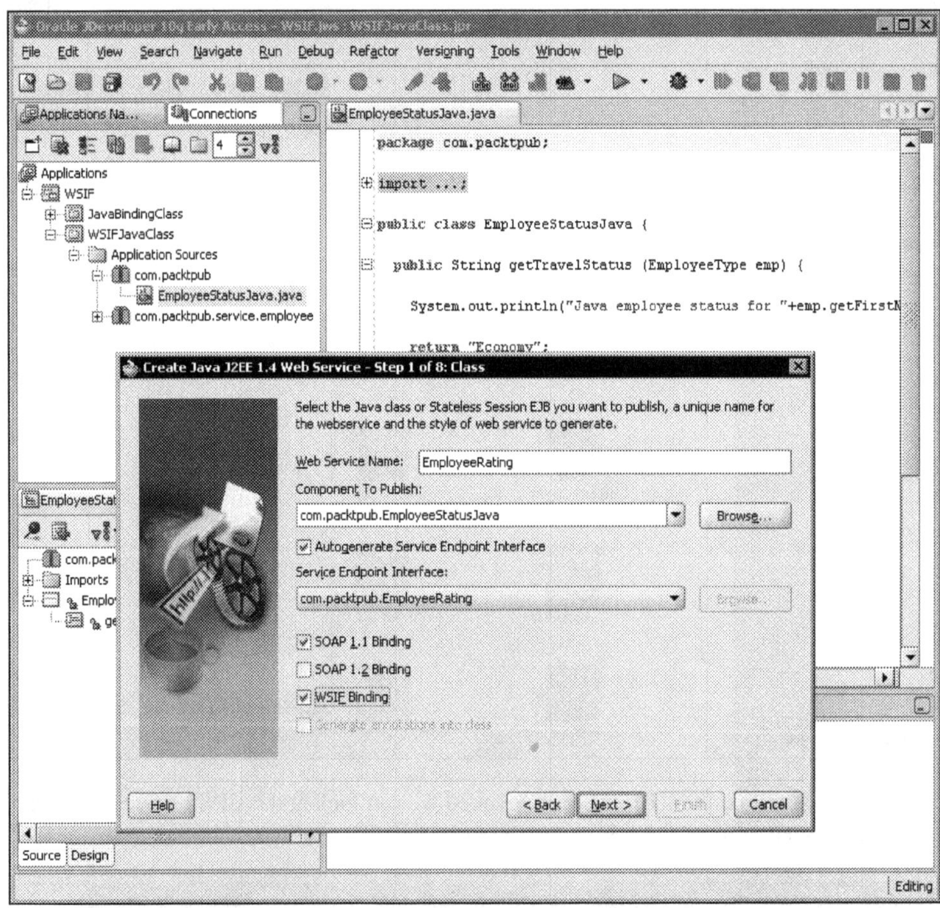

We then have to specify several details, including the SOAP message format, custom data mappings, etc. We can leave most of these at their default values. However, we have to specify the methods that we would like to expose. After finishing the wizard, the WSDL with the WSIF bindings is generated. Looking into the generated WSDL shows that it is pretty much the same as the one we have written by hand.

With this, we have concluded our discussion on WSIF. We have seen that WSIF is an important technology that enables integration of resources other than web services into BPEL. In the next section we will look at another method for integrating Java into BPEL—Java code embedding.

Java Code Embedding

Java code embedding is another method for integrating Java code and resources into BPEL processes. It allows us to embed Java code snippets directly into BPEL process code. This provides the opportunity to use Java for certain aspects where BPEL does not provide an appropriate activity. It also provides a way to use Java code to call other Java resources (EJBs, JCA, JMS, etc.). Compared to WSIF, Java code embedding has several drawbacks. The most important is that it requires proprietary extensions to BPEL code, thus limiting the portability of BPEL processes.

To embed Java code snippets into BPEL, Oracle provides a custom BPEL activity called `<exec>`, defined in the `http://schemas.oracle.com/bpel/extension` namespace. This namespace is usually declared with the `bpelx` prefix, so we write the activity as `<bpelx:exec>`.

The BPEL server will execute the Java code embedded in the `<exec>` activity within its JTA (Java Transaction API) transaction context. If the embedded Java code calls EJBs (session or entity beans), the transactional context will be automatically propagated. If an exception occurs during the execution of the embedded Java code, the exception will automatically be converted to a BPEL fault and thrown to the BPEL process.

The `<exec>` activity supports three attributes (in addition to the BPEL standard attributes):

- `import`: This is used to import Java packages.
- `language`: Denotes the used language. Currently the only supported language is Java, but support for other languages such as C# may be added.
- `version`: Denotes the version of the language. The supported version of Java is 1.4.

The `<exec>` activity also provides built-in methods we can use in the embedded Java code. They allow us to access and update BPEL variables, get JNDI access, update the audit trail, and set priorities and other parameters. These built-in methods are explained in the following table:

Method	Description

`Object getVariableData(String name)`
`Object getVariableData(String name, String partOrQuery)`
`Object getVariableData(String name, String part, String query)`
	Access BPEL variables

`void setVariableData(String name, Object value)`
`void setVariableData(String name, String part, Object value)`
`void setVariableData(String name, String part, String query, Object value)`
	Update BPEL variables

`void addAuditTrailEntry(String message, Object detail)` `void addAuditTrailEntry(Throwable t)`	Add an entry or an exception to the audit trail
`Object lookup(String name)`	JNDI lookup
`Locator getLocator()`	Access to BPEL Process Manager Locator service
`long getInstanceId()`	Returns the process instance unique ID

Method	Description
`void setTitle(String title)` `String getTitle()`	Set/get the title of the process instance
`void setStatus(String status)` `String getStatus()`	Set/get the status of the process instance
`void setPriority(int priority)` `int getPriority()`	Set/get the priority of the process instance
`void setCreator(String creator)` `String getCreator()`	Set/get the creator of the process instance
`void setCustomKey(String customKey)` `String getCustomKey()`	Get/set the custom key for the process instance
`void setMetadata(String metadata)` `String getMetadata()`	Get/set the metadata of the process instance
`void setIndex(int i, String value )` `String getIndex(int i)`	Get/set the search index; `i` can range from 1 to 6
`File getContentFile(String rPath)`	Access to the files stored in the BPEL suitcase (JAR)
`String getPreference(String key)`	Access to the preferences defined in the `bpel.xml` deployment descriptor

Invoking a Java Class from Embedded Code

In the next example, we will invoke the `getTravelStatus()` method from the Employee travel status Java class (`EmployeeStatusJava`) that we developed in the WSIF example. We will embed Java code within the BPEL code using the <exec> activity. Instead of a Java class we could call other resources, such as EJB, JMS, JCA, etc., or simply perform a calculation or other operation for which Java is more suitable than BPEL.

Now let us modify the BPEL code. To use the <exec> activity, we first declare the namespace:

```
<process name="Travel"
         targetNamespace="http://packtpub.com/bpel/travel/"
         xmlns="http://schemas.xmlsoap.org/ws/2003/03/business-process/"
         xmlns:bpws="http://schemas.xmlsoap.org/ws/2003/03/business-process/"
         xmlns:trv="http://packtpub.com/bpel/travel/"
         xmlns:emp="http://packtpub.com/service/employee/"
         xmlns:aln="http://packtpub.com/service/airline/"
         xmlns:bpelx="http://schemas.oracle.com/bpel/extension" >
...
```

Then we make the necessary Java imports. We have to import the DOM Element and our class:

```
...
   <bpelx:exec import="org.w3c.dom.Element"/>
   <bpelx:exec import="com.packtpub.EmployeeStatusJava"/>
   <bpelx:exec import="com.packtpub.service.employee.*"/>
...
```

> We can use BPEL Designer to add the <exec> activity to our code.

Finally we replace the `<invoke>` of the Employee web service with the Java embedded code. In Java, we first create a new `EmployeeStatusJava` object. Then we use the `getVariableData()` function to retrieve the `employee` part from the BPEL variable `EmployeeTravelStatusRequest` and create the XML façade `EmployeeType`. Next we invoke the `getTravelStatus()` method. We then add an entry to the trail. Finally we set the `EmployeeTravelStatusResponse` BPEL variable using the `setVariableData()` function:

```
...
<!-- Invoke the EmployeeStatus Java class instead of a web service -->
<bpelx:exec name="invokeJavaExec" language="java" version="1.4">
  <![CDATA[

    try {

      EmployeeStatusJava e = new EmployeeStatusJava();

      Element empRequest = (Element)getVariableData(
                              "EmployeeTravelStatusRequest",
                              "employee","/employee");

      EmployeeType emp = EmployeeTypeFactory.createFacade(empRequest);

      String empStatus = e.getTravelStatus(emp);

      addAuditTrailEntry("Employee status is: " + empStatus);

      setVariableData("EmployeeTravelStatusResponse", "travelClass",
                      "/travelClass", empStatus);
    }
    catch(Exception e)
    {
      addAuditTrailEntry(e);
    }
  ]]>
</bpelx:exec>
```

We have seen that embedding Java code in BPEL is quite straightforward. Unlike WSIF, we have to manually access the BPEL variables and create the corresponding façades. Instead of the XML façade, we could use the DOM directly to access the data elements such as first name, last name, or department.

For this example to work, we have to pack the Java class file in the BPEL process suitcase JAR archive. We have to store it into the `BPEL-INF/classes` directory. We can use **obant** to compile and deploy the example:

```
Developer Prompt

Z:\Chapter6\6_JavaEmbedding>obant

Z:\Chapter6\6_JavaEmbedding>SETLOCAL
Buildfile: build.xml

CompileJava:
  [schemac] schemac> parsing schema file 'Z:\Chapter6\6_JavaEmbedding/../2_WSIFJ
avaClass/Employee.wsdl' ...
  [schemac] schemac> Loaded schemas from wsdl located at Z:\Chapter6\6_JavaEmbed
ding/../2_WSIFJavaClass/Employee.wsdl
  [schemac] schemac> generating XML business document ...
  [schemac] schemac> compiling XML business documents ...

main:
    [bpelc] validating "Z:\Chapter6\6_JavaEmbedding\Travel.bpel" ...
    [bpelc] BPEL suitcase deployed to: C:\OraBPELPM_1\integration\orabpel\domain
s\default\deploy

all:

BUILD SUCCESSFUL
Total time: 34 seconds

Z:\Chapter6\6_JavaEmbedding>ENDLOCAL

Z:\Chapter6\6_JavaEmbedding>_
```

We will use the BPEL Console to start the process and observe the visual flow, where we can see that the Java embedded code has been executed, as shown in the following screen. To verify that the Java class has been invoked we can observe the output at the server console window.

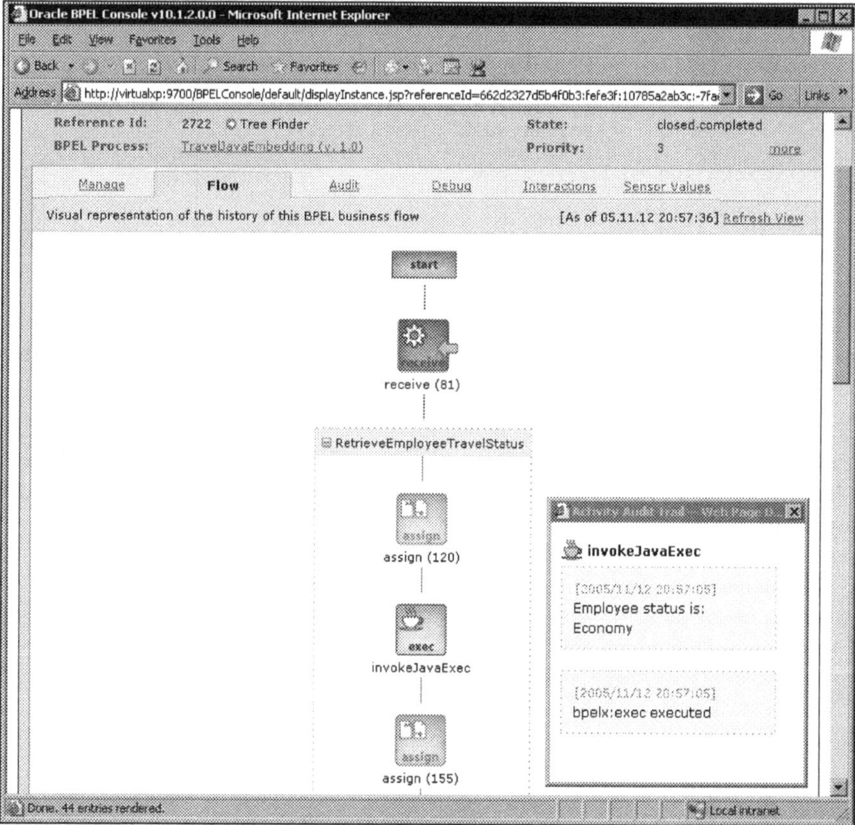

When choosing between Java embedding and WSIF, WSIF is often a better choice because it does not require proprietary extensions to BPEL and only requires modifications in WSDL. WSIF is also more flexible because if a service technology changes (for example a Java class is rewritten as a web service), a modification in WSDL is adequate.

In the next section, we will look at the Notification service.

Notification Service

Business processes sometimes require that notifications are sent to the users or participants. For example, our Travel process might want to notify the employee (via email) which flight ticket he/she has been allocated. Another use case is when an exception occurs in a business process. Then we can use notifications by email or by other channels to notify the responsible person and seek intervention.

The BPEL specification does not provide a mechanism for sending emails or other notifications. Therefore, normally we would need to create a web service (partner link) that is capable of sending and/or receiving notifications. This web service would provide port types with operations for sending and receiving notifications and we would use `<invoke>` and `<receive>` activities to invoke them—similar to any other service.

Fortunately, Oracle BPEL Process Manager already provides a Notification service. It provides support for the following channels:

- **Email**: We can use emails for one-way notifications, require a response by email, or use an incoming email for starting a BPEL process.
- **Voice messages, short message service (SMS), fax, or pager messages**: For these an external server can be used. BPEL Process Manager is preconfigured to use the wireless and voice component provided by Oracle Application Server Wireless.

The Notification service exposes its operations through WSDL and Java interfaces. The overall architecture of the Notification service is shown in the following figure:

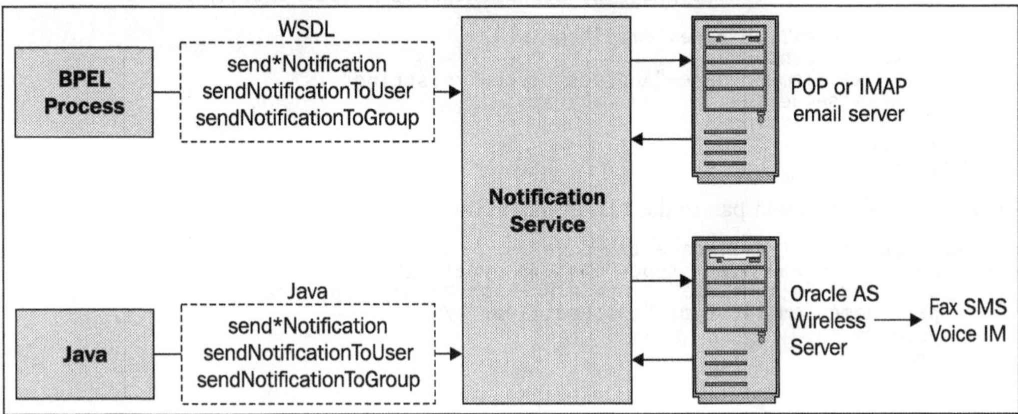

To use the Notification service in our process we have to create a partner link and invoke the provided operations. Through the WSDL interface, the Notification service exposes the `NotificationService` port type. It provides the following operations:

- `send*Notification`, where `*` can be `Email`, `Fax`, `SMS`, `Voice`, `Pager`, or `IM` (Instant Messaging).
- `sendNotificationToUser`, used to send notification to BPEL Process Manager users.
- `sendNotificationToGroup`, used to send notifications to a group of users.

The operations take various input messages. The `sendEmailNotification` operation, for example, takes the `EmailNotificationRequest` input message, which is of type `EmailPayloadType`. The latter is defined in the corresponding `NotificationService` XML Schema and consists of elements such as from address, to address, subject, body, etc.

In addition, the Notification service also provides a Java interface (API). It is implemented as the Java class `oracle.tip.pc.services.notification.NotificationService`, which provides methods with the same name as the WSDL interface. Notification service uses a WSIF binding to expose the operations through WSDL.

Email Example

To demonstrate how to use the Notification service we will add email confirmation to our Travel process example. Originally, our process selected the best ticket offer by comparing offers from American and Delta Airlines web services and invoked a callback to the client. We will add the email confirmation just before the client callback.

Before we start modifying the BPEL code, we need to make modifications to the `TravelRequest` message in the travel process WSDL. We must add the email address to which our process will send the confirmation. Therefore, we first define an `EmailType` (in the `Travel.wsdl` file):

```
<types>
  <xs:schema elementFormDefault="qualified"
             targetNamespace="http://packtpub.com/bpel/travel/">

    <xs:complexType name="EmailType">
      <xs:sequence>
        <xs:element name="Address" type="xs:string" />
      </xs:sequence>
    </xs:complexType>
  </xs:schema>
</types>
```

Next, we add a new `email` part to the `TravelRequestMessage`:

```
<message name="TravelRequestMessage">
  <part name="employee" type="emp:EmployeeType" />
  <part name="flightData" type="aln:FlightRequestType" />
  <part name="email" type="tns:EmailType" />
</message>
```

Notification Wizard

Now we are ready to modify the BPEL source code (`Travel.bpel` file). We will add a scope and within it, we will create the email variable, assign the values, and invoke the Notification service to send the email.

The easiest way to add the Notification service to the BPEL process is to use the JDeveloper BPEL Designer, which provides a convenient wizard. We will drag-and-drop the **Notification** activity from the **Process Activities Component Palette** to the process between the `CheckFlightAvailability` scope and the `CallbackClient` scope, as shown in the following screen:

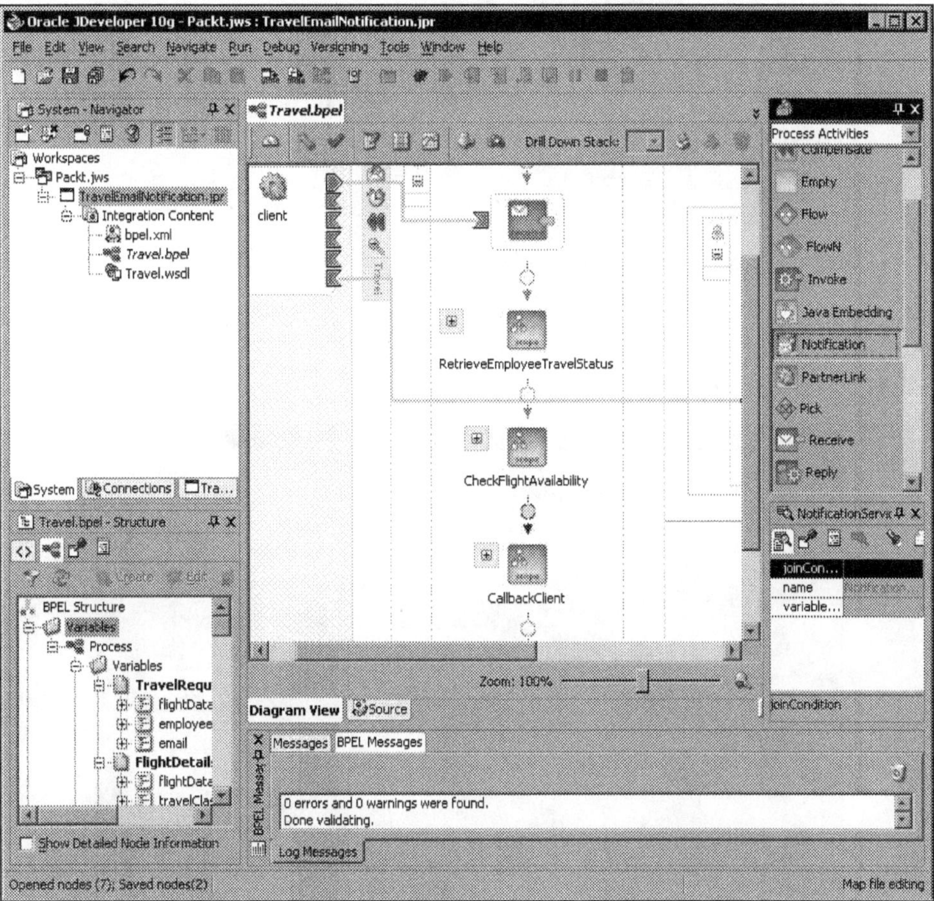

The Notification Wizard will open, and will guide us through the creation of the variables, their assignments, and service invocation. The wizard will also add a fault handler. After pressing **Next** on the first screen we have to select the type of service we will use. We select **EMail**:

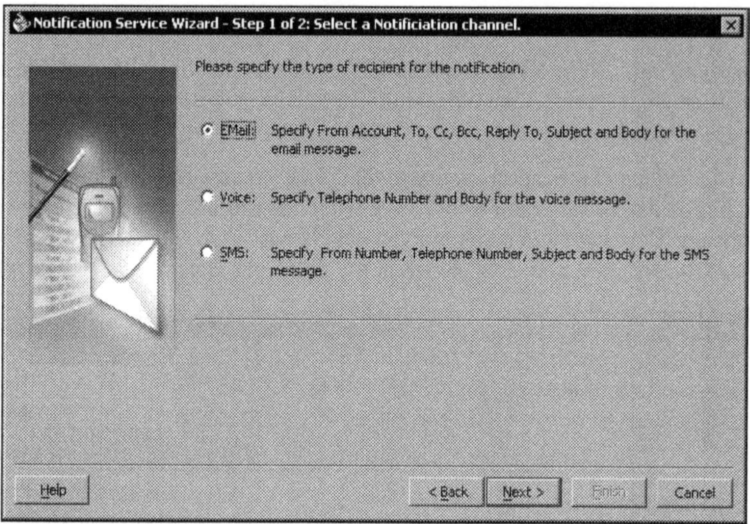

In the next step, we have to specify the email details, including the email account used for sending the mail (from account), to address, Cc, and Bcc, reply to address, subject, and message body. We could use static values for all these fields (and just type them in), but this would make little sense. Rather we will use the values from BPEL variables, which we will access with functions, such as `getVariableData()`. We can also use other available XPath and extension functions:

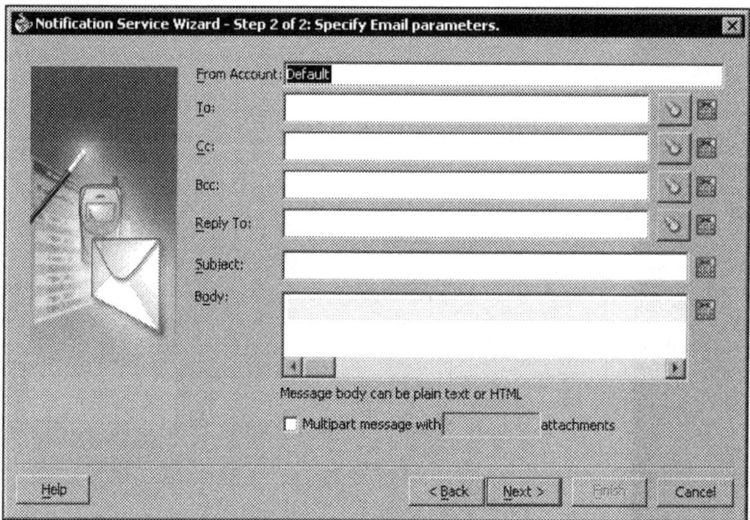

Let us now discuss the fields that we have to specify. The From Account specifies the account that the BPEL process will use to send emails. This email account is configured in the file `ns_emails.xml`, which is located in the `C:\OraBPELPM_1\integration\orabpel\system\services\config` directory. We have to specify the To: email address, and the details regarding the incoming and the outgoing mail server.

Next, we have to specify the addresses the mail will be sent to. For the To address we will use the input, provided by the client. Therefore, we will start the XPath Expression Builder using the right-most icon. We will navigate to the Variables/TravelRequest/email/email/trv:Address and press the left arrow icon to crate the XPath expression:

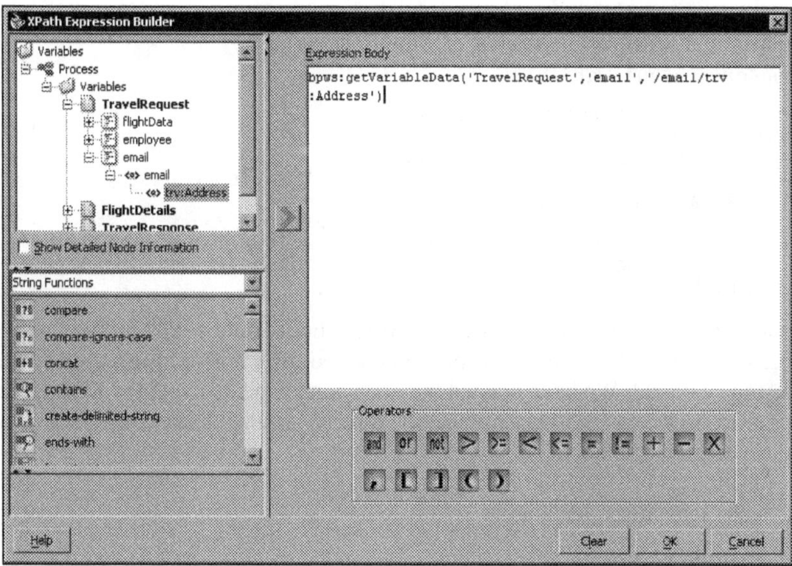

Alternatively, we could use the email address from a BPEL user account—by using the flashlight icon (first from the left). In the same way, we will declare values for subject and body, and finish the wizard, as shown in the screenshot below:

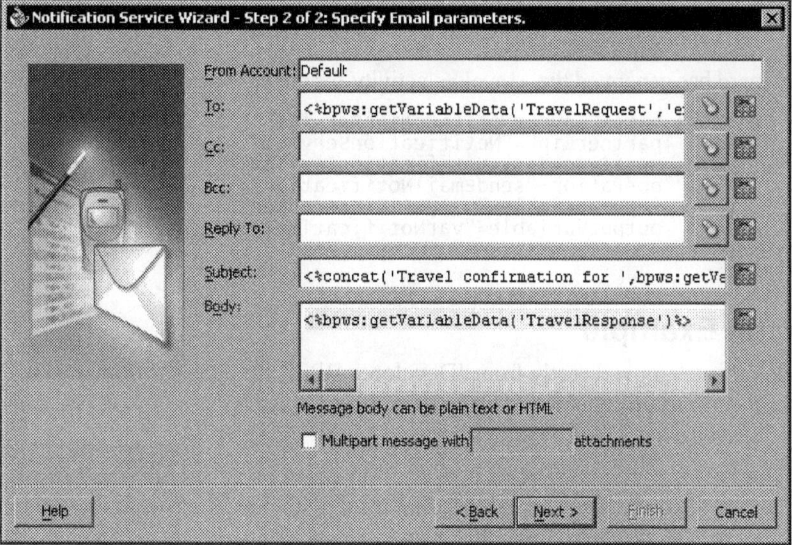

Review of Code

The wizard has added the namespace used by the Notification service: xmlns:ns5="http://xmlns.oracle.com/ias/pcbpel/NotificationService". It has also generated a scope, called NotificationService. Within the scope, three variables have been generated: the input variable varNotificationReq containing the email payload, the varNotificationResponse, containing the response from the Notification service, and the fault variable NotificationServiceFaultVariable:

```
<scope name="NotificationService">
  <variables>
    <variable name="varNotificationReq"
              messageType="ns5:EmailNotificationRequest"/>
    <variable name="varNotificationResponse"
              messageType="ns5:ArrayOfResponse"/>
    <variable name="NotificationServiceFaultVariable"
              messageType="ns5:NotificationServiceErrorMessage"/>
  </variables>
```

An empty fault handler has also been generated, which should not be left empty in real-world scenarios. Then, the <assign> activity has been generated, which is used to assign the values to the email message payload. We have created the <copy> statements using the XPath Expression Builder. Alternatively, we can edit the source code directly. In the code excerpt below, we show the part used to assign the subject:

```
  <sequence>
    <assign name="Assign">
      ...
      <copy>
        <from expression="concat('Travel confirmation for
                      ',bpws:getVariableData('TravelRequest',
                      'employee','/employee/emp:FirstName'),'
                      ',bpws:getVariableData('TravelRequest',
                      'employee','/employee/emp:LastName'))"/>
        <to variable="varNotificationReq" part="EmailPayload"
                           query="/EmailPayload/ns5:Subject"/>
      </copy>
      ...
```

Finally, the wizard has generated the <invoke> activity for the sendEmailNotification operation:

```
    <invoke name="InvokeNotificationService"
            partnerLink="NotificationService"
            portType="ns5:NotificationService"
            operation="sendEmailNotification"
            inputVariable="varNotificationReq"
            outputVariable="varNotificationResponse"/>
  </sequence>
</scope>
```

Testing the Example

We can deploy this example directly from JDeveloper BPEL Designer or from the Developer Prompt using the **obant** utility. After starting the process using BPEL Console, we can verify that the email has arrived.

> Please be sure to configure the email account used by the BPEL process located in the ns_emails.xml file before running this example.

The source code of this and all examples can be downloaded from `http://www.packtpub.com/`.

Mail and JMS Services

For compatibility with previous versions, BPEL Process Manager also provides Mail and JMS (Java Message Service) services. Note that these services have been replaced by the Notification service in the latest release. The Mail and JMS services are very similar to the Notification service. They provide their operations through WSDL and are actually wrappers for the underlying Java email and JMS services. In order to use them with our own processes we create partner links and invoke the operations on the corresponding port types.

The Mail service offers two port types: `MailService` and `MailServiceCallback`. The `MailService` port type is used to send email messages (using the `sendMessage` operation) and to subscribe (or unsubscribe) to incoming messages (using `subscribe` and `unsubscribe` operations). The `MailServiceCallback` port type is a callback interface that should be implemented by our BPEL process. It provides the `onMessage` operation through which our process is notified about an incoming email message. All operations require parameters (input messages). Their exact structure can be seen from the Mail service WSDL, located at the following URL: `http://localhost:9700/orabpel/xmllib/MailService.wsdl`.

The JMS service can be used to integrate BPEL processes with applications using JMS. It is similar to the Mail service and offers two port types: `JMSService` and `JMSServiceCallback`. The `JMSService` port type provides `sendMessage`, `subscribe`, and `unsubscribe` operations. The `JMSServiceCallback` interface provides the `onMessage` operation. Their exact structure can be seen from the JMS service WSDL, located at the following URL: `http://localhost:9700/orabpel/xmllib/JMSService.wsdl`.

In the next section, we will look at the Workflow service.

Workflow Service

Real-world business processes often require human interactions. For example, we might want to extend the Travel business process so that a person approves (or declines) the final ticket selection before the result is returned to the employee. Other examples include confirming stock prices, choosing loan offers, etc. The BPEL specification does not provide a standard way to include human interaction in BPEL processes. However, Oracle BPEL Process Manager provides the **Workflow service**. Workflow is a built-in BPEL service that enables human interaction in BPEL processes in a relatively easy way. Similar to the Notification service, the Workflow service exposes the interfaces through WSDL, and BPEL processes invoke it just like any other service.

BPEL processes use the Workflow service to assign tasks to users. More specifically, tasks can be assigned to users or roles. Assigning tasks to roles is more flexible as every user in a certain role can review the task to complete it (please refer to the Identity service later in this chapter for more information on users and roles). Once the user has completed the task, the BPEL process receives a callback from the Workflow service with the result of the user action. The BPEL process continues to execute.

The Workflow service has several possibilities regarding how users can review the tasks that have been assigned to them, and take corresponding action. The most straightforward approach is to use the **Worklist application**. This application comes with the BPEL Process Manager and allows users to review tasks, see task details, and take the decision to complete the task.

If the Worklist application is not appropriate, we can develop our own user interface in Java (using JSP, JSF, Swing, etc.) or almost any other environment that supports web services (such as .NET). In this respect the Workflow service is very flexible and we can use a portal, such as Oracle Portal, a web application, or almost any other application to review the tasks.

The third possibility is to use email for task reviews. We use emails over the Notification service, described earlier in this chapter. The figure below shows the overall architecture of the Workflow service:

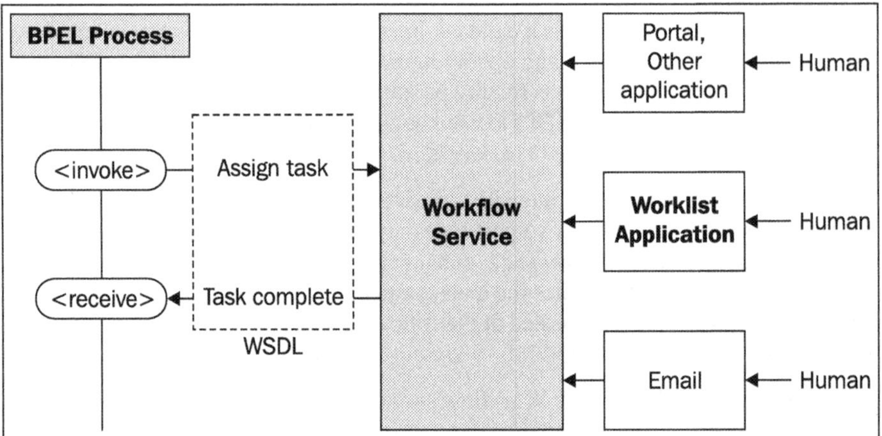

The Workflow service provided by Oracle BPEL Process Manager consists of two major components:

- `TaskActionHandler`: This is a predeployed process used by other BPEL processes to assign tasks to users and get responses.
- `TaskManager` (`TaskManagementService`): This is a predeployed process that takes care of task management and persistence. Through this service, applications used to review tasks can update, complete, and reassign them.

The Workflow service also makes use of the Identity and Notification services and the Worklist application.

Workflow Patterns

To simplify the development of workflows Oracle BPEL Process Manager provides a library of workflow patterns. Workflow patterns define typical scenarios of human interactions with BPEL processes. JDeveloper BPEL Designer provides a Workflow wizard, which simplifies the inclusion of workflows into BPEL processes. Let us first look at the supported workflow patterns:

- **Simple workflow**: Used if a single user action is required, such as confirmation, decision, etc. A timeout can be specified. Simple workflow has two extension patterns:
    - **Escalation**: Provides the ability to escalate the task to another user or role if the original user does not complete the task in the specified amount of time.
    - **Renewal**: Provides the ability to extend the timeout if the user does not complete the task in the specified time.
- **Sequential workflow**: Used if multiple users have to act in a sequence. A management chain or a list of users can be specified. Sequential workflow has one extension pattern:
    - **Escalation**: Same functionality as above.
- **Parallel workflow**: Used if multiple users have to act in parallel (for example, if multiple users have to provide their opinion or vote). The percentage of required user responses can be specified. This pattern has an extension pattern:
    - **Final reviewer**: Used when a final reviewer has to act after parallel users have provided feedback.
- **Ad-hoc (dynamic) workflow**: Used to assign the task to one user, who can then route the task to an other user. The task is completed when the user does not route it forward.
- **FYI workflow**: Used if a user only needs to be notified about a task, but a user response is not required.
- **Task continuation**: Used to build complex workflow patterns as a chain of simple patterns (those described above).
- **User Task Macro**: Used for compatibility with User Task functionality from previous versions of BPEL Process Manager.

Example

To demonstrate how to use the Workflow service we will modify our Travel process example. We will add a simple workflow, where the user will need to approve or decline the selected airline ticket. We will use the Workflow wizard provided by the JDeveloper BPEL Designer.

We will add the user interaction just before the callback to the client. To achieve this we will drag-and-drop the User Task activity from the Process Activities Component Palette to the process, as shown in the screenshot overleaf:

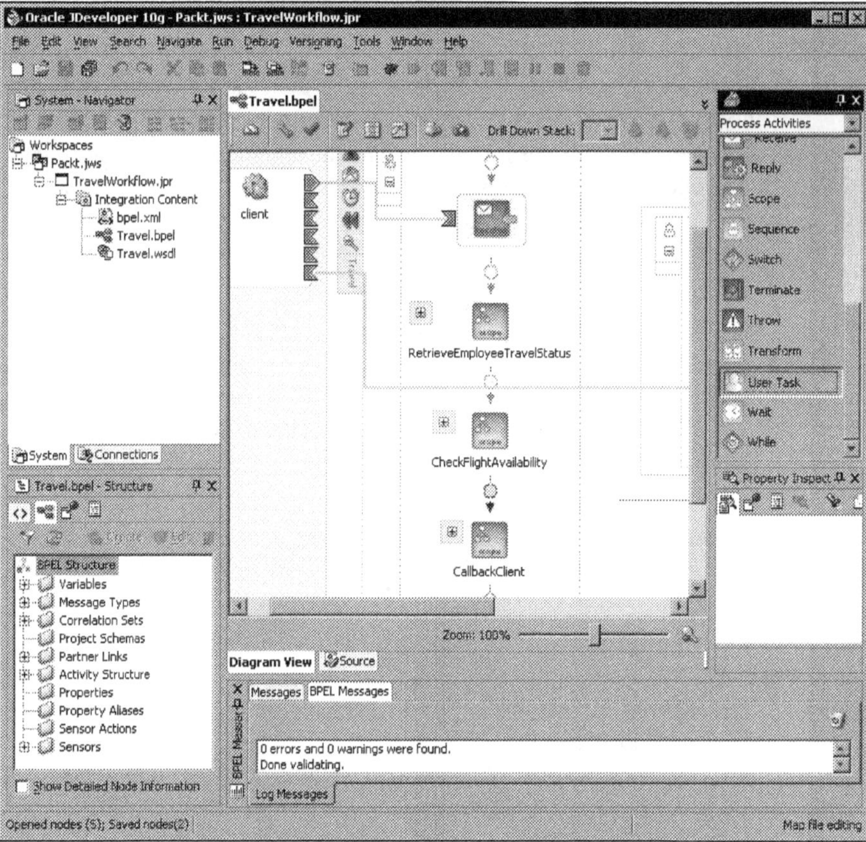

The Workflow Wizard window will appear. We select the Create New Workflow option:

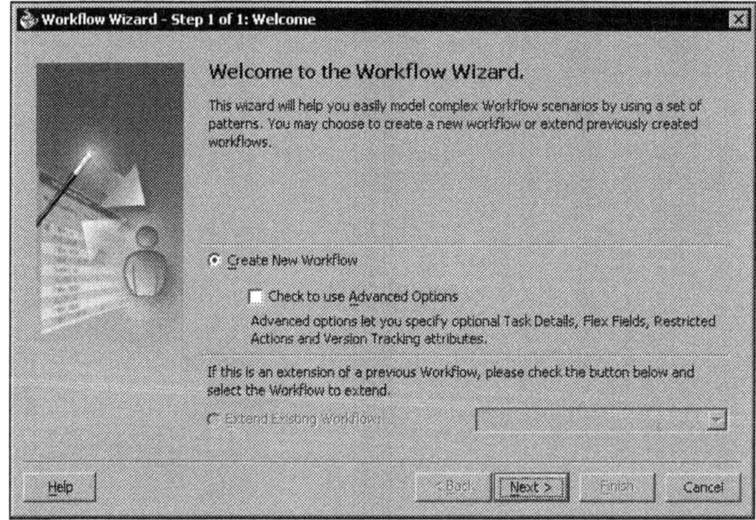

After clicking **Next** we will see the screen for selecting the workflow pattern. We select the **Simple Workflow** pattern for our example. For a description of workflow patterns, please refer to the previous section.

We name the workflow `TravelApproval` and will use the recommended name TravelApprovalVar for the variable name:

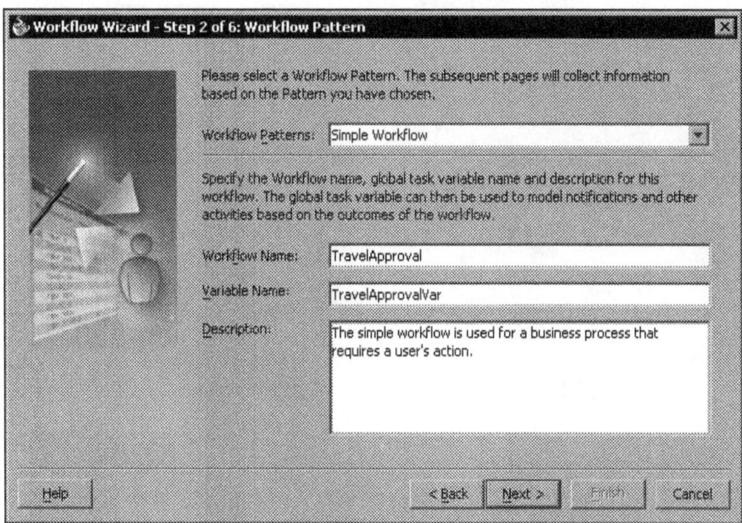

In the next step, we specify the task details. We have to enter the task name, the payload that will be displayed to the user, the task creator, and the expiration duration:

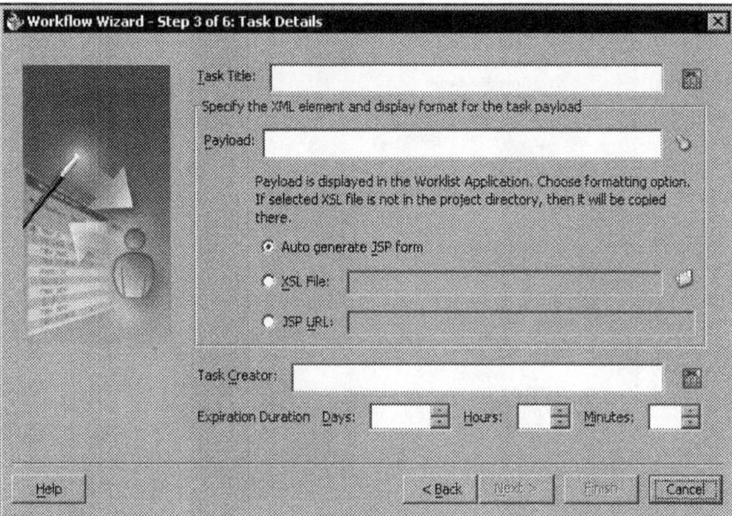

First, we enter the Task Title. We enter the text "Ticket approval for ". Then we use the XPath Expression Builder (by clicking the icon) to add the first and last name:

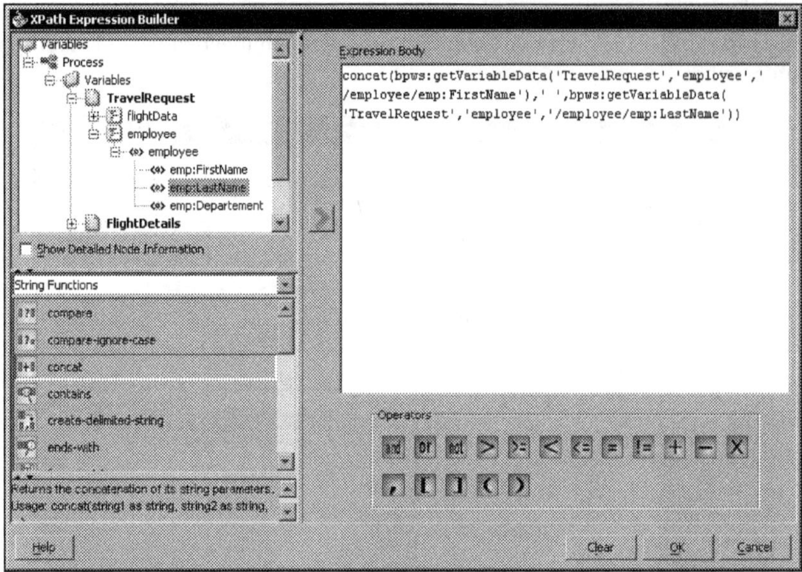

Next, we specify the payload. We use the Variable XPath Builder (by clicking the icon) to select the payload:

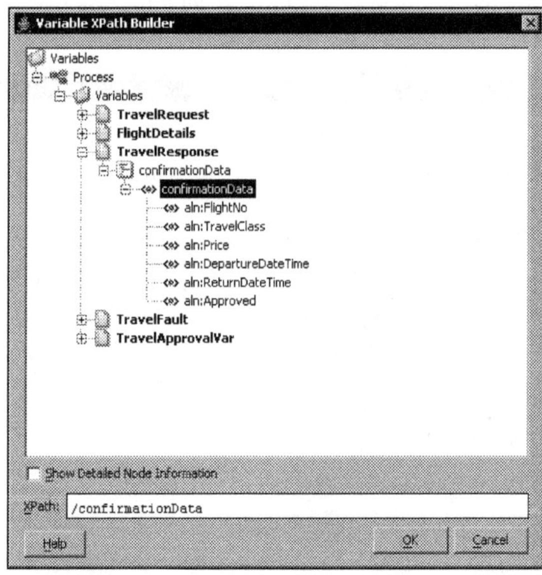

We use the Auto generate JSP form option to generate the user interface. Alternatively, we could use a XSLT transformation or provide the URL of a custom developed JSP.

We leave the Task Creator field empty. If it is left empty, the username of the user who initiated the BPEL process is used.

Finally, we specify the Expiration Duration—we select 1 hour. The filled screen is shown below:

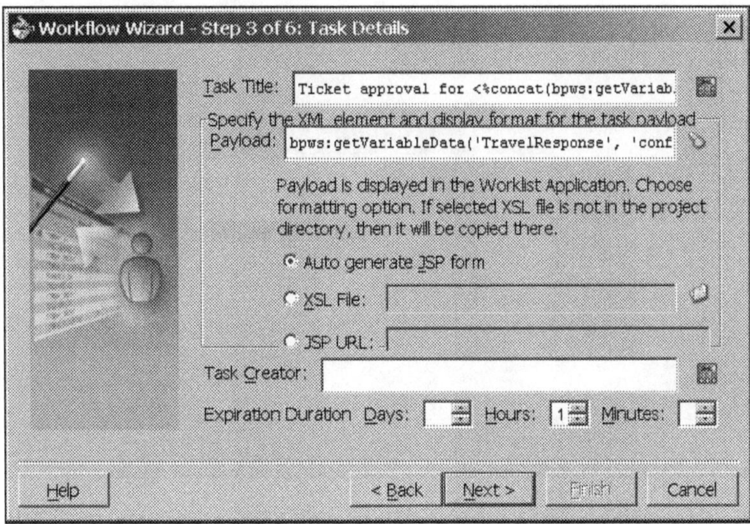

After clicking Next we will see the Task Outcomes window. Here we have to specify the outcomes a user can select. First, we delete the provided Accept and Reject. Then we add Approve and Decline outcomes:

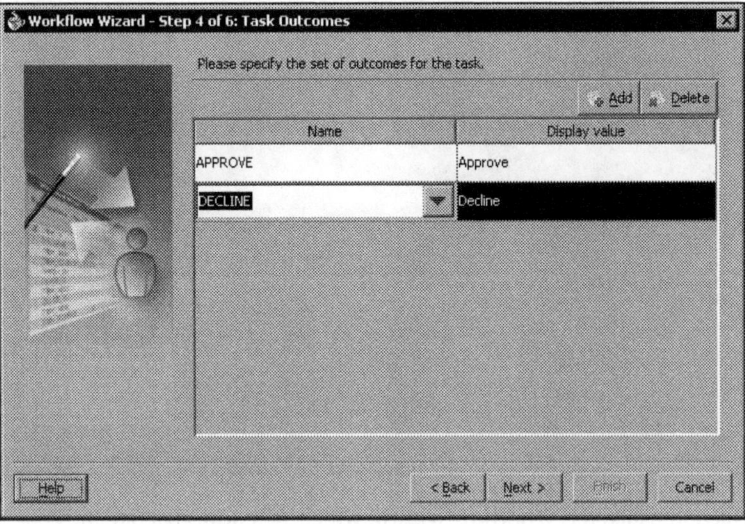

After clicking **Next** we will see the **Task Notifications** window. Here we use the default values, except for the **Recipient**, where we specify **Approvers**:

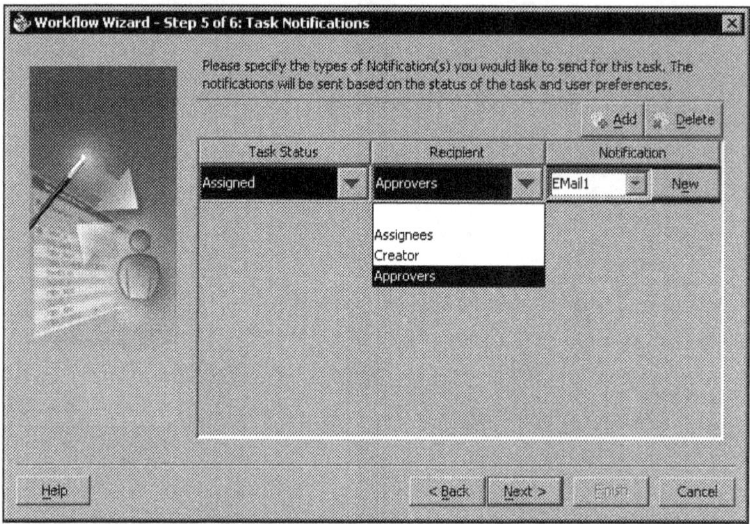

Finally, we have to specify a user or a group of users (role) for assigning the task. We can use the flashlight icon to browse users using the **Identity Lookup Dialog**. To simplify the example we will assign the task to the `admin` user:

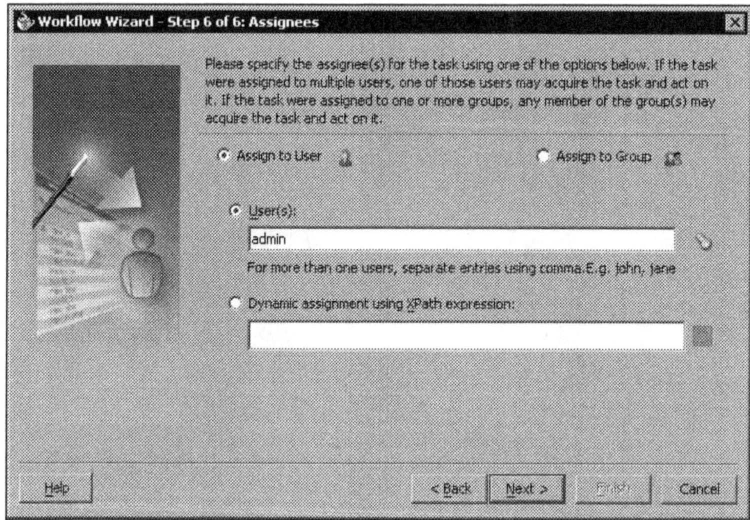

With this, we have finished the Workflow wizard, which will now generate the code.

Checking User Outcome

Let us now look at the generated code. We can see that in addition to the `TravelApproval` scope a switch has been created, where various workflow outcomes are evaluated. In our case these are `APPROVE`, `DECLINE`, and otherwise:

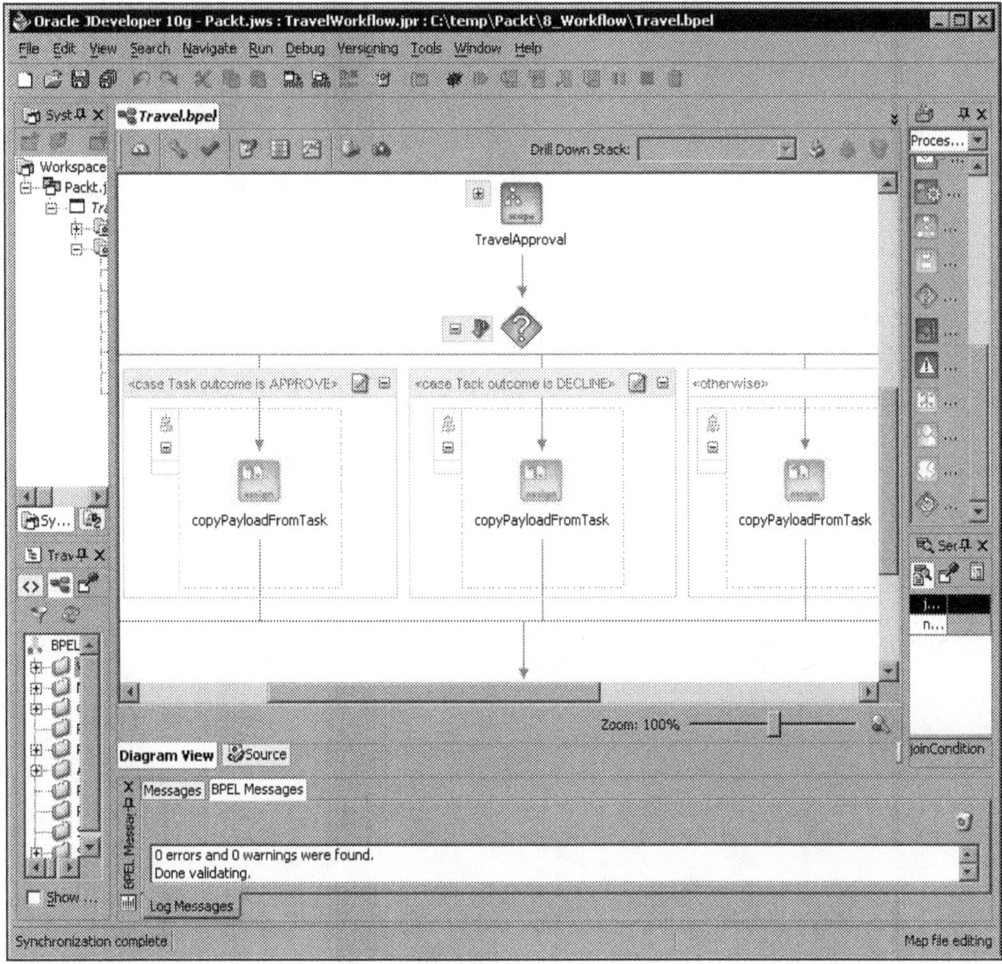

We will now edit the `<assign>` activities for each case. For `APPROVE` we assign `true` to the `Approved` element of the `TravelReponse` variable. To achieve this, we click on the `copyPayloadFromTask` `<assign>` activity. The **Assign** window will open. We edit the copy rule, select **Expression** for the **From** clause, and navigate to the `Approved` element of the **To** clause, as shown in the screenshot overleaf:

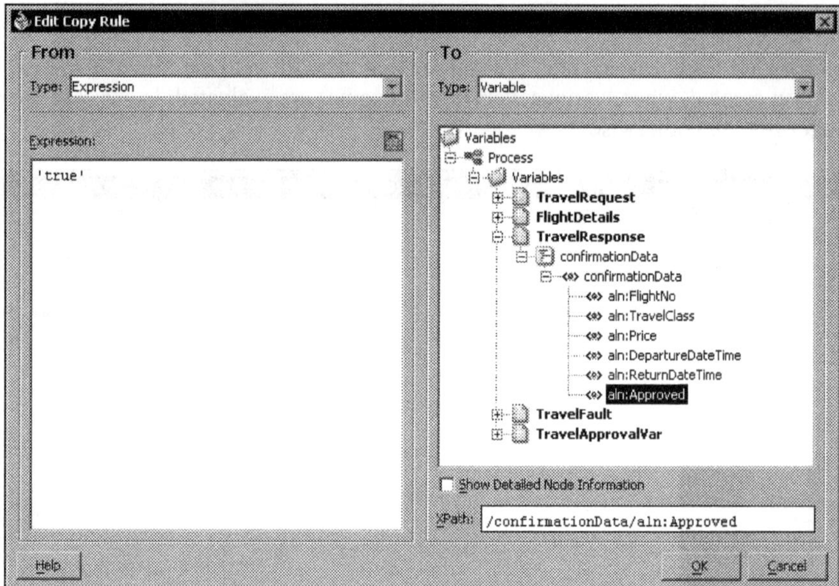

In a similar way we edit the other two assignments and enter `false` for the `Approved` element.

Worklist Application to Approve Ticket

We can deploy this example either from the BPEL Designer or from the command prompt using **`obant`**. After successful deployment, we can use the BPEL Console to initiate the process. From the visual flow we can see that the process has not completed but is waiting for human interaction:

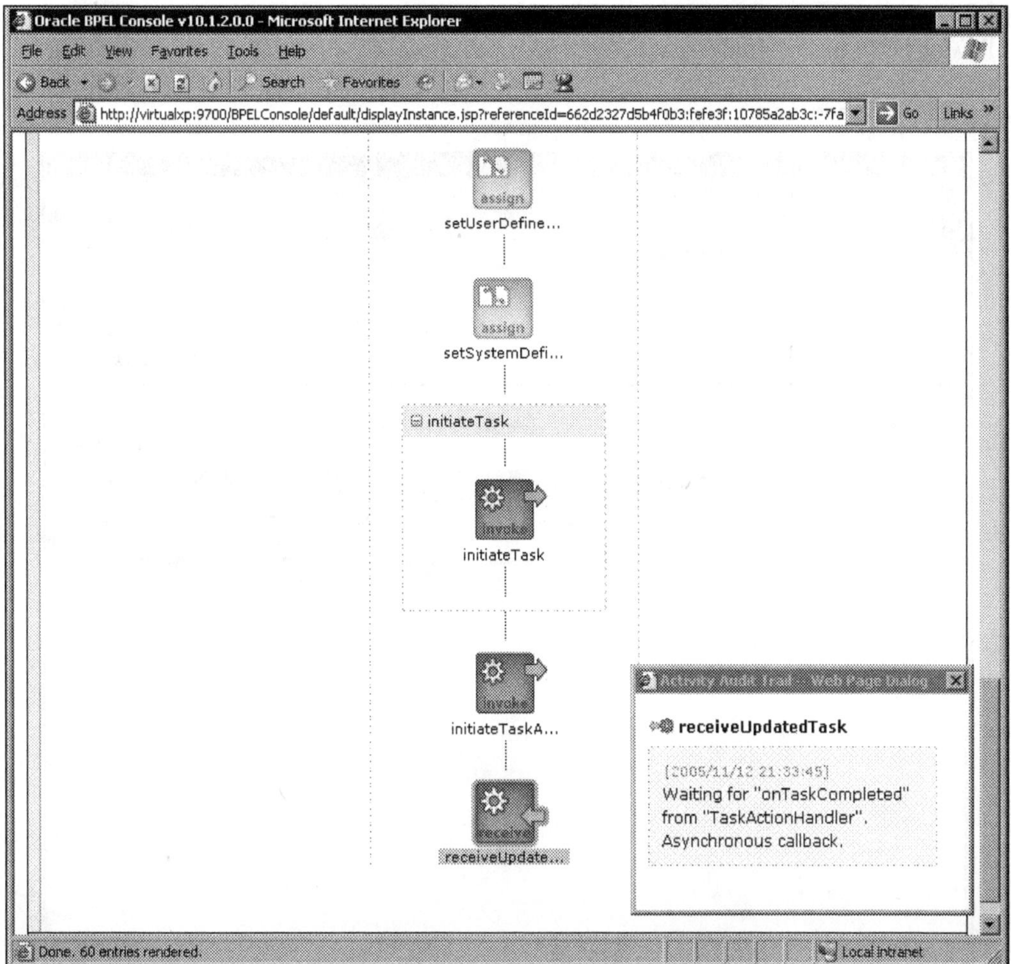
Oracle BPEL Console v10.1.2.0.0 - Microsoft Internet Explorer
File Edit View Favorites Tools Help
Back Search Favorites
Address http://virtualxp:9700/BPELConsole/default/displayInstance.jsp?referenceId=662d2327d5b4f0b3:fefe3f:10785a2ab3c:-7fa
Go Links
assign
setUserDefine...
assign
setSystemDefi...
initiateTask
invoke
initiateTask
invoke
initiateTaskA...
receive
receiveUpdate...
receiveUpdatedTask
[2005/11/12 21:33:45]
Waiting for "onTaskCompleted" from "TaskActionHandler". Asynchronous callback.
Done. 60 entries rendered.
Local intranet

To approve or decline the ticket we use the Worklist application. It can be accessed at the following URL: `http://localhost:9700/integration/worklistapp/Login`. We should log in using the `admin` username and `welcome` password. After successful login, we will see that a task is assigned for the `admin` user:

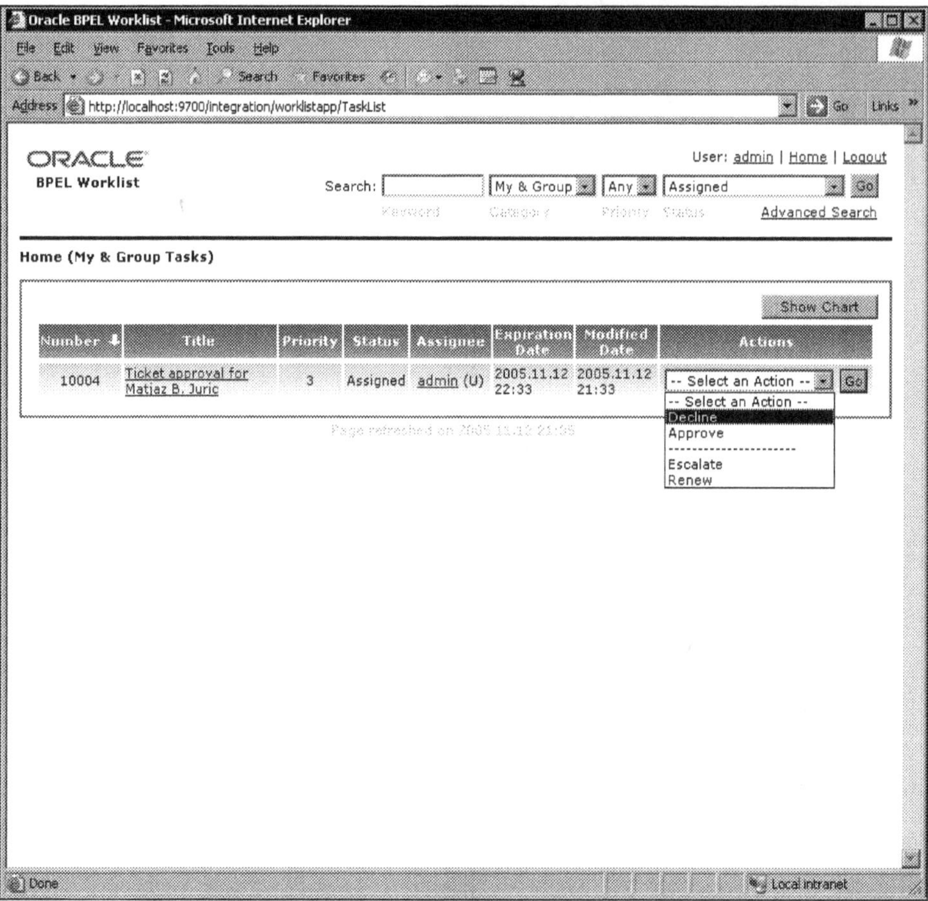

We have the choice to approve or decline the ticket. Clicking on the task title we can see the task details:

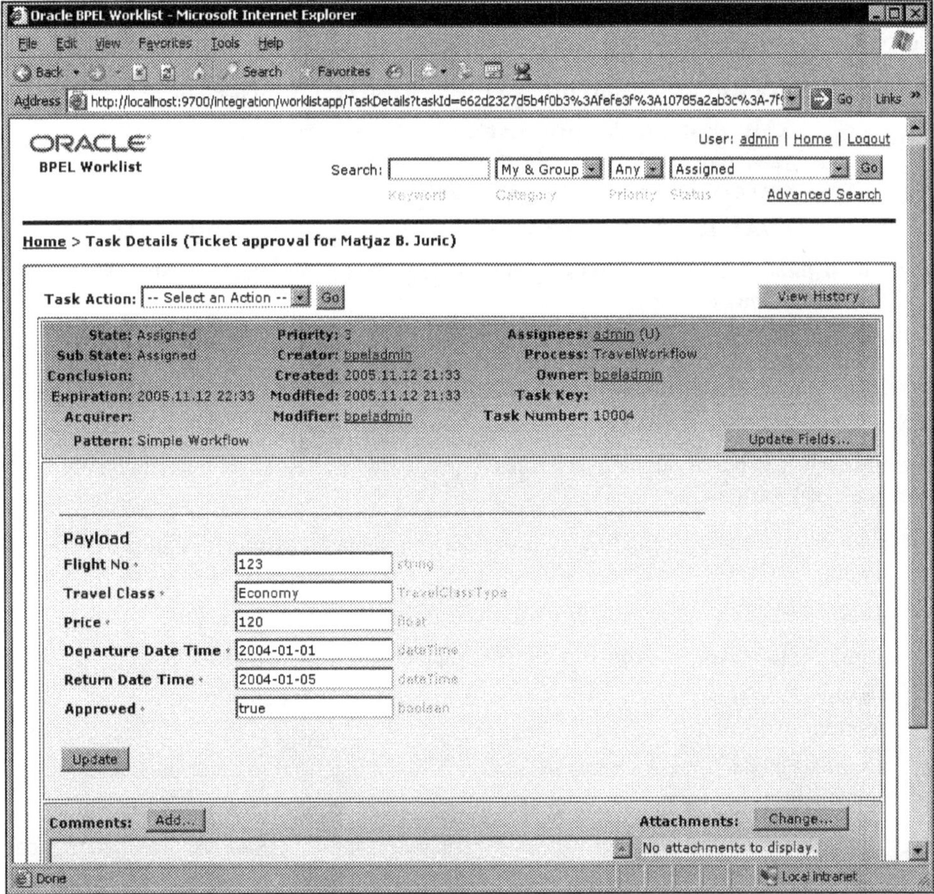

Depending whether we approve or decline the ticket, the BPEL Console shows whether the process has completed successfully or an exception has been thrown.

With this, we have concluded our example on the Workflow service. In a similar way we could develop more complex workflows and use other workflow patterns. Next, we will look at the Identity service.

Identity Service

Sometimes in BPEL processes we will need to authenticate and authorize users, particularly if we use the Workflow service. The Identity service is a web service layer on top of the Oracle JAAS (Java Authentication and Authorization Service) Provider. The Identity service provides access to the application server security infrastructure through the web services layer, using a set of extension functions for XPath expressions.

The Identity service is used to perform authentication, authorization, and retrieve user properties, such as contact information, email, phone, etc. It supports three types of security providers:

- **JAZN (Java Authorization) provider**, which can be XML-based or LDAP-based:
    - **XML-based JAZN provider** uses the `user-properties.xml` and `jazn-data.xml` files in the `C:\OraBPELPM_1\integration\orabpel\system\services\config` directory.
    - **LDAP-based JAZN provider** is based on the Oracle Internet Directory.
- **Third-party LDAP providers**, such as Microsoft Active Directory, Sun Directory Server, or Open LDAP
- **Custom repository plug-ins**

Please refer to Oracle documentation for more information on how to configure different providers and how to manage users.

The Identity service is based on the users' roles. It predefines certain roles that can be used with workflows for task assignments:

- `BPMPublic` (or `PUBLIC`): Allows a user to act on the tasks that are assigned to him/her.
- `BPMWorkflowReassign`: Allows a user to reassign tasks to other users.
- `BPMWorkflowSuspend`: Allows a user to suspend and resume a process.
- `BPMWorkflowViewHistory`: Allows a user to see a complete history of the task approval sequence.
- `BPMWorkflowAdmin` and `BPMSystemAdmin`: Allow a user to reassign, suspend, and view history.

To access the user data from BPEL processes several extension functions are provided that can be used in XPath expressions. They are defined in the `http://schemas.oracle.com/xpath/extension` namespace, for which the `ora` prefix is usually used. The most important functions are listed in the table below:

Method	Description
`ora:lookupUser(userId)`	Returns data about a user.
`ora:lookupGroup(groupId)`	Returns data about a user group.
`ora:getUserProperty(userId, attributeName)`	Returns a property of a user. The property can be `givenName`, `middleName`, `sn`, `displayName`, `mail`, `telephoneNumber`, `homephone`, `mobile`, `facsimileTelephoneNumber`, `pager`, `preferredLanguage`, or `manager`.
`ora:getGroupProperty(groupId, attributeName)`	Returns a property of a group. The property can be `displayName` or `mail`.

Method	Description
ora:getManager(userId)	Returns the manager of a user.
ora:getReportees(userId)	Returns direct reportees of a user.
ora:getUsersInGroup(groupId)	Returns all users in a group.
ora:getUserRoles(userId, roleType)	Returns the roles of a user. The role type can be ApplicationRole, EnterpriseRole, or AnyRole.
ora:isUserInRole(userId, roleName)	Checks if a user has a role.

BPEL Server APIs

Until now, we have discussed how to develop, deploy, and manage BPEL processes using Oracle BPEL Process Manager. We have also discussed how to integrate BPEL with Java resources. In complex real-world scenarios we may also need to invoke BPEL processes from Java (for example, custom-developed JSPs) or access the BPEL Server functionalities from Java. For example, we might want to develop our own console through which users could monitor active processes, start new process instances, set priorities, etc.

To realize these requirements, BPEL Server provides access to its functionalities through a set of APIs. Oracle BPEL Server has been developed in Java, therefore these APIs are Java packages and can be used by developers. Using them, we can develop our own applications that interact with the server and invoke processes, provide information about the state of the process instances, enable their management, and provide other useful information. Oracle provides Javadoc files to help learn how to use these APIs. The BPEL Console also uses these APIs and the source code is provided (a set of JSPs). Developers can use it to learn how to use the APIs.

The most important BPEL Process Manager APIs are:

- `com.oracle.bpel.client`: Provides interfaces and classes for accessing server functionality, such as performing operations on activities and introspecting processes deployed on a server domain.
- `com.oracle.bpel.client.auth`: Used to authenticate against a server domain or for administrative authentication.
- `com.oracle.bpel.client.dispatch`: Used to invoke processes (create process instances) that are deployed on a server domain from Java (for example from JSPs).
- `com.oracle.bpel.client.util`: Contains utility classes for HTML and SQL interaction.

Summary

In this chapter, we have provided a detailed overview of the advanced features provided by the Oracle BPEL Process Manager 10g. We have overviewed the extension functions and activities, such as the built-in XSLT and XSQL engines that we can use in our BPEL processes. We have become familiar with the Web Services Invocation Framework through which we can include resources other than web services into our BPEL processes by simply specifying the service bindings. WSIF provides bindings for Java classes, EJBs, JCA, HTTP, and sockets. Oracle BPEL Process Manager also provides Java code embedding and a set of Java APIs through which we can invoke and manage BPEL processes from Java applications. We have overviewed the Notification service for sending notifications over email, SMS, voice, and other channels; the Workflow service for including human interaction into BPEL processes; and the Identity service for user authentication and authorization.

All these features extend the usability of BPEL considerably. We have seen that Oracle BPEL Process Manager offers a comprehensive, powerful, and relatively easy-to-use environment for the development and deployment of BPEL processes.

In the next chapter, we will look at Microsoft BizTalk server.

7
MS BizTalk Server

Overview

BizTalk Server is part of Microsoft's Windows Server System family of products that enable you to integrate systems, employees, and trading partners. It is an integration server product (Middleware) used to connect different applications, systems, or business processes within an organization (EAI) or between organizations (B2B). It is also be used to aggregate services to build a Service-Oriented Architecture (SOA).

Microsoft initially planned to bundle BizTalk Server 2004 with the e-business suite, code named 'Jupiter', along with other related server products such as Content Management Server, Commerce Server, and Host Integration Server. However, later Microsoft changed plans and continued to release them as standalone products based on customer feedback.

BizTalk Server 2004 has changed significantly from its predecessors. It uses XML extensively to deal with messages. It has been built using the Microsoft .NET Framework and reengineered for improved performance and security. The tools for developing BizTalk applications and artifacts such as Schemas, Maps, and Orchestrations are now seamlessly integrated into **Visual Studio .NET** when BizTalk is installed in the development environment, so that the developers can avoid having to learn another development environment and at the same time leverage their existing skills with Visual Studio .NET. Some of the major features or improvements include:

- **Content-Based Routing** (CBR) where messages can be routed based on the values of certain fields inside the message
- Support for **BPEL4WS**
- Support for **WSDL**
- Support for **XSD**
- Support for **XSLT**
- **A Health and Activity Tracking** (HAT) tool for tracking and debugging of Orchestrations and messages
- **A Business Rules Engine** for abstracting business rules from the business process
- **Business Activity Monitoring** for real-time monitoring of business process in the production environment

- **Business Activity Services** including **Trading Partner Management** for integration with other business processes
- **Human Workflow Services** for workflow systems involving human intervention, such as approvals, data entry, and collaborations

Support for BPEL and XLANG/s

BizTalk supports BPEL as a business process exchange format, to exchange the business process definition with other vendors. BizTalk does not natively execute BPEL, but can export business processes to BPEL and also import external BPEL files that define business processes.

In BizTalk, the business process is built visually using the Orchestration Designer inside Visual Studio and is internally stored and represented using XLANG/s.

XLANG/s is Microsoft's proprietary language for defining business processes in BizTalk Server 2004. It is an improved version of XLANG (used in earlier versions of BizTalk), with support for the .NET framework and for invoking .NET components. It is not mandatory for a developer to learn the underlying XLANG/s to build business processes as it is automatically generated by the Orchestration Designer.

While BPEL is platform neutral by design, XLANG/s is very specific to BizTalk and the .NET platform and as such is able to provide advanced functionalities and a broader range of services than BPEL. However, this also means that if you plan to export business processes to BPEL, you should carefully avoid using features specific to BizTalk and XLANG/s, such as message transformation using maps or calling .NET components from within an Orchestration.

> The current release of BizTalk Server 2004 supports BPEL4WS version 1.1 only. It will not import or export BPEL4WS version 1.0.

Architecture

BizTalk is a message-oriented middleware, which means that all the communication between BizTalk and any external system happens by exchanging messages. In BizTalk, all messages are internally converted to XMLthat adheres to the specified XML Schema Definition (XSD).

The architecture of BizTalk server 2004 can be broadly divided into the **Messaging System** and **Business Processes** (Orchestrations). While Messaging involves receiving, storing, and forwarding of messages and interacting with various external systems, Orchestration is where the business logic is executed.

The following figure describes the architecture graphically:

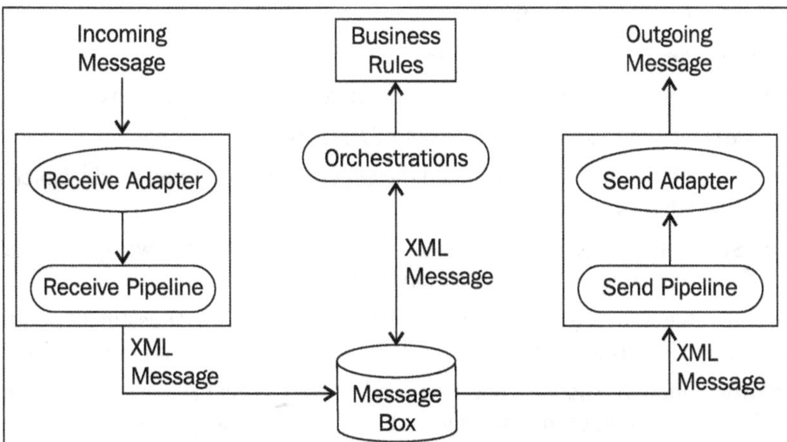

A message is received into BizTalk using a suitable **Receive Adapter** at one of the many possible **Receive Locations** of a defined **Receive Port**. Once the message is received, it is passed through a suitable **Receive Pipeline** where the message is processed in stages. The output of the pipeline can be one or more messages that are normalized and converted to XML format. The message from the pipeline is persisted into the **MessageBox,** which is an SQL Server database. From the MessageBox, messages are routed to **Orchestrations** or directly to the **Send Ports** depending on the subscription. There may be multiple Orchestrations and send ports waiting for a particular message, so when a message arrives into the MessageBox, it is forwarded to whoever has subscribed to that message. The Orchestration is where the process and business logic is implemented; it can do things like transform messages using Maps and call external services. Orchestrations can even call upon the Microsoft **Rules Engine** to apply the necessary business rules. The output from the Orchestration is usually a transformed message that is persisted back into the MessageBox to be routed to the appropriate destination using a suitable **Send Adapter**. Before sending the message out to the target system using the send adapter, the output message undergoes processing in stages inside the **Send Pipeline** where the message is converted form XML format to the format required by the target system.

> Some of the components and features such as Receive Locations, Adapters, Pipelines, MessageBox, Maps, Rules Engine, etc., are specific to the architecture of BizTalk and do not directly relate to BPEL. They are mentioned here for the sake of completeness.

Ports

BizTalk uses different kinds of ports, through which it exchanges messages with the outside world. These are the physical ports specific to BizTalk and are not be confused with the logical ports of the Orchestration (`<partnerLinks>` in BPEL). The logical ports are mapped to the physical ports at the time of deployment, by a process known as binding.

The following physical ports are available to BizTalk:

- **Receive Ports**: Used to receive messages into BizTalk.
- **One-Way Port**: Can only receive messages.
- **Request-Response Port**: Can receive as well as send back a response.
- **Send Ports**: Used to send messages out of BizTalk.
- **Static One-Way Port**: Can only send messages, and has a fixed send adapter and destination address.
- **Static Solicit-Response Port**: Can send as well as get an acknowledgment back, and has a fixed send adapter and destination address.
- **Dynamic One-Way Port**: Can only send messages; the actual destination of the message and the protocol/adapter to be used is determined at run time.
- **Dynamic Solicit-Response Port**: Can send as well as get back an acknowledgment; the actual destination of the message and the protocol/adapter to be used is determined at run time.

The physical ports can be created during development using **BizTalk Explorer** inside Visual Studio and during deployment using the **BizTalk Deployment Wizard**.

Receive Locations

As mentioned earlier, messages are received into BizTalk at a receive location of a receive port. A receive port can have multiple receive locations, each with its own receive adapter and receive pipeline, so that it can receive incoming messages by various means and in various formats.

For example, consider a scenario where a company's HRMS (Human Resource Management System) uses BizTalk to collect data about its employees from various systems. All of these systems have no knowledge about the HRMS as they were built at different times. As a result data retrieved from these systems will be in different formats and structures. One application may simply output a flat file at a regular interval, while another system exposes a web service that can return data in XML format. Yet another system may expose an API to communicate with the outside world, while the others may not have any interfacing capabilities at all, and would require that the data be picked up directly from their data store. In such cases it is useful to have multiple receive locations on a single receive port, so that each receive location can deal with a specific interface type.

Adapters

Adapters are used by BizTalk to interface with the outside world, for example to connect to external applications or systems. BizTalk provides built-in adapters to communicate with external systems using protocols like SOAP, HTTP, SMTP, and FTP. It can also communicate with SQL Server and the Windows file system using the SQL and FILE adapters respectively. However, if you need to connect to systems that have a proprietary interface/protocol, then you either need to build your own custom adapters using the **Adapter Framework** provided by BizTalk or purchase the adapters from third party vendors.

The purpose of the receive adapter is to listen to incoming messages and hand them over to the receive pipeline to be normalized and converted to XML. Similarly, the send adapter sends messages out of BizTalk after the messages pass through a send pipeline where they are converted to the format required by the target system.

Receive Pipelines

The purpose of the Receive Pipeline is to do some pre-processing on the incoming message to ensure that it is in a form that BizTalk can use. BizTalk requires that all messages be in XML format, so that they are easier to manage and convert to other formats required by the target application. BizTalk achieves this by allowing you to specify an XML Schema Definition (XSD) and requires that all incoming messages from different applications be converted in the receive pipeline to XML format conforming to this schema, before any further processing can take place.

The receive pipeline contains different stages where the incoming messages are pre-processed and converted into XML messages. The figure below shows the various stages of the **Receive Pipeline** and the standard components provided for each of the stages.

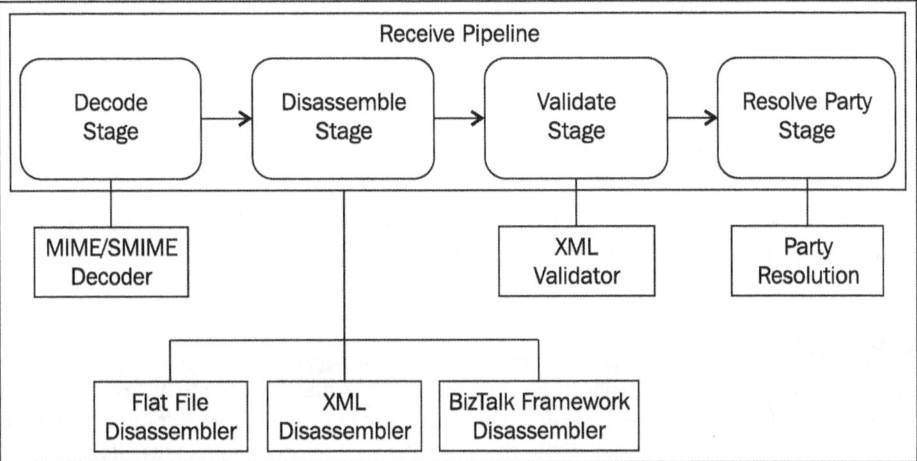

The various stages are:

- **Decode**: Used to decode messages and attachments in either MIME or Secure MIME (S/MIME) format, and to verify their digital signatures.
- **Disassemble:** Used to convert the incoming message formats into the normalized XML format defined by the schema.
- **Validate**: Used to validate the disassembled message against a specified schema
- **Resolve Party**: Determines an identity for the sender of the message.

BizTalk provides a couple of ready-to-use generic receive pipelines called the **PassThruReceive** and the **XMLReceive**. BizTalk also provides standard pipeline components for various stages, so that developers have the option and flexibility of building their own custom pipelines.

Developers can use a new tool in BizTalk 2004 called the **Pipeline Designer** to build a custom pipeline to suite the requirements. If the available pipelines and pipeline components are not suitable for the requirements, the developers can create their own custom pipeline components in .NET for any of the stages mentioned above and use them in the Pipeline Designer to build their own custom pipelines.

Message Contexts

Each message has a message context associated with it. Message contexts are constructed by the **Messaging Engine** and consist of information such as message type, message ID, and receive port name among other things. They can also contain user data from the message itself that are explicitly promoted by the developer.

Promoted Properties

The receive pipeline also performs another function called **Property Promotion** which is nothing but making available values of certain fields of the incoming message inside the Message Context, so that it is easily accessible to BizTalk without having to dig deep into the message. The promoted properties are mainly used for **Content Based Routing** of messages and also to correlate the request and response messages in an asynchronous communication.

For example, an Orchestration may be interested in processing only those purchase orders whose total value is above $1000. In such cases you promote the `TotalAmount` field of the message so that it can be accessed by the messaging engine without loading the whole message into memory to evaluate the subscriptions.

The properties to be promoted are specified in the schema files using **BizTalk Editor** inside Visual Studio. Doing so will actually create a separate **Property Schema** that will contain only the promoted properties. The values are promoted at runtime by the receive pipeline.

Distinguished Fields

Distinguished Fields are quite similar to Promoted Properties and are used to access the content of the message easily without having to load the whole message into memory but only from within an Orchestration. They allow the developer to access the content in an object oriented fashion using the "." (dot) operator as given in the example below.

```
TotalValue = PurchaseOrderMessage.TotalAmount
```

Note that the distinguished fields can be accessed only inside Orchestrations. They do contain the value of the field in the Message Context but are not promoted and hence cannot be used for Message Routing. However Distinguished Fields have their own advantages and must be preferred over Promoted Properties if you intend to use them only inside Orchestrations.

They are lightweight, and do not need a separate Property Schema to be created. Also, Promoted Properties have a limitation that the values must not exceed a length of 255 characters while Distinguished Fields do not have such limitations.

Creating distinguished fields is similar to creating promoted properties in the schema files using BizTalk Editor inside Visual Studio.

The MessageBox

The **MessageBox** is central to the messaging system. Once the incoming message passes through the receive pipeline, it is stored in the MessageBox and then routed to its respective destinations based on the **publish-subscribe mechanism**. The MessageBox is an SQL Server database that stores messages and their contexts. Messages from the MessageBox can either be routed to the Orchestration or to a Send Port for delivery to an external system or both, based on the subscriptions.

How Publish-Subscribe works

When Orchestrations and Send Ports are enlisted, they create a subscription indicating what kind of messages they are interested in. These may include a set of criteria such as "The total amount of a purchase order must be above $1000", "All messages received on port Xyz", etc. When a message arrives into the MessageBox (known as publishing the message) the messaging engine compares the context properties of the message with the available subscriptions and if they are found to match, the message is routed to the appropriate Orchestration or Send Port.

Orchestrations

Orchestration is where the business process resides. In this chapter, we will focus mainly on Orchestration and the related constructs and capabilities, to see how they relate to BPEL. An Orchestration consists of a set of shapes representing actions and control flow similar to a flow-chart diagram. Most of the shapes and constructs in an Orchestration directly correspond to their BPEL equivalents as shown in the table below:

BizTalk Constructs	BPEL Constructs
Send shape	`<invoke>` or `<reply>`
Receive shape	`<receive>`
Port	`<partnerLinks>`, `<partnerLink>`
Role Link	`<partnerLinkType>`, `<role>`
Message Assignment shape	`<assign>`, `<copy>`, `<from>`, `<to>`
Decide shape	`<switch>`, `<case>`, `<otherwise>`
Delay shape	`<wait>`
Listen shape	`<pick>`, `<onMessage>`, `<onAlarm>`
Parallel Actions shape	`<flow>`
Loop shape	`<while>`
Scope shape	`<scope>`
Throw Exception shape	`<throw>`
Compensate shape	`<compensate>`
Suspend shape	Not supported in BPEL
Call Orchestration shape	Not supported in BPEL

BizTalk Constructs	BPEL Constructs
Start Orchestration shape	Not supported in BPEL
Call Rules shape	Not supported in BPEL
Transform shape	Not supported in BPEL
Terminate shape	`<terminate>`
Compensation Block	`<compensationHandler>`
Exception Handler	`<faultHandler>`, `<catch>`, `<catchAll>`
Correlation	`<correlation>`, `<correlations>`, `<correlationSets>`, `<correlationSet>`

Orchestrations are built visually using the Orchestration Designer. It is quite powerful and has the ability to define general programming constructs such as expressions, loops, conditions, and exception handling among other things. In fact it even goes beyond the capabilities of a regular programming language with advanced features such as connecting to web services, parallel execution, message transformation, transaction management, compensation, and correlation. It is also possible to publish the entire business process contained inside the Orchestration as a web service.

Since Orchestrations are visual in nature, it is easy for a Business Analyst to visually verify the business logic without having to dig deep into the developer's code. In fact business analysts can themselves create Orchestrations in Visio by using a snap-in for Visio called **Orchestration Designer for Business Analysts (ODBA)**. This enables business analysts to create Orchestrations and then pass them on to the developers for implementation.

Maps

Orchestration typically performs message transformation using Maps. Maps basically generate XSLT at run time to transform messages from one structure to another. Mapping from source structure to target structure is done using a graphical tool called the **BizTalk Mapper**. This tool allows you to visually map values from the source fields to the target fields by just dragging a line and connecting them. Maps also make use of built-in functions called **Functoids** for various functions like string manipulation, mathematical calculations, date manipulation, and database lookups among other things. It is also possible to create your own custom Functoid that uses inline XSLT or .NET code, or even call an external .NET component.

The maps thus created can be used inside the Orchestration by embedding them inside **Transform shapes**.

Do not get confused between the transformation done by Maps and the format conversion done by the pipelines. Maps deal with XML messages and transform them from one XML structure to another, whereas the pipelines convert messages that are in different formats such a delimited list, positional text, or even another XML format to the XML format specified by the schema (XSD) and vice versa.

> Note that there is no equivalent of **Maps** and **Transform shapes** in BPEL and therefore they must not be used if you plan to export your Orchestration to BPEL.

Business Rules Engine

Another powerful feature of BizTalk Server 2004 is the new **Rules Engine**. The Rules Engine allows for separation of the business process from the frequently changing business rules so that they can be changed as frequently as required without bringing down the whole system. Rules are composed using the **Business Rule Composer** tool that is installed along with BizTalk and not integrated into Visual Studio like the other tools. Microsoft Rules Engine is independent of BizTalk, that is, you can use the Rules Engine independently even from a standalone .NET application such as an ASP.NET-based website, a Windows application, or even a console application. Inside the Orchestration, you can execute the rules either by using an **Expression shape** or the **Call Rules shape**, which is more user-friendly and specifically designed to invoke rules. The basic unit of versioning and deployment for rules is a **Policy**. A Policy can contain one or more rules and you can have many different versions of the same Policy deployed at the same time. The Rules Engine will execute the latest version by default.

> Note that there is no equivalent of the Rules Engine in BPEL and therefore the Call Rules shape must not be used if you plan to export your Orchestration to BPEL.

Send Pipeline

Send Pipelines do the exact opposite of the Receive Pipelines. The XML messages that are ready to be delivered are converted to the format required by the target system. For example the target may be an ERP system implemented using SAP, which expects an IDOC (flat file), in this case the send pipeline will convert the XML message into a flat file using the assemble stage of the pipeline. Similar to the receive pipeline, the send pipeline also has different stages where the outgoing XML message is converted. The figure below shows the various stages of the Send Pipeline and the standard components provided for each of the stages.

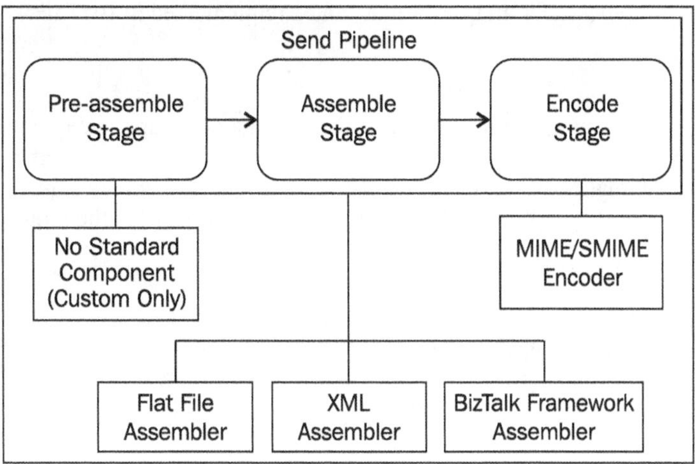

The various stages are:

- **Pre-assemble**: This stage is used to perform any custom action that may be required before the message is assembled. For example, the Assemble stage may require some external data to construct the outgoing message, which may not be part of the incoming message. In such cases, you need to use the pre-assemble stage to perhaps look up a database table, retrieve the data, and pass it on to the Assemble stage.
- **Assemble**: Used to convert the XML message to the format required by the target application.
- **Encode**: Used to wrap outgoing messages into MIME or S/MIME format (encrypt the messages and/or use a digital signature).

As with the receive pipeline, BizTalk also provides a couple of ready-to-use generic send pipelines called the **PassThruTransmit** and the **XMLTransmit** as well as providing standard pipeline components for various stages of the send pipeline.

Similar to the property promotion possible in the receive pipeline, the send pipeline can do something known as **Property Demotion**, which is quite the opposite of property promotion; that is, the data from the message context is copied into the outgoing message.

Finally the converted message is sent to the target system using a **Send Adapter**. Again, just like the receive adapters there are various built-in send adapters to interface with external systems. If you need to connect to systems that have a proprietary interface/protocol, you will have to build your own custom send adapter using the Adapter Framework provided by BizTalk.

Building a Sample Orchestration in BizTalk

Now that you have a fair understanding of BizTalk and its capabilities, let us jump right in and build a sample BizTalk Orchestration. We will use the same scenario as discussed in Chapter 3, of selecting the best insurance offer and see how it can be implemented in BizTalk.

Scenario

BizTalk receives an insurance premium quote request from a client application along with the required details, which it forwards to two external insurance companies. Once the response is received from the external parties indicating the premium each of them have quoted, BizTalk compares them and sends back the response with the lowest premium to the requester.

Implementation

Open a new Empty BizTalk Server Project in Visual Studio .NET and name it InsuranceSelection as shown below.

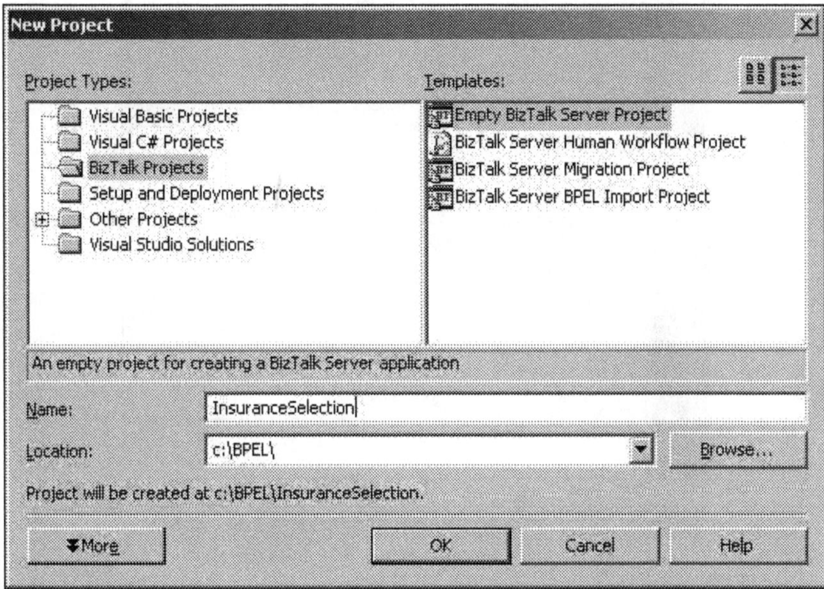

Next we need to build two schemas, one for the request message and one for the response.

The structure of the XML request message is as given below:

```
<InsuranceRequest>
    <Name></Name>
    <DateOfBirth></DateOfBirth>
    <Sex></Sex>
    <InsuredAmount></InsuredAmount>
</InsuranceRequest>
```

The structure of the XML response message is as given below:

```
<InsuranceResponse>
    <PremiumAmount></PremiumAmount>
</InsuranceResponse>
```

To add schemas to the project, right-click on the project name (InsuranceSelection) in the Solution Explorer window and select Add New Item.... In the window that pops up, we can add various BizTalk artifacts such as Schemas, Pipelines, Orchestration, and Maps as shown in the lower figure overleaf. Select a Schema and name it InsuranceRequestSchema.xsd

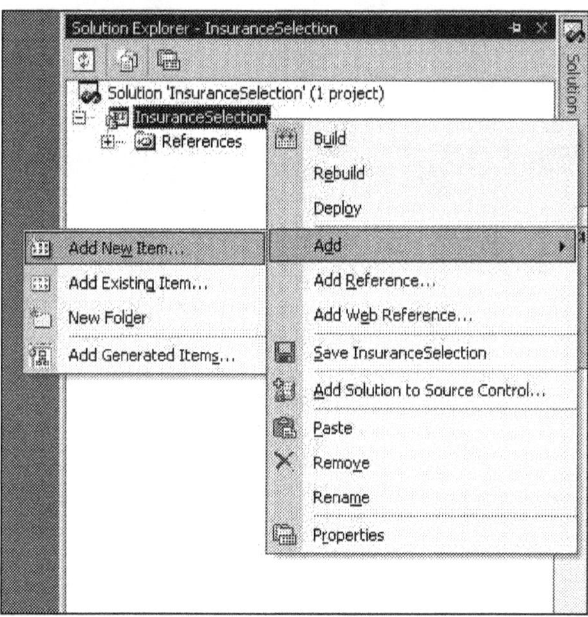

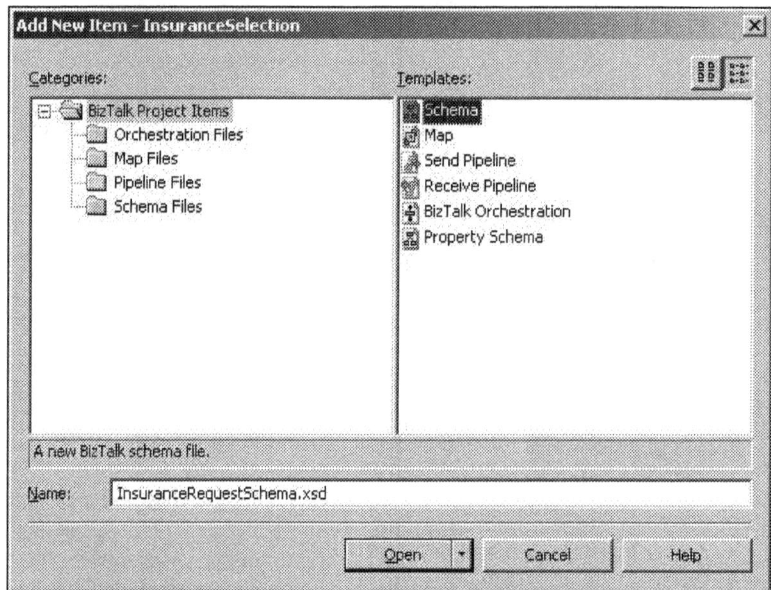

Add another schema and name it InsuranceResponseSchema.xsd

Build the schemas according to the structure we discussed earlier using the BizTalk Schema Editor shown below.

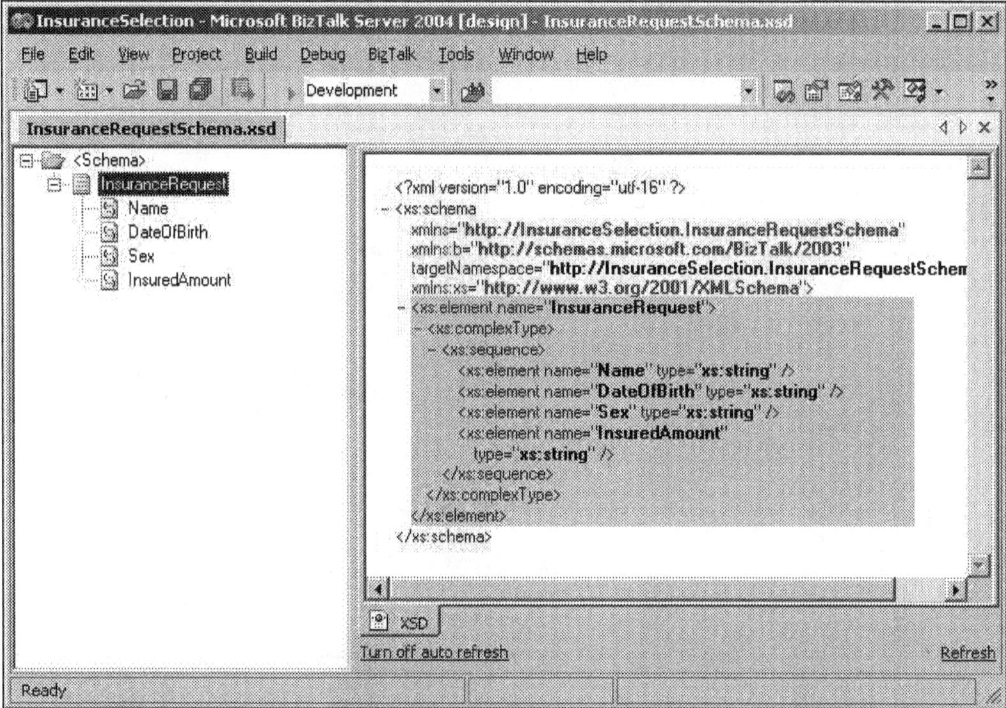

Add an Orchestration to our project in the same way as we added our schemas and name it InsuranceSelectionProcess.odx

Next we will create instance messages for the schemas as mentioned below:

- InsuranceRequestMessage of type InsuranceRequestSchema
- InsuranceAResponseMessage of type InsuranceResponseSchema
- InsuranceBResponseMessage of type InsuranceResponseSchema
- InsuranceSelectedResponseMessage of type InsuranceResponseSchema

To create the messages, make sure that the Orchestration Designer is in the foreground and the Orchestration View window is visible. You can make the Orchestration View window visible by selecting View | Other Windows | Orchestration View on the menu bar.

In the Orchestration View right-click on **Messages** and select **New Message**. Rename the messages and assign the appropriate Message Type (schema) in the properties window for each of the messages as shown below.

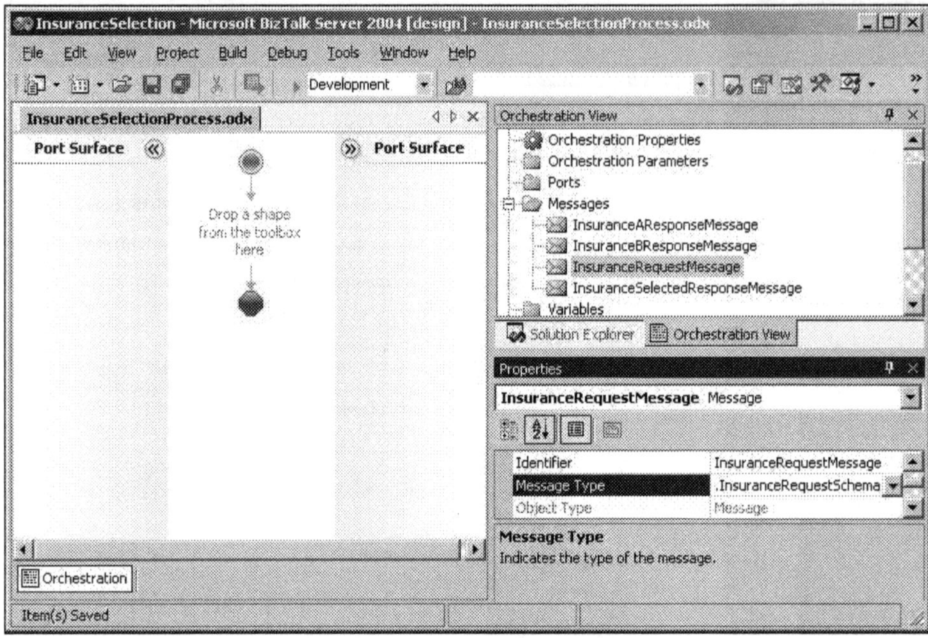

Next we will create our business process by dragging shapes from the Toolbox and adding them to the Orchestration Designer surface as shown opposite.

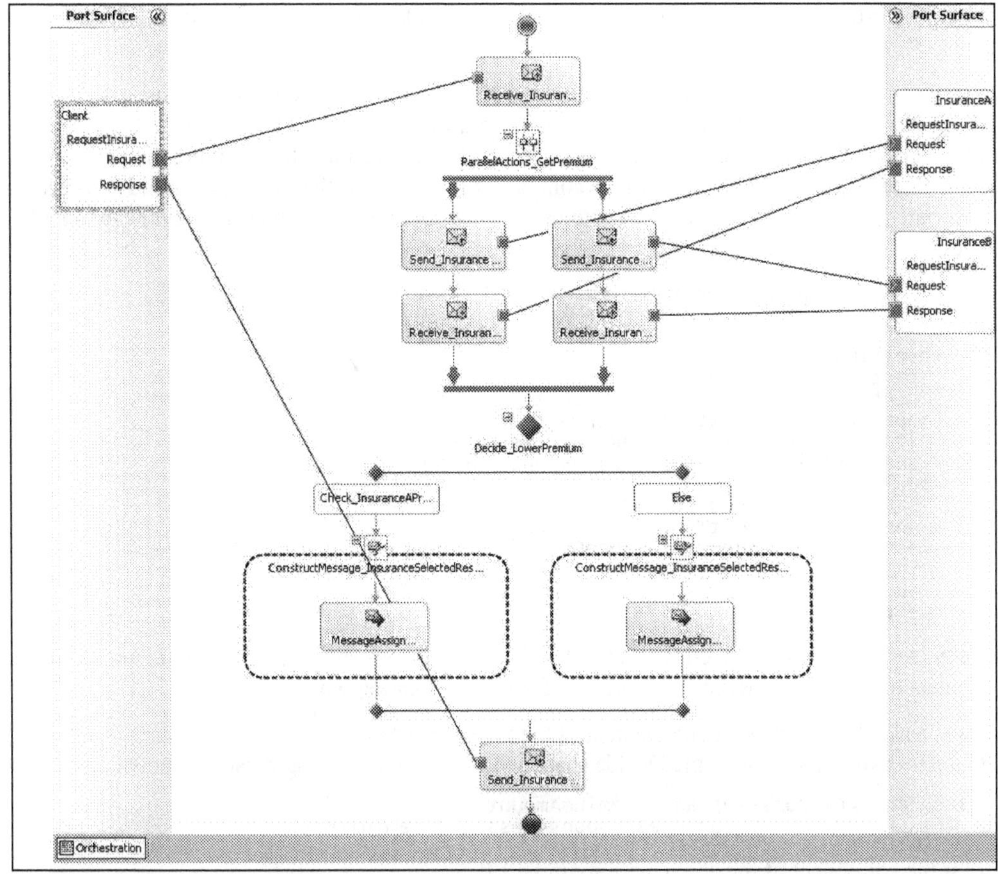

We can see from the figure that we have a Receive shape (`<receive>`) that receives the request from an external client through a Port (`<partnerLink>`). We need to specify the following in the properties window for the Receive shape.

Activate = True (In BPEL, this is equivalent to setting the attribute `createInstance="yes"` on `<receive>`.)

Message = InsuranceRequestMessage (In BPEL, this is equivalent to setting the attribute `variable="InsuranceRequestMessage"` on `<receive>`.)

Connect the Receive shape to Request operation of the Client port.

Here is the equivalent of the above activity in BPEL.

```
<bpel:receive
    partnerLink="Client"
    portType="q1:PortType_Client"
    operation="RequestInsuranceQuote"
    variable="InsuranceRequestMessage"
    createInstance="yes" />
```

The request is then forwarded to two external parties simultaneously using the Parallel Actions shape (<flow>).

We use two Request-Response ports, to send out the requests and receive the response. Using a Request-Response port indicates a synchronous operation. As you can see, we use a Send shape to send a request and a Receive shape to receive the response. We need to configure the Send shape and the Receive shape for both insurance companies in the properties window to send and receive appropriate messages. This is equivalent to using the <invoke> tag with an inputVariable and outputVariable attribute in BPEL

Here is the equivalent of the above activity in BPEL.

```
<bpel:flow>
  <bpel:invoke
    partnerLink="InsuranceA"
    portType="q1:PortType_InsuranceA"
    operation="RequestInsuranceQuote"
    inputVariable="InsuranceRequestMessage"
    outputVariable="InsuranceAResponseMessage" />
  <bpel:invoke
    partnerLink="InsuranceB"
    portType="q1:PortType_InsuranceB"
    operation="RequestInsuranceQuote"
    inputVariable="InsuranceRequestMessage"
    outputVariable="InsuranceBResponseMessage" />
</bpel:flow>
```

Once the responses are received we use a Decide shape to compare the premium amounts. This is equivalent to using the <switch>, <case>, and <otherwise> keywords of BPEL.

We will make the PremiumAmount element of the InsuranceResponseSchema a Distinguished Field, so that it is easily accessible in the Decide shape without explicitly using XPath as shown below.

```
InsuranceAResponseMessage.PremiumAmount <=
                  InsuranceBResponseMessage.PremiumAmount
```

Here is the equivalent of the above activity in BPEL.

```
<bpel:switch>
  <bpel:case
    condition="(
      bpel:getVariableData( 'InsuranceAResponseMessage', 'part', "/*
           [local-name()='InsuranceResponse' and namespace-
           uri()='http://InsuranceSelection.InsuranceResponseSchema']/*
           [local-name()='PremiumAmount' and namespace-uri()='']")
      <=
      bpel:getVariableData( 'InsuranceBResponseMessage', 'part', "/*
           [local-name()='InsuranceResponse' and namespace-
           uri()='http://InsuranceSelection.InsuranceResponseSchema']/*
           [local-name()='PremiumAmount' and namespace-uri()='']")
      )">
</bpel:switch>
```

The response with the lower premium amount is assigned to the outgoing message and sent back to the client. This is done using the Message Assignment shape inside the Construct Message shape. This is equivalent to using the <assign>, <copy>, <from>, and <to> tags in BPEL.

Here is the equivalent of the above activity in BPEL.

```
<bpel:assign>
  <bpel:copy>
```

```
        <bpel:from variable="InsuranceAResponseMessage" part="part" />
        <bpel:to variable="InsuranceSelectedResponseMessage" part="part" />
      </bpel:copy>
    </bpel:assign>
```

Finally the Send shape is used to send the response back to the client, using the synchronous Request-Response port, which is equivalent to the <reply> tag of BPEL.

Here is the activity as a whole in BPEL.

```
<bpel:reply
  partnerLink="Client"
  portType="q1:PortType_Client"
  operation="RequestInsuranceQuote"
  variable="InsuranceSelectedResponseMessage"
 />
```

Exporting Orchestration to BPEL

In the last section we saw how to build an Orchestration in BizTalk. In this section we will export the same to BPEL.

To export the Orchestration to BPEL, we have to do the following:

1. Keeping the Orchestration Designer selected in the foreground, bring up the properties window such that it displays the Orchestration properties.
2. You will see that the Module Exportable property is set to False. Setting this property to True will make two other properties visible in the properties window (Module XML Target Namespace and Orchestration Exportable).
3. Set a value for Module XML Target Namespace such as http://packtpub.com/bpel/example and set the Orchestration Exportable to True. This will make another property visible, called the Orchestration XML Target Namespace, shown in the figure below.

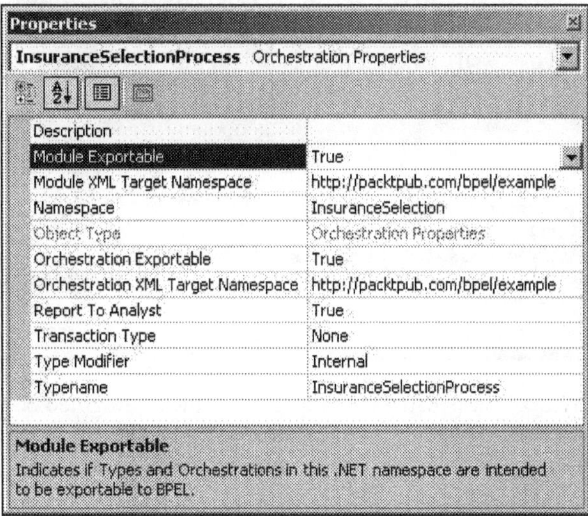

4. Set a value for **Orchestration XML Target Namespace** and you are all set to export the Orchestration to BPEL.
5. In the Solution Explorer window right-click on the Orchestration file (InsuranceSelectionProcess.odx) and select **Export to BPEL**.

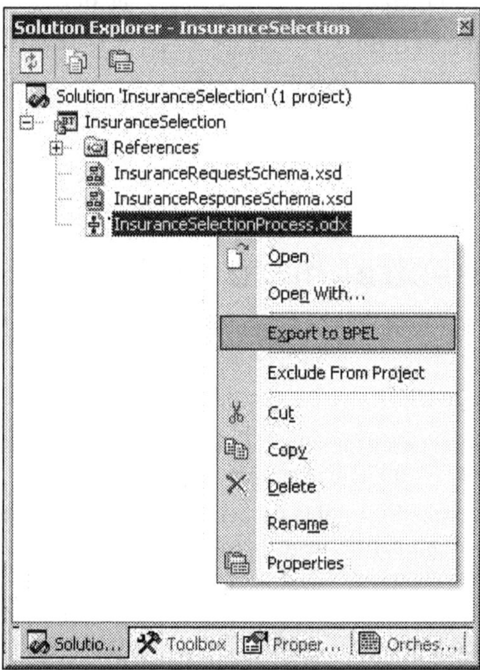

That's it!,If everything went well, you will see in the **Output** window that two files were created as shown below. One will have the extension `.bpel` and will contain the business process in BPEL, and the other file will have a `.wsdl` extension and contain the data types.

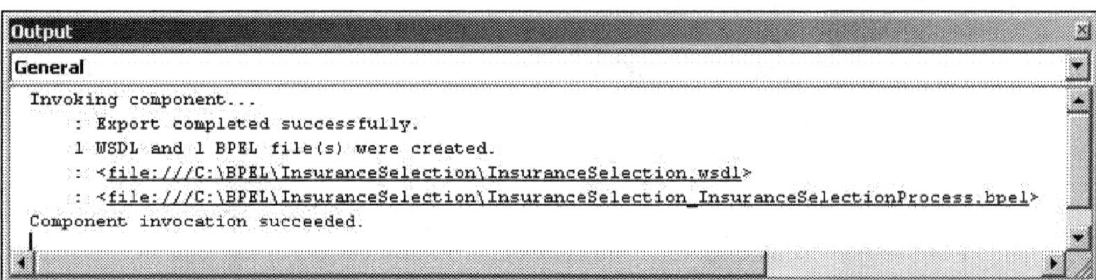

The BPEL generated by BizTalk is listed next (apart from the highlighted comments that have been manually added for documenting the code). Note that it is quite similar to the BPEL we saw in Chapter 3.

```
<?xml version="1.0"?>

<bpel:process xmlns:wsdl="http://schemas.xmlsoap.org/wsdl/"
    xmlns:q1="http://packtpub.com/bpel/example"
    xmlns:xsd="http://www.w3.org/2001/XMLSchema"
    name="InsuranceSelection.InsuranceSelectionProcess"
    targetNamespace="http://packtpub.com/bpel/example"
    xmlns:bpel="http://schemas.xmlsoap.org/ws/2003/03/business-process/">

  <!-- Defines partner links-->
  <bpel:partnerLinks>

    <bpel:partnerLink name="Client"
           partnerLinkType="q1:ClientType"
           myRole="portRole" />

    <bpel:partnerLink name="InsuranceA"
           partnerLinkType="q1:InsuranceAType"
           partnerRole="portRole" />

    <bpel:partnerLink name="InsuranceB"
           partnerLinkType="q1:InsuranceBType"
           partnerRole="portRole" />

  </bpel:partnerLinks>

<!-- Defines variables messages -->
<bpel:variables>
  <bpel:variable name="InsuranceRequestMessage"
   messageType="q1:__messagetype_InsuranceSelection_InsuranceRequestSchema"/>

  <bpel:variable name="InsuranceAResponseMessage"
   messageType="q1:__messagetype_InsuranceSelection_InsuranceResponseSchema"/>

  <bpel:variable name="InsuranceBResponseMessage"
   messageType="q1:__messagetype_InsuranceSelection_InsuranceResponseSchema"/>

  <bpel:variable name="InsuranceSelectedResponseMessage"
   messageType="q1:__messagetype_InsuranceSelection_InsuranceResponseSchema"/>

  </bpel:variables>

  <!-- Defines the business process -->
  <bpel:sequence>

<!-Receives request from client -->
    <bpel:receive partnerLink="Client"
           portType="q1:PortType_Client"
           operation="RequestInsuranceQuote"
           variable="InsuranceRequestMessage"
           createInstance="yes" />

    <!-Invokes external parties simulteneously -->
    <bpel:flow>

      <bpel:invoke partnerLink="InsuranceA"
          portType="q1:PortType_InsuranceA"
          operation="RequestInsuranceQuote"
          inputVariable="InsuranceRequestMessage"
          outputVariable="InsuranceAResponseMessage" />

      <bpel:invoke partnerLink="InsuranceB"
          portType="q1:PortType_InsuranceB"
          operation="RequestInsuranceQuote"
          inputVariable="InsuranceRequestMessage"
          outputVariable="InsuranceBResponseMessage" />
```

```
    </bpel:flow>

    <!—Compares responses -->
    <bpel:switch>
      <bpel:casecondition="(
        bpel:getVariableData( 'InsuranceAResponseMessage', 'part',
&quot;/*[local-name()='InsuranceResponse' and namespace-
uri()='http://InsuranceSelection.InsuranceResponseSchema']/*[local-
name()='PremiumAmount' and namespace-uri()='']&quot;)

          &lt;=

        bpel:getVariableData( 'InsuranceBResponseMessage', 'part',
&quot;/*[local-name()='InsuranceResponse' and namespace-
uri()='http://InsuranceSelection.InsuranceResponseSchema']/*[local-
name()='PremiumAmount' and namespace-uri()='']&quot;) )">

        <!—Assigns InsuranceA response to outgoing message-->
        <bpel:assign>
          <bpel:copy>
            <bpel:from variable="InsuranceAResponseMessage" part="part"/>
            <bpel:to variable="InsuranceSelectedResponseMessage" part="part"/>
          </bpel:copy>
        </bpel:assign>
      </bpel:case>
      <bpel:otherwise>

        <!—Assigns InsuranceB response to outgoing message-->
        <bpel:assign>
          <bpel:copy>
            <bpel:from variable="InsuranceBResponseMessage" part="part" />
            <bpel:to variable="InsuranceSelectedResponseMessage" part="part"/>
          </bpel:copy>
        </bpel:assign>
      </bpel:otherwise>
    </bpel:switch>

    <!—Sends back response to the client (requester) -->
    <bpel:reply partnerLink="Client"
          portType="q1:PortType_Client"
          operation="RequestInsuranceQuote"
          variable="InsuranceSelectedResponseMessage" />

  </bpel:sequence>
</bpel:process>
```

Importing BPEL Processes into BizTalk

Importing BPEL processes into BizTalk is quite easy. BizTalk provides a separate project template called the **BizTalk Server BPEL Import Project**, which will bring up a wizard to take you through the BPEL import procedure step by step. However, there are a few things you need to take care of before importing business processes:

- Ensure that the Name property of the WSDL definition node and that of the BPEL process node are not the same.
- Do not use any XLANG/s reserved words in your BPEL.
- Use only simple types predefined in XSD.

Now let us use the asynchronous travel process example we saw in Chapter 3 to import into BizTalk and see how it goes.

But before we do that we need to make a few modifications to the `.wsdl` files. The `.wsdl` files (`Travel.wsdl`, `Airline.wsdl`, and `Employee.wsdl`) used in the travel process example in Chapter 3 uses the RPC style, whereas BizTalk currently does not support the RPC style and requires that the `.wsdl` files be in Document style. So we first need to convert the `.wsdl` files to Document style.

Converting the `.wsdl` files for the travel process from RPC style to Document style is quite simple; all we need to do is open up the `.wsdl` file in any text editor and do the following:

- Replace the '**type**' keyword in all the message part definitions with the '**element**' keyword as shown below:

  RPC style

  ```
  <message name="TravelRequestMessage">
  <part name="employee" type="emp:EmployeeType" />
  <part name="flightData" type="aln:FlightRequestType" />
  </message>
  ```

  Document style

  ```
  <message name="TravelRequestMessage">
  <part name="employee" element="emp:EmployeeType" />
  <part name="flightData" element="aln:FlightRequestType" />
  </message>
  ```

- Wrap the data type referred to in the message parts inside the element tag as shown below:

  Before

  ```
  <xs:complexType name="EmployeeType">
          <xs:sequence>
                  <xs:element name="FirstName" type="xs:string" />
                  <xs:element name="LastName" type="xs:string" />
                  <xs:element name="Departement" type="xs:string" />
          </xs:sequence>
  </xs:complexType>
  ```

  After

  ```
  <xs:element name="EmployeeType">
    <xs:complexType>
      <xs:sequence>
        <xs:element name="FirstName" type="xs:string" />
        <xs:element name="LastName" type="xs:string" />
        <xs:element name="Departement" type="xs:string" />
      </xs:sequence>
    </xs:complexType>
  </xs:element>
  ```

Now we are ready to import the `.bpel` and the `.wsdl` files into BizTalk. Here are the step-by-step instructions:

1. Open a new BizTalk Server BPEL Import Project in Visual Studio .NET and name it AsyncTravelProcessBPELImport as shown overleaf.

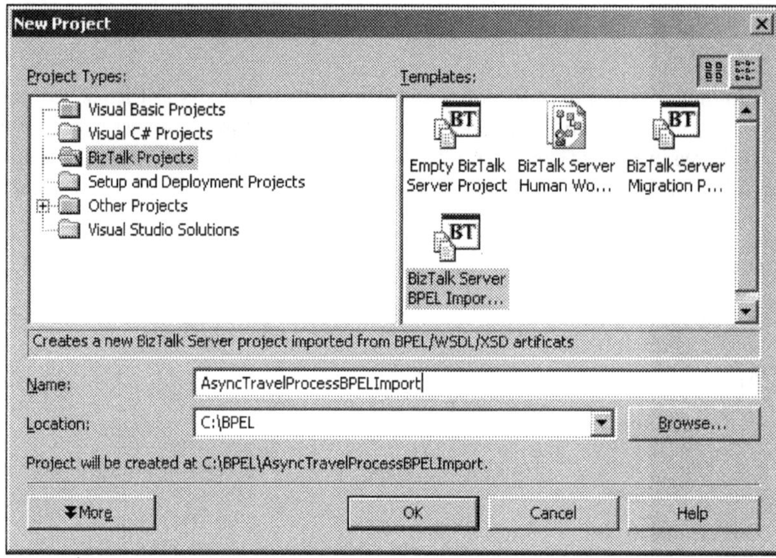

Click OK to bring up the BPEL Import Wizard shown below.

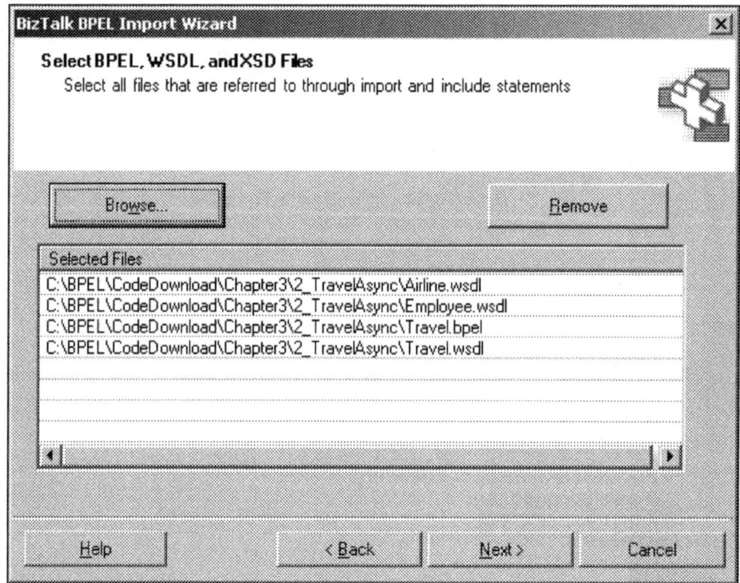

Click Next, and then Finish.

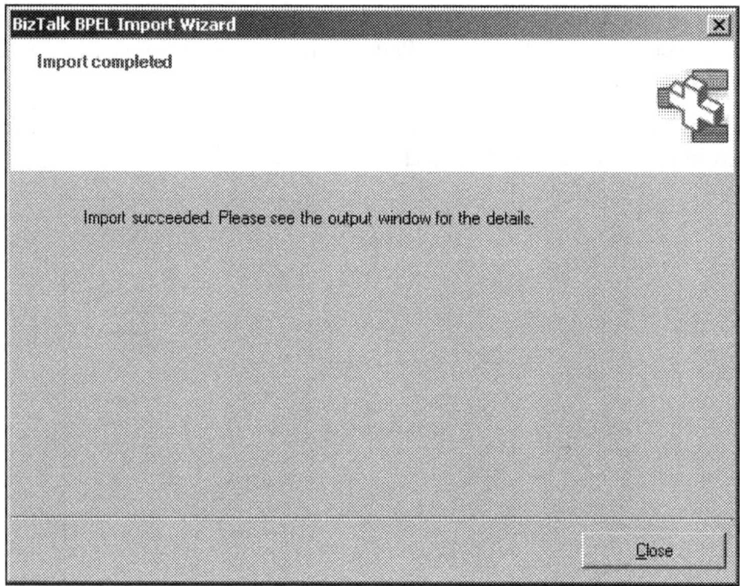

Note: You may find that some constructs have not been correctly converted or have been left as they are, and therefore you may need to make some alterations or manual corrections before the project can be successfully compiled. It is also possible that you may find the conversion less than optimal from BizTalk's perspective and may need some refactoring.

After importing the travel process example, you can see in the Solution Explorer of Visual Studio that the wizard has created four orchestration (`.odx`) files and two schema (`.xsd`) files shown below:

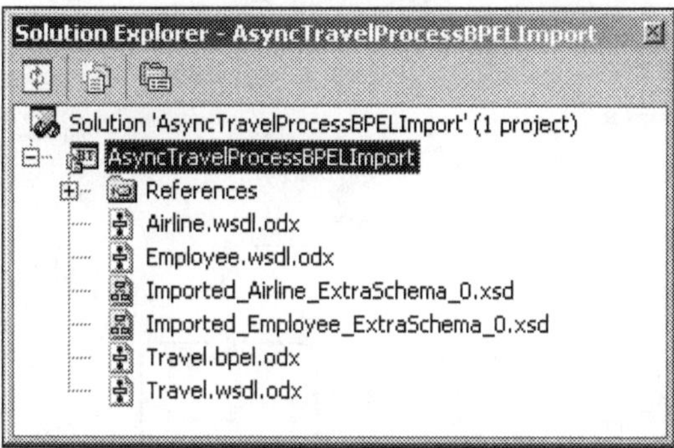

The wizard breaks down each `.wsdl` file into a schema file (`.xsd`) that contains the schema definition and an orchestration file (`.odx`) that contains the other things like Port Types, Message Types, and Partner Link Types (known as Role Link Types in BizTalk). This orchestration file does not contain any business process logic and is only used to define the types.

The `.bpel` file is converted into an orchestration file (`.odx`) that contains the actual business process logic and declarations for things like Partner Links (Ports and Role Links in BizTalk) and Variables (Messages in BizTalk).

Double-click on the Travel.bpel.odx orchestration file in the Solution Explorer and you will see the business process in the Orchestration Designer:

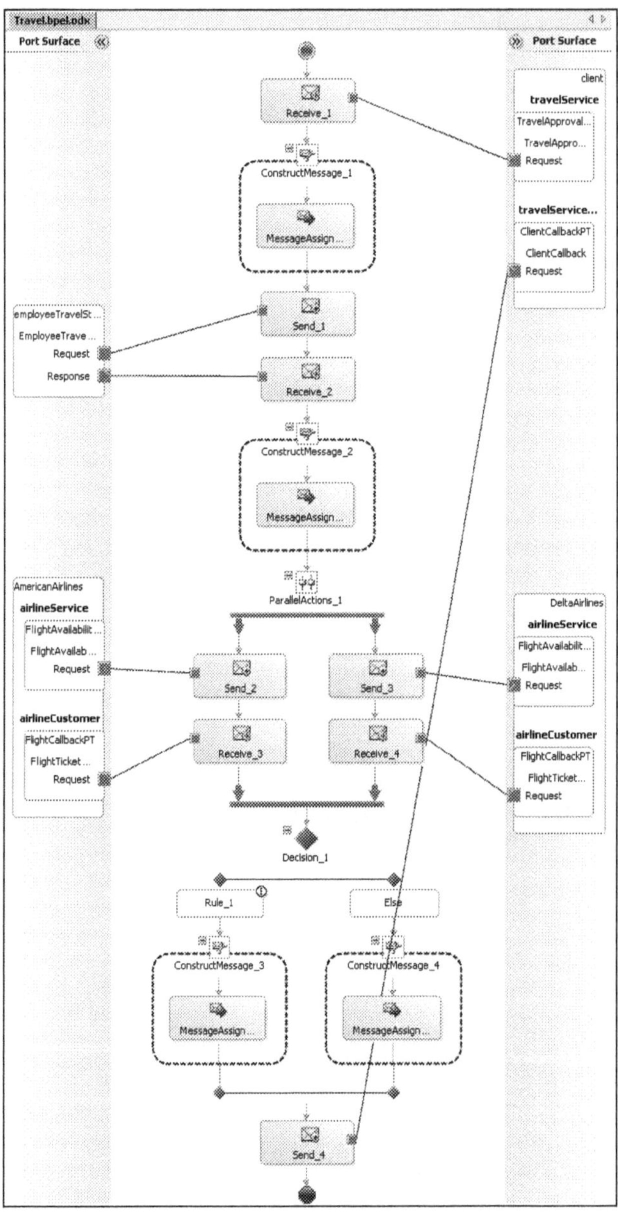

Notice that the wizard has done a wonderful job, and we are able to follow the business process logic just by looking at the Orchestration. However on careful examination you will see a red colored tag on the Rule shape named Rule_1, which indicates that there is an error there. Double-clicking on the Rule shape brings up the BizTalk Expression Editor, which shows you the code inside.

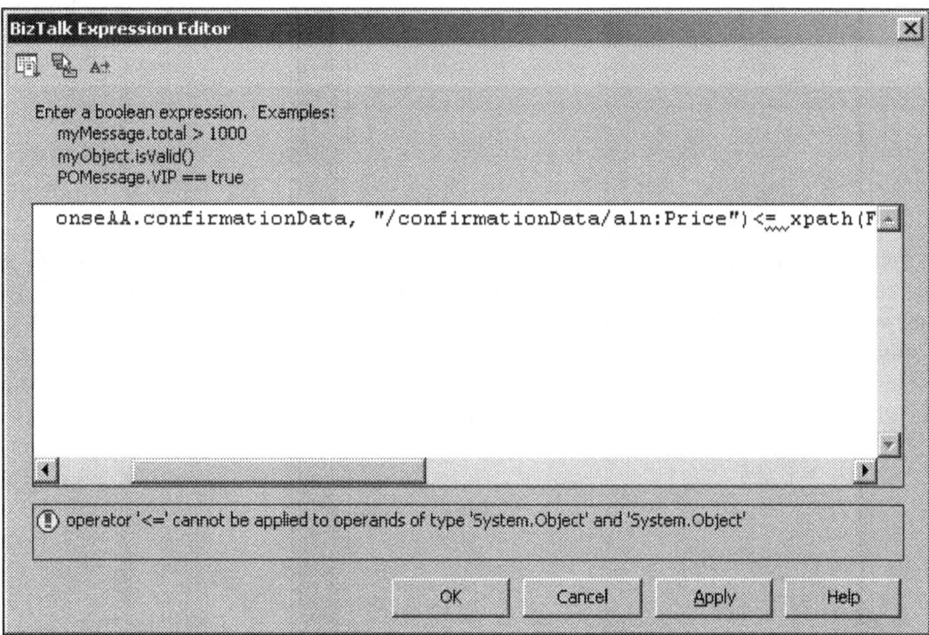

Notice that the BPEL Import Wizard has attempted to convert the code that compares the ticket prices of both airlines as follows.

```
xpath(FlightResponseAA.confirmationData,"/confirmationData/aln:Price")

<=

xpath(FlightResponseDA.confirmationData, "/confirmationData/aln:Price")
```

However, BizTalk complains that you cannot use a '<=' operator on the `System.Object` operands. So we will solve the issue by typecasting each operand with `System.Double` as shown below.

```
(System.Double) xpath(FlightResponseAA.confirmationData,
    "/confirmationData/aln:Price")

<=

(System.Double) xpath(FlightResponseDA.confirmationData,
"/confirmationData/aln:Price")
```

Now you see that the red colored tag is gone, which means there are no errors. Now let us try to compile the project by right-clicking on the project name in the Solution Explorer and selecting Build. Doing so, you see that it still has errors as shown in the screen overleaf:

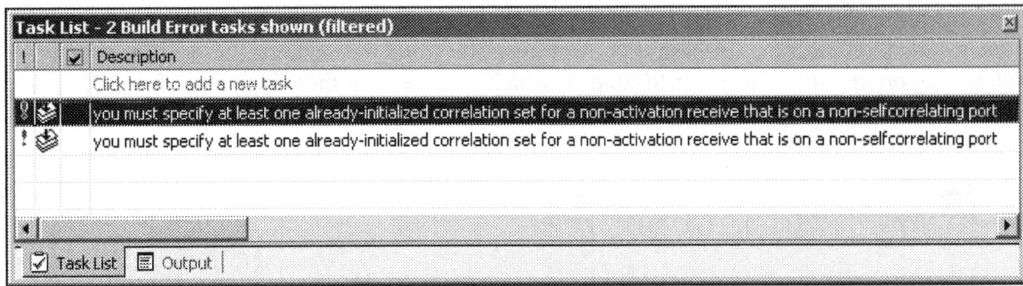

The above error is thrown because you need to specify a correlation of some sort between the `airlineService` and `airlineCustomer` roles for the asynchronous invocation of the `FlightAvailability` operation on both the `AmericanAirlines` and `DeltaAirlines` Role Links.

Let us fix the problem by specifying a correlation on the Send and the Receive shape. Now if you look at the schema of the request message (`FlightDetails`) and the schema of the response message (`FlightResponseAA` or `FlightResponseDA`), you see that there are no common fields on which we could correlate. So we will add a new field called `RequestID` under both `FlightRequestType` and `FlightConfirmationType` of the imported airline schema (Imported_Airline_ExtraSchema_0.xsd) using BizTalk Schema Editor as shown in the figure below.

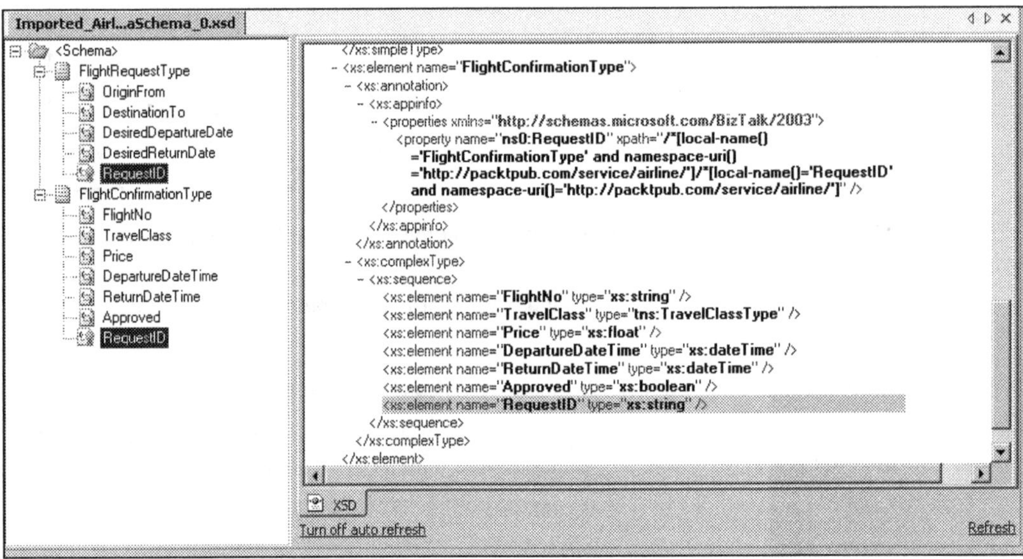

Next we need to promote both the `RequestID` fields we added to be able to use them for correlation. Let us first promote the `RequestID` field of `FlightRequestType` as follows:

- Right-click on the RequestID element in BizTalk schema editor and select Quick Promotion.
- You will see a dialogue box asking you to confirm the creation of a property schema to store the promoted properties. Click OK. This will actually create an element by

the same name (`RequestID`) in the newly created property schema (PropertySchema.xsd).

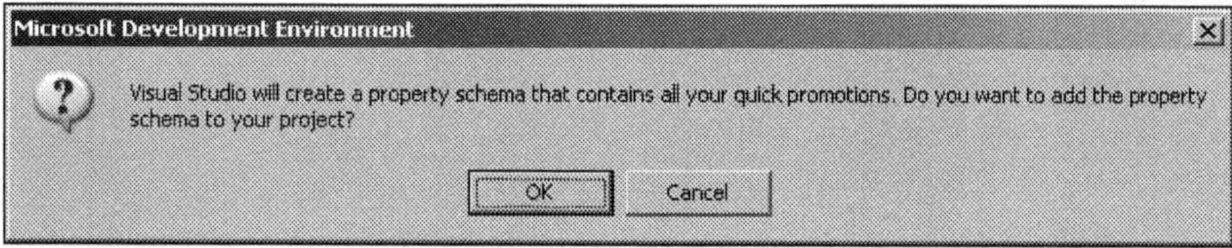

That's it! You have promoted the `RequestID` field of `FlightRequestType`. You will see an icon on the field indicating that it has been promoted.

Now similarly we need to promote the `RequestID` field of `FlightConfirmationType` as follows:

- Right-click on the RequestID node in BizTalk schema editor and select Quick Promotion.
- Since the field name is the same as the one you promoted above, you will see a dialogue box shown below asking you to confirm whether you want to share the same element (`RequestID`) as was created in the property schema earlier. Click OK and you are done.

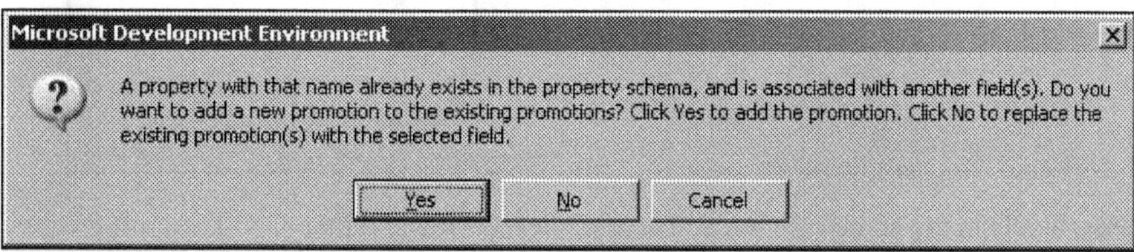

Next we define a correlation type (`<correlationSet>` in BPEL) by right-clicking on Correlation Types and selecting New Correlation Type... in the Orchestration View as shown below.

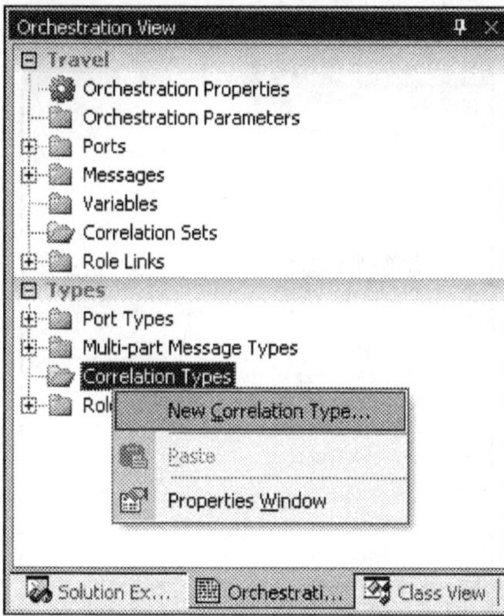

This will open up the Correlation Properties window shown below where you choose the properties that will form the correlation set.

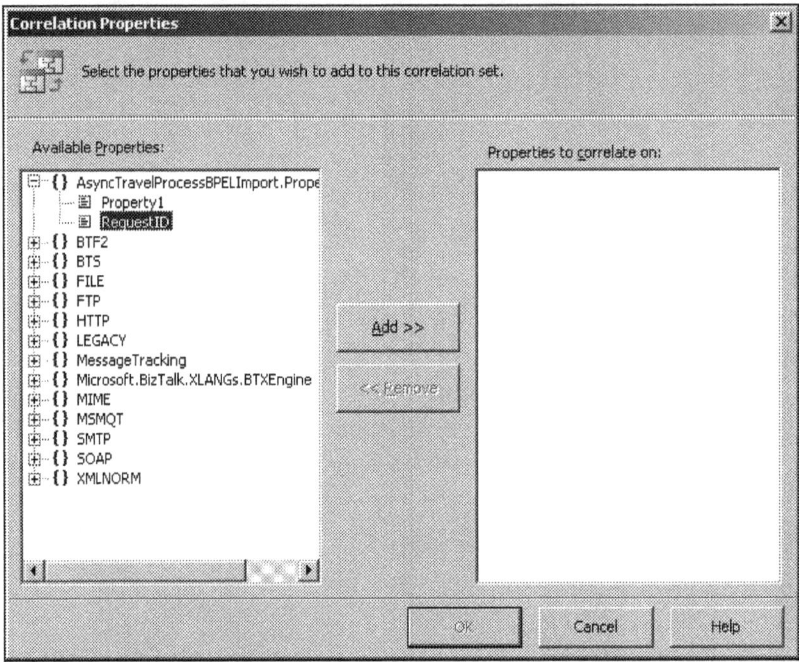

Select RequestID in the screen shown above and click Add>> and then OK. This will create a correlation type called `CorrelationType_1` by default.

Now we need to create two correlation sets (`<correlation>` in BPEL), one for `AmericanAirlines` and one for `DeltaAirlines`, by right-clicking on Correlation Sets and selecting New Correlation Set in the Orchestration View as shown below.

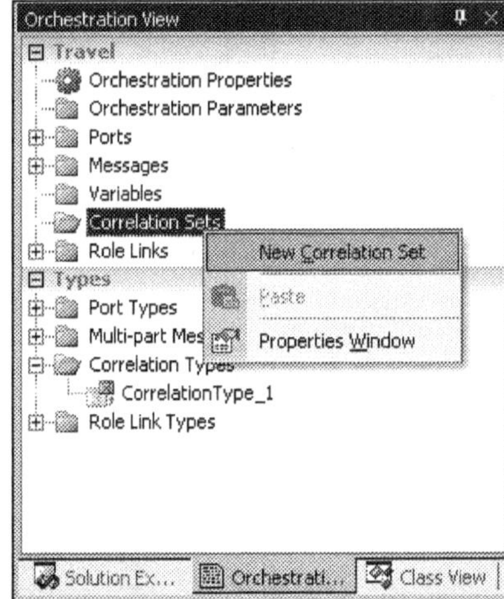

This will create a correlation set called `Correlation_1` by default. Repeat the step to create another one called `Correlation_2`.

Next we will declare both the above correlation sets to be of the correlation type we create earlier (`CorrelationType_1`) by selecting it in the **Properties** window as shown below.

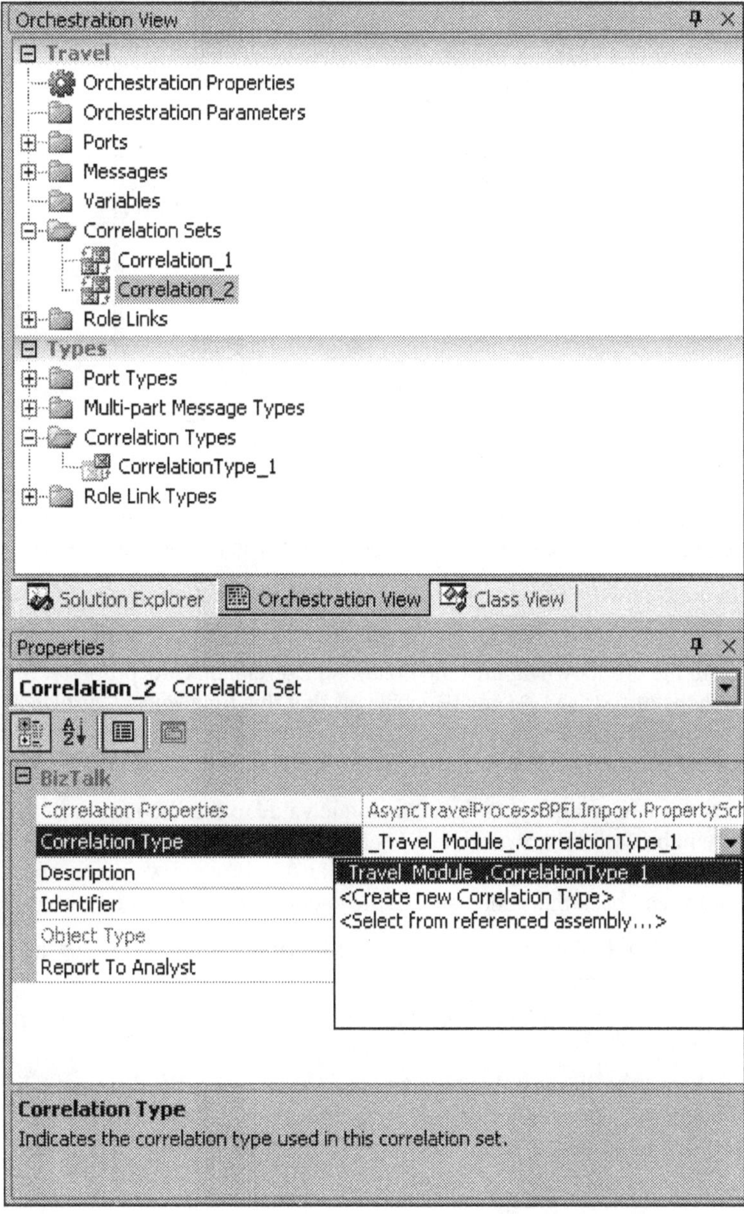

That's it! Now we need to apply the correlation sets to the Send and Receive shapes as follows:

In the Properties window of the Send shape for `AmericanAirlines` (Send_2), select Correlation_1 from the dropdown against the Initializing Correlation Sets property as shown in the figure below.

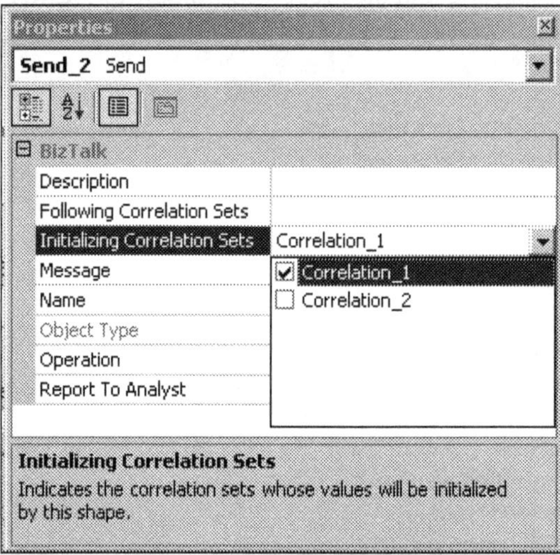

Similarly do it for the Send shape of `DeltaAirlines` (Send_3), but this time select Correlation_2 instead of Correlation_1 from the dropdown against the Initializing Correlation Sets property.

Now we need to configure the Receive shape to receive the correct response as follows:

In the Properties window of the Receive shape for `AmericanAirlines` (Receive_3), select Correlation_1 from the dropdown against the Following Correlation Sets property. Similarly do it for the Receive shape of `DeltaAirlines` (Receive_4), but this time select Correlation_2 instead of Correlation_1 from the dropdown against the Following Correlation Sets property. That's it! You have established the correlations between the request and response messages.

Now remember that we have not yet assigned a unique value to the `RequestID` field of the request message, which will be used for correlation. We can use the `MessageID` available in the Message Context which is actually a **Globally Unique Identifier** (GUID) and we expect the `airlineService` to send back the same value in the `RequestID` field of the response message.

We do this by adding a the following line inside the Message Assignment shape contained in the Construct Message shape (`ConstructMessage_2`)

```
FlightDetails(AsyncTravelProcessBPELImport.PropertySchema.RequestID) =
FlightDetails(BTS.MessageID);
```

Now compile the project to check if there are any more errors. You bet there are…life isn't easy for a software developer! You will see two error messages that say uninitialized 'uses' servicelink 'AmericanAirlines' and uninitialized 'uses' servicelink 'DeltaAirlines'. Now what on earth does that mean?

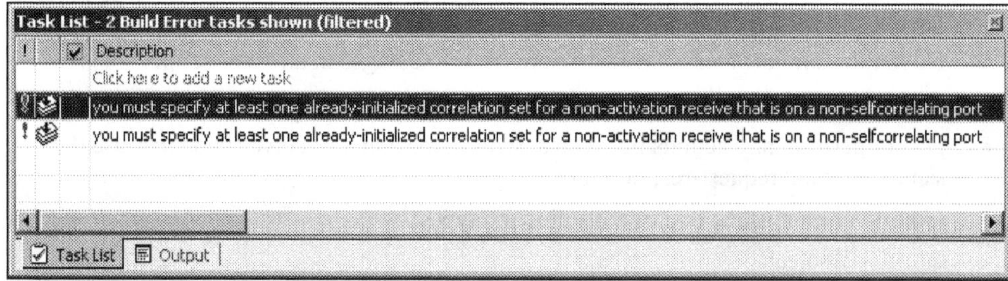
Task List - 2 Build Error tasks shown (filtered)
Description
Click here to add a new task
you must specify at least one already-initialized correlation set for a non-activation receive that is on a non-selfcorrelating port
you must specify at least one already-initialized correlation set for a non-activation receive that is on a non-selfcorrelating port
Task List
Output

To understand this, you first need to know how BizTalk implements Role Links. Role Links are an abstraction between the external service provider or consumer and the business process that allows you to dynamically switch to different external services without making any changes to the Orchestration. It can be configured externally by a BizTalk administrator. As this is a huge topic in itself, we don't intend to go into details here.

For the purpose of this exercise it is sufficient to understand that we need to pass a value to BizTalk that will resolve to the correct provider at run time. We can do this by placing an Expression shape (`Expression_1`) just below the `ConstructMessage_2` shape and adding the following lines inside it.

```
AmericanAirlines(Microsoft.XLANGs.BaseTypes.DestinationParty) = new
    Microsoft.XLANGs.BaseTypes.Party("AmericanAirlines", "OrganizationName");

DeltaAirlines(Microsoft.XLANGs.BaseTypes.DestinationParty) = new
Microsoft.XLANGs.BaseTypes.Party("DeltaAirlines", "OrganizationName");
```

Now compile the project and everything should go smoothly, but before you do that, make sure you set the BPEL Compliance property to **False** in the **Configuration Properties** of the project by right-clicking on the project name in the Solution Explorer and selecting **Properties**.

> Note that we can actually refactor the above solution generated by the BizTalk BPEL Import Wizard to be less complicated and more elegant by using just one orchestration file instead of four and doing away with things like Role Links, Role Link Types, and Multi-part Messages Types.

Do's and Don'ts for BPEL Compliance in BizTalk

The following list contains pointers and best practices that will help ensure that your BizTalk solution is BPEL compliant.

- Do not use the Call Orchestration shape or the Start Orchestration shape.
- Do not use the Transform shape.
- Do not invoke methods on custom .NET components.
- Do not apply a timeout to a long-running transaction.
- Do not pass parameters to Orchestration.
- Do not pass parameters to Callable compensation handlers.

- Do not use the Suspend shape.
- Do not declare local variables, correlations, or messages in an inner scope.
- Do not use Relational operators with type 'Char'.
- Do not perform any actions between a Send shape and a Receive shape that use the same outbound request-response port.
- Literal values must be one of the following types:
    - Boolean
    - Char
    - Byte
    - SByte
    - Int32
    - UInt32
    - Int64
    - UInt64
    - Single
    - Double
    - String
- Arithmetic operators are allowed only on operands of the following numeric types:
    - Byte
    - SByte
    - Int32
    - UInt32
    - Int64
    - UInt64
    - Single
    - Double
- Variable types must be supportable in XPATH.

> Note: Refer to the BizTalk Server Documentation for a detailed list of Do's and Don'ts while importing or exporting to BPEL.

Comparing BizTalk Orchestration Constructs with BPEL

In the sample Orchestration we built in the previous section, we saw a few Orchestration shapes and found that they are quite similar to the BPEL constructs. In this section we will look at them and the others more closely.

Receive and Send Shapes (<receive>, <invoke>, <reply>)

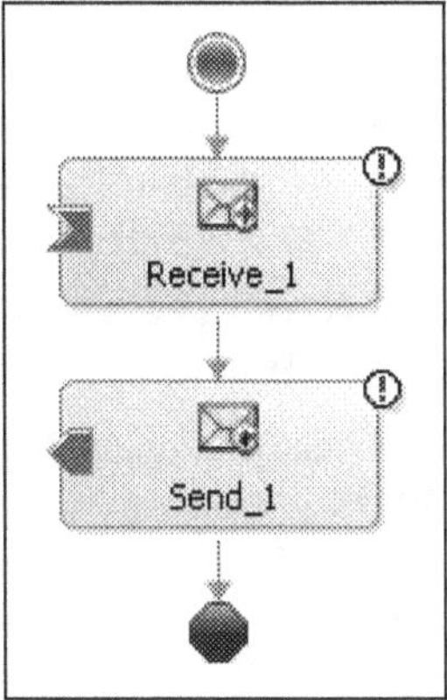

Messages are received and sent to the ports (`partnerLinks`) within the BizTalk Orchestration using the Receive and Send shapes. These are equivalent to the `<receive>`, `<reply>`, or `<invoke>` keywords of BPEL. Note that the same Send shape is used to send messages for both One-Way (Asynchronous `<invoke>`) and Request-Response (Synchronous `<reply>`) calls.

You need configure the Receive shapes by specifying things such as which type of message to receive along with any filter condition, which port to receive from, whether to create a new instance of the Orchestration upon receiving a message, and initializing or following correlation messages among other things. Similar configuration is required for the Send shape as well.

Port and Role Link Shapes (<partnerLink>, <partnerLinkType>, <role>)

Ports and Role Links are the endpoints for messages entering or exiting the Orchestration. They are similar to partner links in BPEL. Configuring the ports includes setting the PortType, Communication Direction (send or receive), Communication Pattern (One-Way or Request-Response), Delivery Notification, and Binding to the physical ports, among other things. When you drop a Port shape or a Role Link shape onto the side panels of the Orchestration Designer surface, the Port Configuration Wizard pops up and assists you in configuring the ports. Role Link is used to group together multiple `PortTypes`, similar to `<partnerLinkType>`.

A receive port is equivalent to a partner link with a `myRole` attribute, while a send port is equivalent to a partner link with a `partnerRole` attribute

Ports are the logical endpoints within an Orchestration, which need to be bound to actual physical ports. The physical port is configured to use pipelines and adapters to transform and send messages to or receive messages from external systems like web services using a transport protocol such as SOAP, HTTP, FTP, etc.

Expression and Message Assignment Shapes (<assign>, <copy>, <from>, <to>)

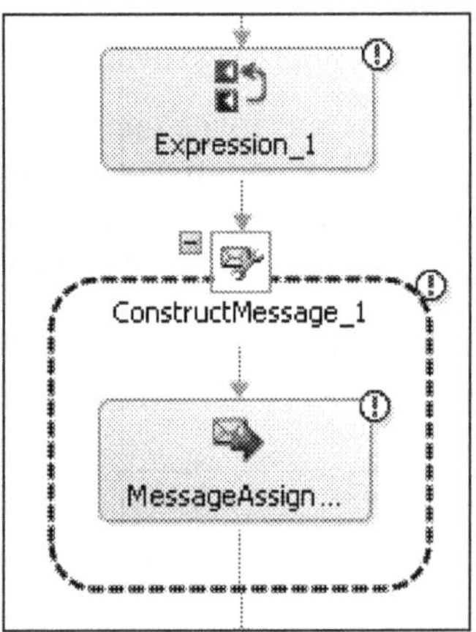

Expression and Message Assignment shapes, as the name suggests, are used to implement business logic that contains expressions, loops, conditions, and assignments. It is possible to use XPath and XLANG/s within these shapes and also to call any external .NET components by defining and instantiating a variable of the particular .NET type.

Note that, unlike in BPEL, a Variable is different from a Message in BizTalk Server 2004. A Message is typically an XML document that is received and sent from within an Orchestration whereas Variables can be of any .NET type including `XmlDocument` type used for holding values/state temporarily inside the Orchestration. Note that even if you are using simple .NET types for Variables such as `System.Int32` or `System.String`, in your Orchestration and export the Orchestration to BPEL, BizTalk wraps them inside an element as shown in the following example, which replaces `type="xs:int"`. BizTalk variables cannot be used to send or receive data. A BizTalk variable is equivalent to the `<variable>` construct with a with a `type` attribute or an `element` attribute as shown below:

```
<variables>
  <variable name="iCount" element="q1:int" />
</variables>
```

Whereas a BizTalk message is equivalent to the `<variable>` construct with a `messageType` attribute as shown below:

```
<variables>
  <variable name="InsuranceRequestMsg" messageType="InsuranceRequestSchema" />
</variables>
```

The Message Assignment shape is used primarily to initialize a Message and can only be placed inside a Construct Message shape. This also means that you cannot assign a value to a message in an Expression shape or any other shape other than a Message Assignment shape.

> Messages in BizTalk are immutable—once a message is created, it cannot be modified. Moreover messages can only be initialized inside a Construct Message shape using a Message Assignment shape or a Transform shape.

Decide Shape (<switch>, <case>, <otherwise>)

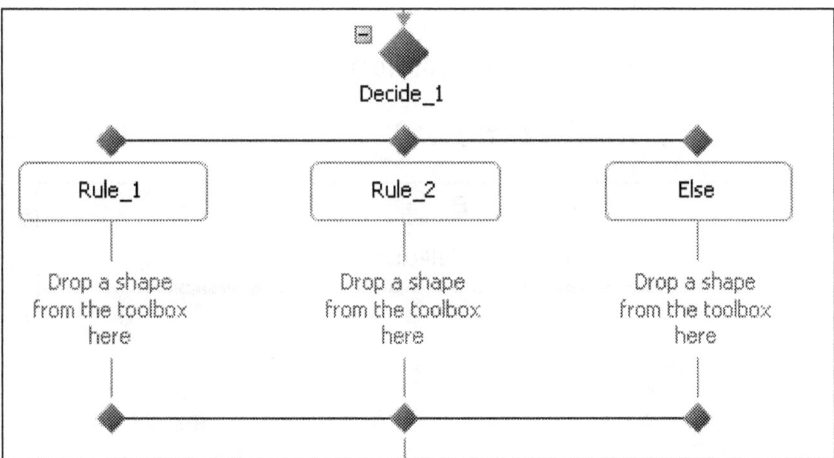

A Decide shape is used for conditional branching. It is similar to an IF/THEN/ELSE/ELSIF programming construct or the `<switch>`, `<case>`, and `<otherwise>` constructs of BPEL. It will always have a minimum of two branches. Each branch (other than the Else branch) will have a Rule shape containing the condition expression to be evaluated. The condition expression of each branch is evaluated and if it satisfies the condition, that branch is executed; otherwise it will evaluate the condition of the next branch (if available) and so on. If none of them satisfy the condition the else branch is executed.

Delay Shape (<wait>)

The Delay shape is equivalent to the `<wait>` activity of BPEL. It is used to delay the execution of the process for a specific length of time (specified by the `System.TimeSpan` class) or until a particular time or date is reached (specified by the `System.DateTime` class).

Note that if you specify the timeout by instantiating the `System.DateTime` class or the `System.TimeSpan` class directly as shown below, you will not be able to export the Orchestration to BPEL since BizTalk will complain that the `new` operator is not permitted under BPEL4WS compliance.

```
new System.TimeSpan(1,0,0,0);
```

Or

```
new System.DateTime(2005,12,25);
```

Instead you need to use the `System.Xml.XmlConvert` class as shown below

```
System.Xml.XmlConvert.ToTimeSpan("2004-12-25")
```

Or

```
System.Xml.XmlConvert.ToDateTime("1,0,0,0")
```

Parallel Actions Shape (<flow>)

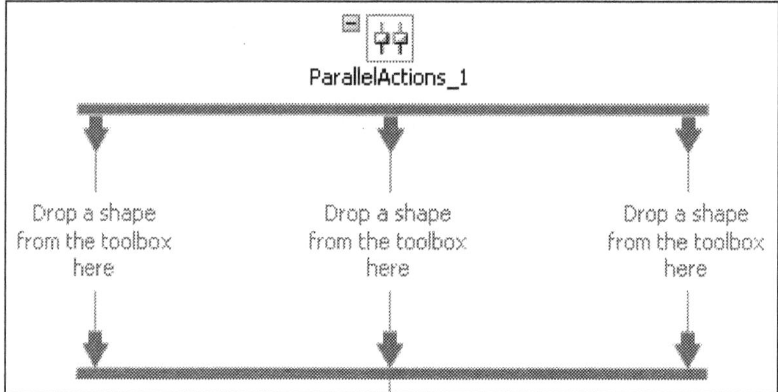

The Parallel Actions shape is used to simultaneously execute multiple actions. It is similar to the `<flow>` activity of BPEL. It is possible to have many parallel branches and the process will wait till all the branches have completed before proceeding further.

Loop Shape (<while>)

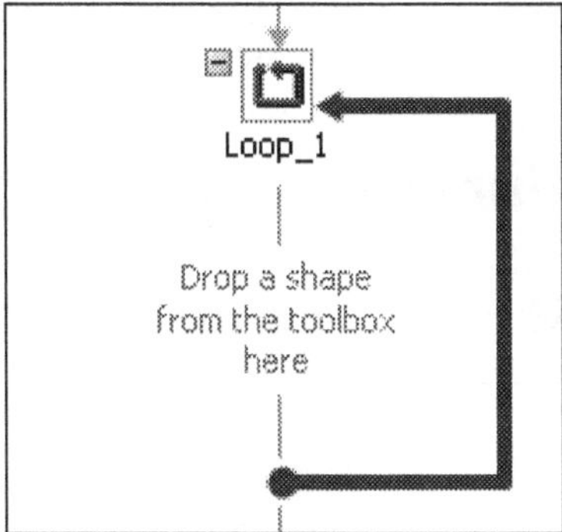

The Loop shape is used to iterate through a set of actions as long as the Boolean condition evaluates to True. This is equivalent to the `<while>` activity of BPEL.

Suspend Shape

A Suspend shape is used to stop a running Orchestration and save its state such that it is possible for the administrator to resume the Orchestration instance. You use the Suspend shape if your Orchestration reaches a condition that is beyond the capabilities of the Orchestration, such that you would rather allow an administrator to look into it and resume the operations based on the administrator's decision. When an Orchestration is suspended an error is logged and it is possible to specify a string containing a brief description along with the error message to help the administrator diagnose the problem. This activity is not available in BPEL.

> The Suspend shape is not supported by BPEL and should not be used if you plan to export the Orchestration to BPEL.

Terminate Shape (<terminate>)

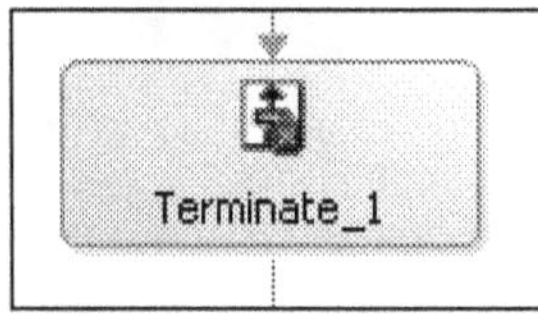

A Terminate shape is used to abruptly stop all activities of a running Orchestration. This is equivalent to the `<terminate>` activity of BPEL. When an Orchestration is terminated an error is logged and it is possible to specify a string containing a brief description along with the error message to help the administrator diagnose the problem.

Advanced BPEL Functions using BizTalk

Listen Shape (<pick>, <onMessage>, <onAlarm>)

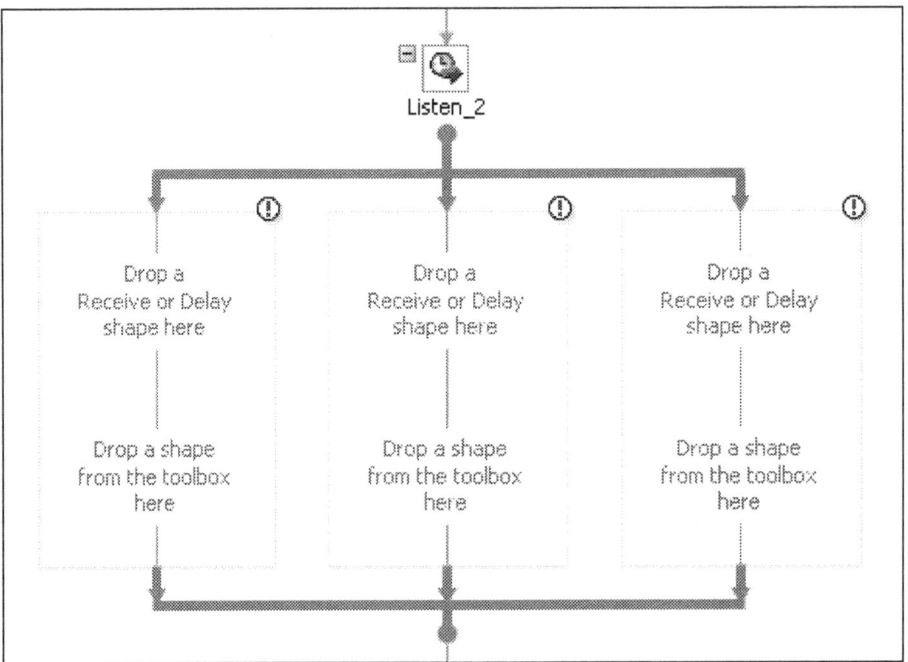

A Listen shape is used when you have to receive a message before proceeding further and also need to specify a timeout period until which BizTalk waits for the message. The Listen shape can have any number of branches each starting with a Receive shape or a Delay shape. Note that you can have all branches starting with a Receive shape in which case there is no timeout period. Alternatively you can have only one branch starting with a Delay shape and the rest must start with a Receive shape. The Listen shape is equivalent to the `<pick>`, `<onMessage>`, and `<onAlarm>` activities of BPEL.

Scope Shape (<scope>)

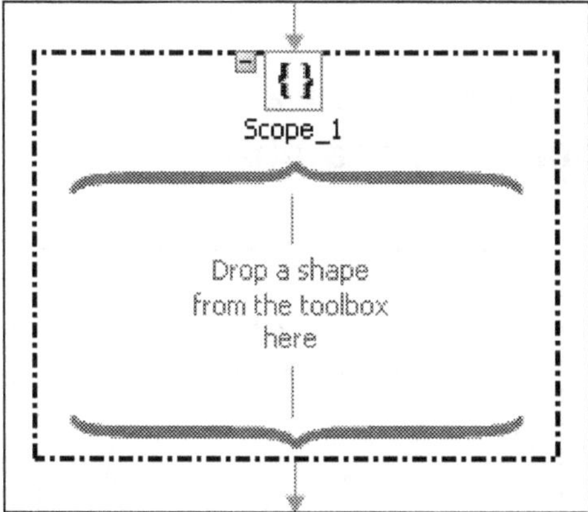

A Scope shape in BizTalk is used to do the following:

- Transaction handling
- Synchronized access to shared data
- Exception handling

A Scope shape has a Boolean Synchronized property, which indicates to BizTalk that all read and write operations on shared data from within the scope must be serialized—avoiding concurrent actions getting into a deadlock. The Synchronized property is equivalent to the `variableAccessSerializable` attribute of the `<scope>` activity in BPEL.

Transaction handling can be achieved by setting the Transaction Type property to Atomic or Long Running (by default it is set to None). Atomic transactions are always synchronized and are similar to the database transaction where either all updates are committed successfully or everything rolls back. BizTalk does not allow you to nest any other transactions within an atomic transaction, nor does it allow you to have any exception handlers. Note that it is possible to have compensation handlers in an atomic scope. Atomic transactions are also used in BizTalk when you need to deal with non-serializable objects within the Orchestration, since atomic scopes are not serialized by BizTalk.

Long Running transactions on the other hand are used when the transactions are expected to take a long time to complete. For example a purchase order approval transaction may take days for manual approval. In such cases the Orchestration waiting for the approval message is **dehydrated** (the state is persisted into a physical store and removed from memory) by the BizTalk engine and **re-hydrated** (the Orchestration is restored) it as soon as the message arrives. A Long Running transaction will not have all the **ACID** properties of an atomic transaction; to be more precise, they do not guarantee the isolation property found in a database transaction. Long Running transactions can contain other Atomic or Long Running transactions. For example all database updates within a Long Running transaction can be encapsulated within an Atomic transaction.

The Scope shape may also have multiple Exception Handlers for handling various exceptions and Compensation Blocks for reversing a successfully committed transaction. Note that Exception Handlers and Compensation Blocks are attached to the end of a Scope shape.

Throw Exception Shape and Exception Handling (<throw>, <faultHandler>, <catch>, <catchAll>)

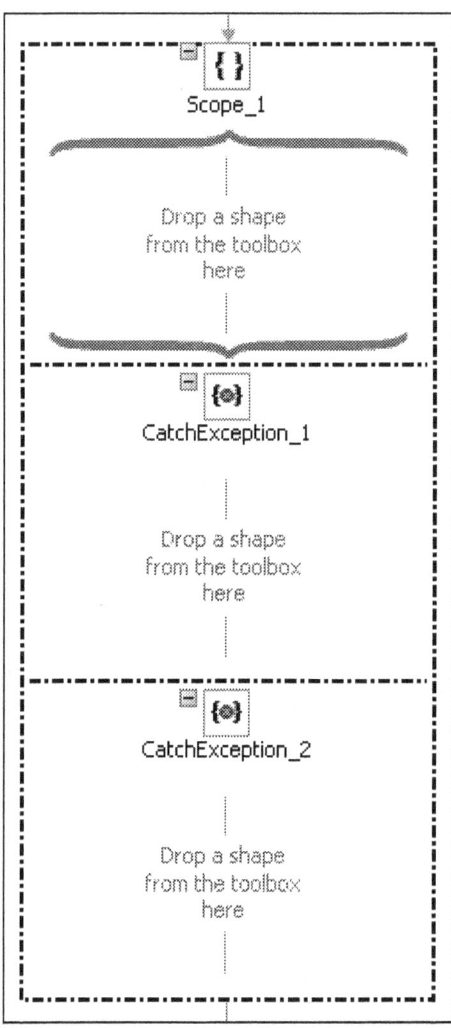

As the name suggests, the **Throw Exception** shape is used to throw or generate an exception from within the Orchestration. This is equivalent to the `<throw>` activity in BPEL. When an exception is thrown, BizTalk searches for an enclosing scope containing a suitable **Exception Handler** block that can handle the exception. The Exception Handler is equivalent to the `<faultHandler>` activity in BPEL. If BizTalk does not find a suitable Exception Handler block in the enclosing scope, it will check in the next higher scope and so on until it finds one. If the Orchestration that generated the exception was called by another Orchestration, BizTalk will even search in that parent Orchestration and finally if no suitable handler is found, the Orchestration terminates. As mentioned earlier, you can have multiple Exception Handlers for a given Scope, but you have to ensure that the most specific exception handler comes first and the less specific ones come later. BizTalk also provides a **General Exception**, which is similar to the `<catchAll>` activity of BPEL.

Compensate Shape and Compensation Block (<compensate>, <compensationHandler>)

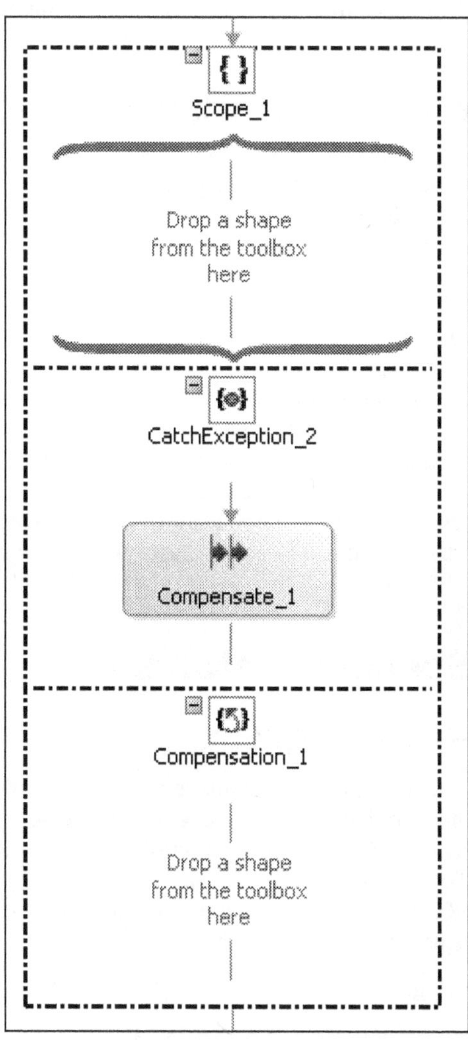

A **Compensation Block** is used to reverse the effects of a transaction after it has been successfully committed. It is equivalent to the `<compensationHandler>` activity of BPEL. This is usually done when an error occurs in the outer transaction scope and as a result the inner transaction needs to be reversed. A compensation block will contain shapes (activities) that perform the necessary actions. BizTalk automatically invokes the actions in a Compensation Block starting from the Compensation Block of the outermost Scope where the error occurred and moves backwards (inwards) invoking all the available Compensation Blocks of the inner scopes. This default behavior can be overridden by calling the Compensation Blocks explicitly using the **Compensate** shape. The Compensate shape is equivalent to the `<compensate>` activity in BPEL. A Compensate shape can be placed either inside a Compensation Block or inside an Exception Handler and can invoke the Compensation Block of the Scope where it is placed or any of the inner Scopes. Each Compensate shape can invoke only one Compensation Block, so you will need multiple Compensate shapes if you have nested Compensation Blocks.

Correlation (<correlations>, <correlationSets>)

Correlation is used to receive all related messages into a single Orchestration instance. Correlation is necessary in certain situations, for example, when aggregating all order items pertaining to a single purchase order. In this case all messages with the same purchase order number will go to a single Orchestration instance. If a message with a different purchase order number arrives, BizTalk will start another instance of the Orchestration to process that message and any other message with that purchase order number. Correlation can be achieved in BizTalk by defining **Correlation Sets** (`<correlations>` in BPEL). A Correlation Set will be of a particular **Correlation Type** (`<correlationSets>` in BPEL). The Correlation Type consists of one or more promoted properties; these promoted properties may be part of the message itself or the message context or any other values *written* into the message context. You can initialize a correlation in either a Receive shape or a Send shape by specifying one or more Correlation Set in the Initializing Correlation Sets property. Once a correlation is initialized you also need to make sure that only correlated messages are received; to achieve this you need to set the Following Correlation Sets property of the subsequent Receive shapes with the same Correlation Sets you used for initializing.

Other BizTalk-Specific Features

Integration with other BizTalk Servers

If your trading partner also uses BizTalk, you can make use of the **Trading Partner Management** feature, a component included in **Business Activity Services (BAS)**. Note that this does not use BPEL. Business Activity Services are a set of services used for managing and collaborating with Trading Partners through SharePoint Services and MS Office tools such as InfoPath. You can create and deploy things like agreements for each trading partner (for example, if PurchaseOrder > $1000, accept the order etc.).

You can configure the following:

- The communication protocol that will be used

- The message format
- The business process that defines the relationship

Information workers can make use of the Business Activity Services interface to create agreements between the trading partners who use BizTalk Server 2004. An agreement describes the relationship between the two parties and contains the business process to be followed, along with the profiles of both parties, like contact information, etc. These agreements and relationships are stored in a database.

Integration with Web Services

BizTalk Server 2004 has native support for web services. It has a built-in SOAP adapter to directly communicate with web services. An Orchestration can consume web services by adding a web reference of the external services' provider from within the Visual Studio .NET environment. It is also possible to easily expose business processes as web services using a tool called **Web Services Publishing Wizard**, so that they can be used by external systems.

Integration with the .NET Framework

Unlike the earlier COM-based versions, BizTalk Server 2004 is built around the .NET framework. You can natively call into the .NET framework from literally every stage of BizTalk architecture. You have the full functionality of the .NET framework at your disposal. You can even connect to other systems like COM / COM+. To call an external .NET component within your Orchestration, all you need to do is declare a variable of the particular .NET type in the Orchestration View and you can instantiate and invoke it from the BizTalk Expression Editor.

Human Workflow Services (HWS)

Human Workflow Services (HWS) is used in workflow activities that involve human intervention such as sign offs and approvals, delegating tasks to people, etc. People who participate in the workflow are known as Actors. Each workflow, also known as an Activity Flow, is composed of one or more Actions, which are implemented as Orchestrations. The Actions in turn contain one or more Tasks that will be executed by the Actors. The user interface for the workflow can be any client that can connect to HWS using web services and even Microsoft Office tools such Word, Outlook, InfoPath, etc.

For example, consider an online leave-processing system. An employee in a company submits a leave request online. The leave request is forwarded to the Human Resource Department of the company where the workflow service looks up the leave history and the available balance and submits it to the HR manager along with the leave request. The HR manager may approve or reject the leave based on the leave policy of the company. If the leave application is rejected, the employee is informed and the workflow is terminated. If on the other hand the HR manager approves the leave, the leave application is again forwarded to the employee's immediate manager who will have the final say in the matter and his or her decision (approval or rejection) is conveyed to the employee through the workflow. The employee also has the facility to check the status of the leave application anytime during the workflow.

Business Activity Monitoring (BAM)

Business Activity Monitoring (BAM) can provide high-level information about the daily business activities to information workers such as business analysts. They can analyze this information to identify bottlenecks or new opportunities in the business among other things.

Health and Activity Tracking (HAT)

The Health and Activity Tracking (HAT) tool, as the name suggests, is used to debug, track, and monitor the activities inside BizTalk. It can do things like:

- Find Messages
- Check whether the messages are getting processed as expected or getting terminated due to some problems
- Inspect the details of instance messages and Orchestrations at any given point of time
- Debug and set Breakpoints inside Orchestrations
- Configure tracking for Ports, Pipelines, Orchestrations, Rules, and Messages

BizTalk Server 2006 and Beyond

Microsoft is planning on two new releases of BizTalk server. The first one will be called **BizTalk Server 2006** (code named **Pathfinder**).

Some of the new features BizTalk Server 2006 may include are:

- Integration with Visual Studio 2005 (.NET 2.0)
- Support for both SQL Server 2000 and SQL Server 2005
- Support for Virtual Server 2005
- Simplified Installation, Migration, and Deployment
- Improved Business Activity Monitoring (BAM)
- Windows 64-bit support
- New Management Console (Visual Studio no longer required for management)
- Wizard for creating Flat File Schema
- New Adapters such as POP3, Sharepoint, MQSeries, and MSMQ
- Enhancement to existing adapters (SMTP, FILE, and HTTP)
- Processing of Larger Messages
- Better Message Handling: Endpoints (Orchestration & Send Ports) can now subscribe to failed messages as well
- New Functoids (IsNil, Nil, and Assert) for Mapping
- XSLT Debugging

The second release, known as **BizTalk vNext**, is due sometime in 2007 or maybe later and is expected to take advantage of the new capabilities of **Windows Vista** (code named **Longhorn**) such as the **Windows Communication Foundation** (formerly **Indigo**) and **Windows Workflow Foundation**.

Summary

BizTalk Server 2004 is a major improvement over its predecessor, and with the support for BPEL, you can expect a lot of interactions and porting of business processes between BizTalk and other products that understand BPEL. In this chapter we studied the architecture of BizTalk Server 2004 and how messages are processed. We briefly touched upon XLANG/s, Microsoft's proprietary language for defining business processes. We then delved into the details of BPEL support offered by BizTalk Server 2004 and saw how most of the Orchestration constructs directly correspond to the BPEL constructs. We also saw how to build an Orchestration and export it to BPEL, as well as how to import BPEL processes into BizTalk. We also learned about things we need to take care of and things we need to avoid in order to successfully export or import a business process. We concluded the chapter by discussing Microsoft's roadmap for the future of BizTalk.

BPEL Syntax Reference

This appendix provides a syntax reference for the BPEL (BPEL4WS) version 1.1 as defined in the specification dated May 5th, 2003 available at the following URLs:

- `http://www.oasis-open.org/committees/download.php/2046/BPEL%20V1-1%20May%205%202003%20Final.pdf`
- `http://dev2dev.bea.com/webservices/BPEL4WS.html`
- `http://www.ibm.com/developerworks/library/specification/ws-bpel/`
- `http://msdn.microsoft.com/library/default.asp?url=/library/en-us/dnbizspec/html/bpel1-1.asp`
- `http://ifr.sap.com/bpel4ws/`
- `http://www.siebel.com/bpel`

In the following sections, you will see the syntax for:

- BPEL activities and elements
- BPEL functions
- Deadline and duration expressions
- Standard elements
- Standard attributes
- Default attribute values
- Standard faults
- Namespaces

Important BPEL Activities and Elements

The following section covers important activity and element tags associated with BPEL processing.

<assign>, <copy>, <from>, <to>

The `<assign>` activity is used to:

- Copy data from one variable to another
- Construct and insert new data using expressions and literal values
- Copy partner link endpoint references

Syntax

```
<assign standard-attributes>
   standard-elements
   <copy>+
      from-spec
      to-spec
   </copy>
</assign>
```

The `from-spec` section can have the following forms:

```
<from variable="ncname" part="ncname"?/>
<from variable="ncname" part="ncname"? query="queryString"?/>
<!-- Executable processes only -->

<from partnerLink="ncname" endpointReference="myRole|partnerRole"/>
<from variable="ncname" property="qname"/>
<from expression="general-expr"/>
<from> ... literal value ... </from>
<from opaque="yes">   <!-- Abstract processes only -->
```

The `to-spec` section can have the following forms:

```
<to variable="ncname" part="ncname"?/>
<to variable="ncname" part="ncname"? query="queryString"?/>
<!-- Executable processes only -->

<to partnerLink="ncname"/>
<to variable="ncname" property="qname"/>
```

Example

```
<assign>
   <copy>
      <from variable="TravelRequest" part="flightData"/>
      <to variable="FlightDetails" part="flightData"/>
   </copy>
   <copy>
      <from variable="EmployeeTravelStatusResponse" part="travelClass"/>
      <to variable="FlightDetails" part="travelClass"/>
   </copy>
</assign>
```

<catch>, <catchAll>

The `<catch>` activities are specified within fault handlers to specify faults that are to be caught and handled. The `<catchAll>` activity is used to catch all faults. Within a fault handler, at least one `<catch>` activity needs to be specified. The optional `<catchAll>` activity can also be specified.

The `<catch>` activity has two attributes that can be used to specify which fault to handle. At least one of them needs to be specified:

- `faultName`: Specifies the name of the fault to handle
- `faultVariable`: Specifies the variable type used for fault data

Syntax

```
<faultHandlers>
   <!-- there must be at least one fault handler or default -->
   <catch faultName="qname"? faultVariable="ncname"?>*
      activity
   </catch>
   <catchAll>?
      activity
   </catchAll>
</faultHandlers>
```

When used to define an inline fault handler for the <invoke> activity, the syntax is as follows:

```
<invoke partnerLink="ncname" portType="qname" operation="ncname"
        inputVariable="ncname"? outputVariable="ncname"?
        standard-attributes>
    standard-elements
    <correlations>?
       <correlation set="ncname" initiate="yes|no"?
                    pattern="in|out|out-in"/>+
    </correlations>
    <catch faultName="qname" faultVariable="ncname"?>*
       activity
    </catch>
    <catchAll>?
       activity
    </catchAll>
    <compensationHandler>?
       activity
    </compensationHandler>
</invoke>
```

Example

```
<faultHandlers>
    <catch faultName="trv:TicketNotApproved" >
       <!-- Perform an activity -->
    </catch>

    <catch faultName="trv:TicketNotApproved" faultVariable="TravelFault" >
       <!-- Perform an activity -->
    </catch>

    <catch faultVariable="TravelFault" >
       <!-- Perform an activity -->
    </catch>

    <catchAll>
       <!-- Perform an activity -->
    </catchAll>
</faultHandlers>
```

<compensate>

To invoke a compensation handler, you use the <compensate> activity. The <compensate> activity has an optional scope attribute that can be used to specify the compensation handler to be invoked. The scope name or activity name (for inline compensation handlers) has to be specified.

Syntax

```
<compensate scope="ncname"? standard-attributes>
   standard-elements
</compensate>
```

Example

```
<compensate scope="TicketConfirmationPayment" />
```

Or

```
<compensate scope="TicketConfirmation" />
```

<compensationHandler>

Compensation handlers are used to define compensation activities. Compensation handlers gather all activities that have to be carried out to compensate another activity and can be defined for the whole process or scope, or can be inlined for the <invoke> activity.

Syntax

```
<compensationHandler>
   activity
</compensationHandler>
```

Example

Compensation handler for a scope:

```
<scope name="TicketConfirmationPayment" >

   <compensationHandler>

      <invoke partnerLink="AmericanAirlines"
              portType="aln:TicketConfirmationPT"
              operation="CancelTicket"
              inputVariable="FlightDetails"
              outputVariable="Cancellation" />

      <invoke partnerLink="AmericanAirlines"
              portType="aln:TicketPaymentPT"
              operation="CancelPayment"
              inputVariable="PaymentDetails"
              outputVariable="PaymentCancellation" />

   </compensationHandler>

   <invoke partnerLink="AmericanAirlines"
           portType="aln:TicketConfirmationPT"
           operation="ConfirmTicket"
           inputVariable="FlightDetails"
           outputVariable="Confirmation" />

   <invoke partnerLink="AmericanAirlines"
           portType="aln:TicketPaymentPT"
           operation="PayTicket"
           inputVariable="PaymentDetails"
           outputVariable="PaymentConfirmation" />
</scope>
```

Inline compensation handler for the <invoke> activity:

```
<invoke name="TicketConfirmation"
        partnerLink="AmericanAirlines"
        portType="aln:TicketConfirmationPT"
        operation="ConfirmTicket"
        inputVariable="FlightDetails"
        outputVariable="Confirmation" >

   <compensationHandler>
```

```
        <invoke partnerLink="AmericanAirlines"
                portType="aln:TicketConfirmationPT"
                operation="CancelTicket"
                inputVariable="FlightDetails"
                outputVariable="Cancellation" >

      </compensationHandler>
   </invoke>
```

<correlations>, <correlation>

The `<correlation>` element is used to associate a correlation set (a collection of key data fields) with an activity. Correlation can be used within the `<receive>`, `<reply>`, `<invoke>`, and `<onMessage>` activities.

Syntax

```
<correlations>
   <correlation set="ncname"
                initiate="yes|no"?
                pattern="in|out|out-in"/>+
</correlations>
```

Example

```
<correlations>
   <correlation set="TicketOrder" initiate="yes" pattern="in" />
</correlations>
```

<correlationSets>, <correlationSet>

A correlation set is a set of properties shared by messages and used for correlation. It is used to associate a message with a business process instance. Each correlation set has a `name` attribute.

Syntax

```
<correlationSets>
   <correlationSet name="ncname" properties="qname-list"/>+
</correlationSets>
```

Example

```
<correlationSets>
  <correlationSet name="VehicleOrder"
                  properties="tns:chassisNo tns:engineNo"/>
  <correlationSet name="TickerOrder"
                  properties="aln:FlightNo"/>
</correlationSets>
```

<empty>

An activity that does nothing is defined by the `<empty>` tag.

Syntax

```
<empty standard-attributes>
   standard-elements
</empty>
```

Example

```
<empty/>
```

<eventHandlers>

Event handlers react to events that occur while the business process is executing. When these events occur, the corresponding event handlers are invoked. Event handlers can be specified for the whole process as well as for each scope.

Syntax

```
<eventHandlers>
   <!-- there must be at least one onMessage or
        onAlarm handler -->
   <onMessage partnerLink="ncname" portType="qname"
              operation="ncname"
              variable="ncname"?>*

      <correlations>?
         <correlation set="ncname" initiate="yes|no">+
      </correlations>
      activity
   </onMessage>
   <onAlarm for="duration-expr"? until="deadline-expr"?>*
      activity
   </onAlarm>
</eventHandlers>
```

Example

```
<process name="BusinessTravelProcess"
         enableInstanceCompensation="yes" ... >

   ...
   <eventHandlers>

      <onMessage partnerLink="client"
                 portType="trv:TravelApprovalPT"
                 operation="CancelTravelApproval"
                 variable="TravelRequest" >

         <terminate/>
      </onMessage>

      <onAlarm for="'PT12H'">
         <terminate/>
      </onAlarm>

   </eventHandlers>
   ...
</process>
```

<faultHandlers>, <faultHandler>

Fault handlers are used to react to faults that occur while the business process activities are executing. They can be specified for the global process or each scope, or inline for `<invoke>` activities. Multiple `<catch>` activities can be specified within the fault handler for specific faults. You need to specify at least one `<catch>` activity. You can optionally specify the `<catchAll>` activity. The syntax and functionality of the `<catch>` activity is the same as described in the earlier section on `<catch>` and `<catchall>`.

Syntax

```
<faultHandlers>
   <!-- There must be at least one fault handler or default -->
```

```
    <catch faultName="qname"? faultVariable="ncname"?>*
       activity
    </catch>
    <catchAll>?
       activity
    </catchAll>
</faultHandlers>
```

An inline fault handler for the <invoke> activity is specified as shown below:

```
<invoke partnerLink="ncname" portType="qname" operation="ncname"
          inputVariable="ncname"? outputVariable="ncname"?
          standard-attributes>
    standard-elements
    <correlations>?
       <correlation set="ncname" initiate="yes|no"?
                    pattern="in|out|out-in"/>+
    </correlations>
    <catch faultName="qname" faultVariable="ncname"?>*
       activity
    </catch>
    <catchAll>?
       activity
    </catchAll>
    <compensationHandler>?
       activity
    </compensationHandler>
</invoke>
```

Example

```
<faultHandlers>
   <catch faultName="trv:TicketNotApproved" >
      <!-- Perform an activity -->
   </catch>

   <catch faultName="trv:TicketNotApproved" faultVariable="TravelFault" >
      <!-- Perform an activity -->
   </catch>

   <catch faultVariable="TravelFault" >
      <!-- Perform an activity -->
   </catch>

   <catchAll>
      <!-- Perform an activity -->
   </catchAll>
</faultHandlers>
```

<flow>

The <flow> activity provides concurrent execution of enclosed activities and their synchronization.

Syntax

```
<flow standard-attributes>
   standard-elements
   <links>?
      <link name="ncname">+
   </links>
   activity+
</flow>
```

Example

```
<flow>
    <!-- Synchronously invoke the Employee Travel Status Web Service -->
    <invoke name="EmployeeTravelStatusSyncInv"
            partnerLink="employeeTravelStatus"
            portType="emp:EmployeeTravelStatusPT"
            operation="EmployeeTravelStatus"
            inputVariable="EmployeeTravelStatusRequest"
            outputVariable="EmployeeTravelStatusResponse" />

    <!-- Prepare the input for AA and DA -->
    ...

    <!-- Async invoke of the AA web service -->
    <invoke name="AmericanAirlinesAsyncInv"
            partnerLink="AmericanAirlines"
            portType="aln:FlightAvailabilityPT"
            operation="FlightAvailability"
            inputVariable="FlightDetails" />

    <!-- Receive the callback -->
    <receive name="AmericanAirlinesCallback"
             partnerLink="AmericanAirlines"
             portType="aln:FlightCallbackPT"
             operation="FlightTicketCallback"
             variable="FlightResponseAA" />

    <!-- Async invoke of the DA web service -->
    <invoke name="DeltaAirlinesAsyncInv"
            partnerLink="DeltaAirlines"
            portType="aln:FlightAvailabilityPT"
            operation="FlightAvailability"
            inputVariable="FlightDetails" />

    <!-- Receive the callback -->
    <receive name="DeltaAirlinesCallback"
             partnerLink="DeltaAirlines"
             portType="aln:FlightCallbackPT"
             operation="FlightTicketCallback"
             variable="FlightResponseDA" />

    <!-- Select the best offer and construct the TravelResponse -->
    ...

    <!-- Make a callback to the client -->
    <invoke name="ClientCallback"
            partnerLink="client"
            portType="trv:ClientCallbackPT"
            operation="ClientCallback"
            inputVariable="TravelResponse" />
</flow>
```

<invoke>

The <invoke> activity is used to invoke the web service operations provided by partners.

Syntax

```
<invoke partnerLink="ncname"
        portType="qname"
        operation="ncname"
        inputVariable="ncname"?
        outputVariable="ncname"?
        standard-attributes>
```

```
    standard-elements
    <correlations>?
       <correlation set="ncname" initiate="yes|no"?
                    pattern="in|out|out-in"/>+
    </correlations>
    <catch faultName="qname" faultVariable="ncname"?>*
       activity
    </catch>
    <catchAll>?
       activity
    </catchAll>
    <compensationHandler>?
       activity
    </compensationHandler>
</invoke>
```

Example

```
<!-- Synchronously invoke the Employee Travel Status Web Service -->
<invoke name="EmployeeTravelStatusSyncInv"
        partnerLink="employeeTravelStatus"
        portType="emp:EmployeeTravelStatusPT"
        operation="EmployeeTravelStatus"
        inputVariable="EmployeeTravelStatusRequest"
        outputVariable="EmployeeTravelStatusResponse" />

<!-- Async invoke of the AA web service -->
<invoke name="AmericanAirlinesAsyncInv"
        partnerLink="AmericanAirlines"
        portType="aln:FlightAvailabilityPT"
        operation="FlightAvailability"
        inputVariable="FlightDetails" />
```

<links>, <link>

Synchronization dependencies in concurrent flows are specified using links.

Syntax

```
<links>
   <link name="ncname">+
</links>
```

Example

```
<links>
   <link name="TravelStatusToTicketRequest" />
   <link name="TicketRequestToTicketConfirmation" />
</links>
```

<onAlarm>

This activity is used in the <pick> and <eventHandlers> activities to specify the occurrence of alarm events.

Syntax

```
<onAlarm (for="duration-expr" | until="deadline-expr")>
   activity
</onAlarm>
```

Example

```
<onAlarm for="'PT30M'">
   <throw faultName="trv:CallbackTimeout" />
</onAlarm>
```

<onMessage>

Used in <pick> and <eventHandlers> activities to specify the occurrence of message events.

Syntax

```
<onMessage partnerLink="ncname" portType="qname"
           operation="ncname" variable="ncname"?>
   <correlations>?
      <correlation set="ncname" initiate="yes|no"?>+
   </correlations>
   activity
</onMessage>
```

Example

```
<onMessage partnerLink="AmericanAirlines"
           portType="aln:FlightCallbackPT"
           operation="FlightTicketCallback"
           variable="FlightResponseAA">
   <!-- Perform an activity -->
</onMessage>
```

<partnerLinks>, <partnerLink>

A business process interacts with services that are modeled as partner links. Each partner link is characterized by a <partnerLinkType>. More than one partner link can be characterized by the same <partnerLinkType>. See the next section for more on <partnerLinkType>.

Syntax

```
<partnerLinks>
   <partnerLink name="ncname" partnerLinkType="qname"
                myRole="ncname"? partnerRole="ncname"?>+
   </partnerLink>
</partnerLinks>
```

Example

```
<partnerLinks>
   <partnerLink name="insurance"
                partnerLinkType="tns:insuranceLT"
                myRole="insuranceRequester"
                partnerRole="insuranceService"/>
</partnerLinks>
```

<partnerLinkType>, <role>

A partner link type characterizes the relationship between two services. It defines roles for each of the services in the conversation between them and specifies the port type provided by each service to receive messages. Partner link types and roles are specified in the WSDL.

Syntax

```
<definitions name="ncname" targetNamespace="uri"
     xmlns="http://schemas.xmlsoap.org/wsdl/"
     xmlns:plnk="http://schemas.xmlsoap.org/ws/2003/05/partner-link/">
     ...
  <plnk:partnerLinkType name="ncname">
    <plnk:role name="ncname">
      <plnk:portType name="qname"/>
    </plnk:role>
    <plnk:role name="ncname">?
```

```
      <plnk:portType name="qname"/>
    </plnk:role>
  </plnk:partnerLinkType>
  ...
</definitions>
```

Example

```
<plnk:partnerLinkType name="flightLT">
  <plnk:role name="airlineService">
    <plnk:portType name="tns:FlightAvailabilityPT" />
  </plnk:role>
  <plnk:role name="airlineCustomer">
    <plnk:portType name="tns:FlightCallbackPT" />
  </plnk:role>
</plnk:partnerLinkType>
```

<partners>

The partner element is used to represent the capabilities required from a business partner. A partner is defined as a set of partner links.

Syntax

```
<partners>
  <partner name="ncname">+
    <partnerLink name="ncname"/>+
  </partner>
</partners>
```

Example

```
<partner name="ServiceProvider">
  <partnerLink name="ReantacarProvider"/>
  <partnerLink name="LodgingProvider"/>
</partner>
```

<pick>

The `<pick>` activity is used to wait for the occurrence of one of a set of events and then perform an activity associated with the event.

Syntax

```
<pick createInstance="yes|no"? standard-attributes>
   standard-elements
   <onMessage partnerLink="ncname" portType="qname"
              operation="ncname" variable="ncname"?>+
      <correlations>?
         <correlation set="ncname" initiate="yes|no"?>+
      </correlations>
      activity
   </onMessage>
   <onAlarm (for="duration-expr" | until="deadline-expr")>*
      activity
   </onAlarm>
</pick>
```

Example

```
<pick>
   <onMessage partnerLink="AmericanAirlines"
              portType="aln:FlightCallbackPT"
              operation="FlightTicketCallback"
              variable="FlightResponseAA">
      <!-- Perform an activity -->
```

```
      </onMessage>

      <onMessage partnerLink="AmericanAirlines"
                 portType="aln:FlightCallbackPT"
                 operation="FlightNotAvaliable"
                 variable="FlightNAResponseAA">
         <!-- Perform an activity -->
      </onMessage>

      <onMessage partnerLink="AmericanAirlines"
                 portType="aln:FlightCallbackPT"
                 operation="TicketNotAvaliable"
                 variable="FlightTNAResponseAA">
         <!-- Perform an activity -->
      </onMessage>

      <onAlarm for="'PT30M'">
         <throw faultName="trv:CallbackTimeout" />
      </onAlarm>
   </pick>
```

<process>

This is the root element of each BPEL process definition.

Syntax

```
<process name="ncname" targetNamespace="uri"
         queryLanguage="anyURI"?
         expressionLanguage="anyURI"?
         suppressJoinFailure="yes|no"?
         enableInstanceCompensation="yes|no"?
         abstractProcess="yes|no"?
         xmlns="http://schemas.xmlsoap.org/ws/2003/03/business-process/">

  <partnerLinks>?
    <!-- Note: At least one role must be specified. -->
    <partnerLink name="ncname" partnerLinkType="qname"
           myRole="ncname"? partnerRole="ncname"?>+
    </partnerLink>
  </partnerLinks>

  <partners>?
     <partner name="ncname">+
      <partnerLink name="ncname"/>+
   </partner>
  </partners>

  <variables>?
    <variable name="ncname" messageType="qname"?
              type="qname"? element="qname"?/>+
  </variables>

  <correlationSets>?
    <correlationSet name="ncname" properties="qname-list"/>+
  </correlationSets>

  <faultHandlers>?
    <!-- Note: There must be at least one fault handler or default. -->
    <catch faultName="qname"? faultVariable="ncname"?>*
      activity
    </catch>
    <catchAll>?
      activity
```

```
    </catchAll>
  </faultHandlers>

  <compensationHandler>?
    activity
  </compensationHandler>

  <eventHandlers>?
    <!-- Note: There must be at least one onMessage or onAlarm handler. -->
    <onMessage partnerLink="ncname" portType="qname"
               operation="ncname" variable="ncname"?>
      <correlations>?
        <correlation set="ncname" initiate="yes|no"?>+
      <correlations>
      activity
    </onMessage>
    <onAlarm for="duration-expr"? until="deadline-expr"?>*
      activity
    </onAlarm>
  </eventHandlers>

  activity
</process>
```

Example

Examples are shown in Chapters 3 and 4.

<property>

Properties are used to create globally unique names and associate them with data types (XML Schema types). Properties have greater significance than the types themselves. Properties are defined in WSDL.

Syntax

```
<wsdl:definitions
    xmlns:bpws="http://schemas.xmlsoap.org/ws/2003/03/business-process/">
    ...
    <bpws:property name="ncname" type="qname"/>
    ...
</wsdl:definitions>
```

Example

```
<bpws:property name="FlightNo" type="xs:string" />
```

<propertyAlias>

Property aliases are used to map global properties to fields in specific message parts. Property aliases are defined in the WSDL.

Syntax

```
<wsdl:definitions
    xmlns:bpws="http://schemas.xmlsoap.org/ws/2003/03/business-process/">
    ...
    <bpws:propertyAlias propertyName="qname"
                        messageType="qname"
                        part="ncname" query="queryString"/>
    ...
</wsdl:definitions>
```

Example

```
<bpws:propertyAlias propertyName="tns:FlightNo"
                    messageType="tns:TravelResponseMessage"
                    part="confirmationData"
                    query="/confirmationData/FlightNo"/>
```

<receive>

A `<receive>` activity is used to receive requests in a BPEL business process to provide services to its partners.

Syntax

```
<receive partnerLink="ncname" portType="qname" operation="ncname"
         variable="ncname"? createInstance="yes|no"?
         standard-attributes>
   standard-elements
   <correlations>?
      <correlation set="ncname" initiate="yes|no"?>+
   </correlations>
</receive>
```

Example

```
<!-- Receive the initial request for business travel from client -->
<receive partnerLink="client"
         portType="trv:TravelApprovalPT"
         operation="TravelApproval"
         variable="TravelRequest" />
```

<reply>

A `<reply>` activity is used to send a response to a request previously accepted through a `<receive>` activity. Responses are used for synchronous request/reply interactions. An asynchronous response is always sent by invoking the corresponding one-way operation on the partner link.

Syntax

```
<reply partnerLink="ncname" portType="qname" operation="ncname"
       variable="ncname"? faultName="qname"?
       standard-attributes>
   standard-elements
   <correlations>?
      <correlation set="ncname" initiate="yes|no"?>+
   </correlations>
</reply>
```

Example

```
<!-- Send a response to the client -->
<reply partnerLink="client"
       portType="trv:TravelApprovalPT"
       operation="TravelApproval"
       variable="TravelResponse"/>
```

<scope>

Scopes define behavior contexts for activities. They provide fault handlers, event handlers, compensation handlers, data variables, and correlation sets for activities.

Syntax

```
<scope variableAccessSerializable="yes|no" standard-attributes>
    standard-elements
    <variables>?
      ...
    </variables>
    <correlationSets>?
      ...
    </correlationSets>
    <faultHandlers>?
      ...
    </faultHandlers>
    <compensationHandler>?
      ...
    </compensationHandler>
    <eventHandlers>?
      ...
    </eventHandlers>
    activity
</scope>
```

Example

```
<scope>

    <faultHandlers>
      <catch faultName="emp:WrongEmployeeName" >
         <!-- Perform an activity -->
      </catch>
      <catch faultName="emp:TravelNotAllowed" faultVariable="Description" >
         <!-- Perform an activity -->
      </catch>
      <catchAll>
         <!-- Perform an activity -->
      </catchAll>
    </faultHandlers>

    <invoke partnerLink="employeeTravelStatus"
            portType="emp:EmployeeTravelStatusPT"
            operation="EmployeeTravelStatus"
            inputVariable="EmployeeTravelStatusRequest"
            outputVariable="EmployeeTravelStatusResponse" />
</scope>
```

<sequence>

A <sequence> activity is used to define activities that need to be performed in a sequential order.

Syntax

```
<sequence standard-attributes>
   standard-elements
   activity+
</sequence>
```

Example

Examples are covered in Chapters 3 and 4.

<source>

<source> elements are used to declare that an activity is the source of one or more links. This is a standard element.

Syntax

```
<source linkName="ncname" transitionCondition="bool-expr"?/>*
```

Example

```
<invoke name="EmployeeTravelStatusSyncInv"
        partnerLink="employeeTravelStatus"
        portType="emp:EmployeeTravelStatusPT"
        operation="EmployeeTravelStatus"
        inputVariable="EmployeeTravelStatusRequest"
        outputVariable="EmployeeTravelStatusResponse" >

    <target linkName="EmployeeInputToEmployeeTravelStatusSyncInv" />
    <source linkName="EmployeeTravelStatusSyncInvToAirlinesInput" />
 </invoke>
```

<switch>, <case>

To express conditional behavior, the <switch> activity is used. It consists of one or more conditional branches defined by <case> elements, followed by an optional <otherwise> element. The case branches of the switch are considered in alphabetical order.

Syntax

```
<switch standard-attributes>
   standard-elements
   <case condition="bool-expr">+
      activity
   </case>
   <otherwise>?
      activity
   </otherwise>
</switch>
```

Example

```
<!-- Select the best offer and construct the TravelResponse -->
<switch>

   <case condition="bpws:getVariableData('FlightResponseAA',
                    'confirmationData','/confirmationData/aln:Price')
                    &lt;= bpws:getVariableData('FlightResponseDA',
                    'confirmationData','/confirmationData/aln:Price')">

           <!-- Select American Airlines -->
           <assign>
             <copy>
               <from variable="FlightResponseAA" />
               <to variable="TravelResponse" />
             </copy>
           </assign>
   </case>

   <otherwise>
           <!-- Select Delta Airlines -->
           <assign>
             <copy>
               <from variable="FlightResponseDA" />
               <to variable="TravelResponse" />
             </copy>
           </assign>
   </otherwise>
</switch>
```

<target>

The <target> element is used to declare that an activity is the target of one or more links. This is a standard element.

Syntax

```
<target linkName="ncname"/>*
```

Example

```
<!-- Select the best offer and construct the TravelResponse -->
<switch name="BestOfferSelect">

   <target linkName="AmericanAirlinesCallbackToBestOfferSelect" />
   <target linkName="DeltaAirlinesCallbackToBestOfferSelect" />

   <case condition="bpws:getVariableData('FlightResponseAA',
                    'confirmationData','/confirmationData/aln:Price')
                    &lt;= bpws:getVariableData('FlightResponseDA',
                    'confirmationData','/confirmationData/aln:Price')">
         <!-- Select American Airlines -->
         <assign>
            <copy>
               <from variable="FlightResponseAA" />
               <to variable="TravelResponse" />
            </copy>
         </assign>
   </case>

   <otherwise>
         <!-- Select Delta Airlines -->
         <assign>
            <copy>
               <from variable="FlightResponseDA" />
               <to variable="TravelResponse" />
            </copy>
         </assign>
   </otherwise>
</switch>
```

<terminate>

The <terminate> activity is used to immediately terminate a business process instance.

Syntax

```
<terminate standard-attributes>
   standard-elements
</terminate>
```

Example

```
<terminate />
```

<throw>

The <throw> activity is used to explicitly signal internal faults.

Syntax

```
<throw faultName="qname" faultVariable="ncname"? standard-attributes>
   standard-elements
</throw>
```

Example

```
<throw faultName="WrongEmployeeName" />

<throw faultName="trv:TicketNotApproved" faultVariable="TravelFault" />
```

<variables>, <variable>

Variables are used to hold messages that constitute the state of a business process. The variable may be of the WSDL message type, an XML Schema simple type, or an XML Schema element.

Syntax

```
<variables>
   <variable name="ncname" messageType="qname"?
             type="qname"? element="qname"?/>+
</variables>
```

Example

```
<variables>
   <variable name="InsuranceRequest"
             messageType="ins:InsuranceRequestMessage"/>
   <variable name="PartialInsuranceDescription"
             element="ins:InsuranceDescription"/>
   <variable name="lastName"
             type="xs:string"/>
</variables>
```

<wait>

A <wait> activity is used to specify a delay for a certain period of time or until a certain deadline is reached.

Syntax

```
<wait (for="duration-expr" | until="deadline-expr") standard-attributes>
   standard-elements
</wait>
```

Examples

```
<wait until="'2004-03-18T21:00:00+01:00'"/>

<wait until="'18:05:30Z'"/>

<wait for="'PT4H10M'"/>

<wait for="'P1M3DT4H10M'"/>

<wait for="'P1Y11M14DT4H10M30S'"/>
```

<while>

A <while> activity is used to define an iterative activity. The iterative activity is performed until the specified Boolean condition no longer holds true.

Syntax

```
<while condition="bool-expr" standard-attributes>
   standard-elements
   activity
</while>
```

Example

```
<while condition=
      "bpws:getVariableData('Counter') &lt;
       bpws:getVariableData('NoOfPassengers')">

      <sequence>

        <!-- Construct the FlightDetails variable with passenger data -->
        ...

        <!-- Invoke the web service -->
        <invoke partnerLink="AmericanAirlines"
              portType="aln:FlightAvailabilityPT"
              operation="FlightAvailability"
              inputVariable="FlightDetails" />

        <receive partnerLink="AmericanAirlines"
              portType="trv:FlightCallbackPT"
              operation="FlightTicketCallback"
              variable="FlightResponseAA" />

        ...
        <!-- Process the results … -->
        ...

        <!-- Increment the counter -->
        <assign>

          <copy>
            <from expression="bpws:getVariableData('Counter') + 1"/>
            <to variable="Counter"/>
          </copy>

        </assign>

      </sequence>

</while>
```

BPEL Functions

This section talks about the important and commonly used functions related to BPEL. These are:

- `getLinkStatus()`
- `getVariableData()`
- `getVariableProperty()`

getLinkStatus()

This function is used to return a Boolean value to indicate the status of a link. Links with positive status are evaluated to `true`, links with negative status to `false`. This function can only be used in join conditions. The `linkName` argument must refer to the name of an incoming link for the activity associated with the join condition.

Syntax

```
bpws:getLinkStatus ('linkName')
```

Example

```
<switch name="BestOfferSelect"

        joinCondition="bpws:getLinkStatus(
                      'AmericanAirlinesCallbackToBestOfferSelect')
                      and
                      bpws:getLinkStatus(
                      'DeltaAirlinesCallbackToBestOfferSelect')" >
                      ...
</switch>
```

getVariableData()

This function is used to extract arbitrary values from variables.

Syntax

```
bpws:getVariableData ('variableName', 'partName'?, 'locationPath'?)
```

Example

```
bpws:getVariableData ('InsuranceRequest',
                      'insuredPersonData')

bpws:getVariableData ('InsuranceRequest',
                      'insuredPersonData',
                      '/insuredPersonData/ins:Age')
```

getVariableProperty()

This function is used to extract global property values from variables.

Syntax

```
bpws:getVariableProperty ('variableName', 'propertyName')
```

Example

```
bpws:getVariableProperty('TicketApproval', 'Class')
```

Deadline and Duration Expressions

To specify deadlines and durations for activities, BPEL uses lexical representations of corresponding XML Schema data types. For setting deadlines, the data types are either `dateTime` or `date`. For setting the duration (a timeout, for instance), you can use the `duration` data type. The lexical representation of expressions should conform to the XPath 1.0 (or the selected query language) specifications. Such expressions should evaluate to values of corresponding XML Schema types: `dateTime` and `date` for deadline and `duration` for duration expressions.

All three data types use lexical representations that conform to the ISO 8601 standard. For more information on this standard, see the ISO web page at `http://www.iso.ch`. The ISO 8601 lexical format uses characters within date and time information. Characters are appended to the numbers and have the following meaning:

- `C` represents centuries.
- `Y` represents years.
- `M` represents months.

- `D` represents days.
- `h` represents hours.
- `m` represents minutes.
- `s` represents seconds. Seconds can be represented in the format `ss.sss` to increase precision.
- `Z` is used to designate Coordinated Universal Time (UTC). It should immediately follow the time-of-day element.

For the `dateTime` expressions, there is an additional designator:

- `T` is used as a time designator that indicates the start of the representation of the time.

For `duration` expressions, the following characters can also be used:

- `P` is used as the time duration designator. Duration expressions always start with `P`.
- `Y` represents the number of years.
- `M` represents the number of months or minutes.
- `D` represents the number of days.
- `H` represents the number of hours.
- `S` represents the number of seconds.

Standard Elements

Each activity has standard optional nested elements `<source>` and `<target>`.

Syntax

```
<source linkName="ncname" transitionCondition="bool-expr"?/>*
<target linkName="ncname"/>*
```

Standard Attributes

Each activity has some standard optional attributes:

- Name
- A join condition
- An indicator to state whether a join fault should be suppressed if it occurs

Syntax

The syntax associated with these attributes within the properties is as follows:

```
name="ncname"?
joinCondition="bool-expr"?
suppressJoinFailure="yes|no"?
```

Default Values of Attributes

In the following table, we cover the default values of some BPEL attributes.

Attribute	Default Value
queryLanguage	http://www.w3.org/TR/1999/REC-xpath-19991116
expressionLanguage	http://www.w3.org/TR/1999/REC-xpath-19991116
suppressJoinFailure	No
variableAccessSerializable	No
abstractProcess	No
initiate	No
createInstance	No
enableInstanceCompensation	No
joinCondition	Disjunction of the status of the incoming links
transitionCondition	True

Standard Faults

The following table is a list of standard faults that commonly arise in BPEL execution.

Fault name	Fault is thrown when:
selectionFailure	A selection operation performed in either a function, such as bpws:getVariableData, or an assignment encounters an error.
conflictingReceive	More than one <receive> activity or equivalent (currently <onMessage> branch in a <pick> activity) are enabled simultaneously for the same partner link, port type, operation, and correlation set(s).
conflictingRequest	More than one synchronous inbound request is active on the same partner link for a particular port type, operation. and correlation set(s).
mismatchedAssignmentFailure	Incompatible types are encountered in an assign activity.
joinFailure	Join condition of an activity evaluates to false.
forcedTermination	A fault occurs in an enclosing scope.
correlationViolation	The contents of messages processed in an <invoke>, <receive>, or <reply> activity do not match specified correlation information.
uninitializedVariable	There is an attempt to access the value of an uninitialized part in a message variable.
repeatedCompensation	An installed compensation handler is invoked more than once.
invalidReply	A reply is sent on a partner link, port type, and operation for which the corresponding <receive> with the same correlation has not been carried out.

Namespaces

In the following table, the BPEL and partner link namespaces are listed.

Prefix	Namespace URL
bpws	http://schemas.xmlsoap.org/ws/2003/03/business-process/
plnk	http://schemas.xmlsoap.org/ws/2003/05/partner-link/

Index

A

abstract business processes, 65
abstract business protocols, 21, 162
abstractProcess attribute
  default value, 342
  process element, 78
acknowledgment interval, reliable messaging, 52
action element, 60, 61, 62
ActiveBPEL Engine, 28
Activities tab, BPEL Console, 185
activity names, 108
adapters, MS Biztalk Server 2004, 278
add partner links, BPEL Designer, 207
add variables, BPEL Designer, 208
addAuditTrailEntry method, exec activity, 249
advantages of orchestration, 20, 21
alarm events, 137, 139
Ant utility, 177
APIs, Oracle BPEL Process Manager, 273
assemble stage, send pipeline, 284
assign activity
  about, 81
  data and array manipulation, Oracle BPEL Process Manager, 218
  transformation, Oracle BPEL Process Manager, 217
  BPEL syntax reference, 321
asynchronous BPEL business process example
  BPEL process definition, 104
  partner link types, 104
  WSDL, 103
asynchronous web services, invoking, 71
atomic transaction, 42
attributes
  BPEL syntax reference, 342
  default values, 342
Audit tag, 182
automation, business processes, 6

B

base re-transmission interval, reliable messaging, 52
BinarySecurityToken element, 35
BizTalk and BPEL equivalents, 306
BizTalk Mapper, 282
Biztalk Server 2004. See MS Biztalk Server 2004
BPEL
  BPEL process, 66
  choreography, 19
  composing business processes, 65
  describing business processes, 21
  example, asynchronous business process, 102
  example, synchronous business process, 85
  features, 18
  further development, 29
  history, 18
  orchestration, 19
  other specifications, 22
  servers, 25
BPEL Compiler, 176
BPEL Console
  about, 170, 178
  Activities tab, 185
  BPEL Domains tab, 192
  Configuration tab, 191
  debugging, 182
  domain administration, 190
  domain management, 187
  functions, 184
  instance auditing, 182
  Instances tab, 185
  Logging tab, 192
  Password tab, 192
  performance tuning, 188
  process management, 178
  server-side administration, 191
  visual flow, 181

BPEL Designer, 171, 193
BPEL Domains tab, BPEL Console, 192
BPEL functions, BPEL syntax reference, 339
BPEL processes
  asynchronous, 72
  partner links, 73
  synchronous, 72
  variables, 78
  WSDL, 76
BPEL Processes tab, BPEL Console, 184
BPEL Server APIs, 273
BPEL servers, 25
BPEL Validation Browser, JDeveloper, 203
BPELand BizTalk equivalents, 306
bpelc command, 177
BPML, 23
BPMPublic role, identity service, 272
BPMSystemAdmin role, identity service, 272
BPMWorkflowAdmin role, identity service, 272
BPMWorkflowReassign role, identity service, 272
BPMWorkflowSuspend role, identity service, 272
BPMWorkflowViewHistory role, identity service, 272
bpws namespace, 343
branching. See conditions
BTP
  about, 46
  atomic transactions, 49
  cohesive transactions, 49
  model, 48
  stack, 48
BTP stack, 48
building BPEL processes, JDeveloper, 204
business activity, 42, 44
Business Activity Services, MS BizTalk Server 2004, 316
business process automation, 17
business process example
  business process definition, 95
  involved web services, 88
  partner link types, 93
  WSDL, 92
business process lifecycle, 143
business processs, abstract, 162
Business Rules Engine, MS Biztalk Server, 283
business transaction scenario, 36
BusinessAgreement coordination protocol, 46
BusinessAgreementWithComplete coordination protocol, 46

C

case element, 84
case element, BPEL syntax reference, 336
catch activity, BPEL syntax reference, 322
catchall activity, BPEL syntax reference, 322
choreography, 20
collaborations, e-business, 31
com.oracle.bpel.client API, Oracle BPEL Server, 273
com.oracle.bpel.client.auth API, Oracle BPEL Server, 273
com.oracle.bpel.client.dispatch API, Oracle BPEL Server, 273
com.oracle.bpel.client.util API, Oracle BPEL Server, 273
compensate activity, BPEL syntax reference, 323
Compensate shape, MS BizTalk Server 2004, 316
compensateHandler activity, BPEL syntax reference, 324
compensation, 132
compensation handlers, 133
compiling, BPEL designer, 212
Completion coordination protocol, 44
CompletionWithAck coordination protocol, 44
composition
  BPEL, 17
  services, 16
  web services, 7
concurrent activities, 150
conditions, 84
configuration tab, BPEL Console, 191
conflictingReceive fault, 342
conflictingRequest fault, 342
constructs
  flow, 70
  invoke, 70
  receive, 70
coordination protocols, atomic transaction
  CompletionWithAck, 44
  OutcomeNotification, 44
  PhaseZero, 44
  Two-Phase Commit, 44
coordination protocols, business activity
  BusinessAgreement, 46
  BusinessAgreementWithComplete, 46
CoordinationContext element, 40
copy command, assign activity, 81
copy data, variables, 81

Copy Rule Editor, BPEL Designer, 211
CORBA, 8
core BPEL engine, BPEL Server, 169
correlations
  about, 145
  correlation sets, 148
  correlations, MS BizTalk Server 2004, 316
correlation element, BPEL syntax reference, 325
correlationSet element, BPEL syntax reference, 325
correlationViolation fault, 342
CreateCoordinationContext element, 40
CreateCoordinationContextResponse element, 41
createInstance attribute, receive activity, 80
createInstance attribute, default value, 342
custom exception serializers, 241
Custom repository plug-ins, identity service, 272

D

Database, Oracle BPEL Process Manager, 171
date data type, 110
dateTime data type, 110
DCE, 8
DCOM, 8
deadline expressions, 110
deadline expressions, BPEL syntax reference, 340
debugging, process management, 182
Decide shape, MS BizTalk Server 2004, 309
defining a business process, 95
defining partner links, 77
Delay shape, MS BizTalk Server 2004, 310
delays, business process, 110
delivery assurance, reliable messaging, 51
deploying processes
  Eclipse BPEL designer, 212
  Oracle BPEL Server, 171
  JDeveloper, 204
  BPEL Console, 186
Deployment Descriptor Properties window, JDeveloper, 206
domain management, BPEL Console, 187
domains administration, BPEL Console, 190
DTC, 32
duration data type, 110
duration expressions, 110
duration expressions, BPEL syntax reference, 340
dynamic parallel flow, Oracle BPEL Process Manager, 222
dynamic partner links, 161

E

ebXML BPSS specification, 22
Eclipse BPEL Designer
  about, 206
  Copy Rule Editor, 211
  Function Wizard, 211
  partner links, 207
  process map, 210
  variables, 208
  XML Type Browser, 209
element attribute, variables, 79
elements
  BPELProcess, 173
  BPELSuitcase, 173
  partnerLinks, 77
  process, 78
  variables, 79
empty activity, 111
empty activity, BPEL syntax reference, 325
enableInstanceCompensation attribute
  default value, 342
  process element, 78
encode stage, send pipeline, 284
endpoint reference, WS-Addressing, 53
enterprise service bus, 10
ESB, 7, 10
event handlers, 140
event managing, 137
event subscription, WS-Eventing, 59
eventHandlers activity, BPEL syntax reference, 326
exception handling, WSIF, 237
exception serializers, custom, 241
exec activity, 249
executable business processes, 65
executable processes, 21
Expires element, 60
Expression shapes, MS BizTalk Server 2004, 308
expressionLanguage attribute, default value, 342
expressionLanguage attribute, process element, 78

extensibility mechanism, WSDL, 76
extension functions, BPEL Process Manager, 215
external security token, 35

F

fault handling
- asynchronous example, 121
- causes of faults, 112
- handling faults, 117
- inline fault handling, 122
- selecting, fault handler, 118
- signaling, 113
- synchronous example, 119
- WSDL faults, 112

faultHandler activity, BPEL syntax reference, 326
faults
- reliable messaging, 52
- standard, 342
- WS-Addressing, 55
- WS-Coordination, 41
- WS-Security, 36
- WSDL, 238

flow activity, BPEL syntax reference, 327
flow construct, 70
flowN activity, Oracle BPEL Process Manager, 222
for attribute, wait activity, 110
forcedTermination fault, 342
forEach activity, 222
Function Wizard, Eclipse BPEL Designer, 211, 216
functoids, 282

G

getContentFile method, exec activity, 250
getIndex method, exec activity, 250
getInstanceId method, exec activity, 249
getLinkStatus function, BPEL syntax reference, 339
getLocator method, exec activity, 249
getPreference method, exec activity, 250
getVariableData function, 84
getVariableData method, exec activity, 249
getVariableData function, BPEL syntax reference, 340
getVariableProperty function, BPEL syntax reference, 340
graphical development, BPEL Designer, 193

H

Health and Activity Tracking, MS BizTalk Server 2004, 318
HTTP protocol, 49
Human Workflow Services, MS BizTalk Server 2004, 317

I

IBM BPWS4J, 28
IBM WebSphere Business Integration Server Foundation, 27
identity service, Oracle BPEL Process Manager, 271
import attribute, exec activity, 249
importing BPEL processes, JDeveloper, 195
inactivity timeout, reliable messaging, 52
in-flight debugging, 182
information systems gap time, 6
initiate attribute, default value, 342
inline fault handling, 122
inputVariable attribute, invoke activity, 80
inspection element, 56
instance auditing, process management, 182
Instances tab, BPEL Console, 185
integration services, BPEL Server, 170
interfaces, BPEL processes. See message flow
invalidReply fault, 342
invoke activity, 80
invoke activity, BPEL syntax reference, 328
invoke asynchronous web service, 71
invoke construct, 70
invoking a java class, WSIF, 230
invoking a web service, 70

J

java code embedding, 249
Java to XML bindings, WSIF, 230
JAZN provider, identity service, 272
JDeveloper
- BPEL Validation Browser, 203
- building and deploying processes, 204
- copy rule editor, 199
- importing BPEL processes, 195
- partner links, 195
- process activities, 198

variables, 196
XPath Expression Builder, 200
XSLT Mapper, 201
JDeveloper BPEL Designer, 194
JMSService port type, Oracle JMS service, 259
JMSServiceCallback port type, Oracle JMS service, 259
join conditions, 158
join failures, 159
joinCondition attribute, default value, 342
joinFailure fault, 342
JTA, 249

L

language attribute, exec activity, 249
ldap:authenticate function, Oracle BPEL Process Manager, 221
ldap:listUsers function, Oracle BPEL Process Manager, 221
ldap:search function, Oracle BPEL Process Manager, 221
LDAP access functions, Oracle BPEL Process Manager, 221
lifecycle,business process, 143
link activity, BPEL syntax reference, 329
link element, 56
links, 150
Listen shape, MS BizTalk Server 2004, 312
Logging tab, BPEL Console, 192
lookup method, exec activity, 249
Loop shape, MS BizTalk Server 2004, 311
looping, 108

M

MailService port type, Oracle Email service, 259
MailServiceCallback port type, Oracle Email service, 259
managing events, 137
mapping properties to messages, 146
MDA, 164
message correlation, 71, 145
message events, 137, 138
message flow
about, 79
invoke activity, 80
receive activity, 80
reply activity, 81
attributes, 80
message properties
about, 145
assignments, 147
extracting, 147
mapping properties to messages, 146
message security, 34
MessageBox, MS Biztalk Server 2004, 281
messageType attribute, variables, 79
messaging, 49
messaging model, 50
Microsoft Biztalk Server 2004, 27
mismatchedAssignmentFailure fault, 342
model driven approach, 164
MS Biztalk Server 2004
about, 27
adapters, 278
architecture, 276
BPEL compliance, 305
Business Activity services, 316
Business Rules engine, 283
Health and Activity Tracking, 318
Human Workflow Services
integration with other BizTalk servers, 316
MessageBox, 281
Parallel Actions shape, 310
ports, 277, 308
receive locations, 278
receive pipelines, 279
receive shapes, 309
sample orchestration, 284
Scope shape, 313
send pipeline, 283
Suspend shape, 311
Terminate shape, 312
Throw Exception shape, 314
Trading Partner Management, 316
XLANG/s, 276
MS BizTalk Server 2006, 318
myRole, partner links, 77

N

name attribute, 108
name attribute, process element, 78
name, partner links, 77
namespaces, BPEL syntax reference, 343
notification service, Oracle BPEL Process Manager, 253

Notification Wizard, Oracle BPEL Process Manager, 255
NotifyTo element, 62

O

OASIS, 46
obant, Ant utility, 177
obsetenv script, 175
onAlarm activity, syntax reference, 329
onMessage activity, BPEL syntax reference, 330
OpenStorm Service Orchestrator, 29
operators, policy, 57
ora:addQuotes function, 220
ora:countNodes function, 219
ora:formatDate function, 221
ora:generateGUID function, 221
ora:getContentAsString function, 220
ora:getConversationId function, 221
ora:getCreator function, 221
ora:getCurrentDate function, 221
ora:getCurrentDateTime function, 221
ora:getCurrentTime function, 221
ora:getElement function, 219
ora:getInstanceId function, 221
ora:getProcessId function, 221
ora:getProcessURL function, 221
ora:integer function, 220
ora:parseEscapedXML function, 220
ora:processXSLT function, 217
ora:processXSQL function, 218
ora:readFile function, 220
Oracle BPEL Console, 170
Oracle BPEL Process Manager
- about, 27
- advanced features, 215
- architecture, 168
- BPEL compiler, 176
- BPEL Console, 170
- BPEL Designer, 171
- BPEL Server, 169
- BPEL Server APIs, 273
- data and array manipulation, 218
- Database, 171
- deploying a process, 171
- dynamic parallel flow, 222
- extension functions, 215
- identity service, 271
- JMS service, 259
- mail service, 259
- notification service, 253
- Oracle-specific functions, 215
- overview, 167
- process descriptor, 172
- query support, 217
- transformation support, 217
- workflow patterns, 260
- Workflow service, 259
- WSIF support, 229
- XML manipulation, 220

Oracle BPEL Server
- about, 169
- core BPEL engine, 169
- integration services, 170
- WSDL bindings, 169

Oracle-specific activities, Oracle BPEL Process Manager
- bpelx:append, 219
- bpelx:copyList, 219
- bpelx:insertBefore, 219

Oracle-specific functions, Oracle BPEL Process Manager, 215
- ora:addQuotes(), 220
- ora:countNodes(), 219
- ora:generateGUID(), 221
- ora:getContentAsString(), 220
- ora:getConversationId(), 221
- ora:getCreator(), 221
- ora:getCurrentDate(), 221
- ora:getCurrentDateTime(), 221
- ora:getCurrentTime(), 221
- ora:getElement(), 219
- ora:getGroupProperty, 272
- ora:getInstanceId(), 221
- ora:getManager, 273
- ora:getProcessId(), 221
- ora:getProcessURL(), 221
- ora:getReportees, 273
- ora:getUserProperty, 272
- ora:getUserRoles, 273
- ora:getUsersInGroup, 273
- ora:integer(), 220
- ora:isUserInRole, 273
- ora:lookupGroup, 272
- ora:lookupUser, 272
- ora:parseEscapedXML(), 220
- ora:readFile(), 220

orchestration, 19
OutcomeNotification coordination protocol, 44
outputVariable attribute, invoke activity, 80

P

Parallel Actions shape, MS BizTalk Server 2004, 310
partner link types, 75
partner links
client partner links, 73
defining links, 77
dynamic partner links, 161
invoked partner links, 73
JDeveloper, 195
parameters, 77
partner link types, 75
types, 75
partner links
BPEL Designer, 207
business process definition, 97
JDeveloper, 195
myRole, 77
name, 77
partnerLinkType, 77
partnerRole, 77
types, 75
partnerLinks activity, BPEL syntax reference, 330
partnerLinks element, 77
partnerLinkType activity, BPEL syntax reference, 330
partnerLinkType, partner links, 77
partnerRole, partner links, 77
partners element, BPEL syntax reference, 331
Password tab, BPEL Console, 192
performance tuning, BPEL Console, 188
PhaseZero coordination protocol, 44
pick activity, 138
pick activity, BPEL syntax reference, 331
plnk namespace, 343
policies, 56
policy assertions, 57
policy inclusion, 58
policy operators, 57
ports, MS Biztalk Server 2004, 277, 308
position function, Xpath, 218
pre-assemble stage, send pipeline, 284
process descriptor, Oracle BPEL Process Manager, 172
process element, 78
process element, BPEL syntax reference, 332
process identification functions, Oracle BPEL Process Manager, 221
process main body, business process definition, 99
process management, BPEL Console, 178
process map, BPEL Designer, 210
process outline, business process definition, 97
property aliases, 146
property demotion, send pipeline, 284
property element, BPEL syntax reference, 333
propertyAlias element, BPEL syntax reference, 333

Q

query support, Oracle BPEL Process Manager, 217
queryLanguage attribute, default value, 342
queryLanguage attribute, process element, 78

R

receive activity, 80
receive activity, BPEL syntax reference, 334
receive construct, 72
receive locations, MS Biztalk Server 2004, 278
receive pipeline, MS Biztalk Server 2004, 279
receive shapes, MS BizTalk Server 2004, 307
Register element, 41
RegisterResponse element, 41
RelatesTo element, 61
Reliable Messaging, 49
renewal, event subscription, 61
repeatedCompensation fault, 342
reply activity, 81
reply activity, BPEL syntax reference, 334
request acknowledgement, reliable messaging, 51
response, event subscription, 60
RM protocol, 49
RPC, 8
Rules Engine, MS Biztalk Server, 283

S

schemac utility, Oracle BPEL Process Manager, 232
scope activity, BPEL syntax reference, 334
Scope shape, MS BizTalk Server 2004, 313
scopes, 123
security, 34

SecurityTokenReference element, 35
selectionFailure fault, 342
send pipeline, MS Biztalk Server 2004, 283
sequence activity, BPEL syntax reference, 335
serializable scopes, 132
server administration, BPEL Console, 190
service composition, 16
service composition with BPEL, 17
service oriented architecture
- interfaces, 13
- loose coupling, 14
- messages, 13
- quality of service, 14
- registries, 14
- service composition, 14
- services, 13
- synchronicity, 13

setCreator method, exec activity, 250
setCustomKey method, exec activity, 250
setIndex method, exec activity, 250
setMetadata method, exec activity, 250
setPriority method, exec activity, 250
setStatus method, exec activity, 250
setTitle method, exec activity, 250
setVariableData method, exec activity, 249
signaling
- about, 113
- asychronous replies, 115
- sychronous replies, 114

SOA, 7, 12
SOAP, 9
source element, 151
source element, BPEL syntax reference, 335, 341
stack, web service standards, 32
standard attributes, elements, 341
standard faults, 342
startOraBPEL script, 175
subscription renewal, WS-Eventing, 61
subscription, event, 59
suppressJoinFailure attribute, process element, 78
Suspend shape, MS BizTalk Server 2004, 311
switch activity, 84
switch activity, syntax reference, 336
synchronous BPEL business process, 85

T

target element, 151
target element, BPEL syntax reference, 337
targetNamespace attribute, process element, 78
terminate activity, 112
terminate activity, BPEL syntax reference, 337
Terminate shape, MS BizTalk Server 2004, 312
termination, business process, 112
third-party LDAP providers, identity service, 272
throw activity, BPEL syntax reference, 337
Throw Exception shape, MS BizTalk Server 2004, 314
Trading Partner Management, MS BizTalk Server 2004, 316
transaction types
- atomic transaction, 42
- business activity, 44

transformation support, Oracle BPEL Process Manager, 217
transition conditions, 157
transitionCondition attribute, default value, 342
Two-Phase Commit coordination protocol, 44
type attribute, variables, 79
types, partner links, 75

U

UDDI, 9
UML to BPEL, 164
uninitializedVariable fault, 342
unsubscribing, 61
unsubscribing, WS-eventing, 61
until attribute, wait activity, 110
user exceptions in Java, 238

V

variable assignments, 81
variable element, BPEL syntax reference, 338
variableAccessSerializable attribute, default value, 342
variables
- assignments, 81
- BPEL Designer, 208
- business process definition, 98
- element attribute, 79
- JDeveloper, 196
- messageType attribute, 79
- type attribute, 79
- types of, 82

version attribute, exec activity, 249

W

wait activity, 110
wait activity, BPEL syntax reference, 338
web service collaboration, 31
Web Services Invocation Framework. *See* **WSIF**
web services technology stack, 9
while activity, 108
while activity, BPEL syntax reference, 338
Workflow service, Oracle BPEL Process Manager, 259
Worklist application, Oracle BPEL Process Manager, 260
WS-Addressing specification, 53
WS-CDL specification, 24
WSCI specification, 24
wscoor:AlreadyRegistered fault, 41
wscoor:ContextRefused fault, 41
wscoor:InvalidParameters fault, 41
wscoor:InvalidProtocol fault, 41
wscoor:InvalidState fault, 41
wscoor:NoActivity fault, 41
WS-Coordination specification, 37
WSDL, 76
WSDL bindings, BPEL Server, 169
WSDL message, variable type, 82
wse:Renew element, 61
wse:Unsubscribe element, 61
WS-Eventing specification, 59
WSFL, 18
WSIF
- about, 228
- advantages, 229
- defining WSIF bindings in WSDL, 233
- exception handling, 237
- invoking a Java class, 233
- Java to XML bindings, 230

WSIF EJB binding, 243
WSIF tab, BPEL Console, 192
WS-Inspection specification, 55
wsp:All policy operator, 57
wsp:ExactlyOne policy operator, 57
wsp:OneOrMore policy operator, 57
wsp:PolicyReference element, 58
wsp:Preference operator, 58
wsp:Usage operator, 58
WS-Policy specification, 56
wsrm:InvalidAcknowledgement fault, 52
wsrm:LastMessageNumberExceeded fault, 52
wsrm:MessageNumberRollover fault, 52
wsrm:SequenceRefused fault, 52
wsrm:UnknownSequence fault, 52
wsse:FailedAuthentication fault, 36
wsse:FailedCheck fault, 36
wsse:InvalidSecurity fault, 36
wsse:InvalidSecurityToken fault, 36
wsse:SecurityTokenUnavailable fault, 36
wsse:UnsupportedAlgorithm fault, 36
wsse:UnsupportedSecurityToken fault, 36
WS-Security specification, 34
WS-Transaction specification, 42

X

XLANG, 18
XLANG/s, 276
XML facades, 231
XML manipulation, Oracle BPEL Process Manager, 220
XML serialization, 231
XML Type Browser, BPEL Designer, 209
xmlns attribute, process element, 78
XPath 2.0 functions, Oracle BPEL Process Manager, 216
XPath Expression Builder, JDeveloper, 200
XSLT Mapper, JDeveloper, 201

Thank you for buying Business Process Execution Language for Web Services Second Edition

About Packt Publishing

Packt, pronounced 'packed', published its first book "*Mastering phpMyAdmin for Effective MySQL Management*" in April 2004 and subsequently continued to specialize in publishing highly focused books on specific technologies and solutions.

Our books and publications share the experiences of your fellow IT professionals in adapting and customizing today's systems, applications, and frameworks. Our solution-based books give you the knowledge and power to customize the software and technologies you're using to get the job done. Packt books are more specific and less general than the IT books you have seen in the past. Our unique business model allows us to bring you more focused information, giving you more of what you need to know, and less of what you don't.

Packt is a modern, yet unique publishing company, which focuses on producing quality, cutting-edge books for communities of developers, administrators, and newbies alike. For more information, please visit our website: `www.packtpub.com`.

Writing for Packt

We welcome all inquiries from people who are interested in authoring. Book proposals should be sent to `authors@packtpub.com`. If your book idea is still at an early stage and you would like to discuss it first before writing a formal book proposal, contact us; one of our commissioning editors will get in touch with you.

We're not just looking for published authors; if you have strong technical skills but no writing experience, our experienced editors can help you develop a writing career, or simply get some additional reward for your expertise.

www.ingramcontent.com/pod-product-compliance
Lightning Source LLC
Chambersburg PA
CBHW080714220326
41598CB00033B/5418